IRELAND FOR KIDS

IRELAND FOR KIDS

Derek Mackenzie-Hook

MAINSTREAM
PUBLISHING

EDINBURGH AND LONDON

To Ronnie and Sam, and their new 'wicked stepmother', Connie.

My thanks to my grown-up, but still wonderful teenage boys! Their needs and expectations have changed dramatically since they assisted with researching the first edition of this book. Their help with this updated version had to account for the tastes and street credibility of the modern teenager, spots and all. Nevertheless, their input and assistance was much appreciated, without which I could not have gathered so much information or acquired the knowledge to formulate such a comprehensive guide, spanning such a range of age groups. The advantages of being older and taller meant they could enjoy a wider range of activities, including the highlight of our research, swimming with Fungi in Dingle Bay.

My thanks also to my new wife Connie, who spent a traumatic honeymoon driving many hundreds of miles around Ireland to research this book.

Copyright © Derek Mackenzie-Hook, 1997

First published in 1997 by
MAINSTREAM PUBLISHING COMPANY (EDINBURGH) LTD
7 Albany Street
Edinburgh EH1 3UG

Revised and updated 2001

ISBN 1 84018 304 7

A catalogue record for this book is available from the British Library

Typeset in Gill Sans and OptiNeulandBlack
Printed and bound in Great Britain by
Creative Print and Design, Wales

CONTENTS

Boundary between Republic of
Ireland and Northern Ireland
Provincial boundaries

County Boundaries

Mayo

Slig

Ro

Connac

Galway

Clare

Limerick

Munst

Kerry

Cork

ACKNOWLEDGEMENTS

I would like to thank the Northern Ireland Tourist Board, Bord Fàilte (Irish Tourist Board) and all the regional Tourist Information Centres for all their help and for providing information to enable me to write this book.

Special thanks go to Catherine McKevitt, Bill Morrison and John Lahisse at Bord Fàilte, Orla Farren at the Northern Ireland Tourist Board, Joris Minne at Macmillan Media, the Irish Farm Holidays Association, the Great Southern Hotels group, the Best Western Hotels group, the Slieve Donard Hotel in Newcastle, Gerry Flynn at Enjoy Ireland Holidays, Ballyhoura Country Holidays, the Fitzgerald family at Abbeyfeale in Co. Limerick, Tom Joyce at Glenbarrow, the Greensmyth family at Westport, Paddy Dillon, Tain Holiday Village, Shamois Leahy at Trabolgan Holiday Park, and the people of Ireland for their warm hospitality.

• • • • •

PREFACE

Not so long ago there was a rather quaint notion that children should be seen and not heard. Try telling that to the kids of today – this is, after all, the age of pester power! Today's children have definite views which they are keen to express. They are both demanding and sophisticated, always searching for new ideas and new things to do. One of the secrets to being a happy child is not to have grown-up parents! Children are children for a very short time whereas grown-ups are grown-ups for a very long time, so it is important to use this childhood time to the full, in terms of both learning and recreation. Recreational needs vary dramatically during these early years and it's important that parents adjust accordingly. This book is a guide to the latest and best that Ireland has to satisfy the needs of the kids of today.

Any family travelling with children is under pressure to keep the youngsters content. As a single parent travelling with two young boys, and having to work at the same time on some occasions, the necessity of going to the right places became doubly important. The idea for this book came about following trips to fulfil writing commissions in Ireland. My two young children, Ronnie and Sam, always accompany me on my trips, acting as navigators, researchers and sometimes photographers. We always plan our trips carefully to include both work and pleasure, but it's not always easy to find child-friendly places to eat, stay or visit at short notice – unless you happen to be in Ireland. We discovered that the people are always welcoming and helpful and, more importantly, that children are made to feel welcome rather than just tolerated.

The boys and I decided that we should share the benefit of our experience with other parents and children, hence this compilation of the best that Ireland has to offer. This book is as much for Irish people themselves as it is for visitors to the country. Whether Ireland is your main holiday destination or just the place for a weekend or daytrip, *Ireland for Kids* will help you locate the ideal attraction to satisfy every member of your family. The fact that St Nicholas himself is reputed to be buried in Co. Kilkenny suggests that Santa's little helpers were Irish. Were they really elves – or leprechauns? After all, where else in the world are the 'Little People' looked after so well!

• • • • •

INTRODUCTION

The hospitality and good humour of the Irish people are legendary. What is perhaps not so well known is the quantity and quality of exciting, innovative and unusual places to visit in each of the 32 counties. There are few countries on earth that can offer so much in such a small area to families with children of all ages. Every county has something to attract both visitors and locals, from historic castles to the latest state-of-the-art technology. More than half the counties have beaches, and even the others are within easy reach of the sea.

Needless to say, however, it would be tragic if Ireland were turned into a Mecca for tourists. It is true that some counties have only a few facilities for children, but that's okay – not everyone wants to be in the company of children and, anyway, attractions in neighbouring counties are never far away. What is important is that the attractions that do exist are fully equipped to cater for the needs of young visitors.

It seems unfortunate sometimes that children today are brought up in a culture that is saturated with technology. Ireland appears to have coped with this situation better than most: while they certainly have the very latest electronic attractions, visitors also have the option to hire a horse-drawn gypsy caravan and tour this wonderland in peace and solitude.

Angling is a major pastime in Ireland and there are many opportunities to spend an excellent day fishing on a lake, river or canal in many parts of the country. Check with a local tackle shop to find out where the best fishing spots are, and if licences or permits are required – in some areas fishing is totally free of charge. Remember that most children enjoy messing about by the water while fishing, so if you want a hassle-free day be sure to find a spot that is safe and relatively quiet where you won't upset any serious anglers.

Ireland for Kids will guide you to the best the country has to offer. You can plan your outings and holidays to accommodate the needs of all the family as there's a wide variety of ideas to choose from which will satisfy all tastes. The listings are broken down into individual counties giving details of the best beaches, the best on offer in cities and towns, the best in historical and cultural sites, and the best in sporting and rural activities. Following are some useful tips for travelling and explanations on how to use this book.

HOW TO USE THIS BOOK

Northern Ireland and the Republic of Ireland are divided into four ancient provinces, each of which is made up of a number of individual counties. Although the island is relatively small – 302 miles (485km) at its longest and 189 miles (304km) at its widest – it has 3,500 miles (5,632km) of coastline and is packed with things to do and see.

The entries in this book are recorded firstly by province, then by county, and are finally broken down into specific activities. You'll find descriptions of where to stay, where to eat, things to do, places to visit and travel information for hundreds of cities, towns and villages listed under each of the 32 counties. Read the introduction to the county first: it will give you a quick overview of the landscape, the big towns and the resorts plus any attractions which must not be missed. An attraction highlighted here in **bold type** indicates that you'll find more information in the 'Places to Visit' listings. The various attractions are divided into sections such as CRAFT CENTRES, SWIMMING-POOLS and HERITAGE CENTRES. Sometimes an attraction can fit into more than one category, so always check if you can't immediately find what you're looking for. For example, ANIMALS, BIRDS AND FISH covers zoos, wildlife parks, aquariums and so on, but if your kids like animals they might also want to look under FARM PARKS, which for the most part also offer tractor rides, farm tours and nature trails. Most entries include specific details about what's on offer throughout the year, a guide to their suitability for different age groups, plus useful details such as opening hours, the cost of admission (more details at the end of this section), phone numbers, addresses and, where necessary, directions to guide you there. It's worth noting that many attractions change their opening hours out of high season, and that last admissions can sometimes be quite a long time before the stated closing time.

Crèches and baby-changing facilities, easy access for disabled people and wheelchair users are mentioned wherever they are known to exist. This information is often omitted from brochures so if these facilities are important to you, it's worth phoning beforehand to check if they are available or if special arrangements can be made. Also, although many attractions have a café or restaurant on the premises, the fact that they are mentioned here is not a guarantee of the quality of the food or the service or even that it will be open during your visit – only that it is available.

The majority of the guest-houses and farmhouse bed & breakfasts in the 'Where to Stay' sections charge under £20 per person per night. I have omitted a guide to the prices of hotels, holiday parks, self-catering holiday homes and caravan and camping sites because they vary so much depending on the quality of facilities, time of year and length of stay. Many offer special deals for long weekends or out-of-season breaks, so look out for these and always be prepared to haggle at the quieter times. Do not overlook travel lodges and hostels – most have family rooms and, although the accommodation is basic, the facilities are good and it often works out as a cheap way of staying in the big cities.

Guide to Admission Charges

£	=	up to £2
££	=	£2 to £3
£££	=	£3 to £4
££££	=	£4 to £5
£££££	=	over £5
F	=	family tickets available

Guide to * Ratings

Some of the entries are highlighted with an asterisk (*). These are entries that we have been able to recommend either from our own personal experiences or which have been recommended by a reliable source. If you discover these to be under- or overrated, please let me know so that I can pass on your experiences to others. This does not imply that entries without star ratings are inferior, it is my wish that this book will generate many responses that will enable many more entries to be personally recommended in future editions.

*	=	good – but not of particular interest to children
**	=	good – but of limited interest to children
***	=	good – of great interest to children
****	=	recommended for a family visit
*****	=	highly recommended for a family visit

Blue Flag Beaches

The best beaches in Europe are awarded Blue Flags. In order to qualify, a beach must have clean, unpolluted water, safe access, life-guards on duty, toilet facilities, wheelchair access and an information centre nearby. You'll find many such wonderful beaches in both the Republic and Northern Ireland!

Tourist Boards and Tourist Information Centres

If there are attractions, accomodation providers, eating place etc., in your area that you would like to see included in this book please send details to the author c/o Mainstream Publishing, 7 Albany Street, Edinburgh EH1 3UG, Scotland.

Your Comments

If you have any experiences, good or bad, of accommodation, places to visit, restaurants and so on, that you would like to share with other readers in future editions of this book, please write to me c/o Main-stream Publishing, 7 Albany Street, Edinburgh EH1 3UG, Scotland

Disclaimer

While every care has been taken in the compilation of this guide, neither the author nor the publisher can accept responsibility for errors or omissions. Where such errors or omissions occur and are brought to the attention of the author, every effort will be made to include corrections in future editions of the guide.

Postscript for Parents

Do remember
- to keep children under control and respect other patrons;
- to avoid places with 'Keep Out' and 'Do Not Touch' signs;
- to be kind to the environment: take nothing but photographs and leave nothing but footprints;
- to make sure you have plenty of food and drink and things to do on a journey;
- to leave time for plenty of comfort stops on a long journey;
- to take a first-aid kit, some medication, a sick-bag, damp cloth and towel on a journey;
- to try and avoid having to stand with children in long queues;
- carefully plan your visits to major attractions during the busy season to avoid peak times if possible;
- before allowing the children to swim in the sea, satisfy yourself as to the safety of the area. Look out for beaches with lifeguards and follow their advice.

Postscript for Kids

Do remember
- to keep the Irish countryside beautiful – take your wrappers and other litter home or use the waste bins;
- that your parents' decision is final;
- that your parents are on holiday too – share the responsibilities and share the fun;
- that coasters and table mats do not have a flying certificate.

Do refrain
- from asking the landlord how many flavours of crisps he has, then asking for the one he hasn't got;
- from drawing faces in the froth on top of Dad's pint of Guinness.

THE PROVINCE OF

CONNACHT

The western province of Connacht, with only five counties, may be the smallest of Ireland's four provinces, but it has much to offer, and Galway, Leitrim, Mayo, Roscommon and Sligo are all very distinctive in their own way. Tourist brochures state that 'Leitrim is lovely' and 'Sligo is surprising', but a more appropriate description may be that 'Leitrim and Sligo are surprisingly lovely'!

• • • • •

COUNTY GALWAY

The county of Galway is a region of superb scenic grandeur and has many top visitor attractions catering for all interests and age groups. It has lots of fine beaches, some of which have been awarded European Blue Flags. Loughrea Lake is a popular venue during the summer, and the Long Point, with its carparks, changing and toilet facilities, is an excellent safe place for swimming. Another good place to swim, which might suit younger children better, is the sandy area at Coorheen.

The vibrant, cosmopolitan and thriving town of Galway is the principal city of Connacht. If you're looking for fun, follow Tinkerbell to the **Peter Pan Funworld,** an action-packed, fully supervised indoor adventure playground. Salthill is the seaside suburb of Galway, and is one of Ireland's leading resorts. The safe beaches and over 2 miles of promenade make this an ideal family resort. After a hard day sampling the delights of the town's many activities, you can take an evening stroll along the promenade and watch the magnificent sunset over Galway Bay. One of the premier family funfairs in Ireland has to be **Leisureland in Salthill.** Rain or shine, this is the place to keep children happy and content.

The city is also the gateway to Connemara, an enthralling country-side where the ancient language and customs of Ireland are preserved. **Connemara National Park** is a wonderful place to take a picnic and explore parts of its 2,000 hectares of bogs, heaths, scenic mountains and grasslands that make up this bonanza of flora and fauna. The facilities here are first class. The **Connemara Heritage and History Centre** is also worth a visit. The centre is about an hour's drive from Galway on the N59 towards the National Park. It suddenly appears, quite unexpectedly in the middle of nowhere, a renovated farm homestead with a small restaurant and craft shop. It's an interesting site to visit, with its prehistoric lake dwelling and dolmen tomb, neolithic site, history presentation and audio-visual room.

There's also a herd of Connemara ponies to see at the centre, but take care as some are for sale, and you may just be persuaded to buy one!

If you are not convinced about buying a Connemara pony then an alternative may catch your eye at the **Turoe Pet Farm and Leisure Park** near Loughrea. The **Delphi Adventure Centre** near Leenane is a well-organised holiday centre with a wide range of activities on offer, run by a dedicated team with a fun-loving approach to creating a unique adventure experience.

The area is well served with public transport, with mainline rail and express bus services to Galway. Regular ferry services operate to the Aran Islands from many harbours along the coast. There is also an air service to all three islands from Galway Airport.

● ● ● ● ●

PLACES TO VISIT

Adventure Centres

DELPHI ADVENTURE CENTRE****
Delphi Adventure Holidays, **Leenane**
Tel: (+353) 095 42307/42232/42246; Fax: (+353) 095 42303
Facilities: indoor sports hall with climbing wall, tennis courts, shop and coffee bar. Included in the price of the activity programmes are specialist clothing and equipment, instruction, hot showers and sauna.
They organise a wide range of adventure holidays for 8- to 17-year-olds from sailing to raft-building and abseiling to tennis, and visitors have a choice of activities each day. The evening entertainment includes beach parties, barbecues, discos, games, live music and ceileidhs. You can also visit the centre either as a day or half-day visitor and choose from a variety of activities, including horseriding. Meals are available at lunchtimes and evenings at very reasonable prices (or you can take your own food). Contact the centre before you visit, both to book and to get advice on what to take with you.

LITTLE KILLARY ADVENTURE CENTRE
Renvyle, **Salruck**
Tel: (+353) 095 43411/42276; Fax: (+353) 095 42314
Open: all year round
Comprehensive range of sea- and land-based activities for half or full days, including waterskiing, sailing, archery and parascending.

Amusement Arcades and Funfairs

LEISURELAND****
Salthill
Tel: (+353) 091 521455; Fax: (+353) 091 521093
Open: June to September
An abundance of fun and entertainment here. The outdoor leisure features include amusements, carnival rides, crazy golf, an adventure

playground, fun house, giant wheel, miniature train rides, ghost train, slides and state-of-the-art virtual-reality games. All the fun of the fair.

Animals, Birds and Fish

OCEANS ALIVE SEALIFE CENTRE
AND SEASIDE PARK
Derryinver, Renvyle Peninsula, Connemara
Tel: (+353) 095 43473
Open: daily, all year. May to November, 10a.m.–7p.m.; December to April, 10a.m.–6p.m.
Admission: A=£££, C=££, F
Facilities: free parking; toilets; tea-room; sealife exhibits; seaside park and picnic areas; pets corner; children's playground; craft shop; local maritime history; scenic and wildlife boat cruises.
An excellent family attraction with both entertaining and educational displays, exhibits, audio-visual material and information panels. The new seaside park with its secluded covers is an ideal spot for a picnic and the children to play.

TROPICAL BUTTERFLY CENTRE****
Costelloe, *near Rossaveal on route R343*
Tel: (+353) 091 572210; Fax: (+353) 091 572370
Open: May to September, Monday to Saturday, 10a.m.–5p.m., Sunday, 2p.m.–6p.m.
Facilities: souvenir shop; coffee shop
The children will enjoy the lush splendour of the tropical enclosure filled with hundreds of free-flying exotic butterflies. Visitors can also watch butterflies emerging from their pupae in the hatchery, and relax over a coffee while viewing the lifecycle of the butterfly on the in-house video. You can also see giant spiders and small reptiles up close – but they're kept safely behind glass!

TUROE PET FARM AND LEISURE PARK*****
Bullaun, **Loughrea,** *on route R350*
Tel/Fax: (+353) 091 841580
Open: Easter and 1 May to 30 September, daily, 10a.m.–8p.m.; April and October, weekends
Admission: A=££, C=£, F
Facilities: nature trails with seating; children's playground; football pitch; indoor picnic area with TV and shop; pets corner; barbecue area; coffee and sweet shop; free car park; toilets and baby-changing room
The farm and leisure park form a delightful rural setting for the famous Turoe Stone, a rare national monument dating back to the 1st or 2nd century BC. The nature walk around the stone is a haven for wildlife and visitors alike. Children will be fascinated by the wishing well and will enjoy feeding the ducks on the pond. This really is a kiddies' paradise, with swings and slides in the playgrounds, a pets corner, a display of old farm machinery, and a tea-shop with home-baking. Remember to take suitable footwear to visit all the different attractions.

Boats and Boat Trips

CORRIB TOURS
*Furbo Hill, **Furbo***
Tel: (+353) 091 592447; Fax: (+353) 091 564899
Or go direct to the boat, Corrib Princess, *at Woodquay*
Daily tours of the River Corrib aboard a luxury cruiser with full commentary and a coffee service. Sailings at 2.30p.m. and 4.30p.m.

Bus Trips

THE FAMOUS CONNEMARA BUS***
*Old Galway, **Connemara***
Tel: (+353) 091 85780
Enjoy a unique sightseeing experience aboard Galway's legendary vintage bus. Departures daily from Eyre Square, Galway.

LALLY COACH HIRE
*19/20 Shop Street, **Galway***
Tel: (+353) 091 562905
Historic and scenic day tours, or 1-hour sightseeing tours of the city of Galway aboard an open-top vintage double-decker bus. (Departs from Eyre Square every hour, from 10.30a.m.)

O'NEACHTAIN DAY TOURS
*Shannagurran, **Spiddal***
Tel: (+353) 091 83188
Scenic day tours departing from Galway Tourist Office.

Castles and Historic Buildings

ATHENRY CASTLE
Athenry
Tel: (+353) 091 844797
Open: mid-June to mid-September, daily, 9.30a.m.–6.30p.m.
Admission: A=££, C=£, F
Facilities: carpark; toilets
A Norman castle with a 3-storey tower surrounded by town walls. There's an audio-visual show and exhibitions inside the castle.

AUGHNANURE CASTLE
Oughterard
Tel: (+353) 091 552214
Open: mid-June to mid-September, daily, 9.30a.m.–6.30p.m.
Admission: A=££, C=£, F
Standing on what is virtually a rocky island close to the shore of Lough Corrib, this castle is a particularly well-preserved example of an Irish tower house.

DUNGUAIRE CASTLE
Kinvara
Tel: (+353) 091 637108
Open: mid-April to September, daily, 9.30a.m.–5.30p.m.
Admission: A=££, C=£, F

This restored castle gives an insight into the lifestyle of the people who lived here from 1520 to modern times.

PORTUMNA CASTLE***
*Near the town of **Portumna** on route N65*
Tel: (+353) 0509 41658
Open: May to June, Tuesday–Sunday, 10a.m.–5p.m.; July to October, daily, 9.30a.m.–6.30p.m.
Admission: A=£, C=£, F
Facilities: carpark nearby; toilets; shop; tea-room
A great semi-fortified house with exhibitions in the castle and gate-house. Nice gardens.

THOOR BALLYLEE VISITOR CENTRE
Thoor Ballylee, 20 miles (32km) south of Galway City off route N18
Tel: (+353) 091 631436
Open: Easter to October, daily, 10a.m.–6p.m.
Admission: A=££, C=free
Facilities: bookshop/craftshop; gardens; picnic area; tea-rooms
A superbly restored tower house that was once the home of the poet W.B. Yeats. Visitors will enjoy the audio-visual presentations.

Cathedrals and Abbeys

KYLEMORE ABBEY
Connemara
Tel: (+353) 095 41113; Fax: (+353) 095 41368
Open: all year round, daily, 9a.m.–6p.m. (restaurant/craft shop, 17 March to 31 October, daily, 9.30a.m.–6p.m.)
Admission: A=££
Facilities: toilets; craft shop; pottery; restaurant
This abbey is the only monastic home of the Irish Benedictine nuns. It offers the warmth and hospitality of its peaceful setting to visitors from all over the world. The restaurant has the best of home-cooking, and a range of the abbey's distinctive pottery can be seen in the studio.

Country Parks

CONNEMARA NATIONAL PARK*****
Letterfrack
Tel: (+353) 095 41054/41006
Park *open: all year round*
Visitor centre *open: May and September, daily, 10a.m.–5.30p.m.; June, daily, 10a.m.–6.30p.m.; July and August, daily, 9.30a.m.–6.30p.m.*
Admission: A=£££, C=£, F
Facilities: toilets with disabled access; baby-changing room; free parking; indoor and outdoor picnic areas; tea-rooms
An excellent place to spend a day with the children. The visitor and exhibition centre has an audio-visual show of the park plus 3-D models and large-scale displays, self-guiding nature trails, an excellent tea-room and an indoor picnic area with a kitchen and washing facilities. Try to visit on a Tuesday or Thursday when special activities such as nature days, games, art lessons, lectures and Connemara pony information are arranged for children over 4.

COOLE PARK***
Gort
Tel: (+353) 091 631804
Open: Easter to mid-June, Tuesday to Sunday, 10a.m.–5p.m.; mid-June to end August, daily, 9.30a.m.–6.30p.m.; September, daily, 10a.m.–5p.m.
Admission: A=££, C=£, F
Facilities: disabled access; toilets; baby-changing room; carpark; tea-room
This estate is now a national nature reserve and has a unique range of habitats. There are some excellent nature trails and lakeside walks as well as an audio-visual presentation and exhibitions in the centre. Look out for the famous 'autograph tree' with the carved signatures of George Bernard Shaw and Douglas Hyde, Ireland's first president, amongst many other famous names.

RINVILLE PARK***
Oranmore, *near Galway*
Tel: (+353) 091 563151
Admission: free
This is an excellent family leisure area and shouldn't be missed whether you're staying in the vicinity or just passing through and looking for a peaceful, scenic spot for a break. Rinville Park has 6 miles (9.6km) of walks through woodland, open farmland and by the seaside. There's a playground in the grounds of Rinville's old walled orchard, picnic facilities near the courtyard, and a coffee shop in one of the estate's 19th-century stone farm buildings.

Craft Centres

ROUNDSTONE MUSIC AND CRAFTS****
IDA Craft Centre, Roundstone, **Connemara**
Tel: (+353) 095 35808; Fax: (+353) 095 35980
Open: March to October, daily, 9a.m.–7p.m.;November to February, Mon–Sat, 9a.m.–7p.m.
Facilities: craft shop; workshop; coffee shop and fashions
Here you can see one of Ireland's oldest musical instruments being made, the bodhran (an Irish drum, pronounced *bow-rawn*). Many musicians playing traditional Celtic music throughout the world use the beautifully hand-crafted bodhrans made here by Malachy Kearns (also known as 'Malachy Bodhran), including The Chieftains, Christy Moore and the Riverdance ensemble. The instruments are decorated with Celtic designs, initials, family crests etc, of your own choice, and you can even have the kids' names painted on to one while you wait, free of charge.

SPIDDAL CRAFT CENTRE***
Spiddal
Tel: (+353) 091 553376
Open: Monday to Saturday, 9a.m.–6p.m.; Sunday, 2p.m.–6p.m.
Admission: free
Facilities: craft shops; café and bistro with home baking; toilets, parking
An attractive complex of workshops producing a variety of crafts not generally available in other retail shops, and ideally located opposite the beach.

HEY, DOODLE, DOODLE***
2 Eyre Street, Galway
Tel: (+353) 091 561906
*Open: Summer, Mon to Wed, 11a.m.–6p.m.; Thur to Sat, 11a.m.–8p.m.;
Sun, 12noon–6p.m.; winter, Mon to Sat, 11a.m.–6p.m.; Sun,
12noon–5p.m.*
*Admission: A=£££££, C=££ (for one hour of painting time including
tuition, plus the price of the piece)*
Children and parents can create their own designs on ready-made
plain pottery. Pieces are glazed, kiln-fired and ready to be collected
24/48 hours later.

Equestrian Facilities

CASHEL EQUESTRIAN CENTRE
Cashel
Tel: (+353) 095 31082
Daily and weekly courses for unaccompanied children. Scenic
mountain treks.

CLEGGAN TREKKING CENTRE
Cleggan
Tel: (+353) 095 44746
Trekking on sandy beaches, including a 2-hour trek to the beautiful
Omey Island.

CLONBOO RIDING SCHOOL
Corrundulla
Tel: (+353) 091 791362
Small, family-run riding school offering day- and week-long courses
for children and half-hour sessions for tots and accompanying
adults.

ROCKMOUNT RIDING CENTRE
Claregalway
Tel/Fax: (+353) 091 798147
Offers trekking, hacking and instruction. Large indoor arena.

Festivals and Events

BALLINASLOE INTERNATIONAL HORSE FAIR AND FESTIVAL**
Ballinasloe
Tel: (+353) 0905 43453
On: end of September/early October (phone for exact date and times)
Europe's oldest international horse fair plays host to many events.
Apart from the many equestrian events, you'll find street
entertainment, amusements and side shows, puppet shows and a
children's workshop.

CHILDREN'S DAY at AUGHRIM INTERPRETATIVE CENTRE***
Near Ballinasloe
Tel/Fax: (+353) 0905 73939
On: second Sunday in June (phone for exact date and times)
Facilities: book/craft shop; restaurant; toilets

GALWAY ARTS FESTIVAL***
Galway
Tel: (+353) 091 562480
On: mid-July
This 15-day festival includes an exciting programme of international theatre, music, films, street theatre and exhibitions together with a children's festival with puppets, clowns and events.

Forest and Amenity Walks

ARDNAGEEHA AND PIGEON HOLE WOOD
*Near **Cong***
Facilities: carpark; picnic site; seats; fishing

CONG WOOD**
Cong
During the final years of his life and reign, Rory O'Connor, the last of the High Kings of Ireland, lived across the River Cong in the old abbey. The Cong and Ashford grounds are famous today for being the location of the film *The Quiet Man*. The area also incorporates a place known as the 'wilderness', which is traversed by a maze of roads, huge stone walls and a tower. Forest walks, seats and fishing are available here, but note there is an entrance fee if you enter via the Ashford Castle grounds.

PORTUMNA FOREST PARK***
***Portumna**, Lough Derg*
Facilities: carpark; toilets; forest and lakeside walks
The name Portumna derives from the Irish *port omna*, meaning the 'landing place of the oak tree'. There are observation points and an excellent nature trail here, and children will enjoy climbing the tower to gain a bird's-eye view of the forest and Lough Derg.

Gardens

PORTUMNA CASTLE GARDENS
*Near **Portumna***
Tel: (353) 0509 41287
Open: all year round, 8a.m.–4.30p.m.
Facilities: shop; tea-room
see CASTLES

Heritage Centres

ARAN HERITAGE CENTRE
*Kilronan, Inishmore, **Aran Islands***
Tel: (+353) 099 61355
Open: April to September, daily, 10a.m.–5p.m.
Admission: A=££, C=£, F
Facilities: book/craft shop; restaurant; toilets
The centre interprets the history and culture of Ireland's largest island group and its people.

AUGHRIM INTERPRETATIVE CENTRE
*Near **Ballinasloe***

Tel/Fax: (+353) 0905 73939
Open: Easter to October, daily, 10a.m.–6p.m.
Admission: A=££, C=£, F
Facilities: book/craft shop; restaurant; toilets
The brilliantly constructed Aughrim Experience enables visitors to relive one of the bloodiest and most important battles in Irish history, the 1691 Battle of Aughrim.

CONNEMARA HERITAGE AND HISTORY CENTRE
*Lettershea, **Clifden***
Tel/Fax: (+353) 095 21246
Open: March to November, daily, 10a.m.–6p.m.
Facilities: craft shop; restaurant; toilets
A good example of a pre-Famine farm, this historic site has lots of exhibits to interest all the family. There's a farm homestead, a prehistoric lake dwelling and dolmen tomb, and a neolithic site.

Ireland at Work – Past and Present

TUAM MILL MUSEUM
*Shop Street, **Tuam***
Tel: (+353) 093 24463
A restored corn mill and miller's house provide the basis for this museum. The mill is in full working order and the adjacent house is used to exhibit models illustrating the history of milling in the area.

LEENANE CULTURAL CENTRE**
Leenane
Tel/Fax: (+353) 095 42323
Open: April to September
Admission: A=££, C=£
Facilities: craft shop; restaurant; audio-visual display
Interpretative centre based on the local sheep industry which shows you the various stages of woolcraft (carding, spinning, weaving, felting and dyeing). The history of sheep in Ireland can be viewed in a beautiful setting overlooking Killary harbour.

Leisure Centres and Adventure Playgrounds

F1 KARTING***
*Deerpark Industrial Estate, **Oranmore***
Tel: (+353) 091 792200
Open: All year, daily, 10a.m.–10p.m.
Admission: A=£££££, C=£££££
Facilities: free parking; toilets; showers/changing-rooms; café; special kart for disabled drivers.
Ireland's biggest custom-built karting circuit facility includes a special children's track for children over six years.

GALWAY LEISURE WORLD***
*Headford Road, **Galway***
Tel: (+353) 091 562820
Open: daily, 10a.m.–midnight

Computerised 10-pin bowling, kiddies' adventureland, laser games.
Bar and catering.

PETER PAN FUNWORLD****
*Corbett Commercial Centre, Wellpark, **Galway***
Tel: (+353) 091 756505
Open: daily, 10a.m.–7p.m.
Admission: C=££
This miniature Disneyworld is a fully supervised, exciting indoor
play-centre with activities for children of all ages. It has distinct areas
for different age groups, each with a range of activities that include
tunnel and freefall slides, ball pools, a bouncy castle, aerial glides,
rope bridges, scramble nets, a haunted cave etc.

Museums

PEACOCKES COMPLEX
Maam Cross
Tel: (+353) 091 82306
A replica building from the film *The Quiet Man* houses a museum of
furniture and household items from a century ago. Set in woodland
beside the Peacockes complex with its craft shop, restaurant and bar.

Shopping Centres

EYRE SQUARE SHOPPING CENTRE***
*Eyre Square, **Galway***
Tel: (+353) 091 568302
Facilities: toilets; baby-changing rooms; good disabled access
This place has everything – except a crèche! It's the only shopping
centre in Ireland with a 'vidiwall', a giant screen displaying the latest in
music and local and national tourist information. The centre hosts
exhibitions and events for adults and children throughout
the year such as live music, animated shows and a children's arts festival in July. Late-night openings are on Thursday and Friday, until 9p.m.

THE CORNSTORE
*Middle Street, **Galway***
A shopping centre with a wide variety of interesting shops which
contain some unique treasures.

Swimming-Pools

LEISURELAND****
Salthill
Tel: (+353) 091 521455; Fax: (+353) 091 521093
Open: daily all year (seasonal times apply)
Admission: A=£££, C=££, F
*Facilities: shop; ice-cream parlour; poolside restaurant; outdoor funfair
during summer season*
The pool area is designed for all the family, with several sections to
cater for different age groups. The Treasure Cove has a beach pool,
pirate ships, water cannon, a bubble pool and a 65m waterslide.
There's also a learner pool for toddlers and a unique 25m pool
with an adjustable floor to control the depth.

Theatres

GALWAY CHILDREN'S THEATRE****
The Kids Kafé, Seapoint, **Salthill**
Tel: (+353) 091 524388
Open: summer only
Admission: ££
Four shows a day. There's also a café for children.

Walking Routes

WESTERN HERITAGE
Galway
Tel: (+353) 091 521699/563081
Guided walks of the city of Galway.

• • • • •

PLACES TO EAT

Cafés and Restaurants

THE ARAN FISHERMAN'S RESTAURANT
Kilronan, **Aran Islands**
Tel: (+353) 099 61104; Fax: (+353) 099 61225
A varied menu uses organically grown vegetables and salads from the islands. Children's menu available all day.

AVOCA HANDWEAVERS VISITOR CENTRE RESTAURANT****
Connemara, **Letterfrack**
Tel: (+353) 095 41048
Situated on the rugged Connemara coastline, the restaurant is open 7 days and serves a delicious selection of home-made foods all day. They have high chairs and baby changing facilities.

DESTRY'S
The Square, **Clifden**
Tel: (+353) 095 21722
This is the place to enjoy 5-star fish'n'chips in a child-friendly, pleasant environment.

MITCHELL'S RESTAURANT
Market Street, **Clifden**
Tel: (+353) 095 21867
Open: daily, 11.30a.m.–10.30p.m.
A good choice of food, including a snack menu until 6p.m., and a children's menu.

CAFE KYLEMORE
Eyre Square Centre, **Galway**
The café offers a selection of good value children's meals.

GBC RESTAURANT AND COFFEE SHOP
*7 Williamsgate Street, **Galway***
Tel: (+353) 091 563087
***Coffee shop** open: 8a.m.–9p.m.; **restaurant** open: noon–10p.m.*
Family restaurant with high-chairs and a children's menu.

MACKEN'S CAFE AND RESTAURANT
*The Cornstore, Middle Street, **Galway***
Tel: (+353) 091 565789
An excellent family restaurant serving everything from light snacks to evening meals. They have a good range of home-made soups and bread, salads and lunch specials.

SCOTTY'S CASUAL GOURMET
*1 Middle Street, **Galway***
Tel: (+353) 091 566400
Open: summer, Monday to Saturday, 11a.m.–11p.m.; winter till 7p.m.
Galway's only authentic American diner. Everything on the menu is also available to take away.

SEV'NTH HEAV'N
*Courthouse Lane, Quay Street, **Galway***
Tel: (+353) 091 563838
Open: daily, noon–12.30a.m.
Good choice of food including vegetarian options and wonderful desserts and ice-creams. Children's menu.

O'FATHARTA SEAFOOD RESTAURANT
*Main Street, **Oughterard***
Tel: (+353) 091 82692
Children's menu available.

THE GALLEON RESTAURANT
*Beside the church in **Salthill***
Tel: (+353) 091 521266
Open: daily, noon–midnight
Serving lunch and evening specials. Children's menu available.

DEL-RIO'S GRILL
*Opposite the church in **Salthill***
Tel: (+353) 091 523174
Kiddies' menu available.

Fast-Food Restaurants

ABRAKABABRA
*32 Eyre Square, **Galway***
Tel: (+353) 091 562922
Magic food if you say the magic word!

McDONAGH'S FISH AND CHIPS
*22 Quay Street, **Galway***
Tel: (+353) 091 565001
Renowned as one of Ireland's finest fish restaurants.

McDONALD'S
*Headford Road Retail Centre, **Galway** (drive-through)*
Tel: (+353) 091 563215

SUPERMAC'S
*Newcastle Road, **Galway***
Tel: (+353) 091 522755

*Headford Road, **Galway***
Tel: (+353) 091 563660

*Eyre Square, **Galway***
Tel: (+353) 091 566555

*Cross Street, **Galway***
Tel: (+353) 091 567207

*Dublin, Road, Merlin, **Galway***
Tel: (+353) 091 756006

*The Square, **Tuam***
Tel: (+353) 093 28872

*Bridge Street, **Gort***
Tel: (+353) 091 841989

*Main Street, **Loughrea***
Tel: (+353) 091 841989

*The Square, **Athenry***
Tel: (+353) 091 844827

*Main Street, **Ballinasloe***
Tel: (+353) 0905 43814

*Society Street, **Ballinasloe***
Tel: (+353) 09005 43444

Hotels and Pubs

GALWAY RYAN HOTEL****
*Dublin Road, **Galway***
Tel: (+353) 091 753181
An excellent place to stay and eat with the kids. Lots of facilities and a good children's menu.

HOTEL INIS OIRR
Aran Islands
Tel: (+353) 099 75020; Fax: (+353) 099 75099
The hotel is near the beach and offers good food at reasonable prices.

ERRISEASKE HOUSE HOTEL
*Ballyconneely, **Clifden***
Tel: (+353) 095 23553; Fax: (+353) 095 23639
Children welcome; high-chairs available.

PLACES TO STAY

Country Houses and Hotels

CONNEMARA COAST HOTEL
Furbo, **Spiddal**
Tel: (+353) 091 592108; Fax: (+353) 091 592065
Located just outside the city of Galway, the hotel has an indoor
heated swimming-pool, a tennis court, and games and playrooms.

CREGG CASTLE***
Corrandulla, *9 miles (14.5km) from Galway*
Tel: (+353) 091 91434
Open: 1 March to 1 November
Great opportunity to stay in a 17th-century castle set in 165 acres
of wildlife preserve. Child-friendly, welcoming atmosphere with
traditional music played around the open fire in the evenings. Very
reasonably priced.

THE GALWAY RYAN HOTEL****
Dublin Road, **Galway**
Tel: (+353) 091 753181; Fax: (+353) 091 753187
An excellent family-friendly hotel with plenty of facilities for kids –
they welcome children here rather than just tolerate them. The
leisure centre is fully equipped with indoor heated swimming and
toddlers' pools, a jacuzzi, sports hall, gym and tennis courts. There's a
games room and a full programme of organised activities for all
ages. The restaurant has a children's menu.

KILLARY LODGE
Leenane
Tel: (+353) 095 42276; Fax: (+353) 095 42314
Family-friendly house on the shores of Killary harbour. Guests can
use the tennis court, children's games and playrooms.

TOWER HOUSE
16 Threadneedle Road, **Salthill**
Tel/Fax: (+353) 091 526213
Located near Leisureland, the beach and all the other facilities in
Salthill, this guest-house has a playroom and a baby-sitting service.

Farmhouse Accommodation

FORT VIEW HOUSE
Lisheeninane, **Kinvara**
Tel: (+353) 091 37147 (or contact Irish Farm Holidays – see Directory)
Open: 1 March to 31 October
Stay on farm with a horseriding centre nearby. Riding and trekking
are available daily, and there's a games room and facilities for kids.

LECKAVREA VIEW FARMHOUSE
Maam Valley
Tel: (+353) 092 48040 (or contact Irish Farm Holidays – see Directory)
Open: 1 January to 20 December
Lakeside farmhouse overlooking Castle Kirk. Take a boat trip to the castle, and enjoy the games room and playground.

ST ANN'S FARMHOUSE
*Milltown, **Tuam**; on route N17 from Galway to Sligo*
Tel: (+353) 093 51337 (or contact Irish Farm Holidays – see Directory)
Open: 1 April to 31 October
Family-run, old-style farmhouse in peaceful wooded surroundings; facilities for children.

Self-Catering Apartments and Houses

HOTEL CARRAROE COTTAGES
*Carraroe, **Connemara***
Tel: (+353) 091 595116; Fax: (+353) 091 595187
Well-appointed cottages set in the grounds of the Hotel Carraroe in the heart of Connemara Gaeltacht. Guests can use the hotel tennis court, outdoor swimming-pool, restaurant, laundry, children's games room and playground.

ISLAND HOLIDAY COTTAGES
*Annaghvaan, **Lettermore***
Tel: (+353) 091 572348; Fax: (+353) 091 572214
Traditional cottages with access to tennis courts, a play area, games and playrooms.

MARINO COTTAGES
*Furbo, **Spiddal***
Tel/Fax: (+353) 091 592335
Family-run holiday cottages with an on-site equestrian centre, playgrounds, playhouse, shop and laundry. Baby-sitting by arrangement.

Caravan and Camping Parks

HUNTER'S CARAVAN AND CAMPING PARK
*Silver Strand, **Galway***
Tel: (+353) 091 592452
Just 1 mile (1.6km) from Salthill; the beach is nearby.

Hostels

BRU RADHARC NA MARA HOSTEL
*Inishere, **Aran Islands***
Tel: (+353) 099 75087

LEO'S HOSTEL
*Sea View, **Clifden***
Tel: (+353) 095 21429

OLD MONASTERY
*Letterfrack, **Connemara***

Tel/Fax: (+353) 095 41132

INISHBOFIN ISLAND HOSTEL
Inishbofin
Tel: (+353) 095 45855

Bicycle Hire

IRISH CYCLE HIRE – see *Directory*
RALEIGH RENT-A-BIKE – see *Directory*

ROTHAR ARAINN TEO
*Frenchman's Beach, Kilronan, **Aran Islands***
Tel: (+353) 091 61132/61203; Fax: (+353) 091 61313

JOHN MANNION
*Bridge Street, **Clifden***
Tel: (+353) 095 21160

CELTIC RENT-A-BIKE
*Queen Street, **Galway***
Tel/Fax: (+353) 091 566606

CHIEFTAIN'S CYCLE HIRE
*Victoria Place, **Galway***
Tel/Fax: (+353) 091 5674554

FLAHERTY CYCLES
*Upper Dominic Street, **Galway***
Tel: (+353) 091 589230

Car Hire

BUDGET RENT-A-CAR
Ballygar
Tel: (+353) 0903 24668; Fax: (+353) 0903 24759

CAPITOL CAR HIRE
*Jet Station, Headford Road, **Galway***
Tel: (+353) 091 65296; Fax: (+353) 091 61221

Airports

CONNEMARA REGIONAL AIRPORT
Inverin
Tel: (+353) 091 593034; Fax: (+353) 091 593238
Aer Arann organise daily flights to the Aran Islands (the trip takes
just 6 minutes, making it the shortest scheduled flight in the world).

GALWAY AIRPORT
Tel: (+353) 091 752874

Bus Services

TRAVEL CENTRE
Ceannt Station, Galway
Tel: (+353) 091 563555
Travel information: (+353) 091 562000

Rail Services

Athenry – Tel: (+353) 091 844020
Ballinasloe – Tel: (+353) 0905 42105
Galway – Tel: (+353) 091 562730

Ferry Services

ISLAND FERRIES: *Aran Islands – Tel: (+353) 091 561767*

COUNTY LEITRIM

Leitrim, a long narrow area bordered by no fewer than six other counties, is divided into two almost equal parts by the River Shannon and Lough Allen. It belongs to part of an undefined area of Ireland known as the Midlands, which is rather confusing because it does have 2^1/$_2$ miles (4km) of coastline. It is actually better known for being the Cinderella of Irish counties, due to its abundance of rivers and lakes set amongst villages trapped in a time warp. An estate agent might describe it as being 'unspoilt, in need of renovation'!

It is rather fitting that one of the main attractions in the county is **Drumcoura City,** a unique American-style ranch modelled on the traditional 'Old West'. This is a wonderful experience for families who enjoy horses, but whether you are an experienced rider or not, you will be taught how to become a cowboy or cowgirl. Drumcoura is fully equipped to provide visitors with an authentic Western experience; you will be given the opportunity to relive the days of mighty cattle drives, taught how to ride Western-style and how to rope cattle. The ranch has luxury log cabins, a Western saloon and a first-class restaurant. So if you fancy donning the chaparejos, spurs and stetson, practise your *YeeHah* and head for the old corral. It's not cheap to stay here, but it's certainly the adventure of a lifetime.

Most of the roads traversing the county are minor ones, but then the pace of life is such that this only adds to the ambience of this hidden part of Ireland.

● ● ● ● ●

PLACES TO VISIT

Boats and Boat Trips

BALLINAMORE BOATS
Ballinamore
Tel: (+353) 078 44079; Fax: (+353) 078 44600
Open: March to October
Rent a boat for a day or take a 2-hour trip on a luxurious water-bus (wheelchair accessible).

CARRICK CRAFT
The Marina, **Carrick-on-Shannon**
Tel: (+353) 078 20236
A fleet of 2- to 8-berth modern cruisers are available for leisure holidays on the River Shannon.

Castles

PARKE'S CASTLE
Fivemile Bourne, **Dromahair**
Tel: (+353) 071 64149
Open: St Patrick's weekend (mid-March), 10a.m.–5p.m.; Easter and
May, Tuesday to Sunday, 10a.m.–5p.m.; June to September, daily,
9.30a.m.–6.30p.m.; October, daily, 10a.m.–5p.m.
Admission: A=££, C=£, F
Facilities: disabled access to the ground floor; tea-room
A restored plantation castle of the early 17th century, scenically
situated beside Lough Gill. Near the castle is a sweat-house, a kind
of medieval Irish sauna. Look out for the audio-visual show.

Forest and Amenity Walks

DERRYCARNE WOOD
Two miles (3.5km) north of **Dromod** *off route N4*
Facilities: carpark; picnic site; forest and riverside walks

Gardens

LOUGH RYNN HOUSE AND GARDENS***
Mohill
Tel: (+353) 078 31427
Open: end-April to mid-September, daily, 10a.m.–7p.m.
Admission: ££££ per car
Lots of interesting things to do here for all the family in 100 acres
of woodland, ornamental gardens and open pasture. There's also a
600-acre lake. The pleasure grounds and arboretum are laid out
with wide walks leading to the ruins of a 16th-century tower, a
Bronze Age dolmen and a wishing seat. Facilities include a children's
playground, boat rides, craft shop and a fast-food restaurant.

Ireland at Work – Past and Present

SLIABH AN IARANN VISITOR CENTRE
Drumshanbo
Tel: (+353) 078 41522
Open: April to October, Monday to Saturday, 10a.m.–6p.m., Sunday,
2p.m.–6p.m.
Admission: A=£, C=£
The centre has an audio-visual presentation showing features of the
area such as the mining of coal, sweat-houses and the Cavan and
Leitrim Railway.

Leisure Centres and Adventure Playgrounds

LOUGH ALLEN ADVENTURE CENTRE***
Ballinagleragh
Tel: (+078) 43292
A wide range of activities for all the family such as canoeing,
windsurfing, mountain biking, rafting, summer camps, walking, over
periods from 1–2 hours to 1–5 days. Visit the giant Finn McCool's
Rock – find his fingerprints and gain his magic powers!

Equestrian Centres

MOORLANDS EQUESTRIAN AND LEISURE CENTRE***
Drumshanbo
Tel: (+353) 078 41500
Open: all year
Residential riding centre with indoor arena, leisurely treks on private
trails and coffee shop. Unaccompanied children catered for.

Farm Parks

SWAN ISLAND OPEN FARM***
Corawallen
Tel: (+353) 049 4333065
Open: Easter to October, daily, 11a.m.–6p.m.; boat trips all year
Admission: A=££, C=£, F
*Facilities: Toilets, car park, picnic and barbecue areas, restaurant, sweet
and gift shops, children's playground, animal farm, boat trips*
Delightful open farm which specialises in 'steak barbecues'. Situated
on the Garradice Lake with a river boat trip and barbecue specials.

Museums

TEACH DUCHAIS FOLK MUSEUM
*Drumeela, **Carrigallen***
Tel: (+353) 049 4333055
Open: seasonal, Monday to Friday, 10a.m.–1p.m., Sunday, 2p.m.–5p.m.
Facilities: tea-rooms with home-baking

Theatres

CORNMILL THEATRE AND ARTS CENTRE
Carrigallen
Tel: (+353) 049 4339612
The best of theatre, music and art. Telephone for details of
programme.

Walking Routes

THE LEITRIM WAY
The only long-distance waymarked route in the region. The
northern end is near Manorhamilton, and from there it runs south
into the O'Donnell's Rock area. The branch route, the O'Donnell's
Rock Way, can be taken from here back to Manorhamilton. The
main route continues to the town of Dowra, then along the eastern
side of Lough Allen and finally to Drumshanbo.

PLACES TO STAY

Luxury Residential Holidays

SHANNON BARGE LINES
Carrick-on-Shannon
Tel: (+353) 078 20520
Shannon cruises with a difference. If you are a large family or are planning a holiday with another family, this may be the holiday for you. Up to 10 people can charter a skippered, luxury hotel barge on a full-board or self-catering basis. The barges are fully equipped with en-suite cabins, a dining-room and a bar.

Country Houses and Hotels

RIVERSDALE FARM GUEST-HOUSE
Ballinamore
Tel: (+353) 078 44122; Fax: (+353) 078 44813
The facilities here are better than at many hotels. There's an indoor heated swimming-pool, games room and squash court in this family-friendly guest-house.

AISLEIGH GUEST-HOUSE
Dublin Road, Carrick-on-Shannon
Tel/Fax: (+353) 078 20313
Family-friendly guest-house with a games room and baby-sitting service.

HOLLYWELL COUNTRY HOUSE***
Liberty Hill, Carrick-on-Shannon
Tel: (+353) 078 21124
Open: all year
Excellent family-friendly accommodation overlooking the River Shannon.

SHANNON RIVER HOUSE
Aughnahunshin, Roosky
Tel: (+353) 078 38492
Luxurious, friendly house situated on the banks of the River Shannon, with a children's playroom and baby-sitting service.

Farmhouse Accommodation

GLENVIEW HOUSE AND RESTAURANT
Aughoo, Ballinamore
Tel: (+353) 078 44157; Fax: (+353) 078 44814 (or contact Irish Farm Holidays – see Directory)
Large, modernised farmhouse with a games room, children's play-room, cycle hire, baby-sitting service and restaurant.

GORTMOR HOUSE
*Lismakeegan, **Carrick-on-Shannon***
Tel: (+353) 078 20489; Fax: (+353) 078 21439 (or contact Irish
Farm Holidays – see Directory)
Family-run farmhouse with facilities for children.

Self-Catering Apartments and Houses

GLENVIEW SELF-CATERING ENTERPRISE
*Aughoo, **Ballinamore***
Tel: (+353) 078 44157; Fax: (+353) 078 44814 (or contact Irish
Farm Holidays – see Directory)
Open: 1 March to 1 October
A range of well-appointed properties that include a traditional Irish
cottage, ultra-modern bungalows, a house and an apartment. On
site is a games room, children's playroom, cycle hire, baby-sitting
service and restaurant.

BREFFNI HOLIDAY COTTAGES
Dromahaire
Tel: (+353) 071 64103; Fax: (+353) 071 64461
Well-appointed cottages situated in 11 acres of woodlands, gardens
and lawns. There's a children's play area, tennis courts and private
fishing on the site, with shops and pubs nearby.

NORTH LEITRIM GLENS HOLIDAY APARTMENTS
*New Line, **Manorhamilton***
Tel/Fax: (+353) 072 55833
Luxury, family-friendly apartments conveniently situated for
shopping and entertainment.

Caravan and Camping Parks

LOUGH RYNN CARAVAN AND CAMPING PARK
Mohill
Tel: (+353) 078 31844

Hostels

TOWN CLOCK HOSTEL
*Main Street, **Carrick-on-Shannon***
Tel: (+353) 078 20068
Open: 1 May to 30 August

Bicycle Hire

IRISH CYCLE HIRE – see *Directory*
RALEIGH RENT-A-BIKE – see *Directory*

Car Hire

MURRAYS EUROPCAR – see *Directory*

Bus Services

Travel information – Tel: (+353) 01 8366111

Rail Services

Carrick-on-Shannon *– Tel: (+353) 078 20036*
Dromod *– Tel: (+353) 078 38203*

COUNTY MAYO

Mayo is a county with a heritage of unique character. It boasts a wide range of visitor attractions, including the famous **Ceide Fields,** an amazing Stone Age settlement; **Ballintubber Abbey,** the 'abbey that refused to die'; and a **sculpture trail** where Irish and international artists have created their impressions of the local landscape and folklore. Many coastal resorts have the distinction of being awarded Blue Flags because they meet with the stringent EU quality standards.

Croagh Patrick, 6 miles south of Westport, is one of Mayo's most famous landmarks. Pagan worship took place on the mountain as long ago as 3000BC, but it is more renowned for the fact that St Patrick is reputed to have spent the 40 days and nights of Lent on its slopes in AD441 praying and fasting for the people of Ireland. The last Sunday in July sees an annual event known as **Reek Sunday,** when people come from all around on a national pilgrimage to the mountain, many climbing barefoot to celebrate Mass in an oratory on the summit.

Westport has a pleasant boulevard called the Mall, and a well known as Poll an Chapall in the old part of town which, legend claims, will one day rise and flood the town. Until such time as this occurs, Westport continues to be an excellent base for touring County Mayo. **Westport House and Children's Zoo** is definitely worth a visit.

If it's a **boat trip** you're looking for, then a voyage on the *Pirate Queen* ferry to Clare Island is the way to go. It sails daily from Westport Quay on a 90-minute journey to this enchanting island, which has beautiful sandy beaches surrounding the main harbour and Granuaile's Castle, making it safe for swimming and an ideal playground for children. Overlooking the harbour is the small Bay View Hotel, which has two family rooms and an excellent children's menu. So if you're just visiting for the day or looking for a get-away-from-it-all holiday where the kids can roam freely, Clare Island would be a good choice.

On the headland overlooking Clew Bay is Louisburgh. Set in a beautiful area on the wild Atlantic coast, it has two of the many Blue Flag **beaches** in Mayo (others can be found at Louisburgh, Murrisk, Mulrany, Achill, Belmullet and Killala). There is an excellent **forest walk** just outside the town at Old Head, a wide choice of accommodation (including self-catering in traditional Irish cottages) and a number of seafood restaurants and pubs.

Castlebar is the administrative capital of Mayo and its central location makes it an ideal inland base to explore the area. There are lots of attractions here including the **Mayo Roller Bowl** and **North West Karting Centre.**

In the north of the county is the Barony of Erris, a wild, unspoilt region that is one of Europe's least inhabited areas. This is an area steeped in history and legend, and responsible for nurturing many famous playwrights, poets and musicians, a fact reflected by the many traditional **festivals** held here annually. If you pass over the musical bridge at Bellacorrick, stop and let the children run a stone along the top of the bridge and they will make music as fellow travellers have done for 200 years. The Blanket Bogs here are the largest in Europe.

a breathing, unspoilt bogland alive with wildlife and flora. The **Bellacorrick Bog Train,** located on the N59, takes you out into the bog to let you see both the modern harvesting methods and the traditional hand-cutting implements.

Access to the county is good via both mainline rail and express bus services, and directly by air via Knock International Airport.

● ● ● ● ●

PLACES TO VISIT

Adventure Centres

ATLANTIC ADVENTURE CENTRE
Westport
Tel: (+353) 098 64806; Fax: (+353) 098 64905
Open: March to November, daily, 9.30a.m.–9p.m.
Residential and day activities available for all age groups. Watersports include canoeing, windsurfing and paddle-boating. Land-based activities include orienteering, rock-climbing and hill-walking.

Beaches

The county is blessed with many excellent beaches, including the following with Blue Flag status: Louisburgh, Murrisk, Mulrany, Clare Island, Achill, Belmullet, Killala.

Boats and Boat Trips

CLARE ISLAND FERRY SERVICE
Westport Quay
Contact Chris and Kay O'Grady, Bay View Hotel, Clare Island
Tel: (+353) 098 26307
Daily service aboard the *Pirate Queen*, a purpose-built ferry which carries 96 passengers.

INNISKEA ISLAND TOURS
Clogher, **Belmullet**
Tel: (+353) 097 85741
A trip to the scenic Inniskea Islands which are rich in wildlife and archaeological sites.

Heritage Centres
HENNIGAN'S HERITAGE CENTRE***
Located off the N16 between Foxford *and* Swinford
Tel: (+353)094 56756
Open: April to October, daily, 10a.m.–6p.m.
Admission: A=££, C=£
Facilities: toilets; tea-rooms, boat hire
The Centre incorporates an authentic thatched house, an original farmhouse and theme farm where poultry and other farm animals

roam freely. In addition you can hire a boat on the lake or fish for coarse fish.

Cinemas

MAYO MOVIE WORLD
Mayo Roller Bowl, Moneen, Castlebar
Tel: (+353) 094 27777
Four-screen de luxe cinema located within the excellent Mayo Leisure Complex.

Equestrian Facilities

BARLEY HILL STABLES
Bohola
Tel: (+353) 094 84262
Indoor equestrian school with tuition and trekking.

CLAREMORRIS EQUITATION CENTRE
*Galway Road, **Claremorris***
Tel: (+353) 094 62292; Fax: (+353) 094 71684
Open: every day
Has a saddlery shop and indoor arena.

DRUMINDOO STUD AND EQUITATION CENTRE
Westport
Tel: (+353) 098 25616
Trekking and riding lessons for children.

Festivals and Events

BALLINA STREET FESTIVAL***
Ballina
Tel: (+353) 096 70905
On: mid-July (enquire for exact dates and programme of events)
This 10-day festival embraces many aspects of Irish life and provides entertainment for all ages and tastes. Live events are held throughout the town, with music, dancing, storytelling, street entertainers and fireworks displays, all combining to create Ballina's own Mardi Gras. Children are well catered for with a fun-filled education programme, workshops, discos, sports events and a teddy bears' picnic.

BLUES INTERNATIONAL
Castlebar
Tel: (+353) 094 23111
On: bank holiday weekend at the end of May
In addition to the many great bands appearing at venues in the town, a number of side events will occur during the festival, including workshops and street entertainment.

CELEBRATION OF THE SENSES***
Castlebar
Tel: (+353) 094 24421/22680
On: October bank holiday weekend

This multicultural event incorporates attractions for each of the 5 senses – sight, sound, smell, taste and touch – through the dance, music, film, art and food of many countries.

HERITAGE DAY
Castlebar
On: end of August
On Heritage Day the clock is turned back in Castlebar: vintage cars chug through the town, market stalls sell pigs, hens and freshly churned butter, and the streets are filled with the smell of freshly baked soda bread and pungent home-made cheeses.

LINEHALL ARTS CENTRE
Castlebar
Tel: (+353) 094 23733
The centre has a comprehensive arts programme throughout the year. Exhibitions include shows by Mayo artists, a sculpture show and a touring exhibition. There's a variety of theatre shows and musical performances.

REEK SUNDAY
Croagh Patrick
Tel: (+353) 098 25711)
On: last Sunday in July
Thousands of pilgrims come here each year to climb Ireland's Holy Mountain.

SIAMSA SRAIDE SWINFORD ('fun in the streets of Swinford')
Swinford
Tel: (+353) 094 51179
On: August bank holiday period
This is a street festival of pageantry, ceili dancing and heritage displays recalling many of the traditions of east Mayo. A special day is devoted to Swinford's heritage, when visitors are invited to step back in time: shopfronts are changed, vintage cars fill the streets and many historical and heritage items are on display.

Forest and Amenity Walks

BELEEK DEMESNE**
Near Ballina on route R314 to Killala
Facilities: carpark; picnic site; forest and riverside walks

CLYDAGH BRIDGE
Three miles (5km) north of Castlebar on route R310 to Pontoon
Facilities: carpark; picnic site; fishing; riverside walks; waterfall

DRUMMIN
Near Foxford on route R318 to Pontoon
Facilities: carpark; picnic site; forest and lakeshore walks

LETTERKEEN WOOD
Six miles (9.5km) north of Newport
Facilities: carpark; picnic site; ring fort; fishing
The popular Bangor Trail was much used in the 19th century by

travellers and cattle and sheep drovers. An annual walk along the route from Bangor Erris to Newport is held in June.

Heritage Centres

BALLINTUBBER ABBEY**
Ballintubber
Tel: (+353) 094 30934
Open: all year round
The traumatic history of Ireland's only royal abbey has earned it the title 'The Abbey that Refused to Die'. Founded in 1216, it was mercilessly sacked on many occasions throughout the centuries, but despite being left roofless for 250 years, the people of Ballintubber still attended Mass there in wind, rain and snow. Restoration work began in 1846 but had to be abandoned due to the Famine. Today, the work to restore it continues; its simple elegance retains the ancient beauty of the historic site. There is a video display, interpretative centre and guides at the abbey. The grounds are landscaped to portray spiritual themes.

CEIDE FIELDS***
*On R314 coastal road from Ballina, 5 miles (8km) west of **Ballycastle***
Tel: (+353) 096 43325; Fax: (+353) 096 43261
Open: mid-March to May, daily, 10a.m.–5p.m.; June to September, daily, 9.30a.m.–6.30p.m.; October, daily, 10a.m.–5p.m.; November, daily, 10a.m.–4.30p.m.; for winter hours call 01 6613111 ext. 2386
Admission: A=££, C=£, F
Facilities: visitor centre; toilets; disabled access; exhibitions; tea-rooms
Preserved beneath the wild blanket bogland on the north Mayo coast lies the most extensive Stone Age monument in the world, whose field pattern systems and megalithic tombs date from 5,000 years ago. This remarkable place indicates the existence of ancient tribesmen who farmed this area before the bog was formed. The impressive, pyramid-shaped interpretative centre has a viewing area overlooking the site.

CONG ARCHAEOLOGICAL AND HISTORICAL EXHIBITION
*Circular road, **Cong***
Tel: (+353) 092 46089; Fax: (+353) 092 46448
Open: April to September, daily, 9.30a.m.–6p.m.
On display is an innovative permanent exhibition detailing the immense wealth of archaeological and historical interest to be found in Cong and its environs, dating back to prehistoric times.

HENNIGANS HERITAGE CENTRE***
Located off the N16 between Foxford and Swinford
Tel: (+353) 094 56756
Open: April to October, daily, 10a.m.–6p.m.
Admission: A=££, c=£
Facilities: toilets, tearoom, boathire
The centre incorporates an authenic thatched house, an orginal farmhouse, and theme farm where poultry and other farm animals roam freely. In addition you can hire a boat on the lake or fish for coarse fish.

KNOCK MARIAN SHRINE AND BASILICA
Knock
Tel: (+353) 094 88100; Fax: (+353) 094 88295
Knock Shrine attracts over a million visitors every year. Private
pilgrimages take place all year with a special programme of
ceremonies and devotions between April and October (enquire
direct for full details). In 1976 the Basilica of Our Lady, Queen of
Ireland, was opened here, Ireland's largest church. The gable of the
old church where the apparition took place (15 people claimed to
have seen the Blessed Virgin, St John and St Joseph here in 1879)
still remains the focal point of the shrine. Although many people
come here to pray and for spiritual reasons, the place itself is very
beautiful and has a special atmosphere. It is a remarkable fact that
the faith and persistence of Monsignor James Horan, the parish
priest of Knock, who envisaged the town as being an international
pilgrimage centre which could be visited by people from all over
the world, resulted in the opening of Horan International Airport in
1986.

THE NORTH MAYO HERITAGE CENTRE
Enniscoe, *Lough Conn*
Tel: (+353) 096 31809
Open: all year round, Monday to Friday (every day in high season)
The centre is situated in the old farm buildings of Enniscoe House
and has a fine collection of farm machinery and household goods.

THE NORTH MAYO SCULPTURE TRAIL
Along the **coastline of north Mayo** is a sculpture trail where Irish and
international artists have created their impressions of the local
landscape and folklore. The unique trail begins in Ballina and follows the
coastal route through Ballycastle to Belmullet, encompassing a total of
15 sites. A sculpture trail guide map is available from the tourist office.

THE QUIET MAN HERITAGE COTTAGE
Circular road, **Cong**
Tel: (+353) 092 46089; Fax: (+353) 092 46448
Open: seasonal, daily, 9.30a.m.–6p.m.
The Cong area is known as 'Quiet Man Country' after the popular
film starring John Wayne made in this area in 1952. The ground
floor of the cottage has been designed as an exact replica of the
set in Hollywood where the interior scenes were filmed.

Historic Houses

WESTPORT HOUSE AND COUNTRY ESTATE****
Westport
Tel: (+353) 098 25340/27766; Fax: (+353) 098 25206
*Open: **House**, Easter/May, Sat/Sun, 2p.m.–5p.m.; **house and zoo**, June,
Mon–Fri, 2p.m.–6p.m.; **house/zoo/attractions**, June, Sat/Sun, 2p.m.–6p.m.;
July/August, Mon–Sat, 11.30a.m.–6p.m.; Sun, 2p.m.–7p.m.; **house only**,
Sept, 2p.m.–5p.m.*
Admission: house and zoo, A=££££, C=££££, F
*Facilities: disabled access; toilets; baby-changing facilities; children's zoo;
craft and gift shop; foodstore; bar food; fast-food restaurant and old
kitchen tea-room*

Westport House is a magnificent building set in a spectacular location with many interesting things to do and see and a wide range of attractions suitable for visitors of all ages. The gardens feature a children's zoo with ostriches, llamas, camels, deer, rheas and monkeys. Enjoy the ball pond, playground, boating, miniature railway, hill slide, model railway, dungeons, supabounce, tennis courts, par-three nine-hole golf course, swan pedaloes, slippery dip, pitch and putt and a new log flume ride.

Ireland at Work – Past and Present

BELLACORRICK BOG TOURS***
Bellacorrick
Tel: (+353) 096 53002
Open: 1 May to 30 September, Monday to Saturday, 11a.m.–4.30p.m., Sundays, 2p.m.–5p.m.
Charges: A=£££, C=£, F
The bog train at Bellacorrick links the past, the present and the future. The train trip through the bog is accompanied by an account of how energy is generated from Irish peat. It takes you to Ireland's first wind farm, and on the train visitors are informed of the process involved in harvesting peat, the history of how blanket bogs were formed and an account of the flora and fauna associated with bogs. This is an interesting and educational trip, and children will certainly enjoy the train ride.

FOXFORD WOOLLEN MILLS VISITOR CENTRE*
Foxford
Tel: (+353) 094 56756
Open: April, May, June, September and October, Monday to Saturday, 10a.m.–6p.m., Sunday, noon–6p.m.; July and August, Monday to Saturday, 9a.m.–8p.m., Sunday, noon–6p.m.; November to March, Monday to Saturday, 10a.m.–6p.m., Sunday, 2p.m.–6p.m.
Admission: A=£££, C=££, F
Facilities: toilets; baby-changing room; shop; craft and exhibition centre; restaurant
With the aid of art galleries and an audio-visual presentation, the visitor centre traces the success story of this remarkable mill from its humble beginnings in 1892 when it was founded by Mother Agnes, the courageous nun who set about alleviating the plight of the people of Mayo following the Famine, to the thriving craft industry you see today. The story is told through a historical presentation followed by a tour of the mill where skilled craftspeople produce the world-famous Foxford tweeds, rugs and blankets.

Leisure Centres and Adventure Playgrounds

MAYO ROLLER BOWL AND NORTH-WEST KARTING****
Moneen, Castlebar
Tel: (+353) 094 25473/25472
Open: all year round, daily, 10a.m.–midnight
Facilities: disabled access; toilets with baby-changing facilities; snack bar
This modern, spacious complex has something for everyone. Choose from 10-pin bowling with fully computerised lanes that cater for beginners and experienced bowlers, indoor go-karting

with all equipment provided and a fully supervised play area with a ball pond, tunnel slides, climbing frame, a separate toddlers' ball pit and mini slide.

TIR NA NOG VENTURE FUN PARK****
Kiltimagh
Tel: (+353) 094 81494
Open: July to August only, daily, 11a.m.–7p.m.
Admission: A=Free!! C=3
Facilities: Toilets, picnic and play areas with swings, aerial runway, rope bridges, climbing frames etc.
Tir na n'og translates into 'land of youth' and aptly describes the fun park with its enchanting play aras for children aged 3–13 years. Parents can sit and watch their children enjoy the various supervised, safe, environmentally friendly play areas, or study the sculptured artwork in the park, and it's free!! (parent power at last).

Museums

KNOCK FOLK MUSEUM
Knock
Tel: (+353) 094 88100; Fax: (+353) 094 88295
Open: May, June, September and October, daily, 10a.m.–6p.m.; July and August, daily, 10a.m.–7p.m.
Knock Folk Museum is located in beautiful landscaped gardens within the grounds of Knock Shrine, and contains a broad selection of artefacts from rural Ireland in the 19th and early 20th centuries. The museum itself is divided into 15 sections, each devoted to a particular aspect of Irish life. Exhibits include craftsmen, such as the village blacksmith, carpenter, shoemaker etc, a complete thatched cottage, and a sports and transport section.

Swimming-Pools

THE HOTEL WESTPORT AND LEISURE CENTRE***
Westport
Tel: (+353) 098 25122; Fax: (+353) 098 26739
Leisure centre which incorporates a heated swimming-pool, sauna, jacuzzi, steam room and gym. The swimming-pool is open to non-residents at certain times (check directly with hotel as times vary throughout the year).

Walks and Tours

CROAGH PATRICK WALKING TOURS
*Gerry Greensmyth, Belclare, **Westport***
Tel/Fax: (+353) 098 26090
Gerry organises and leads a series of guided walks in the area from the guest-house he runs with his wife Bernie in Belclare (**see COUNTRY HOUSES AND HOTELS**). Although most of the walks are for mature and experienced walkers, he will take older, accompanied children on selected walks by arrangement.

PLACES TO EAT

Cafés and Restaurants

BEEHIVE CRAFT AND COFFEE SHOP
Keel, **Achill**
Tel: (+353) 098 43134
Open: every day

ECHOES
Main Street, **Cong**
Tel: (+353 092 46059
Children welcome. High-chairs and special menus available.

BERNIE'S CAFE
High Street, **Westport**
Tel: (+353) 098 27797
Disabled access, vegetarian and children's menu.

CHINA COURT CHINESE RESTAURANT
Bridge Street, **Westport**
Tel: (+353) 098 28177
Vegetarian and children's menu.

THE URCHIN RESTAURANT
Bridge Street, **Westport**
Tel: (+353) 098 27532
Open: all day
Vegetarian and children's menu.

Fast Food Restaurants
SUPERMAC'S
Main Street, Castlebar
Tel: (+353) 094 27544

Dalton Street, Claremorris
Tel: (+353) 094 62670

Corn Market, Ballinrobe
Tel: (+353) 092 42200

Pearse Street, Ballina
Tel: (+353) 096 72241
McDONALD'S
Lower Westport Road, Castlebar *(Drive-through)*
Tel: (+353) 094 27611

Hotels and Pubs

CASTLEBAR HOTEL
*Castlebar Street, **Westport***
Tel: (+353) 098 25444
Live entertainment most nights in July and August. Disabled access and children's menu.

CLOCK TAVERN RESTAURANT AND BAR
*High Street, **Westport***
Tel: (+353) 098 26870
Open: July, August and September
Live entertainment and children's menu.

HOTEL WESTPORT AND LEISURE CENTRE
*The Demesne, **Westport***
Tel: (+353) 098 25122
Open: all year
Live entertainment, leisure centre, vegetarian and children's menu, disabled access.

• • • • •

PLACES TO STAY

Country Houses and Hotels

GRAY'S GUEST-HOUSE
*Dugort, **Achill Island***
Tel: (+353) 098 43244
Family-friendly house with a games room, table-tennis, visitors' garden and croquet.

DOWNHILL HOTEL***
Ballina
Tel: (+353) 096 21033; Fax: (+353) 096 21338
Family-owned and managed hotel with excellent family rooms and children's facilities and menus. The Eagles leisure club has a swimming-pool with a separate toddlers pool, squash and tennis courts, snooker and fames rooms, gymnasium etc, and run a special Eagles Children's Club in summer.

DOWNHILL INN***
*Sligo Road, **Ballina***
Tel: (+353) 096 7344 Fax: (+353) 096 73411
Open: all year
Owned and run by the owners of the Downhill Hotel, this inn offers good facilities for families and access to the leisure complex.

BAY VIEW HOTEL
Clare Island
Tel: (+353) 098 26307

Friendly hotel with family rooms and a children's menu. Safe beaches nearby.

BELMONT HOTEL
Knock
Tel: (+353) 094 88122; Fax: (+353) 094 88532
Family-friendly hotel with a leisure complex and a children's play-room.

ANCHOR HOUSE
Quay Road, **Newport**
Tel: (+353) 098 41178; Fax: (+353) 098 24903
Family-friendly house with a children's playroom.

NEWPORT HOUSE
Newport
Tel: (+353) 098 41222; Fax: (+353) 09841613
Friendly house with cots, high-chairs, a baby-sitting service and early-evening meals for the children.

BELCLARE LODGE
Gerry and Bernie Greensmyth, Belclare, **Westport**
Tel/Fax: (+353) 098 26090
Family-friendly accommodation.

HOTEL WESTPORT AND LEISURE CENTRE***
Westport
Tel: (+353) 098 25122; Fax: (+353) 098 26739
Set in its own grounds, this family hotel is an ideal place to stay, visit and eat. It has 26 family rooms and an excellent swimming-pool which is open to non-residents at specified times (check directly with the hotel as times vary throughout the year), plus a sauna, jacuzzi, steam-room and gym. The hotel organises a special children's Panda Club during peak times with lots of special things for the kids to do, including a fancydress party! The kids can also have dinner in the restaurant at their own special sitting with their own special menu.

ROSTURK WOODS
Rosturk, Mulrany, **Westport**
Tel: (+353) 098 36264
Open: 20 March to 31 October
Welcoming family home set in secluded mature woodlands and situated on the sandy seashore of Clew Bay between Westport and Mulrany. Horseriding, boat trips, fishing, golf, sailing and swimming are all available nearby.

WESTPORT WOODS HOTEL AND BEECH CLUB LEISURE CENTRE***
Quay Road, **Westport**
Tel: (+353) 098 25811 (Reservations UK/NI – 0800 282007); Fax: (+353) 098 26212
Open: all year round
Family friendly hotel set in mature woodland near the town centre. It has an excellent kiddies club and a new leisure centre with a swimming pool, health and fitness facilities and a running track.

Farmhouse Accommodation

RATHOMA HOUSE
Mrs Nuala Carey, **Westport**
Tel: (+353) 096 32035 (or contact Irish Farm Holidays – see Directory)
Open: all year round
Child-friendly accommodation in a scenic area beside the Ceide
Fields and River Palmerstown, 3 miles (5km) from Killala. Has a
games room, playground and small swimming-pool. Horseriding and
boat hire by arrangement.

Self-Catering Apartments and Houses

WESTERN PRIDE HOLIDAY HOMES
Lough Mask, **Ballinrobe**
Tel: (+353) 092 41671; Fax: (+353) 092 41788
Open: all year round
Holiday homes modelled on the traditional Irish village, surrounded
by woodlands and overlooking the River Robe. Children's play-
ground; baby-sitting available by arrangement. Disabled facilities.

WESTPORT HOUSE COUNTRY ESTATE****
Westport
Tel: (+353) 098 27766; Fax: (+353) 098 25206
Open: Mid-May to early September
Attractive estate houses and apartments, fully modernised yet
retaining lots of character. Amenities include children's playroom,
games room, tennis court and shop, access to house and estate
facilities. (See Historic Houses and Country Estates.)

Caravan and Camping Parks

CARRA CARAVAN AND CAMPING PARK
Belcarra, **Castlebar**
Tel: (+353) 094 32054

HINEY'S CARAVAN AND CAMPING PARK
Crossmolina
Tel: (+353) 096 31262
Located on the shores of Lough Conn, facilities include a children's
playroom.

OLD HEAD FOREST CARAVAN AND CAMPING PARK
Old Head, **Louisburgh**
Tel: (+353) 098 66021; Fax: (+353) 098 66455
Facilities include a tennis court, food shop, launderette, grill bar and
restaurant, children's playground and games room.

PARKLAND CARAVAN AND CAMPING PARK****
Westport Country House
Tel: (+353) 098 27766
See self-catering houses and apartments.

Hostels

THE WAYFARER HOSTEL
Keel, Achill Island
Tel: (+353) 098 43266; Fax: (+353) 098 47253
Open: mid-March to mid-October

SALMON WEIR HOSTEL
Barrett Street, Ballina
Tel: (+353) 096 71903
Open: all year round

OLD MILL HOLIDAY HOSTEL
Barrack Yard, James Street, Westport
Tel: (+353) 098 27045; Fax: (+353) 094 21745

Bicycle Hire

IRISH CYCLE HIRE – see *Directory*
RALEIGH RENT-A-BIKE – see *Directory*

O'MALLEY'S ISLAND SPORTS
Keel PO, Achill Island
Tel: (+353) 098 43125; Fax: (+353) 098 43444

GERRY'S CYCLE CENTRE
Crossmolina Road, Ballina
Tel: (+353) 096 70455

O'CONNORS GARAGE
Cong
Tel/Fax: (+353) 092 46008

P. BREHENY & SONS
Castlebar Street, Westport
Tel: (+353) 098 25020

Car Hire

CASEY AUTO RENTALS
Turlough Road, Castlebar
Tel: (+353) 094 21441; Fax: (+353) 094 23823

DIPLOMAT CARS
Knock International Airport, Charlestown
Tel: (+353) 094 67252; Fax: (+353) 094 67394

Airports

KNOCK INTERNATIONAL AIRPORT
Charlestown
Tel: (+353) 094 67222

Bus Services

BUS EIREANN
*Bus Station, **Ballina***
Tel: (+353) 096 71800/71825

WESTPORT
Tel: (+353) 098 25711

Rail Services

Ballina *– Tel: (+353) 096 71820*
Ballyhaunis *– Tel: (+353) 0907 30009*
Castlebar *– Tel: (+353) 094 21222*
Claremorris *– Tel: (+353) 094 71011*
Westport *– Tel: (+353) 098 25253*

COUNTY ROSCOMMON

County Roscommon is the old capital of the province of Connacht, and the county that gave ancient Ireland its last High King and modern Ireland its first president. Much of this inland county consists of level plains, bogland and river meadows. Its loughs, castles and stately homes provide a variety of wonderful landscapes for the visitor – but sadly there is not much to attract visiting families to stay longer than the occasional day visit.

The town of Roscommon has impressive castle and abbey ruins, both of which are open to explore at any time free of charge. In the north of the county is Boyle, with its magnificent **King House and Abbey.** Formerly home to the Connaught Rangers regiment from 1788 and latterly the Irish Army, King House has undergone extensive restoration to bring it back to its former glory. Exciting special effects and life-size models in recreated scenes combine to take the visitor back through the long and compelling history of the house and the local people. There's a coffee shop, craft shop and tourist information office in the grounds. **Boyle Abbey** is a Cistercian monastery founded in the 12th century.

Younger visitors will enjoy **Tullyboy Animal Farm,** an award-winning working farm. Here children can get involved with farm life, past and present, as they milk and bottle-feed animals. They can ride horses, play in the playground, go on a guided tour, or just wander round and see the ostriches, llamas, miniature ponies, chipmunks, piglets, Icelandic ponies and so on.

Two miles north-east of Boyle is the **Lough Key Forest Park,** a large area of mixed woodland. There is a range of facilities and activities here including boating, fishing, a children's paddling-pool and play area, an observation tower, underground tunnels, picnic sites, nature trails and woodland walks. There's a fully serviced caravan park and camping site, together with a shop and tea-room.

A good network of roads runs through the county, and there are rail and bus services to Boyle and Roscommon.

PLACES TO VISIT

Castles and Historic Houses

KING HOUSE***
Boyle
Tel: (+353) 079 63242; Fax: (+353) 079 63243
Open: 1 May to 30 September, daily, 10a.m.–6p.m.; April and October,
weekends, 10a.m.–6p.m.
Admission: A=££, C=£
Facilities: toilets; disabled access and toilets; free parking; coffee shop;
craft shop
Visit this 18th-century mansion house and explore the world of
the kings, landlords, soldiers and craftsmen who forged its unique
history. The use of interactive displays, such as life-sized models
and special effects, combine with visitor participation to bring
history to life. Children will enjoy this hands-on, participatory
attraction.

ROSCOMMON CASTLE AND ABBEY
The county town of Roscommon has impressive castle and abbey
ruins, both of which are open to explore at any time free of
charge.

STROKESTOWN PARK HOUSE
Strokestown
Tel: (+353) 078 33013
Open: April to October, daily, 11a.m.–5.30p.m.
Admission: separate entrance charges for the house, museum and
garden; concessions are available if you visit more than one attraction
Strokestown Park House was constructed in the 1740s. Built in the
Palladian style, the house is complete with its original contents and
is a good example what interiors were like in the 18th and 19th
centuries. The house has been restored and is open to the public,
and has a tea-room in the old kitchen and full restaurant facilities in
the main season (**see** GARDENS **and** MUSEUMS).

Farm Parks

TULLYBOY ANIMAL FARM****
Tullyboy, **Boyle**
Tel/Fax: (+353) 079 68031
Open: May to September, Monday to Saturday, 10.30a.m.–6p.m.,
Sunday, noon–6p.m.
Admission: A=££, C=£, F
Facilities: toilets; gift shop; museum; coffee shop and restaurant
Set in a beautiful location with views of the Curlew and Arigna
mountains, this farm is centred around an 18th-century farmhouse.
The open farm introduces visitors to country life, and with a large
undercover area a visit here can be enjoyed whatever the weather.

Look out for pony rides, a nature trail, pets corner, hand-milking and bottle-feeding animals, a playground and picnic area.

Forest and Amenity Walks

CORREEN
*Five miles (8km) south-east of **Ballinasloe** on R357 to Shannonbridge*
Facilities: picnic site; seating; forest walks

KNOCKRANNY
*Lough Mealagh, near **Keadue***
Facilities: carpark; picnic site
Some interesting walks, including a visit to the ancient church and graveyard of Kilronan, near which is a stone altar and holy well — according to local belief, it has curative powers.

Gardens

STROKESTOWN PARK GARDENS
Strokestown
Tel: (+353) 078 33013
Open: April to October, daily, 1a.m.–5.30p.m.
Admission: see CASTLES
Visitors will enjoy the walled garden, pleasure garden and kitchen gardens. There is a tea-room in the old kitchen and full restaurant facilities in the main season.

Heritage Centres

BOYLE ABBEY
Boyle
Tel: (+353) 079 62604
Open: April to October, daily, 9.30a.m.–6.30p.m.
Admission: A=£, C=£, F
An impressive ruin of a Cistercian monastery which was founded in the 12th century and used to accommodate a military garrison during the 17th and 18th centuries. A restored gatehouse dating from the 1500s contains an interesting exhibition.

Leisure Centres and Adventure Playgrounds

LOUGH KEY FOREST PARK***
*Two miles (3.2km) east of **Boyle** on route N4 to Carrick-on-Shannon*
Tel: (353) 079 62363
Open: daily all year round (but some facilities are seasonal)
Charges: F=£££
This is an excellent area of mixed woodland with forest walks and nature trails, lakes and islands, and parkland in a place rich in history and sites of archaeological interest. Within the park itself are several ring forts and some of the islands in the lake contain interesting medieval ruins. You can take lake cruises and hire boats, visit an observation tower and tunnel, ruins of an old estate chapel and temple, an ice house, fairy bridge and wishing chair. There's also a tea-room and shop and a caravan and camping park.

Museums

ROSCOMMON COUNTY MUSEUM
The Square, **Roscommon**
Tel: (+353) 0903 63856
Open: April to October, Mon–Sat, 10a.m.–5.30p.m.
Admission: free
The museum houses a swide range of interesting artifacts, cottage industry crafts and farm machinery. There is also a Heritage Trail of Roscommon Town on display.

STROKESTOWN PARK FAMINE MUSEUM
Strokestown
Tel: (+353) 078 33013
Open: April to October, daily, 11a.m.–5.30p.m.
Admission: **see** CASTLES
The museum is located in the stable yards of Strokestown Park, an estate which gained international notoriety during some of the worst months of the Famine when the landlord, Major Dennis Mahon, was assassinated. The Major had attempted to clear 8,000 of his destitute tenants through eviction and assisted emigration to Canada. The museum also challenges visitors to reflect on the ongoing spectacle of contemporary global poverty and hunger.

● ● ● ● ●

PLACES TO EAT

SHEEPWALK BAR AND RESTAURANT***
Frenchpark (R36 south of **Boyle***)*
Tel: (+353) 0907 70391
Open: all year
Children are welcome here, and there are high chairs and special children's meals available.

● ● ● ● ●

PLACES TO STAY

Country Houses and Hotels

HODSON BAY HOTEL
Lough Ree, *near* **Athlone**
Tel: (+353) 0902 92444
Beautifully located, friendly hotel on the shores of Lough Ree. It has a modern leisure complex with a heated swimming-pool, and out-door facilities include a tennis court, golf and horseriding. There are children's facilities and a baby-sitting service.

REESIDE

Barrymore, *near Athlone*
Tel: (+353) 0902 92051
Open: all year round
Country home set in 2 acres of grounds. There's a snooker room, a boat and a canoe. Baby-sitting service available.

FOREST PARK HOUSE

Carrick Road, **Boyle**
Tel/Fax: (+353) 079 62227
Well-appointed house adjoining Lough Key Forest Park. Baby-sitting service available.

MOUNT CARMEL GUEST-HOUSE

Rooskey-on-Shannon
Tel/Fax: (+353) 078 38434
Period house set in 11 acres of grounds on the banks of a river. There's a children's playroom and baby-sitting service.

Farmhouse Accommodation

SCREGG HOUSE

Carrick-on-Shannon
Tel: (+353) 078 20210 (or contact Irish Farm Holidays – see Directory)
Open: Easter to 15 October
Luxury farm residence with spacious gardens in quiet rural area. It has a games room and a tea-room, and a painting studio with spectacular mountain views.

CHURCH VIEW HOUSE

Strokestown
Tel/Fax: (+353) 078 33047 (or contact Irish Farm Holidays – see Directory)
Open: 1 April to end of October
Country residence set in beautiful surroundings on a working farm. There are children's facilities and a pony for guests to ride.

Self-Catering Apartments and Houses

THE GRANARY

Ballyglass, **Castlerea** *(or contact Enjoy Ireland Holidays – see Directory)*
Detached 2-bedroom apartment in lovely country area. Facilities for children and baby-sitting service available.

ABBEY MEWS

Boyle *(contact Enjoy Ireland Holidays – see Directory)*
Three well-appointed Georgian houses near Boyle Abbey and the river. Facilities for children and baby-sitting service available.

Caravan and Camping Parks

LOUGH KEY CARAVAN PARK

Rockingham; *2 miles (3.2km) east of Boyle on route N4 to Carrick-on-Shannon*
Tel: (+353) 079 62212

A fully serviced caravan park and camping site within the confines of Lough Key Forest Park. It has a children's play area, shop and tea-room, and small boats available for hire.

Bicycle Hire

IRISH CYCLE HIRE – see *Directory*
RALEIGH RENT-A-BIKE – see *Directory*

BRENDAN SHEERIN
Main Street, **Boyle**
Tel: (+353) 079 62010

Car Hire

MURRAYS EUROPCAR – see *Directory*

Bus Services

Travel information – Tel: (+353) 01 8366111

Rail Services

Boyle *– Tel: (+353) 079 62027*
Castlerea *– Tel: (+353) 0907 20031*

COUNTY SLIGO

County Sligo has a fine variety of scenery with its beautiful coastline, majestic mountains and lakes. Rosses Point and Mullaghmore are both Blue Flag beaches and ideal locations for a quiet day at the seaside where children can simply play in the sand and paddle. Inland is Sligo's most famous mountain, the loaf-shaped Benbulben, and in Lough Gill can be seen the lake-isle of Innisfree, immortalised in William Butler Yeats's poem. The county is renowned for its many connections with Yeats and his family, two of whom were world-renowned painters.

The town of Sligo is the second largest in the province of Connacht and is attractively situated between Lough Gill and Sligo Bay. Its attractions include the **Yeats Visitor Centre** and the **Sligo County Museum**. The **Hawk's Well Theatre** provides a continuous programme of entertainment throughout the year. **Sligo Abbey** is an interesting ruin worthy of exploration; the beautifully carved high altar is the only example of a sculpted altar to survive in an Irish monastic church. Legend has it that during the 1641 rebellion worshippers saved the abbey's silver bell and threw it into Lough Gill, and only those free from sin can hear its peal. In the summer months you can take a cruise on the lough aboard a **water-bus**. There's a selection of tours to choose from, including a trip to Parke's Castle at the eastern end of the lake or a sunset cruise to see the castle floodlit at night. There's even a live recital of Yeats's poetry to accompany you on the journey – and if you have been really good you might just hear the peal of a bell!

Jolly Rogers Pirate Playworld is a magical adventure playground for children, while Sligo's newest family visitor attraction is **Gillighan's World of Miniatures** (formerly known as Lilliputs' Great Land of Small), based in the grounds of Markree Castle. This wonderland of make-believe is now being moved to a new site at Knocknashee, appropriately known as the 'Hill of the Fairies', and will be developed to house Ireland's most unique model village and theme park. The new site will open in early June 1997 and will introduce visitors to the mythological background of the Tuatha dé Danann, their kings, sorcerers, champions, poets and goddess Danu, from whom they take their name. Gillighan's Animal Kingdom will feature domesticated farm animals and provide a hands-on experience for children to enjoy close contact with nature and rural farm life. Gillighan's World of Adventure will be an adventure playground for children up to the age of 12, providing fun and experimentation in a safe and natural environment. A visit here will surely be a unique, enjoyable experience for all the family.

Woodville is an open 140-acre working farm in a picturesque parkland setting on the fringes of the town of Sligo.

The county has a good network of major roads and is serviced by mainline rail services from Dublin, express bus services and Sligo Airport via Dublin.

PLACES TO VISIT

Boats and Boat Trips

YEATS WATER-BUS**
Wild Rose Leisure, **Fivemilebourne**
Tel: (+353) 071 64266
Open: April to October, 9.30a.m.–9p.m.
Charges: A=££££, C=£
A complete tour of Lough Gill accompanied by live recitals of W.B.
Yeats's poems. The tour includes a visit to Parkes Castle and Church
Island. Full bar service, tea, coffee and snacks available.

Equestrian Centre

SLIGO RIDING CENTRE
Carrowmore *(3 miles from Sligo town on the Atlantic coastline)*
Tel: (+353) 071 61353
Open: all year
One of Ireland's foremost equestrian complexes offers all riding
facilities and has an indoor arena and coffee shop.

Farm Parks

WOODVILLE FARM**
Woodville, *near Sligo*
Tel: (+353) 071 62741
*Open: June, weekends and bank holidays, 2p.m.–5p.m.; July and August,
daily, 2p.m.–5p.m.*
Admission: A=££, C=£, F
Facilities: toilets; indoor and outdoor picnic areas; museum; nature trail
Woodville is a 140-acre working farm in a picturesque setting. The
site has a well-laid-out nature trail in mature woodland, an indoor
picnic area, a farm museum, and animal enclosures with a variety of
pets and animals on show. All the facilities are wheelchair-
accessible.

Forest and Amenity Walks

CARNS
Near **Sligo,** *off route N4 to Collooney*
Facilities: picnic site; carpark
A pleasant forest walk on the edge of the town of Sligo, overlooking
Lough Gill. There are some interesting stone cairns, one of which is
believed to be the burial site of Eoghan Bel, King of Connaught, who
was buried here after the Battle of Sligo in the 6th century.

DEERPARK
Four miles (6.5km) east of **Sligo** *on minor road to Colgagh*
Facilities: picnic site; carpark; forest walks; excellent viewing points

There are many points of interest here including a stone circle, a cashel and souterrain and a wedge tomb.

DOONEY ROCK
*On the shores of **Lough Gill**, 3 miles (5km) south-east of Sligo on route R287 to Dromahaire*
Facilities: carpark; picnic sites; forest walks; viewing points
An excellent walk through woodland to a viewing point and the top of Dooney Rock, which inspired W.B. Yeats to pen 'The Fiddler of Dooney'.

HAZELWOOD
*Three miles (5km) east of **Sligo** on route R286 to Dromahaire; turn right on north shore of Lough Gill*
Interesting wooden sculptures have been erected at intervals along the forest walk. Facilities include picnic sites, forest and lakeside walks.

SLISH WOOD**
*On the shores of Lough Gill, 3 miles (5km) west of **Dromahaire** on route R287 to Sligo*
Facilities: carpark; picnic site; forest and lakeside walks
There is a paddling-pool in the small river beside the carpark.

Heritage Centres

SLIGO ABBEY*
Sligo
Tel: (+353) 071 46406
Open: mid-June to mid-September, daily, 9.30a.m.–6.30p.m.
Admission: A=£, C=£, F
Like many a Norman town in Ireland, Sligo once had a castle and abbey. The former has long since disappeared, but the abbey has been preserved and is well worth a visit.

Historic Houses

LISSADELL HOUSE
Drumcliffe
Tel: (+353) 071 63150
Open: June to mid-September, Monday to Saturday, 10.30a.m.–12.15p.m. and 2p.m.–4.15p.m.
Admission: A=££, C=£
This large Georgian mansion is the home of the Gore-Booth family, friends of W.B. Yeats.

Leisure Centres and Adventure Playgrounds

GILLIGHAN'S WORLD OF MINIATURES*****
Knocknashee
Tel: (+353) 096 30286
Open: check locally for seasonal times and special Christmas events
Facilities: toilets; disabled access; baby-changing areas; outdoor picnic areas (picnic boxes available or bring your own); souvenir and gift shop
The children not only look like giants in this miniature wonderland,

they are made to feel like giants. They will enjoy the adventure playground, pet farm; bird and butterfly house and craft workshops, and there's a great viewing platform with panoramic vistas of the Hill of Knocknashee. The whole complex is geared up to accommodate, educate and entertain children of all ages.

JOLLY ROGER'S PIRATE PLAYWORLD****
Adelaide Street, **Sligo**
Tel: (+353) 071 69008
Open: during school holidays, daily, 10a.m.–7p.m.; during school term, Tuesday to Friday, 2p.m.–7p.m., weekends, 10a.m.–7p.m.
Admission: C=£££
Yet another great adventureland for the kids. This is a fully super-vised play area that caters for all ages with all the usual energy-sapping play areas, including a soft-play section for the under-5s, roller squeezes, scrambling nets, biff bags, rope bridges, pendulum swings, crawl tunnels, the pirates' plunge, smugglers' chute and giant freefall slide, plus an ice-cream parlour, snack bar, coffee shop and mothers' room.

SLIGO SPORTS COMPLEX
Cleveragh Road, **Sligo**
Tel: (+353) 071 60539
The centre has a swimming-pool and gym. Check locally for times of public access.

Museums

CULKIN'S EMIGRATION MUSEUM**
Cannaghanally, **Dromore West**
Tel: (+353) 096 47152
Open: June to September, daily, 10a.m.–5p.m.; Sunday, 1p.m.–5p.m.
Emigration, for whatever reason, is a part of Irish culture. Ireland's loss has in many cases been other countries' gain, and there are many parts of the world that have been influenced and shaped by the people of Ireland. The museum stands on the site where once stood the gateway to new worlds in the form of Daniel Culkin's Shipping and Emigration Agency. It houses a host of artefacts and features that will help visitors relive a poignant era when emigration was the only hope for a better life.

SLIGO COUNTY MUSEUM AND ART GALLERY
Stephen Street, **Sligo**
Tel: (+353) 071 42212
Open: seasonal opening times
Many interesting exhibits on display and there is a special section devoted to the Yeats family connections with Sligo, including a copy of the poet's Nobel Prize medal. Wheelchair access to museum only.

Swimming-pools

WATERPOINT***
Enniscrone
Tel: (+353) 096 369999
Open: All year; summer, Mon–Fri, 10a.m.–10p.m.; Sat/Sun,

11a.m.–8p.m.; winter, Mon/Fri, 2p.m.–10p.m.; Sat/Sun, 11.am.–6p.m.
Admission: A=£££, C=££, F
Excellent new swimming-pool complex with a kiddies pool, waterslides, snack bar, sauna, jacuzzi, etc.

Theatres

THE HAWK'S WELL THEATRE
Temple Street, Sligo
Tel: (+353) 071 61526
Has performances all year round – phone for details.

• • • • •

PLACES TO EAT

Cafés and Restaurants

GLEBE HOUSE
Collooney
Tel: (+353) 071 67787
Children welcome. High-chairs, half-price menu and accommodation available.

THE HAPPY EATER CAFE AND TAKE-AWAY
Lord Edward Street, Sligo
Tel: (+353) 071 62607
Open: Monday to Wednesday, 11a.m.–2a.m., Thursday to Sunday, 11a.m.–3.30a.m.

TEAHOUSE RESTAURANT
O'Connell Centre, O'Connell Street, Sligo
Tel: (+353) 071 45331
Open: winter, Monday to Saturday, 9.30a.m.–6.30p.m.; summer, Monday to Saturday, 9.30a.m.–10p.m.

Fast-Food Restaurants

McDONALDS
22 O'Connell Street, Sligo
TEL: (+353) 071 47554

Hotels and Pubs

BEACH HOTEL
Mullaghmore
Tel: (+353) 071 66103
Open daily from breakfast to dinner. Restaurant, bar food and children's meals available.

OCEAN VIEW HOTEL
Strandhill
Tel: (+353) 071 68115
Open for breakfast, lunch and dinner. Children's menu available.

• • • • •

PLACES TO STAY

Country Houses and Hotels

MILLHOUSE
*Keenaghan, **Ballymote***
Tel: (+353) 071 83449
Friendly house with a playroom, tennis court and baby-sitting.

MARKREE CASTLE
Collooney
Tel: (+353) 071 67800; Fax: (+353) 071 67840
Sligo's oldest inhabited house with magnificent gardens and a warm welcome. Riding and instruction available for guests, and facilities for children.

RINROE HOUSE
Inniscrone
Tel: (+353) 096 36183; Fax: (+353) 096 36703
Beautiful family home set in 20 acres of grounds stretching to the sea. There's a play area, horseriding and a baby-sitting service.

THE YEATS COUNTRY HOTEL AND LEISURE CENTRE
Rosses Point
Tel: (+353) 071 77211
Open: all year
The hotel organises special family weekends and holiday breaks and caters for the kids with its Children's KO club, swimming-pool with kiddies' pool and baby-sitting service.

ATLANTC HOTEL
Enniscrone
Tel: (+353) 096 36119
Family-run hotel overlooking the beach. Children's playground and facilities nearby.

GOWAN BRAE
*Pier Road, **Inniscrone***
Tel: (+353) 096 36396
Georgian-style, family-friendly house set in own private grounds. There's a children's playroom and baby-sitting service.

BELVOIR HOUSE
*Holywell Road, **Sligo***
Tel: (+353) 071 69136

Family-friendly guest-house with a games room. Leisure complex with swimming-pool nearby.

SOUTHERN HOTEL AND LEISURE CENTRE
Strandhill Road, **Sligo**
Tel: (+353) 071 62101; Fax: (+353) 071 60328
Right in the heart of the town of Sligo, the hotel has a fully equipped leisure centre with an indoor heated swimming-pool, jacuzzi and gym.

Farmhouse Accommodation

GLEN VIEW
Enniskillen Road, **Drum East;** *near Glencar Lake and waterfall on route N16, 4 miles (6.4km) from Sligo*
Tel: (+353) 071 43770 (or contact Irish Farm Holidays – see Directory)
Open: 1 April to 31 October
Comfortable farm bungalow in scenic setting, with facilities for children and a baby-sitting service.

DUNFORE FARMHOUSE
Ballinfull, near Lissadell, **Maugherow**
Tel: (+353) 071 63137; Fax: (+353) 071 63574 (or contact Irish Farm Holidays – see Directory)
Open: all year round
Peaceful location near Lissadell beach. There's a games room, children's facilities and gardens with a putting green and lawn croquet.

Self-Catering Apartments and Houses

THE THATCHED COTTAGE
Ballinfull, *Ardtarmon Self-Catering Holidays (contact Enjoy Ireland Holidays – see Directory)*
Renovated thatched cottage set in mature grounds beside country house on farm. Has facilities for children and a baby-sitting service.

CARROWHUBBUCK HOLIDAY VILLAGE
Enniscrone *(contact Enjoy Ireland Holidays – see Directory)*
Well-appointed cottages overlooking Killala Bay. Facilities for children and a baby-sitting service available.

Caravan and Camping Parks

GREENLANDS CARAVAN AND CAMPING PARK
Six miles (9.6km) from **Sligo** *off route N15 (R291 to Rosses Point)*
Tel/Fax: (+353) 071 45618
Open: Easter and mid-May to mid-September
Beautifully situated on sandhills overlooking 2 Blue Flag beaches. There's a TV and games room, and a children's playroom.

Hostels

EDEN HILL HOLIDAY HOSTEL
Pearse Road, **Sligo**
Tel/Fax: (+353) 071 43204
Open: all year round

Bicycle Hire

IRISH CYCLE HIRE – *see Directory*
RALEIGH RENT-A-BIKE – *see Directory*

WEST COAST CYCLES
Quigabara, **Enniscrone**
Tel: (+353) 096 36593

CONWAY BROTHERS
6 High Street, **Sligo**
Tel: (+353) 071 61370; Fax: (+353) 071 44171

Car Hire

MURRAYS EUROPCAR – *see Directory*

Airports

SLIGO AIRPORT
Tel: (+353) 071 68280/68407

Bus Services

McDiarmada Station, **Sligo**
Tel: (+353) 071 60066

Rail Services

Ballymote *– Tel: (+353) 071 83311*
Collooney *– Tel: (+353) 071 67126*
Sligo *– Tel: (+353) 071 69888*

THE PROVINCE OF

LEINSTER

Radiating from the capital city of Dublin in beautiful bands of contrasting scenery, this area is probably the most varied of Ireland's regions. Its diverse range of historical attractions includes castles, abbeys, fortresses and settlements that recall the passage of Celts, Vikings, Normans and Anglo-Saxons. This south-eastern quarter of the country is made up of 12 counties. On the east coast, Louth, Meath and Wicklow share not only a magnificent coastline with an array of fine resorts and wonderful scenery, but also a fascinating collection of ancient and early Christian monuments that include the famous 6th-century monastic site at **Glendalough.** The south-eastern county of Wexford has the longest coastline in Leinster, dotted with many fine resorts, and is home to the wonderful **Irish National Heritage Park,** a superb place to visit with children.

The inland counties of Longford, Westmeath, Kildare, Offaly, Laois, Carlow and Kilkenny all have their own unique charm. Longford, Offaly, Carlow and Westmeath make up an unspoiled water playground; Kildare is the home of the Irish horse, including Arkle, the most famous horse Ireland has produced; Kilkenny, with Ireland's medieval capital at its heart, is a county full of history and natural wonders; Laois has the magnificent Slieve Bloom mountain rising from its plains and an ancient fortification at the **Rock of Dunamase;** finally, the icing on the cake of all this wealth is Dublin itself, a capital city as sophisticated as any other, but one which remains as intimate as a village and as friendly as the local pub. The attractive villages, bustling towns, fishing harbours and scenic coastline of County Dublin are as attractive and charming as the city is vibrant and exciting.

● ● ● ● ●

COUNTY CARLOW

This is a county with a wealth of beautiful scenery and outdoor activities. Carlow is often referred to as the 'Dolmen County' on account of the massive megalithic tombs scattered throughout (a dolmen consists of three or more uprights supporting a heavy roofing stone, known as the capstone). Outdoor activities include angling and boating on stretches of two of the great Irish rivers, the Barrow and the Slaney; plus horseriding, pony-trekking, walking and cycling through miles of unspoiled landscape where the visitor meets the county's ancient and historical past at every turn.

If it's the latest technology, state-of-the-art attractions or seaside resorts your children are looking for, you will need to travel a short distance out of the county to find them. Locally you will find tennis, badminton and squash courts, an indoor heated swimming-pool and a cinema in the town of Carlow, and outdoor pools at Bagenalstown and Bunclody. The **Ballykeenan Pet Farm and Aviary** at Myshall would make an interesting day out for youngsters. Once a famous working farm, the old stone outbuildings are now home to a wide variety of farm animals and exotic birds.

There are many gardens and historic houses in County Carlow open to visitors, but some have very limited opening hours even in the summer season, so check locally or with the tourist office before setting off to visit. An example is the **Altamont Gardens** near Kilbride, among the most beautiful and romantic gardens in Ireland, but which are only open on Sunday afternoons (other times by arrangement). They do, however, run a series of residential weekend courses that include gardening, painting and nature studies in which non-residents can participate for the day.

Access throughout the county is very good via road and rail. Expressway buses connect the major towns, with provincial services for the villages. Mainline rail services operate from Dublin, and Waterford and Dublin Airports are nearby.

• • • • •

PLACES TO VISIT

Ancient Monuments

AGHADE
Near Tullow
A large holed stone of great antiquity is sited here, perhaps once part of a megalithic tomb. For over 2,000 years it was believed that sick infants passed through the 6-inch hole would be restored to health.

BROWN'S HILL DOLMEN
Rathvilly Road, Carlow
Open access via carpark
The location, setting and purpose of this megalithic structure, the capstone of which is believed to be the largest in Europe, has been the subject of conjecture for centuries. It probably marks the burial place of a local king of long ago, but a number of myths and legends suggest many other purposes.

Castles

BALLYMOON CASTLE
Near Muine Bheag (formerly Bagenalstown)
Open access
The imposing ruins of a castle with an entrance gate and formidable square towers.

CARLOW CASTLE

Carlow

An impressive ruin overlooking the River Barrow in the town of Carlow. The present remains are the west wall of the keep with 2 of its former towers. Having withstood repeated attacks during various periods of history, an ambitious local doctor tried to convert the castle into an asylum in 1814. He attempted to demolish the interior with the use of explosive charges – but the blast demolished all but the remains you see today.

Country Parks

CLONMORE LEISURE PARK**

Hacketstown

Tel: (+353) 0508 71244

Attractions include a 9-hole golf course, skittles, meggers and bowls. Club hire available.

Equestrian Facilities

THE FORGE RIDING STABLES

Tolerton, 7 miles (11.2km) from Carlow on the Castlecomer road

Tel: (+353) 056 42570

Open: all year round

Woodland treks for beginners and experienced riders. All weather arena available.

Farm Parks

BALLYKEENAN PET FARM AND AVIARY***

Myshall, Ballykeenan

Tel: (+353) 0505 57665

Open: Monday to Saturday, 11a.m.–6p.m., Sunday, 2p.m.–6p.m.

Admission: A=££, C=£

Children will enjoy the experience of seeing and touching a wide variety of exotic birds, farm and pet animals.

Festivals and Events

EIGSE – THE CARLOW ARTS FESTIVAL***

Tel: (+353) 0503 40491

On: June

A 10-day extravaganza of arts, crafts, drama, classical and pop music, and street entertainment. This event is ranked amongst Ireland's top 4 festivals, and is recognised by many as the best visual arts festival in the country.

Forest and Amenity Walks

BAHANA

*Three miles (5km) south of **Barrow Bridge***

Fishing, forest and canalside walks.

Gardens

ALTAMONT GARDENS**
*Six miles (9.6km) south of **Tullow** on the Bunclody road*
Tel: (+353) 0503 59128
Open: April to October, Sunday and bank holidays, 2p.m.–6p.m.
Admission: ££ (free for children under 10)
Facilities: disabled access; toilets; tea-rooms
Beautiful gardens with lots of features that make it ideal for a family outing. There's a small formal garden, lawns graced by wandering peacocks, guinea-fowl and Chinese silkies, the broad walk bordered with roses and yews leading down to the informal gardens and lake. From the lake there are some splendid walks leading off in different directions. Spend some time here exploring as many as you can – they are all scenic and have their own particular beauty at different times of the year. Don't miss out on the home-made teas served in the sheltered courtyard using Altamont farm produce.

Leisure Centres and Adventure Playgrounds

CARLOW SUPERBOWL
*Lismard Centre, Barrack Street, **Carlow***
Tel: (+353) 0503 41555
Open: all year round

Museums

HILLVIEW MUSEUM
*Corries, **Bagenalstown***
Tel: (+353) 0503 21795
Open: Monday to Friday, 2p.m.–6p.m.
Admission: A=£, C=£
Fascinating collection of household artefacts and vintage farm machinery.

THE COTTAGE COLLECTION
*Ardattin, **Tullow***
Tel: (+353) 0503 55639
Open: daily, 2p.m.–5p.m.
Admission: £
A wonderful collection of domestic appliances from bygone times, many dating back to the beginning of this century. The unique collection includes vintage radios from the early 1920s, gramophones, sewing machines, irons and many other items of interest.

THE COUNTY CARLOW MUSEUM
*Town Hall, Centaur Street, **Carlow***
Tel: (+353) 0503 31324
Open: Tuesday to Saturday, 9.30a.m.–1p.m. and 2p.m.–5.30p.m., Sunday, 2.30p.m.–5.30p.m.
Admission: A=£, C=£
Exhibits provide a rare glimpse into County Carlow's past with items from many different centuries.

Swimming-Pools

GRAIGUECULLEN SWIMMING-POOL
Graiguecullen
Tel: (+353) 0503 40330
Open: all year round (check locally for times)
Indoor heated swimming-pool.

BAGENALSTOWN and BUNCLODY
Open: summer (check locally for times)
Outdoor pools.

Theatres

BRIDEWELL LANE THEATRE
*Buzz's Bar, Tullow Street, **Carlow***
Tel: (+353) 0503 43307
Open: check locally for details of performances
The theatre hosts a wide variety of productions, and it is well
worth enquiring about current performances during your visit to
the area.

Walking Routes

THE BARROW WAY
Total distance: 68 miles (109 km)
The route begins at **Lowtown** in County Kildare and follows the
towpaths of the Barrow and Grand Canal through to **St Mullins**.
There are some excellent sections of the route that can be
followed at various points throughout the county.

• • • • •

PLACES TO EAT

Cafés and Restaurants

SHAPLA TANDOORI RESTAURANT
*Hanover Court, Kennedy Avenue, **Carlow***
Tel: (+353) 0503 30037
Open: every day
Take-away menu available.

THE CENTRAL CAFE
*The Square, **Tullow***
Tel: (+353) 0503 52022
Open daily for light snacks and grills.

Fast-Food Restaurants

SUPERMAC'S
*Burrin Street, **Carlow***
Tel: (+353) 0503 30444

Hotels and Pubs

THE MANOR HOUSE
*Market Square, **Bagenalstown***
Tel: (+353) 0503 21085
Full bar menu available throughout the day.

THE GREEN DRAKE INN
*Main Street, **Borris***
Tel: (+353) 0503 73116
Comprehensive bar and snack menu available.

BUZZ'S BAR
*Tullow Street, **Carlow***
Tel: (+353) 0503 43307
An extensive healthy lunch menu available daily.

THE TARA ARMS
*Church Street, **Tullow***
Tel: (+353) 0503 51305
Home-cooked food available throughout the day. Bar meals and carvery lunches.

• • • • •

PLACES TO STAY

Country Houses and Hotels

BALLYVERGAL GUEST-HOUSE
On the N9 Carlow to Dublin road
Tel: (+353) 0503 43634; Fax: (+353) 0503 40386
Open: all year round
Children's playgound and baby-sitting service available

LANE COURT HOTEL
*Kilkenny Road, 1 mile (1.6km) from **Carlow***
Tel: (+353) 0503 42002; Fax: (+353) 0503 42765
Open: all year round
Small family hotel in a woodland setting. There's a playground and a baby-sitting service available.

ROSS NA MULLEN
*Portlaoise Road, **Carlow***
Tel: (+353) 0503 42064; Fax: (+353) 0503 30718
Open: all year round
Quiet, peaceful setting close to the town centre (1km). Baby-sitting service available.

TOM AND GERRY'S
*6 Oaklawns, Dublin Road, **Carlow***
Tel/Fax: (+353) 0503 40557

Open: all year round
Modern house, close to town centre, with a warm Irish welcome.
Baby-sitting service available.

LABURNUM LODGE
*Bunclody Road, **Tullow***
Tel: (+353) 0503 51718
Open: 1 March to 31 October
Elegant Georgian house set in the scenic Slaney valley. Baby-sitting
service available.

Farmhouse Accommodation

SHERWOOD PARK HOUSE
*Kilbride, Ballon, **Tullow***
Tel: (+353) 0503 59117; Fax: (+353) 0503 59355 (or contact Irish
Farm Holidays – see Directory)
Open: all year round
Welcoming Georgian family house located on a 100-acre mixed
farm just off the main N80 route. There's a tennis court and
facilities for children.

Hostels

OTTERHOLT RIVERSIDE HOSTEL
*Otterholt, Kilkenny Road, **Carlow***
Tel: (+353) 0503 30404; Fax: (+353) 0503 41318
Open: 1 June to 15 September

Bicycle Hire

IRISH CYCLE HIRE – see *Directory*
RALEIGH RENT-A-BIKE – see *Directory*

A.E. COLEMAN
*Dublin Street, **Carlow***
Tel: (+353) 0503 31273

Car Hire

PRATT'S GARAGE
*Pollerton Road, **Carlow***
Tel: (+353) 0503 32333

Bus Services

BUS EIREANN, *National travel information:Tel: (+353) 01 8366111*
RAPID EXPRESS. *Local services:Tel: (+353) 0503 43081*

Rail Services

Carlow – *Tel: (+353) 0503 31633*
Muine Bheag *(formerly Bagenalstown)* – *Tel: (+353) 0503 21302*

COUNTY DUBLIN

Many of this county's main attractions are to be found in the city of Dublin itself, the magnificent capital of the Republic of Ireland. The city is spread over the broad valley of the River Liffey, and the beautiful surroundings of the rest of the county are easily accessible from here. A short journey will take you to a pleasant beach or the Dublin mountains. As you would expect to find in one of Europe's finest capitals, the visitor attractions in Dublin are numerous and exceptional. **Dublin Zoo,** for example, is outstanding, while **Viking Adventure** takes visitors on an exciting, live and interactive journey through time that brings the city's colourful history to life in a thrilling way.

If you are in the city on a Saturday I would strongly recommend a visit to the **Ark,** a cultural centre for children located in the **Temple Bar** district. While the children enjoy the Ark's intimate theatre and storytelling sessions, parents can take the opportunity to explore this, the city's cultural quarter. First developed in the 19th century, with narrow cobbled streets running close to the banks of the Liffey, the area is full of atmosphere, character and charm. Stroll around the pedestrianised streets and see how artists, designers and young entrepreneurs with creative ideas have set up small art galleries, cafés, theatres and colourful shops. There are often performances taking place at Temple Bar Square and Meeting House Square, and it's here that you will find the best selection of restaurants and live music venues in Dublin. It's also a great place at Christmas.

There are many interesting museums in Dublin, but the two that will probably be of most interest to children are the **Natural History Museum** and the **National Wax Museum.**

Outside the city, **Newbridge House** at Donabate, an 18th-century manor house set in 350 acres of parkland is well worth a visit. **Malahide Castle** has much to offer the visitor too, but children will be most interested in the **Fry Model Railway Museum** in the castle grounds.

Further north, on the elevated coastline between Skerries and Balbriggan, is the **Ardgillan Demesne.** This park consists of 194 acres of rolling pasture land, mixed woodland and gardens with magnificent views of the coastline overlooking the bay of Drogheda. A sanctuary for many species of mammals and birds and a wonderful place to walk and explore, it's a great place to spend the day.

The Dublin Community and Youth Information Centre in Sackville Place is a useful contact for obtaining current news about various happenings around the city. They have information on street entertainment, park concerts and demonstrations and floor displays in the major stores and shopping centres. Open: Monday to Wednesday, 9.30a.m.–6p.m., Thursday to Saturday, 9.30a.m. to 5p.m.; Tel: (+353) 01 8786844; Fax: (+353) 01 8786610.

PLACES TO VISIT

Amusement Arcades and Funfairs

DR QUIRKEY'S EMPORIUM**
O'Connell Street, Dublin
Latest state-of-the-art technology fun centre.

Animals, Birds and Fish

DUBLIN ZOO*****
Phoenix Park, Dublin 8
Tel: (+353) 01 6771425; Fax: (+353) 01 6771660
Open: summer, Monday to Saturday, 9.30a.m.–6p.m., Sunday, 10.30a.m.–6p.m.; winter, Monday to Friday, 9.30a.m.–4p.m., Saturday, 9.30a.m.–5p.m., Sunday, 10.30a.m.–5p.m.
Admission: A=£££££, C=£££, F (free for children under 3)
Facilities: disabled access; baby-changing room; fast-food restaurant; café bar; lakeside café open in summer for snacks; ice-cream kiosks; picnic facilities; gift shop
A superb place with a huge number of attractions. Check out the Discovery Centre (featuring the world's biggest egg), the Zoo Train (which will take you for a ride around 30 acres of grounds and colourful gardens), the Reptile House (with its collection of croco-diles, snakes and tortoises) and the play areas (with tree-houses and slides). There are many rare and endangered species on view with comprehensive information panels throughout. Don't miss the daily meet-the-keeper sessions and feeding programme (weekends only in winter). Check the information panel at the zoo entrance for times. And for hungry humans, there are picnic tables and ice-cream kiosks scattered around the grounds of the zoo as well as a fast-food restaurant and a café-bar. There are loads of things to do and see here that will appeal to all the family.

Beaches

The Northside Dublin beaches are sandy and clean, but they are popular and get very busy. **Portmarnock** has an excellent beach with miles of golden sand with donkey rides and a small fair on the beach. The nearby harness racing is a very interesting spectacle and well worth a visit on a Sunday. **Donabate** is another good beach with miles of dunes to explore and have a picnic or barbecue, but the tides here are dangerous so it's not suitable for swimming. **Loughshinney** is the place for children to have fun in the water. It has a pretty miniature harbour and a safe, life-guarded beach.

Castles and Historic Houses

ARDGILLAN CASTLE AND DEMESNE**
Balbriggan

Tel: (+353) 01 8492212
Castle open: April to September, Tuesday to Sunday (and bank holidays),
11a.m.–6p.m.; October to March, Wednesday to Sunday (and bank
holidays), 11a.m.–4.30p.m.; 20 December to 31 January, Sunday only,
2p.m.–4p.m.; **Park** open: all year round, daily, 10a.m.–dusk
Admission: A=££, C=£, F (park admission free)
Facilities: wheelchair access to ground floor of castle only; toilets; tea-
rooms within the castle; picnic areas
Ardgillan is situated on the elevated coastline between Balbriggan
and Skerries and enjoys magnificent views of the countryside and
the bay of Drogheda. The ground-floor rooms of the castle are
furnished in Georgian/Victorian style, the kitchens are at basement
level and the first floor is an exhibition area. The park has 194 acres
of mixed woodland and gardens.

AYESHA CASTLE**
Killiney Hill
Tel/Fax: (+353) 01 2852323
Open: April and May, Tuesday to Thursday, 2p.m.–5p.m.; June and July,
weekends, 11a.m.–3p.m.
Admission: A=££, C=£
Entertaining tours of the castle and gardens are provided by the
owners. You can also stay in the castle in a self-catering apartment
(see WHERE TO STAY).

DUBLIN CASTLE**
Dame Street, Dublin 2
Tel: (+353) 01 6777129; Fax: (+353) 01 6797831
Open: Monday to Friday, 10a.m.–5p.m.; weekends and bank holidays,
2p.m.–5p.m. (Note: times may vary due to state business functions)
Admission: A=££, C=£, F
Facilities: toilets; restaurant; craft shop
An impressive heritage site with plenty to interest visitors. The castle
stands on a ridge at the junction of the River Liffey and its tributary
the Poddle, where the original fortification was most probably an
early Gaelic ring fort. A Viking fortress later stood on this strategic
site, part of which can be seen at the Undercroft. Some apartments
are used for state functions, so they will be closed to the public on
such occasions. But there is still plenty to see and explore.

MALAHIDE CASTLE***
Malahide
Tel: (+353) 01 8462184; Fax: (+353) 01 8462537
Open: April to October, Monday to Saturday, 10a.m.–5p.m., Sunday and
bank holidays, 11a.m.–6p.m.; November to March, Monday to Friday,
10a.m.–5p.m., Sat/Sun/bank holidays, 2p.m.–5p.m.
Admission: A=£££, C=£ (under 12), ££ (12–18), F
Facilities: disabled access; toilets; craft shop; restaurant; souvenir shop;
botanic gardens; picnic area; parkland walks; adventure playground
Set in 250 acres of parkland in the pretty seaside town of Malahide
north of Dublin, Malahide Castle was both a fortress and a private
home for nearly 800 years. The house is furnished with beautiful
period furniture together with an extensive collection of Irish
portrait paintings, recording the history of the Talbot family and
giving their own account of Ireland's stormy historic past. One of

the legends tells of the Battle of Boyne in 1690, when 14 members of the family who breakfasted together in the Great Hall were never to return as all were dead by nightfall (**see GARDENS**).

NEWBRIDGE HOUSE***
Donabate, *12 miles (19km) north of Dublin on N1*
Tel: (+353) 01 8436534
Open: April to September, Tuesday to Friday, 10a.m.–5p.m., Saturday, 11a.m.–6p.m., Sunday and bank holidays, 2p.m.–6p.m.; October to March, weekends and bank holidays, 2p.m.–5p.m.
Admission: A=££, C=£, F
Facilities: disabled access; toilets; craft and coffee shop
This delightful manor house boasts one of the finest Georgian interiors in Ireland. Each room open to visitors has its own style of antique and original furniture. In the grounds there's a fully restored courtyard with workshops displaying 19th-century tools, and a 29-acre traditional farm complete with farmyard animals.

Cathedrals

ST PATRICK'S CATHEDRAL
*Patrick's Close, **Dublin 8***
Tel: (+353) 01 4754817; Fax: (+353) 01 4546374
Open: Monday to Friday, 9a.m.–6p.m., Saturday, 9a.m.–5p.m., Sunday, 10a.m.–4.30p.m.
Admission: £
St Patrick's Cathedral stands on the oldest Christian site in Dublin – a church has stood here since AD450. Jonathan Swift, who was Dean of St Patrick's, is buried here, and his pulpit, table and chair can be viewed. The impressive building houses many interesting artefacts, including Celtic gravestones, medieval brasses and tiles, and memorials to famous Irishmen. The massive west tower dates from 1370 and contains the largest ringing peal of bells in Ireland.

Cinemas

THE SQUARE
*Towncentre Tallaght, **Dublin***
Tel: (+353) 01 4525944
12-screen cinema.

PARNELL CENTRE – **see LEISURE CENTRES**

Crèches

THE SQUARE SHOPPING COMPLEX
*Towncentre Tallaght, **Dublin***
Tel: (+353) 01 4525944

Environment and Ecology Centres

ENFO – INFORMATION ON THE ENVIRONMENT***
*17 St Andrew Street, **Dublin 2***
Tel: (+353) 01 6793144; Fax: (+353) 01 6795204
Open: all year round, Monday to Saturday, 10a.m.–5p.m.

Enfo is a public information service providing easy access to wide-ranging and authoritative information on environmental matters. Facilities include exhibitions, videos, a query-answering service and leaflets about the environment in Ireland. The centre produces excellent worksheets and newsletters for children.

Craft Centres

HEY, DOODLE, DOODLE***
*14 Crown Alley, Temple Bar, **Dublin***
Tel: (+353) 01 6727382
Open: Summer, Mon–Wed, 11a.m.–6p.m.; Thur–Sat, 11a.m.–8p.m.; Sun, 12noon–8p.m.; winter, Mon–Sat, 11a.m.–6p.m.; Sun, 12noon–5p.m.
Admission: A=£££££, C=££ (For one hour of painting time including tuition, plus the price of the piece.)
Children and parents can create their own designs on ready-made plain pottery. Pieces are glazed, kiln fired and ready to be collected 24–28 hours later.

Equestrian Facilities

BRIDESTREAM RIDING CENTRE
Kilcock
Tel: (+353) 01 6287261

CARRICKMINES EQUESTRIAN CENTRE
Foxrock
Tel: (+353) 01 2955990

MALAHIDE RIDING STABLES
Malahide
Tel: (+353) 01 8463622

RIDING IN DUNDRUM
Dublin
Tel: (+353) 01 2986112

Festivals and Events

TEMPLE BAR CHRISTMAS CELEBRATIONS*****
Dublin
Tel: (+353) 01 6715717; Fax: (+353) 01 6772525
Information Centre open: June to August, Monday to Friday, 9a.m.–6p.m., Saturday, 11a.m.–6p.m., Sunday, noon–6p.m.; September to May, Monday to Friday, 9a.m.–6p.m.
Events and festivals take place throughout the year. Contact the Temple Bar Information Centre direct for a detailed programme of events.

Forest and Amenity Walks

HELLFIRE CLUB FOREST
*Four miles (6.4km) south of **Rathfarnham** on route R116 to Glencullen*
A variety of forest walks with scenic views. At the summit are the

ruins of the Hellfire Club, traditionally named after a group of 'wild young gentlemen' who used it as a meeting place after being barred from a local tavern for bad behaviour.

TICKNOCK
*Near **Sandyford** on route R113 to Tallaght*
There are walks throughout the forest with outstanding views of Dublin and the surrounding countryside.

Gardens

FERNHILL GARDENS
*Sandyford, 2 miles (3.2km) from **Dundrum** on the Enniskerry road*
Tel: (+353) 01 2956000
Open: April to September, Tuesday to Saturday, 11a.m.–5p.m., Sunday (garden only), 2p.m.–6p.m.
Admission: A=££, C=£, F
Facilities: toilets; wheelchair access to lower sections; picnic areas
Excellent walks through a variety of garden habitats and scenic views. Plant sales.

HOWTH CASTLE DEMESNE***
Howth
Tel: (+353) 01 8322624
Demesne open: all year round, daily, 8a.m.–dusk
Transport museum open: weekends and bank holidays, 2p.m.–5p.m.
Admission: free to park
A wild hillside garden at its best in late spring when the blooms of over 2,000 varieties of rhododendron make a spectacular display on the cliff-face. The castle is not open to the public, but there is an interesting transport museum in the grounds.

NATIONAL BOTANIC GARDENS***
*Botanic Road, Glasnevin, **Dublin 9***
Tel: (+353) 01 8377596; Fax: (+353) 01 8360080
Open: summer, Monday to Saturday, 9a.m.–6p.m., Sunday, 11a.m.–6p.m.; winter, Monday to Saturday, 10a.m.–4.30p.m., Sunday, 11a.m.–4.30p.m.
Admission: free
These magnificent gardens spread over 50 acres on the south bank of the River Tolka contain many interesting features, including an arboretum, riverside walks, rock garden and burren areas, pond, extensive herbaceous borders and annual display of decorative plants. There's also a large palm house, a new alpine house and a complex for ferns, tropical water plants and succulents.

TALBOT GARDENS**
*Malahide Castle, **Malahide***
Tel: (+353) 01 8450940
Demesne open: all year round, daily, 10a.m. to dusk
Admission: free
Access to Castle and Fry Model Railway (**see CASTLES *and* TRAINS**).

ZOOLOGICAL GARDENS***
*Phoenix Park, **Dublin***

Open: all year round, daily, 9.30a.m.–4p.m.
Mature gardens with an abundance of trees, shrubs and flowers, and a lake for seals (*see* ANIMALS, BIRDS AND FISH *and* PARKS).

Heritage Centres

KILMAINHAM GAOL
Kilmainham, Dublin 8
Tel: (+353) 01 4535984; Fax: (+353) 01 4532037
Open: all year round, daily
Admission: A=££, C=£, F
The restored prison gives visitors a vivid insight into some of the most important stages of Ireland's quest for independence.

CEOL – THE IRISH TRADITIONAL MUSIC CENTRE***
Smithfield Village, Dublin 7
Tel: (+353) 01 817 3820 Fax: (+353) 01 817 3821
Open: All year, Mon–Sat, 9.30a.m.–6.30p.m.; Sunday and bank holidays, 10.30a.m.–6.30p.m.
Admission: A=£££, C=££, F
Ceol offers the visitor a unique insight into Irish traditional music, and the interactive destination celebrates the music, song and dance from its roots and energy to its diverse personalities. In the 180-degree-wide screen auditorium visitors are talen on a whistlestop tour across the whole of Ireland, celebrating its musical heritage.

THE HOT PRESS IRISH MUSIC HALL OF FAME****
57 Middle Abbey Street, Dublin 1
Tel: (+353) 01 878 3345; Fax: (+353) 01 878 2225
Open: All year, daily, 10a.m.–7p.m.
Admission: A=£££££, C=££££
Facilities: Toilets; disabled access; 'Jam' restaurant (as in music, not butties)
This is the ultimate Irish music experience as visitors embark on a memorable musical adventure capturing the highlights in the story of Irish music featuring U2, The Corrs, Van Morrison etc. The kids will enjoy the Rock and Stroll trail, and a few parents might enjoy the experience too. (Allow 90 minutes for the tour.)

VIKING ADVENTURE***
Temple Bar, Dublin 2
Tel: (+353) 01 6796040; Fax: (+353) 01 6796033
Open: all year, Tuesday to Saturday, 10a.m.–4.30p.m.
Admission: A=££££, C=£££, F (free for children under 3)
Facilities: toilets; craft and coffee shop
Viking Adventure's Norse guides take you on a journey through time to bring Dublin's colourful history to life in a thrilling journey of discovery. You can talk to Vikings as they go about their daily business, stroll through their town and visit their homes and work-places. The centre also houses an extensive collection of artefacts discovered during the excavation of the site in the heart of the 10th-century Viking city. This is an engaging exhibition and inter-active adventure which will entertain and enlighten all ages.

WATERWAYS VISITOR CENTRE**

*Ringsend, Grand Canal Basin, Pearse Street Bridge, **Dublin***
Tel: (+353) 01 6777510; Fax: (+353) 01 6777514
Open: June to September, daily, 9.30a.m.–6.30p.m.; October to May,
Wednesday to Sunday, 12.30p.m.–5p.m.
Admission: A=£, C=£, F

The centre houses an exhibition designed to introduce the visitor
to the story of Ireland's inland waterways and the range of diverse
activities and experiences they offer.

Leisure Centres and Adventure Playgrounds

BAMBAMS JUNGLELAND
*81 Lower Kilmacud Road, **Stillorgan***
Tel: (+353) 01 2884529
Open: Monday to Friday, 12.30p.m.–7p.m., weekends, 10.30a.m.–
7p.m.
Admission: under-4s=££, over-4s=£££

BOWLING CENTRE
Stillorgan
Tel: (+353) 01 2881656
Computer and video games, playground, coffee and snack bar.

CAPTAIN VENTURE
*The Square, **Dublin***
Tel: (+353) 01 596039

CLONDALKIN SPORTS AND LEISURE CENTRE
*Nangor Road, Clondalkin, **Dublin 22***
Tel: (+353) 01 4574858
Open: all year round, daily
Gymnasium, ball courts and swimming-pool.

DUBLIN ICE RINK
*Dolphin's Barn, South Circular Road, **Dublin 8***
Tel: (+353) 01 4534153
Open: all year round, daily, 10a.m.–10p.m. (check for session times)
Admission: £££ (skate hire included in admission charge)

GIRAFFE'S
*Coolmine Industrial Park, **Clonsilla***
Tel: (+353) 01 8205526
and
*Feltrim Industrial Estate, **Swords***
Tel: (+353) 01 8408749

INJUN FALLS
*Belgard Road, **Tallaght***
Tel: (+353) 01 597440

LEISUREPLEX***
*Malahide Road, **Coolock***
Tel: (+353) 01 8485722
Open: all year round, daily, 24 hours

Facilities: children's play areas; restaurant; bowling alley; laser games; snooker and pool and video games

LEISUREPLEX TALLAGHT SPORTS WORLD***
*Village Green, Tallaght, **Dublin 24***
Tel: (+353) 01 4599411
Open: all year round, daily, 24 hours
Facilities: children's play areas; restaurant; bowling alley; laser games; snooker and pool and video games.

OMNI ADVENTURE WORLD
*Omni Centre, **Santry***
Tel: (+353) 01 8428844

PARNELL CENTRE
*Parnell Street, **Dublin 1***
A new and very advanced entertainment centre with a 9-screen cinema, various bars and restaurants, a futuristic family entertainment centre and Ireland's first IMAX theatre, a giant screen film experience in a sophisticated theatre venue.

THE FUN FACTORY
*Monkstown Road, **Dun Laoghaire***
Tel: (+353) 01 2843344

WALLY WABBITS
*Pye Centre, Dundrum, **Dublin 14***
Tel: (+353) 01 2983470
Open: school days, 2p.m.–6p.m., holidays and weekends, 10a.m.–6p.m.
Admission: £££ (reductions for groups of 2 or more children)

Museums

DUBLIN WRITERS' MUSEUM
*18–19 Parnell Square, **Dublin 1***
Tel: (+353) 01 8722077
Open: all year round, Monday to Saturday, 10a.m.–5p.m., Sunday/bank holidays, 11a.m.– 5p.m.
Admission: A=£££, C=£ (under 12), ££ (12–18), F
An opportunity to explore Dublin's and Ireland's rich literary heritage. One room has an exhibition of contemporary children's literature.

GUINNESS MUSEUM
*Guinness Hop Store, St James' Gate, **Dublin 8***
Tel: (+353) 01 4084800; Fax: (+353) 01 4084965
Open: April to September, Monday to Saturday, 9.30a.m.–5p.m.; Sundays and public holidays, 10.30a.m.–4.30p.m.; October to March, Monday to Saturday, 9.30a.m.–4p.m.; Sundays and public holidays, 12noon–4p.m.
Admission: A=£££££, C=£, F
Facilities: disabled access; parking; audio-visual presentations; visitor centre; souvenir shop
This is the home of Guinness stout and houses the World of Guinness Exhibition. There is also the choice of a bar where you

can sample some of Ireland's famous brew, or the coffee shop!

FRY MODEL RAILWAY MUSEUM***
*Malahide Castle, **Malahide***
Tel: (+353) 01 8463779; Fax: (+353) 01 8462537
Open: April to September, Monday to Saturday, 10a.m.–5p.m.; Sunday and bank holidays, 2p.m.–6p.m.; (Closed Fridays during April, May and September); October to March, Sat/Sun/bank holidays, 2p.m.–5p.m.
Admission: A=££, C=£ (under 12), ££ (12–18), F
Facilities: toilets; book shop and model shop; golf and pitch'n'putt
The Fry Model Railway Museum has a unique collection of hand-made models of Irish trains from the beginning of rail travel to modern times. The beautifully engineered models are from a collection originally built up in the 1920s and '30s by Cyril Fry, a railway engineer and draughtsman. Each piece is assembled with great attention to detail and includes examples from the earliest railway developments. They are run on a Grand Transport complex with stations, bridges, trams and buses and barges on the River Liffey, and will interest both children and adults. Combined with a visit to the castle, gardens and grounds, this is a great place for a day out (**see CASTLES *and* GARDENS**).

MUSEUM OF CHILDHOOD***
*20 Palmerston Road, Rathmines, **Dublin 8***
Tel: (+353) 01 4973223
Open: all year round
Admission: A=£, C=£
The museum houses a collection of memorabilia from nurseries all over the world. The toys go back several centuries, and include toy soldiers, dolls'-houses, brass beds and a 3-faced doll.

NATIONAL GALLERY OF IRELAND***
*Merrion Square West, **Dublin 2***
Tel: (+353) 01 6615133
Open: all year round, Monday to Saturday, 10a.m.–5.30p.m. (till 8.30p.m. on Thursday), Sunday, 2p.m.–5p.m.
Admission: free
Facilities: disabled access; guided tours; shop; self-service restaurant
Fine national art collection especially strong on 19th-century Irish art and old masters. Periodic painting classes and special activities are organised for children – check locally for details.

NATIONAL MUSEUM OF IRELAND and
NATURAL HISTORY MUSEUM***
*Kildare Street/Merrion Street, **Dublin 2***
Tel: (+353) 01 6777444
Open: all year round, Tuesday to Saturday, 10a.m.–5p.m., Sunday, 2p.m.–5p.m.
Admission: free
Facilities: shop and café; wheelchair access to ground floor only
The museum contains artefacts and masterpieces dating from 2000BC to the 20th century. Look out for the 'Ireland's Gold' exhibition, which features the finest collection of prehistoric gold artefacts in Europe, and displays on Ireland in the prehistoric and Viking ages. The Natural History Museum is a zoological museum

containing collections illustrating the wildlife of Ireland.

NATIONAL MARITIME MUSEUM OF IRELAND
Haigh Terrace, **Dun Laoghaire**
Tel: (+353) 01 800969
Open: May to September, Tuesday to Sunday, 2.30p.m.–5.30p.m.; April,
October and November, weekends, 2.30p.m.–5.30p.m.
Admission: A=£, C=£
Limited disabled access
On display are a number of historical models, including a longboat
from a French ship captured at Bantry in 1796.

NATIONAL WAX MUSEUM****
Granby Row, Parnell Square, **Dublin 1**
Tel: (+353) 01 8726340
Open: Monday to Saturday, 10a.m.–6p.m., Sunday, noon–6p.m.
Admission: A=£££, C=££, F
Discover a world where fantasy and reality combine and heroes of
the past and present come alive before your eyes. Ireland's only
wax exhibition has a Kingdom of Fairytales which children can
wander through to find the magical lamp and the all-powerful genie,
or they can visit the Hall of Megastars to see heroes from the
world of rock'n'roll in the shape of Michael Jackson, Madonna and
Elvis. For those who enjoy the sound of clanging chains and blood-
curdling screams there's the Chamber of Horrors. And don't miss
the chance to experience the excitement of the Adventure
Tunnels. This is an ideal venue for a family outing.

GAA MUSEUM***
New Stand, Croke Park, **Dublin 3**
Tel: (+353) 01 855 8176; Fax: (+353) 01 855 8104
Open: May to Sept, daily, 9.30a.m.–5p.m.; Oct to April, Tues to Sat,
10am.–5p.m.; Sun, 12noon–5p.m.
Admisssion: A=£££, C=£, F
Facilities in stadium
The GAA Museum in Croke Park has been designed to facilitate an
experience of an integral part of Irish life and heritage. Touchscreen
technology brings you the historic moments, the great names and
games, and interactives allow you to test yourself in the skills of
Ireland's most popular psorts.

NUMBER TWENTY-NINE
Lower Fitzwilliam Street, **Dublin**
Tel: (+353) 01 7026165
Open: all year round, Tuesday to Saturday, 10a.m.–5p.m., Sunday,
2p.m.–5p.m.
Admission: A=££ (free for children under 16)
A place to discover the daily lifestyle of early 19th-century Dublin.
The atmosphere and furnishings of a typical house of the period
1790–1820 can be experienced in a unique collection of artefacts
and works of art of the time that include exhibits in the nursery
and playrooms.

Parks

MARLAY PARK***
Rathfarnham, *in the south-west suburbs of Dublin*
Tel: (+353) 01 4942083
Lakeland park with an interesting collection of craft workshops in the converted stables of a grand house. Under-10s can ride on a model railway, and there are tennis courts and a pitch'n'putt course for older kids.

PHOENIX PARK****
Dublin
Tel: (+353) 01 6613111
Park *open: all year round, daily*
Visitor centre *open: March, October and November, 9.30a.m.–5p.m.; April and May, 9.30a.m.–5.30p.m.; June to September, 9.30a.m.– 6.30p.m.; December to February, 9.30a.m.–4.30p.m.*
The largest enclosed park in Europe with 712 hectares containing Dublin Zoo, a visitor centre, the People's Gardens, a pond for sailing model boats, a 17th-century tower house and a 205ft obelisk commemorating the Duke of Wellington. But most of all the park is known for its acres and acres of open parkland, rich in wildlife and 4-legged natural lawn mowers: the grazing deer and cattle.

ST STEPHEN'S GREEN**
Dublin 2
Tel: (+353) 01 4757816
Open: all year round, daily
Admission: free
One of Ireland's oldest public parks, with tree-lined walks, colourful flowerbeds, a children's playground, a lake, a garden for the visually impaired, and bandstand performances in the summer months.

TYMON PARK**
Tallaght, **Dublin**
Open: daylight hours
A purpose-built park near the massive Square Shopping Complex. The River Poddle runs through it and there's a children's area, playing fields and scenic vistas of the Dublin and Wicklow mountains.

Shopping Centres

MOORE STREET OPEN MARKET
Dublin
This colourful and lively street is the scene of Dublin's famous barrow vendors. A visit here is an ideal way to experience another form of street entertainment and get a flavour of Dublin through the wit of its people.

TEMPLE BAR*****
Dublin
Tel: (+353) 01 6715717; Fax: (+353) 01 6772525
The blend of cultural centres, galleries, bars, restaurants, cafés and shops and the mixture of old and contemporary architecture combine

to give Temple Bar a unique ambience. The area is full of character and charm and the streets are pedestrianised, so to really appreciate all that the area has to offer take some time to stroll around. Meeting House Square is a spectacular open-air performance area surrounded by a cluster of innovative cultural centres such as the Irish Film Centre, the Photography Centre and Gallery of Photography, and the Ark (a children's cultural centre). Performances on the square incorporate theatre and music, many of which are free of charge and take place during the summer months (see FESTIVALS and THEATRES).

THE SQUARE****
Towncentre Tallaght, Dublin
Tel: (+353) 01 4525944
Open: Monday to Saturday, 9a.m.–6p.m. (till 9p.m., Wednesday to Friday)
The largest shopping centre in Ireland has 140 shops, 10 restaurants and a 12-screen cinema. There is something for everyone under the one roof, and the use of natural light and large areas of trees and shrubs gives the illusion of being outdoors on a pleasant day. Even children will enjoy shopping here, as the centre has a crèche and full baby-care facilities, ice-cream parlours, a soda fountain, fast-food restaurants, escalators and moving walkways, and laser games.

Swimming-Pools

DUBLIN CORPORATION SWIMMING-POOLS
Open: summer, Monday to Friday, 11.30a.m.–3p.m. and 4p.m.–8p.m., Saturday, 10a.m.–1p.m. and 2p.m.–6p.m., Sunday, 10a.m.–2p.m.

BALLYFERMOT, *Le Fanu Park* – *Tel: (+353) 01 6266504*
BALLYMUN SHOPPING CENTRE – *Tel: (+353) 01 8421368*
COOLOCK SHOPPING CENTRE – *Tel: (+353) 01 8477743*
CRUMLIN, *Willie Pearse Park* – *Tel: (+353) 01 4555792*
FINGLAS, *Mellowes Road* – *Tel: (+353) 01 8348005*
MARKIEVICZ, *Townsend Street* – *Tel: (+353) 01 6770503*
RATHMINES – *Tel: (+353) 01 4961275*
SEAN McDERMOTT STREET – *Tel: (+353) 01 8720752*

The following are private pools; phone for session times:
DUNDRUM FAMILY RECREATION CENTRE – *Tel: 01 2984654*
PORTMARNOCK SPORTS CENTRE – *Tel: (+353) 01 8462086*

Theatres

LAMBERT PUPPET THEATRE****
Clifton Lane, Monkstown
Tel: (+353) 01 2800974
On: Saturday, 3.30p.m.
Shows presented by the famous Lambert family provide great entertainment. The show changes every month, with seasonal specials.

THE ARK CULTURAL CENTRE FOR CHILDREN*****
Temple Bar, Dublin
Tel: (+353) 01 6707788; Fax: (+353) 01 6707758

Open: adults can attend between 5p.m.–7p.m. on Thursday, and visiting children can attend the programme of events on Saturday
The centre presents an excellent series of storytelling sessions, workshops and theatre for children. Contact the centre direct for a current programme of events (**see** SHOPPING CENTRES).

Walking Routes

DUBLIN HERITAGE TRAIL***
An excellent way to see the city is to follow a signposted walking tour. The trail into old Dublin begins at College Green, where the Vikings built their Thingmote and 18th-century Ireland had its parliament. The route follows the centres of power and influence that have shaped the history of Dublin, through to districts such as Liberties and Temple Bar where today's Dubliners continue the traditions of the past thousand years. Alternatively, you can follow the route on board Dublin Bus who operate a heritage trail tour of the city. The hourly service stops at 10 places where passengers can alight to visit a point of interest and catch a later bus to visit the next stop on the tour. The ticket is valid for a whole day so you can get on and off as often as you please.

• • • • •

PLACES TO EAT

Cafés and Restaurants

CLERY'S DEPARTMENT STORE
*O'Connell Street, **Dublin***
Open: Monday to Saturday, 9.30a.m.–5p.m.
Basement café, tea-rooms on the first floor and an excellent rooftop restaurant.

THE BELFRY CAFÉ
*Dublin Tourism Centre, Suffolk Street, **Dublin 2***
Tel: (+353) 01 6799641
Located right in the heart of the city above the new Dublin Tourism Centre.

THE BAD ASS CAFÉ
*9–11 Crown Alley, Temple Bar, **Dublin***
Tel: (+353) 01 6712596
Open: All day, every day
This informal, popular eatery caters for all tastes.

WELL FED CAFE
*Dublin Resource Centre, 6 Crow Street, **Dublin***
Tel: (+353) 01 6772234
Vegetarian restaurant.

ELEPHANT AND CASTLE
*18 Temple Bar, **Dublin***

Tel: (+353) 01 6793121
Open: Monday to Friday, 8a.m.–11.30p.m., Saturday, 10.30a.m.–
midnight, Sunday, noon–11.30p.m.
A good selection of excellent food served all day. Children catered
for and welcomed.

Fast-Food Restaurants

BESHOFF'S
Westmoreland Street, **Dublin**
Open: daily, 11.30a.m.–midnight
A good place for fish and chips.

McDONALD'S
Frascati Shopping Centre, **Blackrock**
Tel: (+353) 01 2781422
Open: daily, 7.30a.m.–midnight
and
The Mill Shopping Centre, **Clondalkin**
Tel: (+353) 01 4577875
Open: daily, 7.30a.m.–midnight
and
The Llac Shopping Centre, Henry Street, **Dublin**
Tel: (+353) 01 8728295
Open: daily, 7.30a.m.–midnight
and
Upper O'Connell Street, **Dublin**
Tel: (+353) 01 8724487
Open: daily, 7.30a.m.–midnight
and
The Swan Centre, Rathmines, **Dublin 6**
Tel: (+353) 01 4965533
Open: daily, 7.30a.m.–midnight
and
30 Upper George Street, **Dun Laoghaire**
Tel: (+353) 01 2804087
Open: daily, 7.30a.m.–midnight
and
Nutgrove Shopping Centre, Rathfarnham, **Dublin 16**
Tel: (+353) 01 4933057
Open: daily, 7.30a.m.–midnight
and
The Square, Tallaght, **Dublin 24**
Tel: (+353) 01 4598835
Open: daily, 7.30a.m.–midnight

The Plaxa, **Swords**
Tel: (+353) 01 8903004

Font Hill Road, **Palmerstown**
Tel: (+353) 01 6264265

Maple Centre, Navan Road, **Dublin**
Tel: (+353) 01 8687271

14–16 Mary's Street, **Dublin**
Tel: (+353) 01 8744101

Blanchardstown Shopping Centre, **Dublin**
Tel: (+353) 01 8221856

27 Ranelagh, **Dublin**
Tel: (+353) 01 4967472

Blachardstown, **Dublin** *(Drive-through)*
Tel: (+353) 01 8223227

Cranley Centre, Naas Road, **Dublin** *(Drive-through)*
Tel: (+353) 01 4564809

Belgard Road, Tallaght, **Dublin** *(Drive-through)*
Tel: (+353) 01 4596852

50 Lower O'Connell Street, **Dublin**
Tel: (+353) 018720050

Omni Park Shopping Centre, Santry, **Dublin** *(Drive-through)*
Tel: (+353) 01 8621332

10–11 Grafton Street, **Dublin**
Tel: (+353) 01 6778393

144 Phibsboro Road, **Dublin**
Tel: (+353) 01 8300755

Stillorgan Shopping Centre, **Stillorgan**
Tel: (+353) 01 2883977

Kylemore Road, **Dublin** *(Drive-through)*
Tel: (+353) 01 4505722

Donaghmede Shopping Centre, Donaghmede, **Dublin** *(Drive-through)*
Tel: (+353) 01 8485189

Kilmore Road, Artaine, **Dublin** *(Drive-through)*
Tel: (+353) 01 8327370

SUPERMAC'S
O'Connell Street, **Dublin 1**
Tel: (+353) 01 8721828

Main Street, Blackrock Village
Tel: (+353) 01 2883019

HARRY RAMSDEN'S
Naas Road, **Dublin**
Tel: (+353) 01 4600233
World-famous fish and chips available seven days a week.

PLACES TO STAY

Country Houses and Hotels

JURY'S INN
*Christchurch Place, **Dublin 8***
Tel: (+353) 01 4750111; Fax: (+353) 01 4750488
Open: all year round
This is a fixed-rate hotel right in the heart of Dublin, with an informal restaurant and modern, attractive en-suite rooms that will accommodate 2 adults and 2 children for a total cost of between £30 and £35 per room. This is a perfect arrangement for low-budget family accommodation.

FORTE TRAVELODGE
*Pinnock Hill, Swords bypass, Belfast Road, **Swords***
Tel: Freephone (UK) 0800 850950, (Eire) 1800 709709
Comfortable, award-winning accommodation with well-appointed family rooms on a fixed-rate basis for around £40 per room. Breakfast is available for an extra charge. Sited next to a Little Chef restaurant.

THE DUNES HOTEL
*Balcarrick, **Donabate***
Tel: (+353) 01 8436153; Fax: (+353) 01 8436111
Open: all year round
Family-run hotel located on Corballis beach. Has a games room and facilities for children.

THE ANCHOR GUEST-HOUSE
*49 Lower Gardiner Street, **Dublin***
Tel: (+353) 01 8786913; Fax: (+353) 01 8788038
Open: all year round (except Christmas)
Family-friendly guest-house with facilities for children.

CHARLEVILLE LODGE
*268–272 North Circular Road, Phibsboro, **Dublin 7***
Tel: (+353) 01 8386633; Fax: (+353) 01 8385854
Family-friendly guest-house with facilities for children.

CLIFDEN HOUSE
*32 Gardiner Place, **Dublin 1***
Tel: (+353) 01 8746364; Fax: (+353) 01 8746122
Open: all year round
Refurbished home in the city centre with family rooms.

CLONTARF COURT HOTEL
*225 Clontarf Road, Clontarf, **Dublin 3** (on the coast road to Howth)*
Tel/Fax: (+353) 01 8332680
Open: all year round
Family-run hotel with facilities for children.

HOTEL ISAACS
*Store Street, **Dublin 1***
Tel: (+353) 01 8550067; Fax: (+353) 01 8365390
Open: all year round
Family-friendly hotel with facilities for children.

O'SHEA'S HOTEL
*19 Talbot Street, **Dublin***
Tel: (+353) 01 8365670; Fax: (+353) 01 8365214
Open: all year round
Family-friendly hotel with facilities for children.

VICTOR HOTEL
*Rochestown Avenue, **Dun Laoghaire***
Tel: (+353) 01 2853555; Fax: (+353) 01 2853914
Open: all year round
Family-friendly hotel with facilities for children including multi-channel TVs and a leisure complex.

CARRIAGE HOUSE*****
Lusk
Tel: (+353) 01 8438857; Fax: (+353) 01 8438933
Open: all year round
This beautiful country home has just 5 bedrooms but has its own leisure centre, indoor heated swimming-pool and playground.

Farmhouse Accommodation

WOODVIEW FARMHOUSE
*Margaretstown, **Skerries***
Tel: (+353) 01 8491528 (or contact Irish Farm Holidays – see Directory)
Open: all year round
Large farmhouse with a playground and lots more facilities nearby.

Self-Catering Apartments and Houses

UCD VILLAGE CAMPUS
*Belfield, **Dublin 4***
Tel: (+353) 01 2697111; Fax: (+353) 01 2697704
Open: from mid-June to mid-September
Located within the landscaped grounds of University College Dublin, this is a superior development of 3- and 4-bedroom self-catering apartments. Campus bar, restaurants and coffee shop available for guests. Children are welcome and the apartments are available for single-night and weekly lettings.

WHITEHALL
*Ms P. Rutledge, 117 Ballymun Road, **Dublin 9***
Tel: (+353) 01 8378333
Fully equipped 4-bedroom semi-detached house. Sleeps 6.

AYESHA CASTLE***
Killiney
Tel/Fax: (+353) 01 2852323
A large apartment in the west wing of Ayesha Castle. There are

great views of Killiney Bay, access to a secluded garden and wood-lands. Children are welcome and a baby-sitting service is available.

Caravan and Camping Parks

CAMAC VALLEY CARAVAN AND CAMPING PARK***
*Corkagh Park, Naas Road, Clondalkin, **Dublin 22***
Tel: (+353) 01 4640644; Fax: (+353) 01 4640643
Open: all year round
Located in the beautiful grounds of Corkagh Regional Park, this attractive site has a shop, laundry, campers' kitchen and playground.

Hostels

ABRAHAM HOUSE
*82/83 Lower Gardiner Street, **Dublin 1***
Tel: (+353) 01 8550600; Fax: (+353) 01 8550598
Open: all year round

GLOBETROTTERS TOURIST HOSTEL
*46–48 Lower Gardiner Street, **Dublin***
Tel: (+353) 01 8735893; Fax: (+353) 01 8788787
Open: all year round

KINLAY HOUSE CHRISTCHURCH
*2–12 Lord Edward Street, **Dublin 2***
Tel: (+353) 01 6796644; Fax: (+353) 01 6797437
Open: all year round

OLD SCHOOL HOUSE
*Eblana Avenue, **Dun Laoghaire***
Tel: (+353) 01 2808777; Fax: (+353) 01 2842266
Open: all year round

Gardens

BALLINDOOLIN HOUSE AND GARDENS
Carbury
Tel: (+353) 0405 31430
Open: May to September, 12noon–6p.m. (closed Mondays)
Admission: A=££, C=£
Period house with a restaurant, walled garden, pleasure gardens, nature trail and children's farmyard.

Bicycle Hire

IRISH CYCLE HIRE – see *Directory*
RALEIGH RENT-A-BIKE – see *Directory*

C. HARDING FOR BIKES
*30 Batchelor's Walk, **Dublin 1***
Tel: (+353) 01 8732455; Fax: (+353) 01 8733622

OE DALY CYCLES
*Lower Main Street, Dundrum, **Dublin 14***
Tel: (+353) 01 2981485

LITTLE SPORT LTD
*3 Merville Ave, Fairview, **Dublin 3***
Tel: (+353) 01 8332405; Fax: (+353) 01 8330044

CGL
*9 Townyard Lane, **Malahide***
Tel: (+353) 01 8454275

Car Hire

ARGUS RENT-A-CAR
*Argus House, 59 Terenure Road East, **Dublin 6***
Tel: (+353) 01 904444; Fax: (+353) 01 906328

ATLAS CAR RENTALS
Dublin Airport
Tel: (+353) 01 8444859; Fax: (+353) 01 8407302

SOUTH COUNTY CAR RENTALS
*Rochestown Avenue, **Dun Laoghaire***
Tel: (+353) 01 2806005; Fax: (+353) 01 2857016

Airports

DUBLIN
Tel: (+353) 01 8444900

Bus Services

BUSARAS
*Store Street, **Dublin***
Tel: (+353) 01 8302222; Travel information – Tel: (+353) 01 8366111

DUBLIN BUS
*Upper O'Connell Street, **Dublin***
Tel: (+353) 01 8734222

Rail Services

Dublin (Connolly) *– Tel: (+353) 01 7032355*
Dublin (Houston) *– Tel: (+353) 01 7032126;*
Travel information – Tel: (+353) 01 8366222

COUNTY KILDARE

Kildare is known as the 'Home of the Horse', and many of the attractions around the county reflect this. The Irish Derby is run here at the Curragh; the **horse museum at Tully** near the town of Kildare features Arkle, one of the most famous horses Ireland has produced. This beautiful inland county is littered with majestic stud farms and riding schools, and the emerald pastures are graced by thoroughbred horses grazing the lush green grass. If your chosen mode of transport is four wheels rather than four legs, there are plenty of other attractions around the county for families to visit. There are some beautiful gardens, historic houses and heritage centres, museums, watersports and peatlands. Its central location makes it ideal for visiting the southeast of Ireland and it's only an hour's drive from Dublin.

Kildare has some lovely towns. Naas has excellent facilities and services; Newbridge on the River Liffey, a former garrison town, is now rapidly expanding as a centre of enterprise and industry; and Kildare is recognised throughout the world as the capital of Ireland's horse industry. The town has many attractions, but perhaps the best is the **Irish National Stud and Japanese Gardens.** These gardens – internationally acclaimed as the finest of their kind in Europe – make this a great place to spend a day.

If your kids are interested in horses, they'll love the world renowned **Kellett's Riding School** in Kill, 16 miles (26km) west of Dublin. North of Kill is the village of Straffan, home to the **Morell Open Farm** and its wide range of animals. There's also a pets corner and an animal hospital.

Also in Straffan is the **Lodge Park Heritage Centre and Steam Museum.** It has prototype railway engines and displays of industrial stationary engines. The **Straffan Butterfly Farm** is Ireland's first live tropical butterfly exhibition, and brilliantly combines conservation with education.

North of Naas is the **Ardkill Farm and Bog** at Carbury. There's fun for all the family here with the usual array of farm animals to feed and cuddle. As well as taking part in many organised events here, you can wander down the Old Bog Road to visit the Ardkill Bog and see its wildlife and history.

South of Naas on the N9 is the **Crookstown Historical and Heritage Centre** in the old mill at Ballytore. The mill has now been converted into a heritage centre, and even the mill-wheel restored to full working order.

Peat has been a vital part of rural life in Ireland for centuries, and **Peatland World,** just north of Kildare, is located in the historic Bog of Allen. This informative centre and museum is a good way for the children to learn something about this interesting phenomenon.

There is a good network of major roads throughout the county, including the N4, N7, N9 and N78. Most of the major towns are served by bus and rail, and the villages by provincial bus services. Dublin Airport is on the doorstep of the county.

PLACES TO VISIT

Boats and Boat Trips

ROBERTSTOWN CANAL BARGE TRIPS
*The Eustace, **Robertstown***
Tel: (+353) 045 860808
Open: April to September, daily, from 9a.m.
Canal tours on a refurbished barge will let you discover the
splendour of the Grand Canal countryside.

Castles and Historic Houses

CASTLETOWN HOUSE
Celbridge
Tel: (+353) 01 6288252; Fax: (+353) 01 6271811
*Open: April to September, daily, 10a.m.–6p.m. (Saturday from 11a.m.,
Sunday and bank holidays from 2p.m.); October, Monday to Friday,
10a.m.–5p.m., Sunday and bank holidays from 2p.m.; November to
March, Sunday and bank holidays, 2p.m.–5p.m.*
Admission (including guided tour): A=££, C=£, F
Facilities: disabled access; toilets; coffee shop
Ireland's largest and finest Palladian country house, built in 1722 for
the speaker of the Irish House of Commons, has a fine collection of
18th-century furniture and paintings.

Cinemas

DARA TWIN CINEMA
Naas
Tel: (+353) 045 97382

OSCAR CINEMA
Newbridge
Tel: (+353) 045 431284

Country Parks

CELBRIDGE ABBEY GROUNDS****
Celbridge
Tel: (+353) 01 6288350; Fax: (+353) 01 6270790
Open: March to October, Tuesday to Sunday, noon–6p.m.
Admission: A=£, C=£, F
*Facilities: toilets; disabled access; free parking; information centre in the
courtyard; tea-room; gardens and garden centre; picnic area*
This is an excellent, well-laid-out park with informative presen-
tations, route guides and a diverse range of attractions. The abbey
grounds were planted by the daughter of the Lord Mayor of Dublin
in 1697 for her friend and admirer Jonathan Swift, author of
Gulliver's Travels. Today these magnificent grounds on the banks of

the River Liffey are being developed as a historical, cultural and environmental amenity for the public. The whole area is very child-friendly and has many interesting attractions: a model railway runs along 300ft of authentic country landscapes, past industrial and domestic buildings; the ancient Rockbridge is reputed to be the oldest remaining stone bridge over the Liffey; and Vanessa's Bower is a picturesque island just below the bridge. There's also a picnic area, garden centre, a superb enclosed adventure playground, and donkey and trap rides. The tea-rooms serve home-cooked food in a delightfully restored 17th-century gatehouse. The children's facilities are well maintained and enjoyable, and parents are also well catered for, making this an excellent venue for a day out. Note: the abbey is a private residence and not open to the public.

Craft Centres

IRISH PEWTERMILL and MOONE HIGH CROSS CENTRE
*Timolin, **Moone***
Tel/Fax: (+353) 0507 24164
Open: summer, daily, 10a.m.–5p.m.; winter, Monday to Friday, 10a.m.–4.30p.m.
Admission: free
Visitors can see Irish pewter jewellery, gifts and tableware being made by hand at the 1,000-year-old mill. The stories of Moone High Cross and abbey are told in the Nun's Room.

Environment and Ecology Centres

PEATLAND WORLD***
*Lullymore, Bog of Allen, **Rathangan***
Tel: (+353) 045 860133; Fax: (+353) 045 860481
Open: all year round, Monday to Friday, 9.30a.m.–5p.m.; also open at weekends from April to October, 2p.m.–6p.m.
Admission: A=££, C=£, F
Facilities: toilets; restaurant; crafts and book shop
At Peatland World the whole family can learn something of turf production through the ages, something that has been associated with the area since prehistoric times. On display are ancient artefacts that were preserved in the bogland; a typical Irish kitchen from the early 1900s with a turf fire; and turf-cutting implements and equipment. Children will enjoy the video room with tapes on conservation nature, and energy production. The flora and fauna of the boglands are explained through exhibits showing plants, animals, birds and insect life and the formation and make-up of the Bog of Allen.

Equestrian Facilities

KILL INTERNATIONAL EQUESTRIAN CENTRE***
*(Formerly Kellett's Riding School), **Kill***
Tel: (+353) 045 877208; Fax: (+353) 045 877704
Open: all year round
Facilities: riding tuition for all ages and levels of experience; residential accommodation; 2 indoor riding arenas and an outdoor manège; horses available for trekking; coffee shop; recreation centre
Situated on 100 acres of grassland, this world-famous purpose-built

equestrian centre is one of Europe's most modern, and offers specialist instruction both for experienced riders and complete beginners of all ages – so there's no excuse for parents not joining in! It also offers superb residential accommodation.

OLD MILL RIDING CENTRE
Kill
Tel: (+353) 045 877053
Open: all year round
Tuition for adults and children; indoor and outdoor arenas; summer camp for children.

Farm Parks

ARDENODE DEER FARM
*Ardenode Lodge, **Ballymore Eustace***
Tel: (+353) 045 864428
Open: Easter to September, tours on Wednesday and Saturday commence at 3p.m.
Tour charges: A=££, C(under 12)=£, F
Conducted tours only of this interesting farm to see herds of deer being raised commercially.

ARDKILL FARM AND BOG***
Carbury
Tel: (+353) 0405 53009
Open: all year round (except August), daily, 2p.m.–5p.m.
Admission: A=££, C=£ (afternoon-tea included in admission price)
Facilities: walks; picnic area; large under-cover area; sheep-shearing demonstrations (May to June, weekends, 4p.m.)
Families are really made to feel welcome here and there is much to see and do that will interest everyone. Children are encouraged to handle and feed the animals, they can see eggs being hatched and join an egg hunt. Make sure children are dressed appropriately to handle animals and walk around a farm.

MORELL OPEN FARM***
*Turnings, **Straffan***
Tel: (+353) 01 6288636
Open: all year round, daily, 10a.m.–5p.m. (till 6p.m. in summer)
Admission: A=££, C=£
Facilities: disabled access; toilets; pets corner; attractive picnic area by a shallow stream; animal hospital
A wonderful opportunity for children to see and touch a wide variety of animals (rare breed sheep, pigs, goats and cows, rare poultry, ducks and geese, an exotic collection of foreign birds, rare Egyptian geese, pheasants from China and the Himalayas, plus peacocks and ornamental ducks), learn about breeds and the welfare of animals and wildlife. Make sure everyone is appropriately dressed and has wellingtons.

STRAFFAN BUTTERFLY FARM***
*Ovidstown, **Straffan***
Tel: (+353) 01 6271109
Open: May to September, daily, noon–5.30p.m.

Admission: A=££, C=£, F
Facilities: wheelchair access to all the displays; toilets; picnic area; free parking; gift shop
The large exhibition areas contain butterflies from all over the world with a special emphasis on education and living displays. It's a great opportunity to see some of the world's most exotic creatures, observe their lifecycles, learn something of their habitats and how to tell the difference between a moth and a butterfly. There's also a glass-fronted display of tarantulas, scorpions, stick insects and reptiles. In the tropical butterfly house visitors can relax among colourful blooms and exotic plants while butterflies flutter all around. This is a fascinating experience that all the family will enjoy.

Festivals

FESTIVAL OF NAAS
Naas
On: April
Street events, cycle races, theatre, music and dancing.

RATHANGAN WELCOMING FESTIVAL
Rathangan
On: late May and early June
A village festival to welcome summer visitors. There's a parade with floats, pageant, music and entertainment.

Forest and Amenity Walks

DONADEA FOREST PARK**
*Five miles (8km) south of **Kilcock** on route R407 to Naas*
A series of forest walks and nature trails. A shop opens during the summer, and there are toilets, a carpark and a picnic site nearby.

MOORE ABBEY
*Located adjacent to **Monasterevan** on route R417 to Athy*
Facilities: carpark; picnic site
There's an excellent view of the Moore Abbey house from the wood

Gardens

JAPANESE GARDENS***
*Tully, **Kildare***
Tel: (+353) 045 522963; Fax: (+353) 045 522129
Open: mid-February to mid-November, daily, 9.30a.m.–6p.m.
Admission: A=£££, C=££, F
Facilities: disabled access; toilets and baby-changing room; restaurant; craft shop; garden centre; visitor centre
The only true Japanese Garden in Ireland is here, adjacent to the National Stud at Kildare (SEE HERITAGE CENTRES). The many special features of this magical setting, including beautiful walks and access to the National Stud, make it a unique attraction. Visitors can take a leisurely stroll through the sophisticated yet relaxing gardens which portray the story of 'The Life of Man'.

BALLINDOOLIN HOUSE AND GARDEN
Carbury
Tel: (+353) 0405 31430
Open: May to September, 12p.m.–6p.m., (closed Mondays)
Admission: A=££, C=£
Period house with restaurant, walled garden, pleasure gardens, nature trail and children's farmyard.

Heritage Centres

CROOKSTOWN HISTORICAL AND HERITAGE CENTRE
*The Mill, **Ballytore***
Tel: (+353) 0507 23222
Open: April to September, daily, 10a.m.–7p.m.; October to March, Sunday only, 10a.m.–4p.m.
Admission: A=££, C=£, F
Facilities: tea-room
Historical and heritage visitor centre with exhibitions of milling and baking through the ages. There's also local history exhibits, a folk life display illustrating agriculture and domestic life, and an art gallery.

LULLYMORE HERITAGE PARK
*Lullymore, **Rathangan***
Tel: (+353) 045 870136
Open: all year round, Monday to Friday, 10a.m.–6p.m., weekends, 2p.m.–6p.m.
Admission: A=££, C=£, F
This interesting community project displays an early Christian centre, peat settlement and neolithic farmstead.

IRISH NATIONAL STUD***
*Tully, **Kildare***
Tel: (+353) 045 522963; Fax: (+353) 045 522129
Open: mid-February to mid-November, daily, 9.30a.m.–6p.m.
Admission: A=£££, C=££, F
Facilities: disabled access; toilets and baby-changing room; restaurant; craft shop; museum; children's Lego area
An excellent centre with many facilities and opportunities to see a diverse range of attractions. There's a great visitor centre, beautiful walks through the grounds of Tully Farm and access to the Japanese Garden (see GARDENS), and a museum that serves as a historical archive to the Stud farm's successes and contains the skeleton of the legendary Arkle. A wonderful place to spend a relaxing day out.

Leisure Centres and Adventure Playgrounds

MONDELLO PARK MOTOR-RACING CIRCUIT
*Donore, **Naas***
Tel: (+353) 045 860200; Fax: (+353) 045 860195
Open: all year round
A chance to sample the excitement of Ireland's premier motor-racing circuit. There are high-speed events throughout the year. If you would like to put your own skills to the test, you can enrol on the motor-racing introductory course run by the Racing School.

NEWBRIDGE INDOOR KARTING CENTRE
Newbridge
Tel: (+353) 045 436204

Swimming-Pools

Indoor swimming-pool, **Athy** – *Tel: (+353) 0507 31524*
Indoor swimming-pool, **Naas** – *Tel: (+353) 045 876119*
There are also pools at Kildare and Newbridge – *Tel: (+353) 0507 31859 for further details.*

Trains and Model Railways

LODGE PARK HERITAGE CENTRE AND STEAM MUSEUM***
Straffan
Tel: (+353) 01 6273155; Fax: (+353) 01 6273477
Open: April, May and September, Sunday and bank holidays only, 2.30p.m.–5.30p.m.; June to August, Tuesday to Sunday, 2p.m.–6p.m.
Admission: A=£££, C=££, F
Facilities: disabled access; toilets; shop; tea-room
Some interesting exhibits, such as working steam engines and historic models, which have a great fascination for children, particularly the hands-on area. The 18th-century walled garden and Lodge Park are open from June to August.

• • • • •

PLACES TO EAT

Fast-food Restaurants

McDONALD'S
2 North Main Street, Naas
Tel: (+353) 045 881444

Edward Street, Newbridge
Tel: (+353) 045 486161

SUPERMAC'S
Emily Square, Athy
Tel: (+353) 0507 32202

Main Street, Maynooth
Tel: (+353) 01 6289170

PLACES TO STAY

Country Houses and Hotels

THE GABLES GUEST-HOUSE AND LEISURE CENTRE
*Ryston, Kilcullen Road, **Newbridge***
Tel: (+353) 045 435330; Fax: (+353) 045 435355
This family-run guest-house on the banks of the Liffey has a relaxed,
friendly atmosphere as well as its own leisure centre.

Farmhouse Accommodation

BALLINDRUM FARM
*Ballindrum, **Athy***
Tel/Fax: (+353) 0507 26294
Family-friendly farmhouse with children's facilities and free guided
walks around the farm.

MOATE LODGE
*Off Dublin Road, **Athy***
Tel: (+353) 0507 26137 (or contact Irish Farm Holidays – see Directory)
Open: all year round
An 18th-century Georgian house of charm and character with
facilities for children.

BARBERSTOWN HOUSE
Straffan
Tel: (+353) 01 6274007 (or contact Irish Farm Holidays – see Directory)
Open: 1 March to 30 November
Elegantly restored 18th-century farmhouse in a scenic setting with
facilities for children.

Self-Catering Apartments and Houses

KILRUSH HOLIDAY HOMES
*Narraghmore, **Athy***
Tel: (+353) 0507 26631
You can rent 1- and 2-bedroom apartments in this 18th-century
refurbished house set on a 120-acre estate. Facilities include a
games room, children's playroom and tennis court.

Bicycle Hire

IRISH CYCLE HIRE – *see Directory*
RALEIGH RENT-A-BIKE – *see Directory*

JOHN CAHILL
*Sallins Road, **Naas***
Tel: (+353) 045 879655; Fax: (+353) 045 874055

Car Hire

MURRAYS EUROPCAR – see *Directory*

Bus Services

Travel information – Tel: (+353) 01 8366111

Rail Services

Athy – Tel: (+353) 0507 31966
Kildare – Tel: (+353) 045 521224
Maynooth – Tel: (+353) 01 6285509
Newbridge – Tel: (+353) 045 431219

COUNTY KILKENNY

Home to Ireland's medieval capital, centre of civilisation and culture for more than 1,500 years; heritage and environmental harmony are recurring themes throughout the county of Kilkenny. Here you'll find an abundance of fascinating historic sites, abbeys, forest parks, natural wonders, scenic locations and visitor attractions in every corner of this south-eastern county. The river valleys, forests, mountains and undiscovered areas are great places to visit and explore; the bustling towns and unspoilt villages provide a perfect base to visit local attractions or the adjacent coastal counties of Wexford and Waterford. But the county holds one of the greatest secrets of all time, a secret I will only share with fellow parents: the **grave of Santa Claus** is reputed to be in County Kilkenny! Tradition has it that the remains of the great St Nicholas himself, the patron saint of children, were brought from Turkey and buried in the old cemetery near Belmore House, Thomastown (see p.93).

The city of Kilkenny has been at the heart of Irish civilisation and culture for more than 15 centuries, and here is where you will find ancient and historic reminders preserved from as long ago as the 7th century, as well as many other interesting places to explore.

A most unusual attraction (and one that children will enjoy because they can actually create something), is the **Kilkenny Brass Rubbing Centre,** in a superbly restored Tudor house in Kilkenny. The **CityScope Exhibition and Smallworld Miniatures** is another fascinating display worthy of a visit. And don't miss **Kilkenny Castle**.

For action kids there's the thrilling **Countryside Leisure Activity Centre** at Bonnetsrath, just 2 miles outside Kilkenny. This action-packed centre has activities ranging from archery to quad motorbikes. Light snacks, tea and coffee are available on the site.

Seven miles north of Kilkenny, near the delightful forest park at Jenkinstown, is **Dunmore Cave.** Consisting of a series of chambers formed over millions of years, this outstanding natural limestone cave contains some of the finest calcite formations in Ireland.

At Tullaroan, 6 miles (10km) west of Kilkenny, the **Brod Tullaroan** (incorporating the Lory Meagher Heritage Centre and Kilkenny County GAA Museum) has Ireland's only exhibition centre and museum dedicated to a county's exploits in Gaelic games. It has a wealth of sporting history. The heritage centre, a 17th-century two-storey thatched mansion, has been restored to the way it was in 1884, and provides a unique insight into how a typical Irish family might have lived.

Seven miles south of Kilkenny is the **Nore Valley Park Open Farm** at Bennettsbridge, which has plenty to do for all age groups.

The county has a good network of main roads and is well serviced by bus and mainline rail. Nearest airports are at Waterford and Dublin.

PLACES TO VISIT

Boats and Boat Trips

GRAIGUENAMANAGH
Tel: (+353) 0503 24798
Open: March to October, daily
Barge cruises on the scenic River Barrow.

Castles

KILKENNY CASTLE AND BUTLER GALLERY***
Kilkenny
Tel: (+353) 056 21450; Fax: (+353) 056 63955
Castle open: April and May, daily, 10.30a.m.–5p.m.; June to September, daily, 10a.m.–7p.m.; October to March, Tuesday to Saturday, 10.30a.m.–5p.m. (closed at lunch-time), Sunday, 11a.m.–5p.m.
Admission: A=£££, C=£, F
Gardens open: all year round, admission free
Facilities: disabled access to ground floor of castle and gardens only; toilets; parking; coffee shop and restaurant; video presentations; bookshop; well-equipped outdoor children's playground; picnic area
This impressive 12th-century castle, set in picturesque parklands, has undergone major restoration work and has many interesting features. Guided tours around the castle take in the imposing 150ft-long picture gallery, the library, drawing-room, bedroom and sitting-room, all decorated in 1830s splendour. There's much fun to be had in the magnificent 50-acre landscaped park that surrounds the castle. Here you'll find a playground, picnic area and formal rose garden. The castle restaurant is open during the summer season.

Cathedrals and Abbeys

DUISKE ABBEY and ABBEY CENTRE
Graiguenamanagh
Tel: (+353) 0503 24238
Open: all year round, daily, 10a.m.–5p.m. (weekends from 2p.m.)
Admission: offerings invited
Facilities: toilets; disabled access; bookshop
Duiske is a fine example of an early Cistercian abbey (AD1204), featuring many fine lancet windows. In the adjacent centre there is an exhibition of contemporary Christian art and local historic artefacts.

JERPOINT ABBEY
Thomastown
Tel: (+353) 056 24623
Open: mid-April to mid-June, daily, 10a.m.–1p.m. and 2p.m.–5p.m.; mid-June to September, daily, 9.30a.m.–6.30p.m.; October, daily, 10a.m.–1p.m. and 2p.m.–5p.m.

Admission: A=££, C=£, F
Facilities: disabled access; visitor centre; toilets; shop
An outstanding Cistercian abbey, believed to be the finest monastic ruin in Ireland. Founded in the 12th century, it has unique cloister carvings. In this peaceful riverside setting visitors can also view the abbey's 14th-century tower and a range of domestic buildings, such as the kitchen, refectory and chapterhouse.

ST CANICE'S CATHEDRAL AND ROUND TOWER
Irishtown, **Kilkenny**
Tel: (+353) 056 64971
Open: Easter to September, daily, 9a.m.–1p.m. and 2p.m.–6p.m. (Sunday afternoons only); October to Easter, daily, 10a.m.–1p.m. and 2p.m.–4p.m. (Sunday afternoons only)
Admission: cathedral – free; tower – A=£, C=£
Facilities: toilets; disabled access
Completed in 1285, this impressive cathedral with its rich carvings and colourful stained glass is the second-longest cathedral in Ireland. The adjacent 9th-century round tower is a marvellous structure. Visitors are allowed to climb the narrow steps to the top, but you'll need to be sure-footed and have a head for heights!

Caves

DUNMORE CAVE***
Ballyfoyle
Tel: (+353) 056 67726
Open: mid-March to mid-June, daily, 10a.m.–5p.m.; mid-June to mid-September, daily, 10a.m.–7p.m.; mid-September to October, daily, 10a.m.–5p.m.; November to mid-March, weekends and bank holidays, 10a.m.–5p.m.
Admission: A=££, C=£, F
Facilities: toilets; shop; exhibition centre
This is a fully developed show cave consisting of a series of chambers connected by short passageways, some of which are quite narrow. The children will enjoy exploring this underground labyrinth where spectacular formations of limestone are a major feature, particularly the famous Market Cross formation which is said to be 800 million years old and still growing. There's a well-appointed exhibition centre at the cave entrance which deals extensively with the formation of caves in general, and the history of Dunmore Cave in particular. Viking coins and other archaeo-logical remains have been discovered in the cave, indicating its early importance for use as a safe place of refuge.

Cinemas

REGENT CINEMA
William Street, **Kilkenny**
Tel: (+353) 056 21239

Craft Centres

KILKENNY BRASS-RUBBING CENTRE***
Rothe House, Parliament Street, **Kilkenny**

Tel: (+353) 056 70002
Open: April to October, daily, 10.30a.m.–5p.m. (Sunday from 3p.m.)
At a modest cost, parents and children can spend an hour or two in an absorbing, relaxing and enjoyable activity in an authentic Tudor environment. Materials and guidance are provided so that everyone can create images spanning the history of Ireland and Northern Europe. No artistic ability, special skill or experience is required and every participant will take away an 18"x10" brass rubbing which they will have created in gold wax on black cartridge paper. In addition, ready-made rubbings and a range of historical and craft gifts can be purchased from the centre.

Equestrian Facilities

THE IRIS KELLETT EQUESTRIAN CENTRE
*Mount Juliet, **Thomastown***
Tel: (+353) 056 24455; Fax: (+353) 056 24522
Open: all year round
Designed to accommodate riders of all standards, the centre takes full advantage of the estate's many natural features and trekking trails.

WARRINGTON TOP FLIGHT EQUESTRIAN CENTRE
***Warrington,** near Kilkenny*
Tel: (+353) 056 22682
Open: all year round
Facilities: changing-room and canteen, ponies and horses for trekking to suit all levels of experience, indoor arena and tuition if required

Farm Parks

NORE VALLEY PARK OPEN FARM***
*Annamult, **Bennettsbridge***
Tel: (+353) 056 27229; Fax: (+353) 056 63955
Open: April to September, Monday to Saturday, 9a.m.–9p.m.
Admission: charges are very reasonable and vary because there are options for visitors to take a conducted tour and families may look around at their own pace. There's also a combined ticket that includes a tour, barbecue and crazy golf
Facilities: toilets; barbecue and picnic area; tea-room; souvenir shop; children's play area; pets corner; caravan and camping park
This unique park has a wide variety of animals to see in a specially designed area with an American-style fort in the centre as a viewing point, which is very popular with children. There are lots of fun things to do here – you can play crazy golf, have a pony or donkey ride, and take a walk along the riverbank. Go appropriately dressed.

Forest and Amenity Walks

JENKINSTOWN PARK
*Six miles (10km) north of **Kilkenny** on route N78*
Facilities: carpark; picnic site; forest walks
Details of the trails are shown on a noticeboard in the carpark.

WOODSTOCK DEMESNE
*In the Nore Valley overlooking the village of **Inistioge***
Facilities: carpark; forest walks; arboretum; extensive lawns; open parkland

Gardens

KILFANE GLEN AND WATERFALL****
*Kilfane, **Thomastown***
Tel: (+353) 056 24558; Fax: (+353) 056 27491
Open: May to September, Tuesday to Sunday, 2p.m.–6p.m.
Admission: A=£££, C=££
Facilities: toilets; teas; picnic area; guided tours
I have to confess that this is my kind of garden – plenty of space for the children to run free in harmony with nature. Recently redis-covered and restored, Kilfane is a magic, wild garden dating from 1790 and designed to display nature at its best. The winding wood-land paths, clifftops, cascading stream, hermit's grotto and waterfall all combine to cast a magic spell on every visitor. Adjoining forest and open spaces are laid out in gravelled walks connecting different planting areas with works of modern art. From the bluebell display in May, to the summer moon garden, to the rich autumnal fall, this is a garden for all seasons.

MOUNT JULIET DEMESNE****
Thomastown
Tel: (+353) 056 24455
Open: all year round
Admission: free
Facilities: disabled access; restaurant
The magnificent 1,500-acre walled demesne is still intact and a part of the grounds has been converted into a championship golf course. There's a wonderful variety of informal gardens to see and explore, and discreetly enquire about a very special grave in the old cemetery near Belmore House! (See p.90.)

THE SENSORY GARDEN
*Dove House, Main Street, **Abbeyleix***
Tel: (+353) 0502 31636/31325
Open: April to September, Mon to Fri, 10a.m.–4p.m.; Sat/Sun/bank holidays, 2p.m.–6p.m.
Admission: Free
Set in the old walled garden of the Brigidine Convent, this garden will appeal to everyone by the stimulation of their senses – vision, smell, touch, taste and sound.

Heritage Centres

BROD TULLAROAN and the LORY MEAGHER HERITAGE CENTRE
*Curragh House, **Tullaroan***
Tel: (+353) 056 69107
Open: March to May and September to November, weekends, 2p.m.–5.30p.m.; June to August, Monday to Friday, 10a.m.– 5.30p.m., week-ends, 2p.m.–5.30p.m.
Admission: A=£££, C=£, F
Facilities: toilets; craft shop; tea-room

This 17th-century thatched mansion provides an insight into the lifestyle of a wealthy Irish farming family of the 1880s. It was once the home of Lory Meagher, a great hurling hero of the 1920s and '30s. Housed in an adjoining building is an exhibition centre and museum dedicated to County Kilkenny's many exploits in Gaelic games. Inside is a special trophy room containing medals and other valuable mementoes of sporting history. The tea-room in the heritage centre is excellent.

HERITAGE HOUSE AND SEXTON HOUSE
Abbeyleix
Tel: (+353) 0502 31653
Open: March to October, Mon to Sat, 10a.m.–6p.m.; Sun/bank holidays, 1p.m.–6p.m.; November to February, Mon to Fri, 9a.m.–5p.m.
Admission: A=££, C=£
Facilities: Toilets; coffee parlour; craft shop
This exhibition centre portrays mjaor local settlements and a reconstructed carpet factory and its links to the *Titanic*. Tickets to the restored Sexton House can be obtained from the Heritage Centre.

CITYSCOPE EXHIBITION and SMALLWORLD MINIATURES***
*Rose Inn Street, **Kilkenny***
Tel: (+353) 056 51500; Fax: (+353) 056 63955
Open: March to September, daily, 9a.m.–5p.m.; October to November, Monday to Friday, 9a.m.–5p.m.
Admission: A=£, C=£
The CityScope exhibition is an accurately reconstructed scale model of Kilkenny as it was in 1640. A computer-controlled battery of tiny lights combine with state-of-the-art electronics to make a 22-minute dramatic presentation telling the evolving story of Ireland's medieval capital. Also in the same building, the Shee Alms-House, is the Smallworld Miniatures Exhibition, which has a fascinating collection of miniature houses from the 16th century to the present.

Leisure Centres and Adventure Playgrounds

COUNTRYSIDE LEISURE AND ACTIVITY CENTRE**
Bonnetswrath, near Kilkenny
Tel: (+353) 056 61791
Open: April to October, daily, 10a.m.–8p.m.
The place to go for a range of activities including archery, shooting and quad biking. The minimum age for participants is 12, although children aged between 8 and 12 can ride quad bikes if an adult drives. Light snacks, tea and coffee are available.

Museums

ROTHE HOUSE
*Parliament Street, **Kilkenny***
Tel/Fax: (+353) 056 22893
Open: January to March, November and December, daily 1p.m.–5p.m. (Sunday from 3p.m.); April to June and September to October, daily, 10.30a.m.–5p.m. (Sunday from 3p.m.); July and August, daily, 10a.m.–

6p.m. (Sunday, 1p.m.–5p.m.)
Admission: A=££, C=£
Facilities: toilets; museum bookshop; coffee shop
Rothe House, a recently restored Tudor merchant's house built in
1594, consists of 3 stone buildings divided by cobbled courtyards.
The city and county museum, a period costume collection and a
genealogical study centre are housed there.

Swimming-Pools

JAMES STEPHEN'S SWIMMING-POOL
Michael Street, Kilkenny
Tel: *(+353) 056 21380*

Theatres

THE WATERGATE THEATRE
Parliament Street, Kilkenny
Tel: (+353) 056 61674

Walks and Tours

GRAIGUENAMANAGH
A pleasant, signposted walk has been established from the town to
the summit of Brandon Hill. Follow the South Leinster Way signs
from the town.

TYNAN TOURS OF KILKENNY CITY
Pat Tynan, 10 Maple Drive, Kilkenny
Tel: (+353) 056 65929
*Open: March to October, 6 tours daily (4 on Sunday); November to
February, Tuesday to Saturday, 3 tours daily*
Charges: A=££, C=£
An informative guide will take you on an introductory tour of the
city's many historic and architectural sites. All tours commence from
Kilkenny Tourist Office. Check direct for times.

• • • • •

PLACES TO STAY

Country Houses and Hotels

THE QUAY GUEST-HOUSE
St Mullins, Craiguenamanagh
Tel: (+353) 051 24665
Old-style, family-friendly house with facilities for children. Situated
on the River Barrow in the historic village of St Mullins. Baby-sitting
service available.

AUBURN LODGE
Bennettsbridge Road, Kilkenny

Tel: (+353) 056 65119; Fax: (+353) 056 52641
Warm, family-friendly country home, with facilities for children and a tennis court. There is a riding school nearby.

DANVILLE HOUSE
Kilkenny; *New Ross road (R700), 1km from city centre*
Tel: (+353) 056 21512 (or contact Irish Farm Holidays – see Directory)
Open: 1 April to 1 November
A 200-year-old Georgian house in a secluded setting on the edge of the city. Extensive, mature gardens with a walled kitchen garden, miniature croquet and facilities for children.

NEWPARK HOTEL AND LEISURE CENTRE
Castlecomer Road, **Kilkenny**
Tel: (+353) 056 22122; Fax: (+353) 056 61111
Open: all year round
Friendly hotel with swimming-pool and children's facilities.

RODINI
Waterford Road, **Kilkenny**
Tel: (+353) 056 21822
Family-friendly bungalow with large family rooms. Baby-sitting service available.

TROYSGATE HOUSE
Kilkenny
Tel: (+353) 056 61100; Fax: (+353) 056 51200
Open: all year round
Troysgate House, formerly the gatehouse of the medieval walled city of Kilkenny, is a charming old inn, incorporating Bambrick's famous traditional pub. The accommodation is suitable for families, and there's a children's playroom and a games room.

Farmhouse Accommodation

GROVE FARMHOUSE
Ballycocksuist, **Inistioge**
Tel: (+353) 056 58467 (or contact Irish Farm Holidays – see Directory)
Open: Easter to October
Magnificent 200-year-old Georgian house set in mature gardens on a family-run mixed farm located on route R700 between Thomastown and Inistioge. Bicycle hire and children's facilities are available.

THE BUNGALOW FARMHOUSE
Clomantagh, Woodsgift, **Urlingford**
Tel: (+353) 056 35215 (or contact Irish Farm Holidays – see Directory)
Open: all year round
Modern bungalow on a mixed stock farm set in scenic countryside just off the Kilkenny to Cashel road, route R693, just under 4 miles (6km) from Urlingford. Family-friendly rooms with facilities for children.

Caravan and Camping Parks

NORE VALLEY CARAVAN AND CAMPING PARK and OPEN FARM
Annamult, **Bennettsbridge**
Tel: (+353) 056 27229; Fax: (+353) 056 63955
Open: I March to 31 October
Free access to the open farm with its children's play areas, barbecue and picnic areas; home-baking and farm produce available; games room, laundry etc. Breakfasts are available from June to August.

Hostels

KILKENNY TOURIST HOTEL
35 Parliament Street, **Kilkenny**
Tel: (+353) 056 63541
Open: all year round

Bicycle Hire

IRISH CYCLE HIRE – see *Directory*
RALEIGH RENT-A-BIKE – see *Directory*

BIKES 'N' BEDS
49 John Street, **Kilkenny**
Tel: (+353) 058 44340; Fax: (+353) 052 36141

J.J. WALL
88 Maudlin Street, **Kilkenny**
Tel: (+353) 056 21236

Car Hire

MURRAYS EUROPCAR – see *Directory*

Bus Services

TOURIST OFFICE
Kilkenny
Tel: (+353) 056 64933

LOCAL SERVICES
Rapid Express
Tel: (+353) 056 31106

Rail Services

Kilkenny – *Tel: (+353) 056 22024*
Thomastown – *Tel: (+353) 056 24218*

COUNTY LAOIS

Known as the crossroads of Ireland, County Laois is full of rural charm. Unless your children are interested in outdoor activities such as horseriding, walking, cycling or angling, however, there's really not a great deal that will appeal to them in this rural paradise. But Laois is bordered by no less than five other counties, so it is an ideal base from which to visit the many attractions across the south of Ireland.

There is a cinema and a swimming-pool in Portlaoise, which is also where you'll find the ancient fortification of **Rock of Dunamase**. The magnificent **Slieve Bloom mountains** dominate the landscape to the extent that it was formerly believed that Ard Erin, the loftiest peak in the range, was the highest point in Ireland – when in fact, at 1,734ft (528m), it falls far short of carrying that honour. They are nevertheless a superb range of mountains in which to walk with children; with around 24 beautiful glens and the waymarked **Slieve Bloom Way,** they are relatively safe and not too strenuous.

Road access to the county is good, mainly via the N7, N8 and N80 roads. Mainline rail services run from Dublin through to Portlaoise and on to the south-west, the nearest airport is Dublin.

●　●　●　●　●

PLACES TO VISIT

Cinemas

COLISEUM TWIN CINEMA
Coliseum Lane, **Portlaoise**
Tel: (+353) 0502 21212

Equestrian Facilities

KERR EQUESTRIAN CENTRE
Cremorgan, Timahoe, **Portlaoise**
Tel: (+353) 0502 27162
Open: March to October, daily
Whether you are an experienced rider or a total beginner, there will be a horse or pony to suit you here. Basic tuition and routes given for trekking through quiet, unspoilt countryside.

PORTLAOISE EQUESTRIAN CENTRE
Timahoe Road, **Portlaoise**
Tel: (+353) 0502 60880

Farm Parks

CASTLETOWN HOUSE OPEN FARM**
Donaghmore
Tel: (+353) 0505 46415; Fax: (+353) 0505 46788
Open: April to September, daily, 11a.m.–6p.m. (Sunday from 2p.m.)
Admission: A=££, C=£, F
Facilities: toilets; pets corner; indoor and outdoor picnic areas; shop; tea-rooms with home-baking; farmhouse accommodation
Plenty of animals and facilities to amuse the children.

Forest and Amenity Walks

CAPPONELLAN WOOD
*One mile (1.6km) south-west of **Durrow** on N8 Cork to Dublin road*
This is a well-used carpark area with picnic facilities – an ideal rest stop on the tiring journey between Cork and Dublin. While there are no official walks starting from the carpark, the surrounding forest roads and paths are ideal for stretching the legs.

GLENBARROW
*Four miles (6.4km) east of **Clonaslee** on route R423 to Mountmellick*
Pleasant riverside and forest walks and a waterfall.

OUGHAVAL WOOD
*One mile (1.6km) from **Stradbally** on the N80 Carlow road*
Mature broadleaf plantation with extensive walks, a carpark and a picnic site.

Gardens

EMO COURT DEMESNE AND ARBORETUM**
***Emo;** north-east of Portlaoise off route N7 to Monasterevan*
Tel: (+353) 0502 26110
***Arboretum** open: all year round, daily, 10.30a.m.–5.30p.m.*
***House** open: April to October, Monday only, 2p.m.–6p.m.*
Admission: A=££, C=£
Facilities: disabled access; toilets; teas on summer Sundays; picnic area
An excellent estate that has been restored with many new plantings. There's a variety of garden areas and a 20-acre lake to walk around.

HEYWOOD GARDENS
*In the grounds of Salesian College near **Ballinakill***
Tel: (+353) 0502 33563
Open: all year round, daily, dawn to dusk
Admission: free
These formal gardens overlook undulating park and countryside. To one side a hidden pergola gives views over the lake, with an avenue of lime trees leading to an oval pool on the other side.

THE SENSORY GARDEN
*Dove House, Main Street, **Abbeyleix***
Tel: (+353) 0502 31636/31325
Open: April to September, Monday to Friday, 10a.m.–4p.m., Saturday,

Sunday and Bank Holidays, 2p.m.–6p.m.
Admission: Free
Set in the old walled garden of the Brigidine Convent, this garden will appeal to everyone by the stimulation of their senses – vision, smell, touch, taste and sound.

Heritage Centres

ROCK OF DUNAMASE***
Portlaoise
A ruined castle sits on the summit of the prominent Rock of Dunamase, lording over the north Laois landscape. Originally a Celtic fortification, it has been the scene of various raids and was part of the dowry of Aoife, daughter of the King of Leinster, on her marriage to the Norman lord, Strongbow.

HERITAGE HOUSE AND SEXTON HOUSE
Abbeyleix
Tel: (+353) 0502 31653
Ope: March to October, Monday to Saturday, 10a.m.–6.pm., Sunday and bank holidays, 1p.m.–6p.m., November to February, Nonday to Friday 9a.m.–5.p.m.
Admission: A=££, C=£
Facilities: toilets; coffee parlour; craft shop
This exihibition centre portrays major local settlements, and a reconstructed carpet factory and its links to the *Titanic*. Tickets to the restored Sexton House can be obtained from the Heritage Centre.

Horse-Drawn Caravans

KILVAHAN HORSE-DRAWN CARAVANS
Timahoe
Tel: (+353) 0502 27048; Fax: (+353) 0502 27225
Open: May to September
A great way to tour around and see the countryside, but you will have to include some activities to keep the children amused. Everything you need is provided, including routes and horse feed.

Museums

DONAGHMORE MUSEUM
Donaghmore, Portlaoise
Tel: (+353) 0505 46212/44196
Open: May to September, daily, 2p.m.–5p.m.
Admission: A=££, C=£, F
This is a restored workhouse, originally built in 1850 at a time of great poverty and deprivation among the local people, arising directly as a result of the great Famine. Today visitors will see the original dormitories, a kitchen and a waiting hall authentically restored. There's also an agricultural museum with artefacts that demonstrate the day-to-day activities of people in rural Ireland during the past 100 years.

Swimming-Pools

PORTARLINGTON SWIMMING-POOL
Portarlington
Tel: (+353) 0502 23149

PORTLAOISE SWIMMING-POOL
Ridge Road, **Portlaoise**
Tel: (+353) 0502 21710

Walking Routes

ROCK OF DUNAMASE***
Portlaoise
An excellent short walk to this magnificent heritage site. Children
will enjoy exploring the ruins, and the views across the north Laois
landscape are spectacular (**see** HERITAGE CENTRES).

SLIEVE BLOOM WAY
An excellent waymarked walking route crossing both the counties
of Laois and Offaly. There are many short routes into beautiful glens
along the way, so pick up a route map and off you go.

● ● ● ● ●

PLACES TO STAY

Country Houses and Hotels

TULLAMOY HOUSE
Stradbally, *off the N80*
Tel: (+353) 0507 27111
A 19th-century stone building. Facilities for children.

Farmhouse Accommodation

CASTLETOWN HOUSE
Donaghmore, *Borris-in-Ossory*
*Tel: (+353) 0505 46415; Fax: (+353) 0505 46788 (or contact Irish
Farm Holidays – see Directory)*
Open: 1 March to 1 December
Early 19th-century farmhouse in scenic surroundings on a 200-acre
farm. Has a games room, an open farm with a variety of animals,
indoor and outdoor picnic facilities, a tuck shop and tea-room.

BEECH HILLS LODGE****
Moher West, *Mountrath*
Tel: (+353) 0502 35097
Family-friendly farmhouse with a children's playroom. The farm has
horses, donkeys, cattle and sheep, and is located in the beautiful
Slieve Bloom mountains.

Self-Catering Apartments and Houses

CLONKELLY HOUSE
Rosenallis
Tel: (+353) 0502 28517
Self-catering accommodation located 2 miles (3.2km) from Glen-barrow and the beginning of the Slieve Bloom Way.

Caravan and Camping Parks

KIRWAN'S CARAVAN AND CAMPING PARK
*Limerick road (N7), **Portlaoise***
Tel: (+353) 0502 21688
Open: 1 April to 15 October
Long-established family-run park with a children's TV and video room, a barbecue area, and all the usual amenities.

Hostels

FARREN HOUSE FARM HOSTEL
*Ballacolla, **Portlaoise***
Tel: (+353) 0502 34032; Fax: (+353) 0502 34008
Open: all year round
Excellent en-suite accommodation in a converted grain loft and stables. Facilities include wheelchair access, a barbecue area, modern kitchen, large dining-room and a laundry.

Bicycle Hire

IRISH CYCLE HIRE – *see Directory*
RALEIGH RENT-A-BIKE – *see Directory*

M. KAVANAGH
*Railway Street, **Portlaoise***
Tel: (+353) 0502 21357

HAMILTON CYCLES
Portlaoise
Tel: (+353) 0502 22643

Car Hire

MURRAYS EUROPCAR – *see Directory*

Bus Services

BUS EIREANN
Travel information – Tel: (+353) 01 8366111

Rail Services

Portarlington – *Tel: (+353) 0502 23128*
Portlaoise – *Tel: (+353) 0502 21303*

COUNTY LONGFORD

Longford, along with Leitrim, Cavan, Westmeath and Offaly, is another one of those counties referred to as part of the Irish Midlands, that undefined area of the country often spurned by tourists and which is, on the whole, quite indifferent to them. Longford has been described as an 'inland county of quiet farmlands and brown bog', and its main town is said to be 'woefully bereft of visitor facilities', so it's not difficult to understand why so few visitors make the journey to Longford.

The descriptions, however, are unjustified. There are some attractive areas for picnics, swimming and angling around Lough Gowna, and some interesting historic sites in the Granard region. The town of Longford is vibrant, with both traditional and modern commercial activities, and it has a **sports and leisure complex** with a heated swimming-pool.

Seven miles (11.2km) south of Longford is the pretty little village of Ardagh. Its **heritage centre** interprets the history of the area with an audio-visual presentation and guided tours. There are also craft shops and a restaurant on the site.

The **Longford Summer Festival,** held in late July and providing fun for all the family with street theatre, tugs-of-war, a funfair and novelty events, is just one festival worth noting. Children will also enjoy the **Granard Harp Festival** in mid-August, the oldest festival in Ireland, dating back to 1784. Its celebration of traditional music and dance provides entertainment for all.

Road access through the county is quite limited, but there is a bus and railway station in the town of Longford. The nearest airport is Dublin.

• • • • •

PLACES TO VISIT

Castles and Historic Houses

CARRIGGLAS MANOR AND GARDENS***
Longford
Tel: (+353) 043 45165; Fax: (+353) 043 41026
Open: June to September, daily (closed Tuesday and Wednesday),
1.30p.m.–5.30p.m.
Admission: A=££££, C=££, F (entry to house, museum and gardens)
Facilities: toilets; museum; guided tours; gift shop; tea-room
A fine gothic revival manor house set in extensive parkland with a magnificent Georgian double courtyard and tiered woodland garden. The grounds are a wonderful example of truly informal gardens where anything is allowed to grow so long as it looks good! The

beautifully restored stableyard houses a fascinating costume museum. There is a charming tea-room serving home-made goodies and light lunches. Also has self-catering accommodation (see WHERE TO STAY).

Cinemas

ODEON CINEMA
Bridge Street, Longford
Tel/Fax: (+353) 043 46457

Equestrian Facilities

AUGHEREA HOUSE EQUESTRIAN CENTRE
Longford
Tel: (+353) 043 41004

CHEZ-NOUS RIDING CENTRE
Arva Road, Drumlish
Tel/Fax: (+353) 043 24368
Open: all year round
Beginners welcome.

Festivals and Events

GRANARD HARP FESTIVAL**
Tel: (+353) 043 86375
On: mid-August
The oldest festival in Ireland, dating back to 1784. Everyone will enjoy the traditional music and dance on show.

LONGFORD SUMMER FESTIVAL***
Tel: (+353) 043 47781
On: late July
Takes place in the town of Longford and provides fun for all the family, with street theatre, tugs-of-war, a funfair and novelty events.

Forest and Amenity Walks

DERRYCASSIN
Four miles (6.5 km) west of Granard on minor road to Ardagh
Woodland setting on the shores of Lough Gowna with a picnic site, lakeside and forest walks.

Heritage Centres

ARDAGH HERITAGE CENTRE**
Ardagh
Tel: (+353) 043 75277; Fax: (+353) 043 75278
Open: all year round, daily, 9a.m.–6p.m.
Admission: A=££, C=£, F
Facilities: disabled access; toilets; restaurant; shop selling local crafts
The story of Ardagh is one of history and literature, which is presented in an interesting exhibition in this magnificent old schoolhouse. Audio-visual presentation.

CORLEA TRACKWAY VISITOR CENTRE*
Kenagh
Tel: (+353) 043 22386
Open: June to September, daily, 9.30a.m.–6.30p.m.
Admission: A=£££, C=£, F
Facilities: disabled access; toilets; tea-rooms; picnic area
This interesting centre interprets the story of the local Iron Age
bog road which was built in 148BC across the boglands close to the
River Shannon. An 18m stretch of this road is on permanent display
along with colourful and informative exhibitions. The road is the
largest of its kind to have been uncovered in Europe.

Swimming-Pools

LONGFORD SPORTS AND LEISURE COMPLEX
*Market Square, **Longford***
Tel: (+353) 043 46536

Theatres

BOG LANE THEATRE
Ballymahon
Tel: (+353) 0902 32252
An 80-seat theatre presenting a variety of interesting productions.

• • • • •

PLACES TO STAY

Farmhouse Accommodation

TOBERPHELIM HOUSE
Granard
Tel: (+353) 043 86568 (or contact Irish Farm Holidays – see Directory)
Open: 1 May to 18 September
Georgian farmhouse on a 200-acre cattle and sheep farm. Warm
hospitality and family rooms; children welcome.

Self-Catering Apartments and Houses

HOLLYBROOK
Drumnaure, *Abbeyshrule*
Tel: (+353) 078 20118
Open: all year round
Fully modernised family home (sleeps 7), set in a picturesque
landscape of mature trees.

CARRIGGLAS MANOR HOLIDAY HOMES
Longford
Tel: (+353) 043 45165; Fax: (+353) 043 41026
Three period cottages/apartments in a restored Georgian farmyard
adjacent to a fine gothic revival manor house set in extensive

parkland. The beautifully restored stableyard houses a fascinating costume and lace museum (see CASTLES AND HISTORIC HOUSES).

CUMISKEY'S TRADITIONAL COTTAGES
*Ennybegs, **Drumlish***
Tel: (+353) 043 23320; Fax: (+353) 043 23516
Open: all year round
Award-winning luxury cottages set amid the lakes of north Longford. Facilities include wheelchair access, multi-channel TVs and a baby-sitting service.

DIAMOND HILL FARM
Moyne
Tel: (+353) 043 35031; Fax: (+353) 043 45796
Has 1- and 3-bedroom apartments in a scenic setting on a working farm. Excellent facilities include a tennis court, crazy golf, sauna, jacuzzi and children's playground.

Bicycle Hire

IRISH CYCLE HIRE – *see Directory*
RALEIGH RENT-A-BIKE – *see Directory*

Car Hire

MURRAYS EUROPCAR – *see Directory*

Airports

ABBEYSHRULE AERODROME
Tel: (+353) 044 57424

Bus Services

***Longford,** Railway Station* – *Tel: (+353) 043 45208*

Rail Services

Edgeworthstown – *Tel: (+353) 043 71031*
Longford – *Tel: (+353) 043 45208*

COUNTY LOUTH

Louth is the smallest county in Ireland, covering only 317 square miles. It is nevertheless an area of contrasting landscape, varying from a scenic coastline running from Baltray to Dundalk (with wide sandy bays and occasional rocky headlands at Clogerhead and Dunany Point) to the mountainous Cooley Peninsula bounded by Dundalk Bay and Carlingford Lough.

County Louth is steeped in myth and legend. Stories abound about the Irish epic, the *Tain Bo Cuailnge*, which tells of a cattle raid by the Queen of Connaught on a farmer with a famous brown bull at Cooley. An area once inhabited by the great giant Finn MacCool whispers stories about the Long Woman's Grave and Clontygora Court Graves of Omeath.

Carlingford is a medieval town of narrow streets and castles nestling at the foot of Slieve Foye on the southern shore of Carlingford Lough, and tradition has it that St Patrick landed near here on his return from Rome. This is an ideal place to visit with children or to use as a base. Its attractive harbour and ancient ruins make it an interesting location to explore and have fun. The towering ruin of **King John's Castle**, a massive fortress, overlooks the pretty harbour, whilst **Taaffe's Castle** consists of a large square keep. It is well worth taking the **town walk** to see all Carlingford has to offer – such as the **Dominican Abbey** and the **Mint**, a 15th-century fortified house.

There is an excellent **adventure centre and holiday hostel** based in Carlingford that runs a series of activity programmes. Full-board or self-catering accommodation is available and the centre is an ISA-recognised teaching establishment, supervised by fully qualified staff.

There are many events and festivals in the town throughout the year. These include one that will capture the imagination of young and old alike throughout the world, the **Great Leprechaun Hunt,** held on Carlingford Mountain in May. Other events include a **medieval festival** in July, when the local community dress up in medieval costume and the streets are filled with entertainers and craft workers displaying their wares and skills; an **oyster festival** in August; and a **folk festival** in September.

Five miles (8km) north of Carlingford, the **Tain Holiday Village** near Omeath is a great place to stay. The village is in a picturesque setting on the shores of the lough. The 10-acre site (with a huge indoor leisure centre) offers numerous attractions for visitors of all ages.

The main Belfast to Dublin road (N1) passes through the length of the county from which a good many feeder roads serve all parts of the area. The main Belfast to Dublin railway also runs through Dundalk, Castlebellingham, Dunleer and Drogheda, and there are two major bus depots serving the county based in Dundalk and Drogheda. The county is about halfway between Belfast and Dublin, and both capital airports are within 50 miles (82km) of here.

PLACES TO VISIT

Activity Centres

CARLINGFORD ADVENTURE CENTRE***
Tholsel Street, **Carlingford**
Tel: (+353) 042 9373100; Fax: (+353) 042 9373651
Open: 1 February to 30 November
This fun adventure centre has something for everyone. The facilities are very good and the activities well organised and professionally supervised. The centre specialises in beginners courses, which are available on a daily or half-day basis, but my guess is that the kids will want to spend at least a full day here. Activities include sailing, canoeing, windsurfing, currach-building, hill-walking, abseiling, team games, tennis and indoor climbing.

Amusement Arcades and Funfairs

AMUSEMENT ARCADE
Shore Road, **Omeath**
Tel: (+353) 042 9375159

Castles

KING JOHN'S CASTLE
Carlingford
A massive fortress commanding the entrance to Carlingford Lough.

TAAFFE'S CASTLE
Carlingford
A well-preserved tower house.

Craft Centres

RIVERSTOWN OLD CORN MILL AND CRAFT CENTRE***
Riverstown Mill, Cooley, **Dundalk**
Tel: (+353) 042 9376157; Fax: (+353) 042 9376361
Open: May to October, Thursday to Sunday, noon–6p.m.
Admission: free
Facilities: crafts centre; coffee shop; restaurant
This is a restored 18th-century water mill sited in the beautiful Cooley Peninsula, surrounded by scenic walks. It also has an animal farm which children will enjoy.

Equestrian Facilities

BELLINGHAM STABLES
Castlebellingham
Tel: (+353) 042 9372175
Approved centre for riders at all levels of experience; beginners

must be over 7 years old. Four-day camps in summer. All-weather arena.

Festivals and Events

GREAT LEPRECHAUN HUNT****
Carlingford Mountain
On: May
Forty Leprechauns are hidden on the mountain in an area marked out by flags, and a reward is paid for each one found. The hunt originated after a local businessman discovered a genuine Leprechaun suit with 4 gold sovereigns in a trouser pocket on the mountain in 1988, a find that has worked wonders for local businesses ever since! The big search is on for the little people, but with prize money amounting to over £3,000 it can be serious stuff. It's great to watch and lots of fun.

MEDIEVAL FESTIVAL***
Carlingford
On: July
The wonderful spectacle of a trip into the past. Streets are transformed into a medieval market place with entertainers, artists, animals, bakers and candlestick-makers, together with the people of Carlingford all dressed in medieval costume.

OMEATH GALA WEEK***
Omeath
On: August
A celebration to mark the homecoming of returned emigrants and friends, this is a week of fun and entertainment for all the family.

CARLINGFORD FESTIVAL***
Carlingford
On: September
A week of street music and dancing with funfairs, sheep fairs, pony-trotting, and a song at every corner.

Farm Parks

ARDEE ANIMAL FARM***
Hunterstown, Ardee
Tel: (+353) 041 56047
Open: Easter to 31 August, daily, 10a.m.–8p.m.
Admission: A=£, C=£, F
Facilities: Toilets; picnic area; children's playground and display of old farm machinery
Lots of animals for the children to see and touch.

Forest and Amenity Walks

SLIEVE FOYE WOODS
*Two miles (3.5km) north-east of **Carlingford** on R173 to Omeath*
Situated on a hill near Carlingford Lough, there are marvellous views overlooking the lough, a picnic site, a carpark and forest walks.

TOWNLEY HALL
*One mile (2km) north of **Ballina** on route R314 to Killala*
Facilities: carpark; picnic area; fishing

Heritage Centres

HOLY TRINITY HERITAGE CENTRE
Carlingford
Tel: (+353) 042 9373454
*Open: March to September, daily, 10a.m.–5p.m.; October to February,
weekends and bank holidays only, 10a.m.–4p.m.*
Admission: A=£, C=£, F

The centre houses exhibits which show the development of the
town from its Norman origins, giving the visitor an insight into
Carlingford's history and encouraging further exploration of the
streets and antiquities of a town full of atmosphere and
character.

DROGHEDA HERITAGE CENTRE****
*Mary Street, **Drogheda***
Tel: (+353) 041 9831153
*Open: all year round, 10a.m.–5p.m., Monday to Friday; 2p.m.–5p.m.
Saturday and Sunday*
Admission: A=££, C=£, F
*Facilities: disabled access; toilets; parking located close to town centre;
audio visual display; craft shop; and The Mollies coffee shop*

This excellent centre captures the many historic tales of Drogheda's
800-year existence and will interest the whole family. Visitors young
and old are encouraged to take an authentic step back in time by
dressing up in period costumes, so even dads can don a genuine
wartime helmet and play the part of a 17th-century Roundhead or
Norman soldier.

OLD MELLIFONT ABBEY
Drogheda
Tel: (+353) 041 9826459
*Open: May to mid-June, mid-September to October, daily, 10a.m.–5p.m.;
mid-June to mid-September, daily, 9.30a.m.–6.30p.m.*
Admission: A=£, C=£, F

This, the first Cistercian monastery in Ireland, was founded in 1142
by St Malachy of Armagh. Its most unusual feature is the octagonal
lavabo, c.1200. The visitor centre has an interesting exhibition.

Leisure Centres

DUNDALK SPORTS CENTRE
Dundalk
Tel: (+353) 042 9331740
Open: all year round, daily

Sports centre with a wide range of activities. Crèche available.

Museums

COUNTY MUSEUM***
*Jocelyn Street, **Dundalk***
Tel: (+353) 041 9327056; Fax: (+353) 041 9327058
Open: all year round, Monday to Saturday, 10.30a.m.–5.30p.m.; Sunday and bank holidays, 2p.m.–6p.m. (closed Mondays October to April)
Admission: A=£££, C=£, F
Facilities: disabled access to all floors; toilets; coffee shops adjacent to the building; children's activity room
The County Museum is housed in a beautifully restored 18th-century warehouse with 4 floors of exhibition space. On display is the industrial heritage of the county and a range of exhibitions on a wide variety of subjects. A 72-seater film theatre shows a short presentation on the history and development of County Louth. There's a specially fitted room for children's activities such as painting, clay-modelling, quizzes etc.

MILLMOUNT MUSEUM AND MARTELLO TOWER
*Millmount, **Drogheda***
Tel: (+353) 041 9833097
Open: all year round, Monday to Saturday, 10a.m.–6p.m.; Sundays and bank holidays, 2.30p.m.–5.30p.m.
Admission: A=£££, C=££, F (includes Museum and Tower)
Facilities: toilets; exhibitions; craft centre; genealogy centre; restaurant
The museum has a range of interesting exhibitions including a folk kitchen, Irish history room, industrial exhibition, medieval room and a collection of geological specimens and curiosities. The Tower provides excellent views of the town and Boyne Valley.

Visitors Centres

STEPHENSTOWN POND AND
AGNES BURNS VISITORS CENTRE****
*Knockbridge (4 miles from **Dundalk**)*
Tel: (+353) 042 9379019
Open: all year round; 1 April to 20 September, daily, 10a.m.–8p.m.; 1 Octiber to 31 March, Monday to Saturday, 10a.m.–6p.m.; Sunday, 11a.m.–6p.m. (note that the playground closes at 4p.m. in winter)
Admission: £1 per car for parking and the pond and playground are free
Facilities: toilets; children's playground; tea/coffee shop
This is a great place for kids, the Stephenstown Pond covers five acres of woodland and the pond provides an oasis for a fascinating variety of wildlife. The Agnes Burns Cottage is a beautifully restored 18th-century cottage where Agnes Burns, the sister of Scotland's national bard, Robert Burns, resided for 18 years. The cottage interprets the life and works of Robert, life on the Stephenstown estate, local history and explores the Scottish/Irish diaspora.

Walking Routes

CARLINGFORD TOWN WALK
An interesting short walk to see the many historic buildings in medieval Carlingford.

THE TAIN TRAIL
A 26km waymarked walk in the beautiful Cooley and Carlingford mountains, beginning from the town of Carlingford.

• • • • •

PLACES TO EAT

Cafés

DREAMY DELIGHTS
Dundalk
Ice-cream parlour for teas and snacks.

Fast-Food Restaurants

McDONALDS
*The Waterfront, Rathmullan Road, **Drogheda***
Tel: (+353) 041 9843495

Dundalk Shopping Centre, Stapleton Drive,
***Dundalk** (Drive-through)*
Tel: (+353) 042 9351100

SUPERMAC'S
*Clonbrassil Street, **Dundalk***
Tel: (+353) 042 34413
and
Emily Square
Athy

Hotels and Pubs

FAIRWAYS HOTEL✳✳✳✳✳
*Dublin Road, **Dundalk***
Tel: (+353) 042 21500; Fax: (+353) 042 21511
Open: All year
This hotel has a choice of family-friendly restaurants serving a good selection of meals and snacks from menus to suit all ages.

FITZPATRICK'S BAR AND RESTAURANT
*Jenkinstown, **Rockmarshall** (Dundalk to Carlingford road)*
Tel: (+353) 042 9376193
Olde worlde style pub with an excellent reputation for its food for all the family.

PLACES TO STAY

Country Houses and Hotels

BALLYMASCANLON HOUSE HOTEL***
*Near **Dundalk** on the Carlingford/Greenore road*
Tel: (+353) 042 9371124; Fax: (+353) 042 9371598
Family friendly hotel with swimming-pool, tennis courts, golf course and superb gardens.

CARRICKDALE HOTEL
*Carrickcarnon, Ravensdale, **Dundalk***
Tel: (+353) 042 9371397; Fax: (+353) 042 9371740
Open: all year round
Family-run hotel with leisure complex, swimming-pool, games room and crèche.

FAIRWAYS HOTEL AND LEISURE CENTRE*****
*Dublin Road, **Dundalk***
Tel: (+353) 041 9321500; Fax: (+353) 041 9321511
Open: all year round
This family-run hotel, set in its own grounds, is an ideal place to stay. It is very child friendly, and they have excellent family rooms, a leisure centre with an indoor heated swimming-pool, sauna, jacuzzi, modern gym, snooker tables and squash, tennis and badminton courts.

Holiday Parks and Villages

TAIN HOLIDAY VILLAGE***
*Omeath, **Carlingford***
Tel: (+353) 042 9375385; Fax: (+353) 042 9375417
Open: mid-March to November
Facilities: fully supervised crèche; shops; licensed restaurant and bar
A well-supervised site with plenty of activities, including a heated indoor swimming-pool with flumes, slides and rafts, an indoor adventure centre with freefall slides, ball pool and climbing ropes etc, and outdoor adventure playgrounds specially designed for younger and older age groups. The village also has games rooms with table-tennis, pool, snooker, TV and video, and an interactive science centre with a hands-on exploration of the world of technology. The Kiddies Club has supervised and organised activities. There is a choice of B&B or self-catering accommodation, plus a touring caravan and camping field.

Castles

SMARMORE CASTLE AND LEISURE CENTRE
*Smarmore, **Ardee***
Tel: (+353) 041 6857167; Fax: (+353) 041 6857650
Open: all year rounf
This is the chance for the kids to stay in a child-friendly castle, complete with child-friendly ghosts. The facilities include family rooms, leisure centre with a swimming-pool and toddlers pool. There's also a restaurant that has children's menus.

Caravan and Camping Parks

GYLES QUAY CARAVAN AND CAMPING PARK
Riverstown
Tel: (+353) 042 9376262
This park gives access to a safe, clean beach, and has a licensed club-house with live entertainment, a pool room, playroom and playgrounc

Hostels

CARLINGFORD ADVENTURE CENTRE AND HOLIDAY HOSTEI
*Tholsel Street, **Carlingford***
Tel: (+353) 042 9373100; Fax: (+353) 042 9373651
Open: 1 February to 30 November

Bicycle Hire

IRISH CYCLE HIRE – see *Directory*
RALEIGH RENT-A-BIKE – see *Directory*

Car Hire

MURRAYS EUROPCAR – see *Directory*

Bus Services

Drogheda, Bus Office – Tel: (+353) 041 9835023
Dundalk, Bus Office – Tel: (+353) 042 9334075

Rail Services

Drogheda – Tel: (+353) 041 9838749
Dundalk – Tel: (+353) 042 9335521

COUNTY MEATH

The county of Meath sits neatly around the north and north-western boundaries of Dublin. It is ideally situated for visiting the capital city, but has much to offer in its own right. The secrets of over 5,000 years of history are held within the scenic beauty of the Boyne valley. Nestling in a wooded part of the River Blackwater valley is the ancient town of Kells. It was here that an illuminated Latin manuscript of the four gospels, the *Book of Kells*, was produced around the beginning of the 9th century. It proved to be one of the greatest works of art that the world has ever seen.

The **passage grave at Newgrange** and its satellite tombs predate the pyramids of Egypt, and the twin seaside resorts of Bettystown and Laytown have beautiful sandy **beaches** on a short strip of coast-line north of Dublin, which is County Meath's only outlet to the sea. A magnificent sandy beach stretches 6 miles (10km) from south of Laytown and heads north through Bettystown to the mouth of the Boyne at Mornington. The **Mosney Holiday Centre** is located just south of Laytown and 26 miles (42km) north of Dublin. This magnificent complex has everything for kids – a waterworld, indoor and outdoor heated swimming-pools, a supervised playground, nature walks, kiddies' rides, fun sports, a pets corner, laserdome, boating lakes, go-karting, mini golf, bumper boats, children's clubs and discos and family entertainment. There are shops and restaurants on the site, baby-sitting facilities and a wide range of accommodation to suit all tastes. Alternatively, you can just visit for the day.

The town of Navan sits in pleasant undulating countryside at the meeting of the Boyne and Blackwater rivers. It has tennis courts and two cinemas. The **Grove Gardens at Fordstown** have alpine beds, rose gardens, a peaceful cedar garden, tea-rooms and a children's play area, making it a superb place to visit.

Road access throughout the county is excellent, with many main routes threading their way to Dublin from every direction. Public transport is plentiful via both rail and bus, and Dublin Airport is virtually on the doorstep.

PLACES TO VISIT

Castles

ST JOHN'S CASTLE
Trim
Tel: (+353) 046 37227
Open: July and August, Monday to Friday, 11.30a.m.–2p.m.
Admission: ££
An imposing 12th-century castle ruin on the banks of the Boyne. The interpretative centre in Mill Street depicts the history and beauty of the castle, the town and its surrounds in an interesting audio-visual show.

Environment and Ecology Centres

SONAIRTE NATIONAL ECOLOGY CENTRE****
*The Ninch, **Laytown***
Tel: (+353) 041 9827572; Fax: (+353) 041 9828130
Open: all year round, Monday to Friday, 9a.m.–5p.m.; Saturday, 11a.m.–5p.m.; Sunday, 11a.m.–6p.m.
Admission: A=££, C=£, F
Facilities: wholefood coffee shop; natural gift shop; organic winery; renewable energy park; picnic area; toilets; adventure playground
With its alternative energy displays, organic garden, riverside nature trail, eco-shop and winery, this is a wonderful opportunity to see ecology in action and to introduce children to a sustainable way of living.

Equestrian Facilities

PELLETSTOWN RIDING CENTRE
*Pelletstown, **Drumree***
Tel: (+353) 01 8259435
Open: all year round
Set in 100 acres of farmland, the centre has both indoor and outdoor facilities and caters for all levels of experience.

BROADMEADOW COUNTRY HOUSE AND
EQUESTRIAN CENTRE
*Bullstown, **Ashbourne***
Tel: (+353) 01 8352819
Open: All year
The centre has a coffee shop, an indoor and outdoor arena, and caters for riders of all ages and levels of experience.

RATHE HOUSE EQUESTRIAN CENTRE
*Rathe House, **Kilmainhamwood***
Tel/Fax: (+353) 046 52376

Farm Parks

NEWGRANGE FARM AND COFFEE SHOP
*Newgrange, **Slane***
Tel: (+353) 041 9824119
Open: Easter to 31 August, daily, 10a.m.–5.30p.m.
Admission: ££, C=££, F
Facilities: disabled access; toilets; indoor and outdoor picnic areas; gift shop; pets corner
Morning coffee and afternoon-tea, home-made cakes and soups served in a beautifully converted building overlooking the farmyard. There is a rural life museum with displays of vintage farm machinery, and farmyard tours and walks are possible.

Festivals

KELLS HERITAGE FESTIVAL
Kells
On: late June/early July
A week of family events, classical music, drama, sports, competitions and parades.

Forest and Amenity Walks

ROSS
*Five miles (8km) west of **Finea** on road to Mountnugent*
Situated on the southern shore of Lough Sheelin, one of Ireland's largest freshwater lakes. There's a carpark and a picnic site.

SUMMERHILL
*Adjacent to **Summerhill** village*
Picturesque woodland setting with walks and a picnic site.

Gardens

BUTTERSTREAM GARDENS
Trim
Tel: (+353) 046 36017
Open: 1 April to 30 September, daily, 11a.m.–6p.m.
Described as the most imaginative garden in Ireland, Butterstream comprises gardens within a garden.

GROVE GARDENS AND TROPICAL BIRD SANCTUARY AND MINI ZOO
***Fordstown**, 5 miles (8km) south of Kells on the Athboy road*
Tel: (+353) 046 34276
Open: Daily, 10a.m.–6p.m. (closed December)
Admission: A=££££, C=££, F
Facilities: disabled access; teas on Sunday
This informal garden has something for everyone: a barbecue area, a tree-house, a summer-house for parents to relax in, and peaceful areas of green lawns surrounded by sweetly scented flowers.

LOUGHCREW HISTORIC GARDENS***
***Oldcastle** (5km from Oldcastle, off the Mullingar road)*

Tel: (+353) 049 8541922
Fax: (+353) 049 8541722
Open: Saturday/Sunday/bank holidays during April/September/October, 12noon–6p.m., daily duirng May/June/July/August, 12noon–6p.m.
Admission: A=£££, C=££
Facilities: car park; toilets; disabled access; book and gift shop; display and education area; tearoom
Children (supervised) are welcome and will be fascinated by the woodland maze, the spectacular watermill cascade, hidden fairies, giant spiders and weird toadstools. There are also nature and history trails.

Heritage Centres

HILL OF TARA
Tara
Tel: (+353) 046 25903
Open: May to mid-June, daily, 10a.m.–5p.m.; mid-June to mid-September, daily, 9.30a.m.–6.30p.m.; mid-September to October, daily, 10a.m.–5p.m.
Admission: A=£, C=£
Though best known as the seat of the High Kings of Ireland, the Hill of Tara has been an important site since the late Stone Age when a passage tomb was constructed there. There is a visitor centre, an audio-visual show and guided tours.

THE POWER AND THE GLORY
Trim Visitor Centre, Trim
Tel: (+353) 046 37227
Open: all year round, daily, 11a.m.–6p.m.
Admission: A=££, C=£, F
An exciting multimedia exhibition gives a vivid picture of the historical background of the magnificent medieval ruins of Trim.

Leisure Centres and Adventure Playgrounds

MOSNEY HOLIDAY CENTRE*****
Mosney, 6 miles (9.6km) south from Drogheda off route N1
Tel: (+353) 041 9829000; Fax: (+353) 041 9829444
Open: 25 May to 30 August for day visitors, 10a.m.–6p.m.
Admission: day visitors, A and C=£££££
Facilities: baby-sitting and crèche facilities; baby-changing room
As well as being one of Ireland's leading family holiday centres, Mosney is also a popular venue for day trips. The centre is ideal because it has so much to do in one location, and you can even travel directly there by train into the on-site railway station. Visitors can look forward to indoor and outdoor leisure pools, a funfair, a supervised playground, a pet farm, a boating lake, pitch'n'putt, nature walks, children's clubs and discos and family entertainment.

PLACES TO EAT

Fast-food Restaurants

McDONALD'S
*37 Trimgate Street, **Navan***
Tel: (+353) 046 73414

SUPERMAC'S
*Kennedy Road, **Navan***
Tel: (+353) 046 73016

• • • • •

PLACES TO STAY

Country Houses and Hotels

BOTHAR ALAINN HOUSE
*Balreask, **Navan**; just over 1 mile (2km) from Navan on the Trim road*
Tel: (+353) 046 28580 (or contact Irish Farm Holidays – see
Directory)
Open: 1 April to 1 September
Spacious modern house with a garden for visitors and facilities for
children.

BROADMEADOW COUNTRY HOUSE AND
EQUESTRIAN CENTRE
*Bullstown, **Ashbourne***
Tel: (+353) 01 8352823
Open: all year round
This is the place to stay if you are interested in horses and riding.
There's also a tennis court and cycling available.

BLOOMFIELD HOUSE HOTEL AND LEISURE CENTRE****
*Tullamore Road, **Mullingar***
Tel: (+353) 044 40894
Fax: (+353) 044 43767
Excellent family friendly hotel with family rooms, children's menus
and good leisure facilities.

WELLINGTON COURT HOTEL
*Summerhill Road, **Trim***
Tel: (+353) 046 31516; Fax: (+353) 046 36002
Family-run hotel with superb accommodation and food. Families
welcome.

Farmhouse Accommodation

MOUNTAINSTOWN
*Castletown, Kilpatrick, **Navan***
Tel: (+353) 046 54154; Fax: (+353) 046 54635
Open: all year round (except Christmas and New Year)
Mountainstown is a beautifully restored Queen Anne house situated on an 800-acre farm with parkland and woodland. Children are welcome on this family-friendly farm where there are horses, donkeys, free roaming peacocks, geese and poultry.

CHERRYFIELD
*Dangan, Summerhill, **Trim***
Tel: (+353) 0405 57034 (or contact Irish Farm Holidays – see Directory)
Open: 1 April to 31 October
Modern farmhouse set in quiet countryside on working dairy farm with facilities for children and a laundry for guests.

Guest Houses and B&Bs

WHITE GABLES****
*Headfort Place, **Kells***
Tel: (+353) 046 40322
Open: all year round
Excellent family friendly accommodation hosted by a cordon bleu cook, hence the exceptional breakfast menu!

Holiday Parks and Villages

MOSNEY HOLIDAY CENTRE*****
***Mosney,** 6 miles (9.6km) south from Drogheda off route N1*
Tel: (+353) 041 9829000; Fax: (+353) 041 9829444
Open: 25 May to 30 August
Facilities: see LEISURE CENTRES
Located at this excellent holiday centre are options for self-catering luxury homes in the fabulous holiday village, compact holiday flats overlooking the lake, holiday suites, half-board accommodation or touring caravans and camping.

Caravan and Camping Parks

BETTYSTOWN CARAVAN AND CAMPING PARK
*Five miles (8km) from **Drogheda** on route R167 to Bettystown*
Tel: (+353) 041 9828167
Open: Easter to September
Peaceful, family-run site with children's playground, launderette, kitchen and thatched pub on site.

Hostels

KELLS HOSTEL
Kells
Tel: (+353) 046 40100; Fax: (+353) 046 40680
Open: all year round

Bicycle Hire

IRISH CYCLE HIRE – *see Directory*
RALEIGH RENT-A-BIKE – *see Directory*

Car Hire

MURRAYS EUROPCAR – *see Directory*

Bus Services

Travel information – Tel: (+353) 01 8366111

Rail Services

Enfield – Tel: (+353) 0405 41010

COUNTY OFFALY

Located right in the heart of Ireland, County Offaly's many attractions are just waiting to be discovered. The highlight of a visit here is the **national monument at Clonmacnoise,** a 6th-century monastic settlement that enjoyed great prestige throughout Europe during the Middle Ages. The county's natural features include the Shannon and its tributary, the Brosna; its internationally famed raised bogs and wetlands; the magnificent mountain range of Slieve Bloom; and the Grand Canal that ambles from east to west through the whole county – in fact, you can hire a boat and cruise across the county at a leisurely pace along the canal.

The **guided bog tour** aboard the Clonmacnoise and West Offaly Railway is a great way to learn about the evolution of raised bogs in Ireland. Also on the site is a museum, picnic areas, a craft shop and coffee shop.

Birr Castle Demesne in the south-west of the county is a wonderful place to take children on a fine day. Laid out around a lake and along the banks of two rivers, the Demesne contains over 1,000 different species of tree and shrub and is a place of outstanding historic interest. The parkland offers riverbanks, waterfalls and the lake, all inhabited by a variety of water birds – a nature lover's paradise. Also in the park are the remains of an observatory containing a giant telescope, which was built in 1845. This amazing piece of engineering attracted astronomers from around the globe. It has been restored and is now operational again, and will be particularly interesting to children not only because of its educational features, but also because of its immense size. The Demesne will also house Ireland's Historic Science Centre which is due to open to the public in the spring of 1998, incorporating the themes of astronomy, engineering and photography.

Many of the towns in Offaly have swimming-pools and other attractions. Tullamore has an outdoor pool and a pitch'n'putt course. The picturesque market town of Edenderry, on the Grand Canal, has an indoor swimming-pool. The prosperous market town of Birr, with its tree-lined malls and quiet Georgian streets on the Camcor River, also has an indoor pool. The pretty village of Banagher on the east bank of the River Shannon has some wonderful boating facilities, including a river-bus to take you on a scenic cruise. There are also tennis and squash courts, an outdoor swimming-pool and the **Crannog Pottery,** which is well worth a visit. So too is the 12th-century **Cloghan Castle** near Lusmagh to the north of Birr. This is the oldest inhabited castle in Ireland open to the public and is currently being restored. The **An Dun Transport and Heritage Museum** at Ballinahown has a unique collection of lovingly restored cars and trucks from the 1920s.

Road access throughout the county is very good and there are rail and bus connections in Tullamore. The nearest airports are Dublin and Galway.

PLACES TO VISIT

Boats and Boat Trips

CELTIC CANAL CRUISERS
Tullamore
Tel: (+353) 0506 21861; Fax: (+353) 0506 51266
The opportunity to drift along the Grand Canal to the Barrow
River aboard 2- to 9-berth canal cruisers.

Cinemas

TULLAMORE OMNIPLEX
*Bridge Street, **Tullamore***
Tel: (+353) 0506 22800

Equestrian Facilities

ANNAHARVEY FARM
Tullamore
Tel: (+353) 0506 43544
Residential and day treks across a 300-acre farm. Tuition available;
indoor and outdoor arenas.

BALLYSHEIL RIDING SCHOOL
*Ballysheil, Belmont, **Birr***
Tel: (+353) 0902 57366
Open: Monday to Saturday
Facilities: toilet; small play area
Children aged 4 to 11 to be accompanied. Children over 11 can
stay for half or full day.

Farm Parks

ASHBROOK OPEN FARM AND AGRICULTURAL MUSEUM***
Shannonbridge
Tel: (+353) 0905 74166
Open: seasonal, daily, 10a.m.–7p.m.
Admission: A=££, C=£, F
*Facilities: toilets, picnic area; pets corner; teas and coffee with home-
baking; children's playground*
Well-laid-out farm with lots of fun things for children to see and do.
As well as an audio-visual display and an array of farm machinery
from bygone days, they can enjoy donkey and cart rides.

LUSMAGH FARM***
*Lusmagh, **Banagher***
Tel: (+353) 0509 51233
Open: May to September, daily, 2p.m.–6p.m.
Admission: A=££, C=£, F

Facilities: large indoor and outdoor picnic areas; teas and coffee served with home-baking in the farmhouse; donkey rides; pets corner
Centred around a 250-year-old farmhouse and museum, the well-maintained Lusmagh Farm has a large variety of pets and animals on show to interest all the family.

Forest and Amenity Walks

GLOSTER/GLASDERRY
*Three miles (5km) north-west of **Roscrea** on route N62 to Birr*
Facilities: carpark; picnic site; forest and lakeside walks

GOLDEN GROVE
*Just over 2 miles (3.5km) from **Roscrea,** off route N62 to Birr*
Facilities: carpark; forest walks; picnic site
The hill, Cnoc na Meas ('Hill of the Banquet'), is reputed to be the site where the last act of cannibalism took place in Ireland.

Gardens

BIRR CASTLE DEMESNE AND
IRELAND'S HISTORIC SCEIENCE CENTRE****
*Rosse Row, **Birr***
Tel: (+353) 0509 20336/22154; Fax: (+353)0509 21583
Open: All year, daily, 9a.m.–6p.m.
Admission: A=£££, C=£, F
Facilities: disabled access; toilets; free parking; coffee shop; garden centre, picnic and play area; demonstrations of the telescope
With its fairytale setting beside the River Camcor, the great estate at Birr has something for everyone. The castle interior remains a private family home, but the grounds attract visitors from all over the world. The formal gardens are noted for their hornbeam alleys and box hedges, which feature in the *Guinness Book of Records* as being the tallest in the world. Beyond the formal gardens and huge greenhouses, paths lead off into woodlands where there are many surprises hidden amongst the trees. There's a fernery, lagoon garden, a lilac walk, a waterfall with a gravity-driven fountain jetting water high above wooden bridges, and look out for the shell well. There's a stretch of informal garden below the castle, with a series of terraces overlooking the river. Located in the centre of the grounds is the enormous telescope created by William, third Earl of Rosse. For three-quarters of a century after it was invented in the 1840s, it was the world's largest telescope.

Heritage Centres

CLONMACNOISE
Shannonbridge
Tel: (+353) 0905 74195; Fax: (+353) 0905 74273
Open: mid-September to mid-March, daily, 10a.m.–5p.m.; mid-March to mid-May, daily, 10a.m.–6p.m.; mid-May to mid-September, daily, 9a.m.–7p.m.
Admission: A=££, C=£, F
Facilities: disabled access; toilets; tea-rooms; visitor centre; museum
Clonmacnoise is Ireland's premier monastic site and one of the

most celebrated of holy places. Located in a tranquil setting on the banks of the River Shannon, visitors are invited to travel back over 1,400 years and visit the famous monastic site founded in AD545. It has towers and churches, 2 exquisitely carved high crosses, a superb visitor centre and museum with exhibitions and audio-visual presentations.

Leisure Centres and Adventure Playgrounds

CANAL VIEW BOAT HIRE***
*Killina, Rahan, **Tullamore;** 2 miles (3.2km) off route N52, Tullamore to Birr road*
Tel: (+353) 0506 55868
Open: all year round
Pedal and row boats for hire on the Grand Canal. Have a picnic or tea with home-baking while the children have fun in the playground.

Museums

AN DUN TRANSPORT AND HERITAGE MUSEUM
*Doon, **Ballinahown***
Tel/Fax: (+353) 0902 30106
Open: Easter to October, Monday to Saturday, 10.30a.m.–6p.m., Sunday, 1p.m.–6p.m.
Admission: A=££, C=£, F
Facilities: souvenir shop; coffee shop
The displays feature a collection of lovingly restored vintage cars, bicycles, farm implements and post-war tractors.

Swimming-Pools

Tullamore has an outdoor swimming-pool.
Edenderry and **Birr** have indoor swimming-pools.

Trains and Model Railways

THE CLONMACNOISE AND WEST OFFALY RAILWAY***
*Bord na Mona, Blackwater, **Shannonbridge***
Tel: (+353) 0905 74114; Fax: (+353) 0905 74210
Open: 1 April to 31 October, daily (hourly on the hour), 10a.m.–5p.m.
Charges: A=£££, C=££, F
Facilities: toilets; wheelchair access throughout; peat machine museum; picnic areas; craft shop; coffee shop
This is a unique opportunity to enjoy a 5-mile (8km) circular guided tour in a comfortable train coach which will give you an insight into a raised bog of major importance – the Blackwater Bog. The journey across this desert of cutaway bog is like a journey through time – as you experience the evolution of a landscape that never stands still. The bogs and wetlands are also home to many plants and animals, including a huge variety of native and migrant birds with a total of 87 species to be seen and heard.

Walking Routes

SILVER RIVER NATURE TRAIL
Cadamstown
A visit to the Silver River Nature Trail takes you on a journey into the remote past and provides an insight into a landscape formed by seas and rivers over 400 million years ago. This geological reserve is a special place and one of considerable beauty and botanical interest. The gorge is steep-sided, so wear suitable footwear and take extra care to keep to the pathways.

SLIEVE BLOOM WAY
Slieve Bloom Display Centre, Outdoor Education Centre, Roscrea Road, Birr
Tel: (+353) 0509 20029
One vast environment park is the best way to describe the Slieve Bloom mountains, with their 17 major valleys, numerous amenity areas and hundreds of kilometres of accessible forest tracks. All of the glens, walks and viewing points are easy to find from the large-scale map of the area, and the display centre tells you more about all the Slieve Bloom's many attractions. The fully waymarked Slieve Bloom Way walking route circles the mountain for 31 miles (50km).

• • • • •

PLACES TO EAT

Fast-food Restaurants

McDONALD'S
Church Road, Tullamore (Drive-through)
Tel: (+353) 0506 24260

SUPERMAC'S
William Street, Tullamore
Tel: (+353) 0506 52034

PLACES TO STAY

Country Houses and Hotels

BROSNA LODGE HOTEL
Banagher-on-Shannon
Tel: (+353) 0509 51350; Fax: (+353) 0509 51521
Country hotel with a restaurant serving children's meals. Baby-sitting service available.

TULLAMORE COURT HOTEL AND LEISURE CENTRE
Tullamore
Tel: (+353) 0506 46666; Fax: (+353) 0506 46677
Open: All year
Excellent hotel with family rooms, fully supervised creche, kids club during high season, and a lesiure centre with heated indoor swimming-pool.

TREASCON LODGE***
Portarlington
Tel: (+353) 0502 43183
Open: all year round
Family-friendly modern home with 2 acres of paddocks and gardens. Family rooms, ponies, tennis court, playground, bicycles and games. Child-minders can be arranged for daytime or evening.

CANAL VIEW COUNTRY HOUSE***
*Killina, Rahan, **Tullamore;** 2 miles (3.2km) off route N52, Tullamore to Birr road*
Tel: (+353) 0506 55868
Open: all year round
Beautifully situated bungalow on the banks of the Grand Canal, with excellent facilities that include pedal and row boats, a sauna, steam room and jacuzzi, and a children's playground.

Farmhouse Accommodation

MINNOCK'S FARMHOUSE
Birr
Tel: (+353) 0509 20591 (or contact Irish Farm Holidays – see Directory)
Open: all year round
Spacious farmhouse set in mature gardens on dairy farm. Facilities for children.

LAUREL LODGE
*Garrymore, **Shannonbridge***
Tel: (+353) 0905 74189 (or contact Irish Farm Holidays – see Directory)
Open: 1 January to 30 November
Modern farmhouse situated in peaceful surroundings with a games room and facilities for children.

Self-Catering Apartments and Houses

PORTAVOLLA LEISURE LODGES
Banagher-on-Shannon
Tel: (+353) 023 33110; Fax: (+353) 023 33131
New, comfortable lodges on the Shannon's banks. Ideal for families.

LIME KILN COTTAGES
*Corgrave South, Lusmagh, **Banagher***
Tel: (+353) 0509 51224
Open: All year
Two-bedoromed luxury cottages in peaceful setting with beautiful gardens and picnic and barbecue area. Safe for families with young children.

Caravan and Camping Parks

GREEN GABLES CARAVAN AND CAMPING PARK
*Geashill, **Tullamore***
Tel/Fax: (+353) 0506 43760
Open: Easter to October
Facilities: disabled and baby-changing facilities; children's play area with toys for toddlers; picnic area with free use of barbecue; tea-room serving snacks all day; laundry room

Hostels

CRANK HOUSE HOSTEL
*Main Street, **Banagher***
Tel: (+353) 0509 51458; Fax: (+353) 0509 51676
Open: all year round

CREIDIM HOUSE HOSTEL
*Kishavannah, **Edenderry***
Tel: (+353) 0405 32166; Fax: (+353) 0405 31327
Open: all year round
Facilities: fully equipped self-catering kitchen and dining-room; family rooms; laundry room; picnic area

Bicycle Hire

IRISH CYCLE HIRE – *see Directory*
RALEIGH RENT-A-BIKE – *see Directory*

Car Hire

MURRAYS EUROPCAR – *see Directory*

Bus Services

Travel information – Tel: (+353) 01 8366111

Rail Services

Clara *– Tel: (+353) 0506 31105*
Tullamore *– Tel: (+353) 0506 21431*

COUNTY WESTMEATH

Westmeath nestles in the heart of Ireland and offers a wide range of rural pursuits for the outdoor enthusiast. There are lots of lakes with scenic wooded shores for boating, fishing and swimming; some low hills ideal for family walking (the highest point is little more than 850ft/259m); and, with much of the county being flat, it is a perfect place for quiet cycles in the countryside with the family.

Every Westmeath lake has a myth or legend associated with it, guaranteed to capture children's imagination. The fairy queen Deirdre is said to have brought back Lough Owel as a present from King Dun of Connacht – she carried it in her white handkerchief over the mountains to the emerald hills of Westmeath. Lough Derravaragh is linked with the tragic legend of the Children of Lir. Their jealous step-mother, Queen Aoife, is said to have pushed the four children into the water by the shore of the lough and turned them into swans. She decreed that they should remain so for the next 900 years. During the centuries of their enchantment, the children kept their human faculties and were endowed with the gift of song, singing so beautifully that all passers-by stopped to listen to them.

In a valley near Lough Lene is the village of Fore and the majestic ruins of **Fore Abbey,** a grand monastery founded in AD630 by St Fechin. It is here that the famous Seven Wonders of Fore are said to be: the monastery in a bog; the mill without a race; the water that flows uphill; the tree that won't burn; the water that won't boil; the anchorite in a stone; and the stone raised by St Fechin's prayers. It's a great place to visit and explore – I wonder if you'll find all seven?

The county has two main towns, Mullingar and Athlone. Mullingar is almost encircled by the magnificent Royal Canal, making angling and boating high on the agenda of attractions. The town is dominated by the **Cathedral of Christ the King,** and has an indoor swimming-pool as well as tennis, badminton and squash courts. Riding centres are located at Rathcolman and Lough Ennell, and you can boat, swim and fish (among other activities) at the **Lilliput–Jonathan Swift Park** on the shores of Lough Ennell. The bustling town of Athlone neatly straddles the ambling River Shannon at the foot of Lough Ree. This is a harbour on Ireland's inland navigation system. It has many family attractions, including **Athlone Castle. Athlone Leisure World** has many tempting attractions, while the **Glendeer Open Pet Farm** at Drum, just west of the town, is a good place to stretch your legs and let the kids run free among deer, ponies, donkeys, cows, sheep, goats, peacocks and other birds. There are pet animals to feed, a picnic area, a tea-room, tuck shop and play area. Adventurous types can don the 'cow horns' and cruise along the Shannon to Lough Ree aboard a **Viking-style longship.**

Road access is good throughout the county via the main N4, N6 and N52 roads feeding many minor roads. Public transport is adequate with bus and rail stations in the main towns, and provincial services serving the outlying villages.

PLACES TO VISIT

Activity Centres

WINEPORT SAILING CENTRE AND RESTAURANT
Glasson, **Athlone**
Tel: (+353) 0902 74944; Fax: (+353) 0902 85471
Open: all year round (restaurant) and seasonal (sailing)
Instruction for beginners and experienced sailors (minimum age
10). The superb restaurant serves delicious food.

Boats and Boat Trips

MV *ROSS* BOAT TRIPS
Jolly Mariner Marina, Coosan, **Athlone**
Tel: (353) 0902 72892
The MV *Ross* carries up to 60 passengers on a 90-minute cruise on
the Shannon. There's an on-board bar, coffee shop and commentary.

THE VIKING SHIP***
Rosanna Cruises, The Strand, **Athlone**
Tel: (+353) 0902 73383
Daily cruises to Lough Ree (90-minute round trip), and twice-
weekly cruises to Clonmacnoise (4-hour round trip), aboard a
Viking ship. Lots of fun and great scenery.

Castles

ATHLONE CASTLE AND VISITOR CENTRE***
St Peter's Square, **Athlone**
Tel: (+353) 0902 72107; Fax: (+353) 0902 72100
Open: April to September, daily, 10a.m.–6p.m.
Admission: A=££, C=£, F
Facilities: toilets; tea-rooms; tourist office
Dating from the 13th century, the impressive Norman castle
dominates the town centre and commands the traditional gateway
to the west of Ireland. There are folk and military museums and
audio-visual presentations.

TULLYNALLY CASTLE**
Castlepollard
Tel: (+353) 044 61159
Gardens *open: April to October, daily, 10a.m.–6p.m.*
Castle *open: mid-July to mid-August daily, 2p.m.–6p.m.*
Admission: castle and gardens, A=£££, C=££; gardens only, A=££, C=£
Facilities: wheelchair access; toilets
The magnificent Tullynally House is the largest castellated house in
Ireland. As well as its fine collection of portraits and furniture, it is
renowned as a museum of 19th-century gadgets and has splendid
Victorian laundries and kitchens. There are excellent walks to take

through pleasure grounds and parkland. Look out for the small grotto with views towards Lough Derravaragh where the Children of Lir swam as swans (see p.127), and the River Sham, an ornamental lake masquerading as a river.

TYRRELLPASS CASTLE
Tyrrellpass
Tel/Fax: (+353) 044 23105
Facilities: museum; restaurant; coffee shop; gift and antiques shop

Cathedrals

CATHEDRAL OF CHRIST THE KING
Mullingar
Tel: (+353) 044 48338
Museum *open: June to September, Thursday and weekends, 3p.m.–4p.m.*
The museum contains many artefacts of historic interest including wonderful mosaics, frescoes, canvases and models of church buildings from the 17th century.

Heritage Sites

FORE ABBEY AND THE SEVEN WONDERS****
Fore
Tel: (+353) 044 40861
Open: All year
Admission: Free
Facilities: toilets; coffee and craft shop
This is a great place for kids to run free and explore. There's the ancient remains of St Feichin's Monastery and the mysterious seven wonders for them to find and investigate.

Craft Centres

MULLINGAR BRONZE AND PEWTER VISITOR CENTRE
*Greatdown, The Downs, **Mullingar***
Tel: (+353) 044 48791; Fax: (+353) 044 43665
Open: Monday to Saturday, 9.30a.m.–6p.m.
Workshop tours: Monday to Friday, 9.30a.m.–4p.m.
Facilities: craft shop and showrooms; coffee shop
An opportunity to see the age-old craft of pewter-making and beautifully sculpted bronze.

Equestrian Facilities

MULLINGAR EQUESTRIAN CENTRE
*Athlone Road, **Mullingar***
Tel/Fax: (+353) 044 48331
Open: all year round
Treks along the wooded shores of Lough Derravaragh for beginners and experienced riders. Residential packages available. Has a large indoor arena, tuition, summer pony camp, and a games room.

Farm Parks

GLENDEER OPEN PET FARM***
Drum, Athlone
Tel: (+353) 0902 37147
Open: April to September, Monday to Saturday, 10a.m.–6p.m., Sunday, noon–6p.m.
Admission: A=££, C=£, F
Facilities: toilets; picnic area; shop; tea-room; nature walk
The farm has a large variety of animals to feed and see which will please all the family. There's also an unspoilt nature walk where a selection of horse-drawn farm machinery can be seen.

Festivals and Events

MULLINGAR FESTIVAL***
Tel: (+353) 044 44044; Fax: (+353) 044 44045
On: second week in July
A week of fun for all the family with street entertainment, music and dance, talent competitions, busking, a 'lark in the park', and the famous Mullingar International Bachelor Competition.

Forest and Amenity Walks

KILPATRICK
On the northern shore of Lough Owel near Ballinafid off route N4
Facilities include a lakeside walk, sailing, swimming and fishing.

MULLAGHMEEN
Five miles (8km) west of Oldcastle on minor road to Finea
The plantation extends to almost 400 hectares, making it the largest broadleaf forest in Ireland. Has extensive forest walks throughout.

Gardens

BELVEDERE HOUSE AND GARDENS**
Just under 4 miles (6km) from Mullingar on the Tullamore road
Tel: (+353) 044 40861
Open: April to October, daily, noon–6p.m.
Admission: A=£, C=£
Facilities: disabled access; picnic area; pets corner
The garden has 3 main areas: the arboretum which slopes down to the shores of Lough Ennel; an enclosed garden with shrubs and trees; and the walled garden.

Leisure Centres and Adventure Playgrounds

ATHLONE LEISURE WORLD***
Grace Road, Athlone
Tel: (+353) 0902 94766
Open: all year round, daily, 10a.m.–11p.m.
Facilities: restaurant and bar; 10-pin bowling; snooker; kiddies' adventure-land; indoor football; indoor kart racing

JONATHAN SWIFT AMENITY PARK**

*Lough Ennell, **Mullingar***
The Lilliput–Jonathan Swift Amenity Park has many facilities in a wonderful setting on the shores of Lough Ennell. You can go boating, swimming or angling, play on a par 3 golf course, and enjoy lakeside walking, a children's play area and a coffee shop.

Museums

LOCKE'S DISTILLERY MUSEUM**
Kilbeggan
Tel/Fax: (+353) 0506 32134
Open: November to March, daily, 10a.m.–4p.m.; April to October, daily, 9a.m.–6p.m.
Admission: A=££, C=£, F
Facilities: baby-changing facilities in carpark toilets; guided tours; picnic area by river; coffee shop (high-chair available)
Established in 1757 and in production until 1953, Locke's is now open as a museum to show you how whiskey was made in times past. Over 85% of the original machinery remains intact, including the waterwheel powered by the Brusna River. It is the only small pot-still whiskey distillery remaining in Ireland. They plan to have special play areas and exhibitions for children in the future.

Swimming-Pools

ATHLONE SWIMMING-POOL
*Retreat Road, **Athlone***
Tel: (+353) 0902 72355

MULLINGAR SWIMMING-POOL
Mullingar
Tel: (+353) 044 40262

• • • • •

PLACES TO EAT

Cafés and Restaurants

THE WINEPORT RESTAURANT
*Glassan, **Athlone***
Tel: (+353) 0902 85466
Children welcome. Special menu includes pizzas, small portions of soup, ice-creams etc.

Fast-Food Restaurants

McDONALD'S
*Irishtown Central, **Athlone***
Tel: (+353) 0902 77020

*Creggan Roundabout, Dublin Road, **Athlone** (Drive-through)*
Tel: (+353) 0902 73390

*21 Pearse Street, **Mullingar***
Tel: (+353) 044 47575

PIZZA PARK
*Church Street, **Athlone***
Tel: (+353) 0902 73241

SUPERMAC'S
*Irishtown, **Athlone***
Tel: (+353) 0902 76433

*Main Street, **Moate***
Tel: (+353) 0902 82171

• • • • •

PLACES TO STAY

Country Houses and Hotels

BLOOMFEILD HOUSE HOTEL AND LESUIRE CENTRE****
*Tullamore Road, **Mullingar***
Te: (+353) 044 40894; Fax: (+353) 044 43767
Excellent family friendly hotel with family rooms, children's menus and good lesuire facilities.

HODSON BAY HOTEL
Athlone
Tel: (+353) 0902 92444; Fax: (+353) 0902 92688
Open: all year round
In a picturesque setting on the shores of Lough Ree, this hotel has some excellent facilities including a leisure centre with an indoor heated swimming-pool, sauna, steam room, gym and tennis court.

LAKESIDE HOTEL AND BALLYKEERAN CRUISERS
*Lakeside Hotel, Ballykeeran, **Athlone***
Tel: (+353) 0902 85163; Fax: (+353) 0902 85431
Open: all year round
Family-run hotel and cruiser hire company on the shores of Lough Ree. Facilities include a children's playroom.

LOUGH OWEL LODGE
***Cullion,** north of Mullingar just off the N4*
Tel/Fax: (+353) 044 48714
Open: March to December
Unusual country home set among mature woodland. Guests can enjoy woodland and lakeside walks, a tennis court, games room and family room, and fishing boats can be hired.

Farmhouse Accommodation

CUMMERSTOWN HOUSE
Collinstown; *9 miles (15km) from Mullingar via R394*
Tel: (+353) 044 66316 (or contact Irish Farm Holidays – see
Directory)
Open: 1 May to 1 October
Spacious farmhouse on stock farm. There are facilities for children,
and Lough Lene and its beaches (Blue Flag) are nearby.

HOUNSLOW HOUSE
Fore, **Castle Pollard**
Tel: (+353) 044 61144
Open: February to November
Family-friendly accommodation with home baking and a games
room with computers.

Holiday Parks and Villages

MULTYFARNHAM HOLIDAY VILLAGE
Multyfarnham, **Mullingar**
Tel: (+353) 044 71359; Fax: (+353) 044 71342
Open: all year round
Facilities: limited wheelchair access; launderette; games room; play area;
tennis courts
Well-appointed luxury bungalows to sleep 5 to 6, all set in their
own landscaped grounds. Each of the 14 bungalows has 3
bedrooms and 2 bathrooms, a fully fitted kitchen, a dishwasher,
multi-channel TV, high-chairs and cots.

Self-Catering Apartments and Houses

RATHCAM COTTAGE
Gaybrook, **Mullingar**
Tel: (+353) 044 22306
Comfortable, peaceful, traditionally furnished cottage situated
amidst parkland and animals on an organic farm. You'll have your
own garden, telephone, washing-machine and outdoor toys. Baby-
sitting service, cots and high-chair are available.

Caravan and Camping Parks

LOUGH REE EAST CARAVAN AND CAMPING PARK
Ballykeeran, **Athlone**
Tel: (+353) 0902 78561
Open: 1 April to 2 October
Family-run park set in the peace and tranquillity of 5 acres on the
shores of Lough Ree, just 2 miles (3.2km) from Athlone. The park
has its own jetty, and boats are available to hire. There's also a
campers' kitchen, a recreation room and play areas for children.

LOUGH ENNELL CARAVAN AND CAMPING PARK
Lough Ennell Holiday Village, Tudenham, Carrick, **Mullingar**
Tel/Fax: (+353) 044 48101
Open: 1 April to 30 September

Facilities: well-equipped play areas; games room; shop; laundry
The village is set in mature woodland close to the lakeside on the Tudenham shore of Lough Ennell.

Bicycle Hire

IRISH CYCLE HIRE – *see Directory*
RALEIGH RENT-A-BIKE – *see Directory*

Car Hire

O'MARA'S RENT-A-CAR
*Galway Road, **Athlone***
Tel: (+353) 0902 92325; Fax: (+353) 0902 94310

HAMILLS RENT-A-CAR
*Dublin Road, **Mullingar***
Tel: (+353) 044 48682; Fax: (+353) 044 41374

Bus Services

***Athlone** Railway Station – Tel: (+353) 0902 73322*

Rail Services

***Athlone** – Tel: (+353) 0902 73300*
***Mullingar** – Tel: (+353) 044 48274*

COUNTY WEXFORD

In County Wexford you will find 150 miles (240km) of coastline washed by both the Irish Sea and the Celtic Sea, with some of the best beaches in Europe and the most sunshine in Ireland. Combine this with the fantastic array of unique attractions designed to captivate the imagination of children of all ages, and it is not too difficult to appreciate why this south-eastern corner of Ireland is a favourite.

There are many reasons to linger here, apart from the many roadside stalls selling punnets of mouth-watering Wexford strawberries. The **Johnstown Castle Gardens** and **Irish Agricultural Museum** are worth visiting. The fairytale castle and gardens are beautiful, and the museum has interesting displays.

The town of Wexford has many attractions that are ideal for family visits. Don't miss the **West Gate Heritage Centre** and **Selskar Abbey**, or the **Fun House**, an indoor adventure play centre for children up to 12 years old. Five minutes from the town centre is the **Irish National Heritage Park**. Here you can wander around a beautiful country park on well-made pushchair-friendly pathways, and explore a heritage site which demonstrates how the Celts, Vikings and Normans lived and how Irish society developed. With winding paths, streams, ponds and wildlife, children can wander safely. It's well worth spending the entire day here.

On the south coast of the county is the **Maritime Museum and Lightship** *Guillemot* at Kilmore Quay, a whole ship just waiting to be explored. Further along the south coast is the Hook Peninsula, a rocky finger that points precariously out into the Celtic Sea at the mouth of Waterford Harbour. The towering **Hook Head Lighthouse** is one of the oldest lighthouses in Europe. The Hook Peninsula is described as 'a self-contained wonderland in the sunniest corner of Ireland', and this craggy, sea-carved peninsula is a veritable maze of tiny beaches and coves.

On the north-western coast of the Hook is the Blue Flag resort of Duncannon, a beautiful little fishing village that is bustling with life as a major tourist venue with over a mile of golden sands. A superb spot to spend a day with the bucket and spade, or take a guided tour of the historic **military fort** that has stood guard over Waterford harbour since 1586, when it was fortified as a precaution against an attack by the Spanish Armada.

Further north, on the main road from the Hook Peninsula to New Ross (R733) is **Dunbrody Abbey and Castle,** an excellent visitor complex that provides hours of fun for all the family.

Just 2 miles east of New Ross is the **Ballylane Open Farm and Nature Reserve.** Take a guided tour and visit the farm shop. The **John F. Kennedy Park and Arboretum,** just a few miles south of New Ross, is a great place to visit and has spectacular views.

Rosslare Strand is a magnificent Blue Flag beach, the sort of place you dream of – a magnificent stretch of sand backed by tea-rooms, hotels, restaurants, pubs, tennis courts, crazy golf, a recreation and windsurfing centre, and a supervised playground. On the east coast of the county, just south-east of Gorey, is the Blue Flag resort of

Courtown. It has over 2 miles of fine sandy beach, plus lots of family amusements. One of the best is the unique **Pirates Cove Adventure Golf Course and Fun Cave.** Gorey is midway between Wexford and Dublin and provides an ideal base to visit the many beaches and resorts along the eastern coastline. The town itself is an excellent shopping centre. Just east is Ballymoney, a quaint little holiday resort with a fine sandy beach. Virtually the whole of this coastline consists of beautiful sandy beaches backed by dunes providing a safe paradise for the bucket and spade brigade. Access isn't always easy, but you can be sure of finding large areas of uninhabited beaches; at Curracloe, for example, there's a 7-mile (11.2km) crescent of sheltered sandy beach.

On the R742 coast road near Ballygarrett is the **Shrule Deer Farm,** while west of Gorey near Askamor is **Young McDonald's Animal Park** which has a wide variety of animals and birds to amuse children and a good adventure playground.

Access throughout the county is very good both by public and private transport. The road network is excellent with first-class roads zigzagging across the county. Expressway bus services connect the major towns, with provincial services serving the villages. Mainline rail services operate from Dublin, Waterford and Limerick into Wexford, and the nearest airports are Dublin and Waterford.

● ● ● ● ●

PLACES TO VISIT

Boats and Boat Trips

THE GALLEY CRUISING RESTAURANTS
New Ross
Tel: (+353) 051 421723
On: May to October, 2-hour cruises from New Ross with lunch and dinner on board; June to August, 2-hour cruises with afternoon-tea
Admission: children under 14 half-price except at dinner
Delicious meals are served in comfortable, heated salons while you cruise along the beautiful Barrow and Nore rivers. It is possible to buy a ticket for cruising only.

Castles

BALLYHACK CASTLE
Ballyhack
Tel: (+353) 051 389468; Fax: (+353) 051 389284
Open: April, May, June and September, Wednesday to Sunday, noon–6p.m.; July and August, daily, 10a.m.–6p.m.
Admission: A=£, C=£, F
The castle, a large tower house, is currently under restoration. The heritage information centre has interesting displays about Crusader knights, medieval monks and Norman nobility.

ENNISCORTHY CASTLE – *see* MUSEUMS

Cathedrals and Abbeys

DUNBRODY ABBEY AND CASTLE VISITOR CENTRE***
*Campile, **New Ross***
Tel: (+353) 051 388603
Open: April, May, June and September, daily, 10a.m.–6p.m.; July to August, daily, 10a.m.–7p.m.
Admission to abbey: A=£, C=£, F; to maze/castle/pitch'n'putt: A=£, C=£, F
Facilities: toilets; walks; craft shop; picnic areas; tea-shop; pitch'n'putt
The abbey is one of the most imposing Cistercian ruins in Ireland. There is an exciting visitor centre and an excellent tea-shop with a small museum that houses the Dunbrody Castle Dolls'-House, a scale replica of the castle. This is a super place to spend a quiet, relaxing day, and children will enjoy the intricate yew hedge maze.

TINTERN ABBEY***
*Near **Saltmills**, Hook Peninsula*
Tel: (+353) 051 562321
Open: all year round, daily, dawn to dusk
Admission: free
A stroll around the beautiful abbey grounds will restore you to peace and tranquillity. This is the place to go with the baby in the backpack or the children for a picnic – there's a maze of ancient paths and woodland trails just waiting to be explored. They will lead you to walled gardens, the ruins of an old mill on the banks of a stream, a fine battlemented bridge, a well and the ruins of a little church. The abbey, church and fortified bridge are currently undergoing a major restoration programme and a visitor centre is going to be opened on the site. The aim is to make this area a major tourist attraction for the future – but I hope it doesn't become too popular and ruin the special ambience this historic site holds for the visitors of today.

Craft Centres

KILTREA BRIDGE POTTERY**
Enniscorthy
Tel: (+353) 054 35107; Fax: (+353) 054 34690
Open: all year round, Monday to Saturday, 9.30a.m.–5.30p.m., Sunday in high season
It is not very often you get the chance to see earthenware clay being skilfully used to produce a whole range of beautiful, hand-thrown pottery. Well worth visiting.

Crèches

FUN HOUSE ADVENTURE PLAYCENTRE***
Wexford *– see* LEISURE CENTRES AND ADVENTURE PLAYGROUNDS

PETTITT'S SUPERMARKET
*St Aidan's Shopping Centre, **Wexford** – see* SHOPPING CENTRES
Facilities: crèche; baby-changing rooms

Equestrian Facilities

BALLINGALE FARM RIDING CENTRE
Taghmon
Tel: (+353) 053 34387; Fax: (+353) 053 34541
Open: all year round
This centre specialises in unaccompanied children's riding holidays and family breaks, and offers lessons, trekking, cross country and beach rides.

BORO HILL HOUSE EQUESTRIAN HOLIDAY CENTRE
*Clonroche, **Enniscorthy***
Tel: (+353) 054 44117; Fax: (+353) 054 44266
Open: all year round
This centre specialises in residential holidays for children, accommodating them either in the house or in fully supervised dormitories, and offers lessons, trekking and cross-country.

CURRACLOE HOUSE EQUESTRIAN CENTRE***
*Curracloe, **Enniscorthy***
Tel: (+353) 053 37129
Open: all year round
Excellent facilities to cater for all levels of expertise. You can enjoy a canter on the spectacular Curracloe Beach or a trek through the famous Wexford Sloblands, viewing the flocks of rare geese and teeming wildfowl there (*see* WILDLIFE PARKS).

HORETOWN EQUESTRIAN CENTRE
Foulksmills
Tel: (+353) 051 565786; Fax: (+353) 051 565633
Open: all year round
Superb outdoor riding and trekking facilities. Choose from daily, weekly and weekend packages. Large indoor arena.

SHELMALIERE RIDING STABLES
*Forth Mountain, **Wexford***
Tel: (+353) 053 39251
Open: all year round
A large selection of ponies and horses are available for riders of any ability. Novices can trek at a leisurely pace on ponies and cobs, while experienced riders can take an exciting gallop along miles of forest trails on quality horses. Advance booking essential. Tuition available.

Farm Parks

BALLYLANE FARM AND NATURE RESERVE**
New Ross
Tel: (+353) 051 25666; Fax: (+353) 051 22898
Open: May to September, daily, 10a.m.–6p.m.
Admission: A=££, C=£, F
Facilities: disabled access; toilets; shops; tea-room; picnic and barbecue areas; play area
Ballylane Farm offers visitors the opportunity to explore Ireland's natural heritage and experience life on a working farm. Learn about crops and see deer, livestock and pets.

SHRULE DEER FARM*
*Shrule, Ballygarrett, **Gorey***
Tel: (+353) 055 27277
*Open: May and September, weekends, 10a.m.–6p.m.; June to August,
daily, 10a.m.–6p.m.*
Admission: A=££, C=£, F
Facilities: toilets; tea-room; playground
A wide variety of animals (goats, pigs, calves, lambs, turkeys, rabbits
and guinea pigs) to see and handle. There are also wonderful herds
of red and sitka deer.

TOBERGAL FARM**
*Boolavogue, **Ferns***
Tel: (+353) 054 66286
*Open: March to October, Monday to Saturday, 10a.m.–7p.m., Sunday,
2p.m.–6p.m.; November to February, weekends, 2p.m.–5p.m.*
Admission: A=£, C=£
A wide variety of animals, birds and wildfowl. Kids will love the duck-
pond, pony rides, nature trails, craft centre and gift shop, demonstra-
tions and exhibits of farm equipment, and the play area with its
tree-house.

YOUNG McDONALD'S ANIMAL PARK***
*Askamore, **Gorey***
Tel: (+353) 055 26312; Fax: (+353) 055 26555
*Open: Easter to 30 September, Monday to Saturday, 10a.m.–6p.m.,
Sunday, noon–6p.m.*
Admission: A=££, C=£, F
Facilities: toilets; adventure playground; coffee shop; tuck shop
The farm has lots to see and do for all the family. There's a museum,
a tree trail, river walk and a maze, as well as lots of animals and birds
– cattle, pigs, sheep, goats, donkeys, deer, rabbits, peacocks, pheasants,
ducks, geese and hens. The adventure playground is excellent.

WOODLANDS HONEY FARM*
Carrickbyrne
Tel: (+353) 051 28287
Open: May to August, daily, 2p.m.–6p.m.
Admission: A=££, C=££
Video show on the life of bees plus demonstrations and honey-
tastings.

Festivals and Events

WEXFORD VIKING FESTIVAL***
Tel: (+353) 053 24210
On: May bank holiday
A look into Wexford's Viking past provides fun for all the family with
street theatre, entertainment and fantastic costumes.

FAIR DAYS FESTIVAL
New Ross
On: June
A week of entertainment and exhibitions which kids will enjoy a lot.

MUSIC FOR WEXFORD
St Iberius Church, **Wexford**
On: July/August
Admission: A=£££, C=£
A series of weekly lunchtime concerts by young Irish musicians in the beautiful setting of St Iberius Church.

STRAWBERRY FAIR***
Enniscorthy
On: early July
Tel: (+353) 054 35142
Eight days of fun, music and *craic* to celebrate the annual strawberry harvest. The whole family will enjoy the street entertainment, exhibitions, music, and the wonderful strawberries and cream.

DUNCANNON SUMMER FESTIVAL***
Duncannon
On: first week in July
Tel: (+353) 051 389109
A festival in this pretty seaside village, built around the historic fort. Lots of outdoor activities, music and games on the street and beach.

GOREY SUMMER FAIR**
Gorey
On: early August
Tel: (+353) 055 21117
Music and entertainment for all the family in the streets of this lovely town.

CAMPILE STREET FESTIVAL**
Near Dunbrody Abbey, **Campile**
On: August weekend
Plenty of carnival games, entertainment and family activities.

TAGOAT STEAM RALLY*
Tagoat
On: Sunday following 15 August
Tel: (+353) 053 31238
Lots of steam and side shows – a great day out for kids and dads!

COURTOWN FAILTE FESTIVALS**
Courtown
Tel: (+353) 055 25140
On: held on 3 weekends, the May and October bank holidays and mid-August weekend
Plenty of activities for all ages: open-air music, majorettes, vintage cars, pony and trap rides, competitions and street parties. (The August festival is particularly family-orientated.)

STORYTELLING FESTIVAL***
Ar mBreacha Raheen, House of Story-telling, **Ballyduff**
Tel: (+353) 054 44148
On: every Tuesday night during July and August
An open house of storytelling, song and dance.

Forest and Amenity Walks

THE JOHN F. KENNEDY ARBORETUM***
Seven miles (12km) south of **New Ross** *off the R733 Duncannon road*
Tel: (+353) 051 388171; Fax: (+353) 051 388172
Open: April and September, daily, 10a.m.–6.30p.m.; May to August, daily,
10a.m.–8p.m.; October to March, daily, 10a.m.–5p.m.
Admission: A=££, C=£, F
Facilities: disabled access; toilets; picnic areas; visitor centre; tea-room
The arboretum is set in 252 hectares of beautiful rolling woodland
on the slopes of Slieve Coillte. There are over 6,000 species of
plants, trees and shrubs, a lake and some excellent walks along a
number of waymarked routes. Pony and trap transport and a
miniature railway operate for the youngsters in summer.

DUNAMORE
Three miles (5.5km) south of **Enniscorthy** *on minor road to Killuran*
Facilities: fishing; forest and riverside walks

TINTERN ABBEY***
Fifteen miles (24km) from **New Ross** *on route R734 to Fethard*
Facilities: carpark; forest walks; access to abbey
see CATHEDRALS AND ABBEYS

Gardens

JOHNSTOWN CASTLE GARDENS**
Murrintown, *south of Wexford off the Rosslare road (N25)*
Tel: (+353) 053 42888
Gardens *open: all year round, daily, 9a.m.–5.30p.m.*
Museum *open: all year round, Monday to Friday, 9a.m.–5p.m. (also*
open weekends from April to October, 2p.m.–5p.m.)
Admission: free to gardens; a modest charge for entry to museum
Facilities: toilets; museum; tea-room at museum in July and August
The fairytale castle at Johnstown fits neatly into the surrounding
setting of lawns, lakes and ornamental towers. Whilst only the
entrance hall to the castle (where information can be obtained) is
open to the public, the 50 acres of ornamental grounds with 3
lakes and a picnic area in the old sunken garden make an ideal
place to spend a sunny afternoon. There are many scenic walks that
include a large rhododendron arboretum, pleasure grounds and a
statue walk. The estate farmyard contains an agricultural museum
with a fabulous display of antique farm implements and rural
transport, as well as large-scale replicas of a blacksmith's, cooper's
and other workshops.

Heritage Centres

DUNCANNON FORT**
Duncannon
Tel: (+353) 051 389454
Open: June to September, daily, 10a.m.–6pm.
Admission: A=£, C=£
Facilities: toilets; wheelchair access
The fort is noted for its dry moat and exterior walls. Restoration

work is still in progress, but there are some very interesting displays and exhibits to see and explore.

IRISH NATIONAL HERITAGE PARK*****
Ferrycraig, *near Waterford*
Tel: (+353) 053 20733; Fax: (+353) 053 20911
Open: mid-March to early November, daily, 10a.m.–7p.m.
Admission: A=£££, C=£££, F
Facilities: disabled access; toilets with baby-changing facilities; picnic areas; craft shop; coffee shop
The park is an open-air museum depicting man's first settlements in Ireland, sweeping across almost 9,000 years of history. Visitors are given a map to follow a clearly defined route around the 16 historical sites set in 35 acres of mature forest. These sites explain Ireland history from the Stone and Bronze Ages, through the Celtic period and concluding with the Viking and Norman influences. Every one is very realistically laid out and usually manned by guides in period dress. The early Norman castle and replica of an Irish monastic round tower are outstanding. There are no 'keep out' or 'do not touch' signs here: children can enter and explore the buildings, touch and investigate the structures and, to their great delight, climb onto the ramparts of the ring fort and into the Viking ships.

WEST GATE HERITAGE CENTRE*
Spawell Road, Wexford
Tel: (+353) 053 46506; Fax: (+353) 053 41911
Open: April to December, Monday to Saturday, 9.30a.m.–1p.m. and 2p.m.–5.30p.m.; July to August, Sunday, 2p.m.–6p.m.
Admission: A=£, C=£
Facilities: toilets; disabled access; exhibitions; audio-visual theatre
Constructed in the last remaining towergate on the walls of the town of Wexford, the West Gate Centre combines with the ancient and historic Selskar Abbey to produce the perfect setting in which to understand the development of the town and its people.

YOLA FARMSTEAD***
Tagoat, Rosslare Harbour
Tel/Fax: (+353) 053 31177
Open: May and October, weekends, 2p.m.–5p.m.; June to September, daily, 9a.m.–5p.m.
Admission: A=££, C=£
Facilities: toilets; disabled access; craft and crystal showroom; coffee shop; playground
Drift back in time to a bygone age as you wander around this fascinating farmstead. There are lots of interesting and fun things to do for all the family. Examine the windmill and the thatched farm buildings; visit the rare species' enclosure and the genealogy centre; and stroll along the flora and fauna walk.

Ireland at Work – Past and Present

CRAANFORD MILLS**
Craanford
Tel: (+353) 055 23124
Open: all year round, daily

A fully restored 17th-century corn-grinding watermill in full working order. The works are on view to visitors together with explanatory exhibits. Excellent, wholesome food is served in the Kiln Loft.

Leisure Centres and Adventure Playgrounds

FUN HOUSE ADVENTURE PLAYCENTRE****
*McCauley's Carpark, Redmond Place, **Wexford***
Tel: (+353) 053 46696
Open: all year round, Monday to Wednesday, 9.30a.m.–6p.m., Thursday and Friday, 9.30a.m.–7p.m., Saturday, 10a.m.–7p.m., Sunday, noon–7p.m.
Admission: ££
Facilities: toilets; baby-changing facilities; coffee shop
This fully supervised adventure playcentre is the ideal place to leave the children for an hour if you need to go shopping or have a quiet cup of coffee. There's plenty to amuse them (including a twin aerial runway, bouncy castle, slides, scramble nets and a ball pond, plus a mini-adventure area, slides and an assortment of toys specifically for the under-5s) in a safe environment.

KARTELL KARTING
*Kelogue Industrial Estate, Rosslare Road, **Wexford***
Tel: (+353) 053 47866; Fax: (+353) 053 47858
Open: daily, noon–11p.m.

PIRATES COVE ADVENTURE GOLF AND FUN CAVE****
*Courtown Harbour, **Courtown***
Tel: (+353) 055 25555 (after-hours enquiries: 055 25280); Fax: (+353) 055 25309
Open: June to August, daily, 11a.m.–11p.m.; rest of year: bowling and Fun Cave only, Sunday, 2p.m.–late (Adventure Golf may open at spring and autumn weekends, subject to weather)
Admission: A=£££, C=££, F
Facilities: picnic areas; golf course; bowling; restaurant with kids' meals
This unique attraction in a wonderful setting of tropical gardens and cascading water is the perfect place for an outing. Full of dramatic colour and light, the waterfalls and foliage add a magical atmosphere to the spectacular setting. The Adventure Golf is marvellous fun for all the family, and the Fun Cave and 10-pin bowling are ideal places to while away an hour or two, especially on a rainy day. The Lagoon Restaurant is the perfect spot to fill up the tank!

Museums

BERKELEY COSTUME AND TOY MUSEUM***
*Berkeley Forest House, **New Ross***
Tel: (+353) 051 21361
Open: May to September, Thursday to Sunday, 11a.m.–6p.m.
Admission: A=£££, C=£
Private collection of 18th- and 19th-century dolls, toys and costumes, displayed in the drawing-rooms of Berkeley Forest House. Children can sometimes ride in Victorian carriages – pulled by goats!

GUILLEMOT LIGHTSHIP MARITIME MUSEUM**
Kilmore Quay

Tel: (+353) 053 29655
Open: May to October, daily, noon–6p.m.
Admission: A=£, C=£, F
The last remaining lightship in Ireland has a museum on board with
exhibits of model ships, coral, maritime pictures, paintings and
records. The ship retains all its original fittings and atmosphere.

NATIONAL MUSEUM OF AGRICULTURE AND RURAL LIFE –
see GARDENS

WEXFORD COUNTY MUSEUM
Enniscorthy
Tel: (+353) 054 35926
*Open: June to September, Monday to Saturday, 10a.m.–1p.m. and
2p.m.–6p.m.; October to November, Monday to Saturday, 2p.m.–5p.m.*
Admission: A=££, C=£, F
Housed in the medieval Enniscorthy Castle, the museum contains
wide range of items depicting mostly 19th- and 20th-century
history.

Parks

NEW ROSS TOWN PARK***
*At **Marsh Meadows** on the New Ross to Rosslare road*
This beautifully landscaped park has a bandstand, picnic areas, tenn
courts, excellent children's playground, toilets and washing facilities.

Shopping Centres and Markets

BULL RING OPEN MARKET
Wexford
Open: all year round, Friday and Saturday, 10a.m.–4.30p.m.
Colourful outdoor market selling a wide range of goodies including
bric-à-brac, books, clothes, home produce and flowers.

ST AIDAN'S SHOPPING CENTRE
Wexford
Late-night shopping on Thursday and Friday till 9p.m.
Pettitt's Supermarket offers free parking, toilets, a crèche and baby-
changing rooms.

Swimming-Pools

BAN MILLS SWIMMING-POOL
Fethard-on-Sea
Tel: (+353) 051 397163

BUNCLODY
Tel: (+353) 054 77459
Outdoor heated swimming-pool.

KENNEDY MEMORIAL SWIMMING-POOL
Barrack Lane, New Ross
Tel: (+353) 051 21169
Indoor heated swimming-pool.

MUNICIPAL SWIMMING-POOL
*Ferrybank, **Wexford***
Tel: (+353) 053 23274
Open: all year round, Monday, 9a.m.–6p.m., Tuesday to Friday, 9a.m.–9p.m., weekends, 10a.m.–6p.m.
Heated indoor swimming-pool, saunas, shop and restaurant.

Theatres

GOREY THEATRE HALL
Gorey
Tel: (+353) 055 21248
Informal performances by the Gorey Little Theatre Group. Check locally for current programme.

Walking Routes

CURRACLOE NATURE TRAIL***
Curracloe
Tel: (+353) 053 42211
Take with you the informative, colourful booklet available locally free of charge on this superb short nature trail through seashore dunes.

WEXFORD COASTAL PATH
Tel: (+353) 053 42211
A long-distance coastal path stretching ***from Kilmichael Point***, north of Courtown harbour, ***to Ballyhack.*** The route is clearly waymarked and free supporting literature is available. Not suitable for young children.

WEXFORD TOWN WALKS
Tel: (+353) 053 46506
On: July and August, Monday to Saturday, 11a.m. and 2.30p.m.
Charges: A=££, C=£
Leaves from the Westgate Heritage Centre.

WEXFORD TOWN
Sam Coe, Tel: (+353) 053 41081
Walking tours each evening leaving from the Talbot and Whites Hotel. No set charge.

Wildlife Parks

WEXFORD WILDFOWL RESERVE***
North Slob
Tel: (+353) 053 23129; Fax: (+353) 053 24785
Open: mid-April to September, daily, 9a.m.–6p.m.; October to mid-April, daily, 10a.m.–5p.m. (the reserve may close occasionally for management operations)
Admission: free
Facilities: toilets; visitor centre; picnic area
The Wexford Slobs are internationally famous for wild geese – around 10,000 Greenland white-fronted geese (over a third of the world population) spend the winter here. Trekking is a great way to view the flocks of wildfowl and geese, and nearby Curracloe House Equestrian Centre will supply the horses.

PLACES TO EAT

Cafés and Restaurants

COUNTRY KITCHEN RESTAURANT AND TAKE-AWAY
Main Street, **Taghmon**
Tel: (+353) 053 34470
Open: Monday to Saturday, 9.30a.m.–9p.m., Sunday, 12.30p.m.–9p.m.
Children's half-price meals or choice from Kiddies' Corner.

CHAN'S RESTAURANT
90 North Main Street, **Wexford**
Tel: (+353) 053 22356
Open: daily for lunch and dinner

THE WOODEN BRASSERIE
25 North Main Street, **Wexford**
Tel: (+353) 053 23669
Open: summer, Monday to Saturday, 8.15a.m.–9p.m., Sunday, 10a.m.–6p.m.; winter, Monday to Saturday, 8.15a.m.–6p.m.
This world of home cooking offers breakfasts and hot lunches, a large range of cakes and gateaux and a take-away service. A good selection of children's meals is available but there are no high-chairs or baby-changing facilities.

Fast-Food Restaurants and Take-Aways

THE BAKED POTATO
18 Rafter Street, **Enniscorthy**
Tel: (+353) 054 34085
Open: Monday to Saturday, 9a.m.–6p.m.
Hot food, snacks and salads served all day.

CHAN'S TAKE-AWAY
15 Selskar Street, **Wexford**
Tel: (+353) 053 46110
Open: daily, 5p.m. till late, plus Friday and Saturday, 12.30p.m.–2.30p.m.

THE BAKED POTATO
7 Redmond Square, **Wexford**
Tel: (+353) 053 22917
Open: Monday to Saturday, 9a.m.–6p.m.
Hot food, snacks and salads served all day.

THE LOTUS HOUSE
70A South Main Street, **Wexford**
Tel: (+353) 053 24273
Chinese restaurant and take-away.

Hotels and Pubs

KELLY'S RESORT HOTEL
Rosslare
Tel: (+353) 053 32114; Fax: (+353) 053 32222
Open: March to December
You'll find an excellent choice of children's meals in this friendly
family hotel. Choose either from the main menu at a reduced price
or from the special children's menu.

• • • • •

PLACES TO STAY

Country Houses and Hotels

COURTOWN HOTEL AND LEISURE COMPLEX
Courtown Harbour, **Gorey**
Tel: (+353) 055 25108; Fax: (+353) 055 25304
Family-run hotel noted for its family atmosphere. The leisure centre
has an indoor heated swimming-pool, jacuzzi, steam room, sauna
and gym. There's also a children's playground.

HILLSIDE HOUSE
Tubberduff, **Gorey**
Tel: (+353) 055 21726
Family-friendly house with facilities for children.

AHARE HOUSE
Castletown, **Inch**
Tel: (+353) 0402 37329
Situated near Kilgorman beach, guests can use the tennis courts,
snooker table, golf practice nets and indoor and outdoor play areas.

ROSSLARE GREAT SOUTHERN HOTEL****
Rosslare Harbour
Tel: (+353) 053 33233; Fax: (+353) 053 33543
Open: all year round
Facilities: family rooms; crèche; baby-minding service
An excellent base for exploring this corner of Ireland. The family
rooms are comfortable and, most importantly, children are made to
feel very welcome here. They are very well catered for with their
own dining-room, playground and well-supervised crèche and baby-
sitting facilities. The hotel has its own leisure complex and swimming-
pool with free swimming lessons during the peak season, a games
room and tennis court. If you are looking for a Christmas holiday
the hotel organises a fun-packed programme of activities and entertainment providing a combination of traditional Irish hospitality with
festive fun.

KELLY'S RESORT HOTEL
Rosslare

Tel: (+353) 053 32114; Fax: (+353) 053 32222
Open: March to December
The famous family-run Kelly's beachside hotel has many facilities for families. The leisure complex has 2 swimming-pools, squash and tennis courts, crazy golf, bowls and croquet lawns, a playground, organised fun tournaments for children and crèche facilities.

Farmhouse Accommodation

INGLESIDE FARMHOUSE
Duncormick
Tel: (+353) 051 563154 (or contact Irish Farm Holidays – see Directory)
Open: March to November
Modern farm bungalow on 90-acre farm with horseriding and trekking for beginners and experienced riders. There's also a pets corner, children's play area, baby-sitting service, farm and beach walks, and boat trips by arrangement.

ASHMOUNT FARMHOUSE
Ballylacey, **Gorey**
Tel: (+353) 0402 37361
Modern farmhouse with enclosed play area, a tennis court, games room and farm animals.

RIVERFIELD FARMHOUSE
Inch, **Gorey**
Tel: (+353) 0402 37232 (or contact Irish Farm Holidays – see Directory)
Open: all year round (except Christmas and New Year)
Happy family home with spacious gardens, enclosed play garden, children's adventure area, baby-sitting service, tennis court, river fishing, small animal paddock and free pony rides.

Holiday Parks and Villages

CARNE BEACH HOLIDAY PARK
Carne
Tel/Fax: (+353) 053 31131
Open: mid-May to mid-September
Facilities: fully equipped mobile homes; caravan and camping pitches; food shop and pub on site; launderette; children's playground; baby-sitting service; children's meals

BURROW HOLIDAY PARK
Rosslare
Tel: (+353) 053 32190; Fax: (+353) 053 32256
Open: Easter to November
Facilities: mini-market; home bakery; take-away food; launderette; evening entertainment in nearby hotel; snooker hall; games room; video games and TV room; adventure playground; tennis courts; mini-golf; self-drive boats
The 14-acre holiday complex has a range of holiday accommodation that includes self-contained mobile homes, hotel rooms and touring caravan and camping sites.

Self-Catering Apartments and Houses

COURTOWN HOTEL AND LEISURE COMPLEX
*Courtown Harbour, **Gorey***
Tel: (+353) 055 25108; Fax: (+353) 055 25304
Self-catering apartments with use of hotel facilities and leisure
complex included.

CLONSHARRA
*Duncannon, **New Ross***
Tel: (+353) 051 389122
Semi-detached farmhouse apartment in the grounds of a farm.
Large courtyard and extensive gardens for children. Videos available.

GLENDINE SELF-CATERING
*Arthurstown, Estuary Village, **New Ross***
Tel: (+353) 051 389258
Spacious, self-contained apartment in a Georgian farmhouse; sleeps 7.
Ideal family base. Baby-sitting arranged.

BAYVIEW HEIGHTS BEACHSIDE HOLIDAY HOUSES
Rosslare
Tel: (+353) 051 561138
Open: all year round
Luxury accommodation in 2- and 3-bedroom houses each with a
12-channel TV, microwave oven, fridge/freezer, washing/drying
service, cot and high-chair and baby-sitting service. Private on-site
amenities include a tennis court, crazy golf/adventure golf course,
indoor games and playrooms, and a playground.

Caravan and Camping Parks

FERRYBANK CAMPING AND CARAVAN PARK***
*The Bridge, **Wexford***
Tel: (+353) 053 44378
Open: Easter to October (swimming-pool open all year)
*Facilities: laundry; shop; TV room; restaurant; heated indoor swimming-
pool; children's playground*

Hostels

BUNCLODY HOLIDAY HOSTEL
*Old Schoolhouse, Ryland Road, **Bunclody***
Tel: (+353) 054 76076
Open: 1 March to 30 September

KILTURK HOSTEL
Kilmore Quay
Tel: (+353) 053 29883
Open: 1 May to 6 October

MacMURROUGH FARM HOSTEL
*MacMurrough, **New Ross***
Tel: (+353) 051 21383
Open: all year round

Bicycle Hire

IRISH CYCLE HIRE – see *Directory*
RALEIGH RENT-A-BIKE – see *Directory*

HAYES CYCLES
108 South Main Street, Wexford
Tel: (+353) 053 22462

THE BIKE SHOP
9 Selskar Street, Wexford
Tel/Fax: (+353) 053 22514

Car Hire

BUDGET RENT-A-CAR
Shannon Motors, New Ross, Wexford
Tel: (+353) 051 21550; Fax: (+353) 051 21235

HERTZ RENT-A-CAR
Ferrybank, Wexford
Tel: (+353) 053 23511; Fax: (+353) 053 22405

Ferries

PASSAGE EAST CAR FERRY
Barrack Street, Passage East, Co. Waterford
Tel: (+353) 051 382480; Fax: (+353) 051 382598
Continuous service – average crossing time 7 minutes.
This drive-on drive-off car ferry service from Ballyhack to Passage
East offers a shortcut between Co. Wexford and Co. Waterford.

Bus Services

Ferry Terminal, Rosslare Harbour – Tel: *(+353) 053 33114*
Tourist Office, Wexford – Tel: *(+353) 053 22522*

Rail Services

Enniscorthy – Tel: *(+353) 054 33488*
Gorey – Tel: *(+353) 055 21105*
Rosslare Harbour – Tel: *(+353) 053 33592*
Rosslare Strand – Tel: *(+353) 053 32262*
Wellingtonbridge – Tel: *(+353) 051 61102*
Wexford – Tel: *(+353) 053 22522*

COUNTY WICKLOW

Known as the 'Garden of Ireland', there is actually far more to Wicklow than just its many magnificent gardens and scenery. The county has wonderful sandy beaches and resorts, many archaeological sites and historical monuments (such as the spectacular **Glendalough,** a centre for pilgrims and visitors since it was founded by St Kevin in the 6th century), and some of the best outdoor fun and leisure centres around. Lots of festivals and events take place throughout the year, celebrating themes as diverse as music, cartoons and village life.

But the county's many exquisite gardens are legendary, making it a veritable paradise for the garden enthusiast. Most are fun places to visit for all the family and are not just designed to suit the specialist visitor. The magnificent **Powerscourt Gardens** near Enniskerry, one of the loveliest and most popular formal gardens in Ireland, is just one example that will enthral the whole family.

Over a third of the 30-mile (48km) Wicklow coastline is fringed with soft golden sand. The southern resorts have some of the best beaches on the east coast. One of these, Brittas Bay, is a very popular resort for day-tripping Dubliners eager to get out of the city on a summer's day, so it does tend to get quite busy. The nearby Jack's Hole, a secluded little seaside resort with wide golden sands, may be a better option if your kids are happy just to paddle in the sea and build castles on the beach. On the extreme south of the Wicklow coast is Arklow. This attractive Viking town at the mouth of the River Avoca is noted for its fishing industry and boat-building, and it has an interesting **maritime museum.** There are splendid beaches stretching north and south of Arklow and a large open-air **swimming-pool and leisure centre** near the north beach. Clogga Beach is about 4 miles (6.5km) south of Arklow. This attractive sandy beach is situated in a bay sheltered by steep cliffs and the Arklow Rock headland.

To the north of Wicklow town the coastline is a mixture of shingle and sand. Newcastle and Kilcoole have some lovely walks on the grassy banks that run along the foreshore, while the twin resorts of Bray and Greystones retain the Victorian charm that has ensured their popularity since the last century. Bray is at the extreme northern end of the county coastline, just 10 miles (16km) south of Dublin. It has a long, safe beach of sand and shingle, backed by a spacious esplanade. The town has lots of **amusement centres** offering games and traditional attractions, and there's a road train to transport you along the esplanade during the high season. Apart from the main beach, you can swim at the North Strand and also the town's indoor heated pool. The **International Leisure Bowl** is another very popular attraction, as is the splendid new **National Aquarium.** Greystones has a pleasant village atmosphere, and its attractive fishing harbour and shingle beach are very popular with anglers and bathers. Boats can be hired and there's a cinema and tennis and badminton courts.

The popular Irish television series *Glenroe* is set in the nearby village of Kilcoole. The **Glenroe Open Farm** is the actual farm where the famous show is filmed. It is now open daily to visitors.

Nine miles (14.5km) south of Bray is **Model World** in the village of Newtownmountkennedy. This unique exhibition looking at Ireland through the ages was created using scale models, and provides fun and recreation for every visitor. While you are in this area you may wish to take the opportunity to visit the **National Garden Exhibition Centre** at Kilquade just a little further north of Newtownmount-kennedy. Unless the children are particularly interested in gardening, though, this is really a visit for mums and dads.

Yet another garden that is well worth a mention is the lovely 20-acre **Mount Usher Gardens** on the banks of the Varty River in the village of Ashford, north of Wicklow town on the N11. There are also riverside walks and trails in the nearby **Devil's Glen.**

In the centre of the county, near Rathdrum, is the **Greenan Farm Museums and Maze,** a fun and educational centre to visit with the children. Another farm with a difference is the **Annamoe Leisure Park and Trout Farm,** which children will thoroughly enjoy.

The **Clara-Lara Fun Park** near Laragh is probably the highlight of any child's trip to Wicklow. The 100-acre outdoor adventure park sits in spectacular surroundings astride the Avonmore river and is quite superb. Children's love of water (unless it's in a bath, of course) is well known, and here practically everything they do will involve getting wet!

Access throughout the county is very good both by public and private transport. The road network is excellent with first-class roads zigzagging across the county. Expressway bus services connect the major towns, with provincial services serving the villages. Mainline rail services operate from Dublin, and Dublin Airport is just next door.

• • • • •

PLACES TO VISIT

Activity Centres

BLESSINGTON LAKES LEISURE PURSUITS CENTRE
Burgage, **Blessington**
Tel: (+353) 045 865092; Fax: (+353) 045 865024
Open: March to December, daily, 10a.m.–dusk
Leisure pursuits include canoeing, boardsailing, tennis, sailing, orienteering, pony-trekking. The minimum age to take part is 8.

Animals, Birds and Fish

THE NATIONAL AQUARIUM*
Bray Esplanade, **Bray**
Tel: (+353) 01 2864688
Open: daily, 10a.m.–6p.m.
Admission: A=££, C=£, F
See 10,000 fish in over 200 tanks, some of which contain 100 tons of water and house over 700 species of sea creatures.

Boats and Boat Trips

BLESSINGTON LAKE CRUISES
Blessington Lake *Adventure Centre pier*
Tel: (+353) 045 865092
The MV *Blessington* takes visitors on tranquil hour-long cruises of the lakes. The commentary explains the history, folklore and geographical wonders surrounding you.

Castles and Historic Houses

AVONDALE HOUSE – **see** FOREST AND AMENITY WALKS

RUSSBOROUGH HOUSE*
Blessington
Tel: (+353) 045 865239; Fax: (+353) 045 865054
Open: April, May and October, bank holidays and Sunday only, 10.30a.m.–5.30p.m.; June to August, daily, 10.30a.m.–5.30p.m.; September, Monday to Saturday, 10.30a.m.–2.30p.m., Sunday, 10.30a.m.–5.30p.m.
Admission: A=£££, C=£
Facilities: wheelchair access; toilets; shop; restaurant; playground; woodland walks; lakeside picnic areas
Outstanding Palladian house reputed to be the finest in Ireland open to the public. The house contains magnificent displays of fine furniture, tapestries, porcelain, silver, bronzes and paintings from the world-famous Beit Collection.

Craft Centres

ARKLOW VALE POTTERY
*South Quay, **Arklow***
Tel: (+353) 0402 32401
Open: daily, 9.30a.m.–4.45p.m.
A major producer of high-quality earthenware exported worldwide. A guided factory tour is available by arrangement during the summer months and the factory shop is open daily to visitors.

WICKLOW VALE POTTERY
Arklow
Tel: (+353) 0402 39442
Open: daily, 10a.m.–6p.m.
Visitors are welcome to walk through the production area and see the potters at work. The showroom has a superb range of Avoca hand-painted ceramics and glassware, and the tea-rooms have wonderful home-baked pastries and lunches.

WILD IRISH CRAFT AND NATURE TRAIL
*Kilquiggan, **Shillelagh***
Tel: (+353) 0503 56228
Open: all year round, daily, 9a.m.–6p.m.
Facilities: craft shop; picnic area
Five-acre nature trail with viewing points, water features and a windmill.

Equestrian Facilities

CLARA VALE RIDING STABLES
Rathdrum
Tel: (+353) 0404 45327
Horseriding and trekking on scenic forest and mountain trails.

LARAGH TREKKING CENTRE
*Laragh East, **Glendalough***
Tel: (+353) 0404 45282
Open: all year round
Horseriding and pony-trekking into beautiful Glendalough. Full-day rides with lunch stops available for experienced riders.

Farm Parks

BALLINAGEE OPEN FARM***
Enniskerry
Tel: (+353) 01 2869154
Open: Easter to Halloween, weekends, 10a.m.–5p.m.
Admission: A=££, C=£, F
A family farm where children are especially welcomed and encouraged to learn about the rural way of life. On view are a wide range of farm and pet animals, and rare breeds of poultry. Visitors will also see raw wool being processed to the finished product.

GLENDALOUGH SPRING WATER FARM*
*Roundwood Road, **Laragh***
Tel: (+353) 0404 45287
Admission: A=££, C=£, F
Open: Easter to September, daily, 11a.m.–5p.m.
This is an open farm featuring a display of farm machinery from previous generations, an 18th-century farmhouse, animals, and a hillside trail covering 15 acres of enchanting mountainside walks.

GLENROE OPEN FARM***
Kilcoole
Tel: (+353) 01 2872288
Open: April to September, Monday to Friday, 10a.m.–5p.m., weekends, 10a.m.–6p.m.; September to March, weekends, 10a.m.–6p.m.
Admission: A=££, C=£, F
The actual farm where Ireland's famous TV soap opera *Glenroe* is filmed is now open to visitors. Attractions include Dinny's cottage, farm animals and a souvenir and home-produce shop.

Festivals and Events

ANNUAL FIREWORKS FESTIVAL
Rathdrum
Tel: (+353) 0404 46262
On: mid-August

AVOCA'S MELODY FAIR
Vale of Avoca
Tel: (+353) 0402 35108

On: last week in May
A celebration of the music of Thomas Moore and a festival of local life with talent competitions and activities.

GLENDALOUGH FESTIVAL OF ARTS
Glendalough
On: June
Tel: (+353) 0404 69117

INTERNATIONAL CARTOON FESTIVAL****
*The Square, **Rathdrum***
Tel: (+353) 0404 46811
On: first week in June
Charges: A=£, C=£
Lots of family entertainment, exhibitions, street theatre, workshops and cartoon competitions for children.

STAR CHILD FESTIVAL
Bray
On: beginning of May
Tel: (+353) 0404 69117
Visual and performing arts by children for children.

STRAWBERRY FAIR
Kilbogget
Tel: (+353) 01 2867128
On: late June
Afternoon of fun followed by music in the evening and a fireworks display at dusk.

WICKLOW TOWN REGATTA FESTIVAL
Wicklow
Tel: (+353) 0404 69117
On: 2 weeks, from the end of July into August.

Fishing

ANGLING AND WILDLIFE PARK***
Aughrim
Tel: (+353) 0402 36552
Open: summer, 8a.m. to dusk; winter, 9a.m. to dusk
Charges: £££££ for 2 hours; day rates available (free for children under 12 if accompanied by a paying adult)
Facilities: toilets; wheelchair access to fishing
Situated alongside the river in the picturesque village of Aughrim, this 4-acre lake stocked with trout and surrounded by a wildlife haven provides an excellent opportunity for a family fishing trip. Coaching is available for beginners and all equipment can be hired.

Forest and Amenity Walks

AVONDALE HOUSE/FOREST PARK AND ARBORETUM***
*Two miles (3.5km) south of **Rathdrum** on route R752 to Arklow*
Tel: (+353) 0404 46111
***House** open: all year round, daily, 11a.m.–6p.m.*

Admission: A=£££, C=£, F
Facilities: toilets; carpark; picnic areas; access to Avondale House with its audio-visual display; tea-room; craft shop
There are 3 marked trails, each offering different scenery and suitable for different levels of ability. Avondale is the cradle of modern Irish forestry and much that has been learned from these plantations has been applied in practice throughout the country.

BALLINAFUNSHOGE
*Eight miles (13km) north-west of **Rathdrum** on minor roads to Glenmalure*
Forest walks, picnic site and, for the experienced walker, the option of a wilderness trek via Mullacor Mountain to Glendalough.

DEVIL'S GLEN
*Two miles (4km) west of **Ashford** on minor road to Glendalough via Nun's Cross*
Facilities: carpark; picnic sites; castle ruins
This is a well-known beauty spot with a deep chasm along which walks have been built at a considerable height. The views from the winding pathways, both of the glen and the Varty River as it tumbles nearly 30m into the Devil's Punchbowl, a deep basin in the rock below, are spectacular. Please be very careful.

DJOUCE WOODS***
*Three miles (5.5km) south of **Enniskerry** on minor road to Roundwood*
Part of the Powerscourt Estate, this is an excellent, well-laid-out area of woodland. There are 3 carparks, forest and mountain walks, lots of wonderful scenery and views of the spectacular Powerscourt Waterfall, the highest in Ireland, crashing 120m into the glen below. The Dargle River tumbles freely from the shoulder of Djouce Mountain, and falls dramatically down the face of the mountain, a magnificent sight when the river is in spate.

GLENART
*Two miles (4km) west of **Arklow** on route R747 to Woodenbridge*
Facilities: carpark; forest walks with viewing points; picnic site
The rhododendron drive is spectacular during early summer.

MEETINGS WOOD
Avoca
*Three miles (5.5km) south of **Rathdrum** on route R752 to Arklow*
Facilities: forest walks; picnic site
This is a popular area near Meeting of the Waters and the remains of a tree under which Thomas Moore is said to have written the song, 'Sweet Vale of Avoca'.

Gardens

MOUNT USHER GARDENS***
Ashford
Tel: (+353) 0404 40116; Fax: (+353) 0404 40205
Open: mid-March to end October, daily, 10.30a.m.–6p.m.
Admission: A=£££, C=££
Facilities: toilets; limited wheelchair access; craft shops; tea-room
Informal gardens planted in harmony with beautiful natural wood-

land make this an ideal spot for family walks. The river, with its weirs and waterfalls, is crossed by attractive suspension bridges, a perfect setting where the whole family can wander around and enjoy the peace and tranquillity of a garden that has been developed from a mere potato patch in 1860 into one of Ireland's finest informal and naturally designed gardens of the day. This is a garden for all seasons, offering a fantastic display of colours from its 5,000 trees and shrubs. The rhododendrons and eucryphias are spectacular, and the maples are especially striking in early autumn. Excellent tea-rooms overlook the river and gardens.

NATIONAL GARDEN EXHIBITION CENTRE
Kilquade
Tel: (+353) 01 2819890; Fax: (+353) 01 2810359
Open: all year round, Monday to Saturday, 10a.m.–6p.m., Sunday, 1p.m.–6p.m.
Admission: A=££, C=free
Facilities: toilets; garden centre; light refreshments
An excellent exhibition for garden enthusiasts.

POWERSCOURT GARDENS, WATERFALL
AND HOUSE EXHIBITION****
Enniskerry
Tel: (+353) 01 204 6000
Open: gardens and house exhibition, daily, 9.30a.m.–5.30p.m., April to October; 9.30a.m.–dusk, November to March; waterfall, daily, 9.30a.m.–7p.m., April to October; 10.30a.m.–dusk, November to March
Admission: garden and house exhibition, A=£££££, C=£££ (under fives free); garden only, A=£££, C=££; house exhibition only, A=£, C=£ (under fives free); waterfall only, A=££, C=£ (under fives free)
Facilities: limited disabled access; toilets; baby-changing room; craft shop; garden centre; restaurant; picnic and play areas
Stretching out over 45 acres, this is more than a mere 'garden'. Originally adorning the 18th-century Powerscourt House (of which just the shell remains following a tragic fire in 1974), the grand scale and delicate detail together with the mixture of Japanese and Italian gardens, steep terraces, flamboyant fountains and statuary all combine to make Powerscourt a fairytale demesne.

Heritage Centres

AGRICULTURAL HERITAGE DISPLAY CENTRE**
Coolakay House, Enniskerry
Tel: (+353) 01 2862433
Open: Easter to November, daily, 9a.m.–6p.m.
Admission: A=££, C=£
Facilities: toilets; farm walks; tea-rooms; restaurant
A fascinating display of implements and machinery dating back to the early 1700s, demonstrating the evolution of farm life.

BRAY. HERITAGE CENTRE
Old Court House, Main Street, Bray
Tel: (+353) 01 2866796
Open: June to September, daily, 9a.m.–6p.m.; October to May, daily, 10a.m.–5p.m.

The downstairs room contains a permanent exhibition on the history of Bray. Upstairs is an exhibition gallery which changes monthly, plus an interesting folklore room.

GLENDALOUGH VISITOR CENTRE****
Glendalough, near Laragh
Tel: (+353) 0404 45352
Open: mid-March to May, daily, 9.30a.m.–6p.m.; June to August, daily, 9a.m.–6.30p.m.; September to mid-October, daily, 9.30a.m.–6p.m.; mid-October to mid-March, daily, 9.30a.m.–5p.m.
Admission: A=££, C=£, F
Facilities: disabled access to visitor centre; toilets; guided tours
Choose a fine day to visit because there are so many historic sites to see and places to walk. Watch the video, look at the exhibitions, take the guided tour around the monastic sites, have lunch and set off on the spectacular walk along the valley to the lakes.

Horse-Drawn Caravans

CLISSMANN HORSE-DRAWN CARAVANS
Carrigmore Farm, **Wicklow**
Tel: (+353) 0404 48188
Open: May to September
A great way to tour and see the countryside, but don't forget to include some activities for the children. Everything you need is provided, including bedding, routes and horse feed.

Leisure Centres and Adventure Playgrounds

ANNAMOE TROUT FARM AND LEISURE PARK***
Annamoe, on the road to Glendalough between Roundwood and Laragh
Tel: (+353) 0404 45470
Open: May and September, weekends, 11.30a.m.–6p.m.; June to August, daily, 10.30a.m.–6.30p.m.
Admission: A=££, C=££
Facilities: play areas; fishing (all tackle provided); barbecue facilities
This 9-acre leisure park is set in a scenic woodland area on the banks of the Avonmore river and features adventure play areas and a shallow (1m-deep) lake with canoes, rafts and swimming. There is a separate stocked lake where you are almost certain to catch trout (equipment is supplied), and a barbecue area to cook the day's catch! Remember that kids will get wet and muddy, so go prepared.

ARKLOW SPORTS AND LEISURE CENTRE
Seaview Avenue, **Arklow**
Tel: (+353) 0402 39016
Open: all year round, Monday to Friday, 9.30a.m.–11.30p.m., Saturday, 9.30a.m.–8.30p.m., Sunday, 9.30a.m.–7.30p.m.
Facilities: multi-purpose sports hall with ball courts; tennis courts; crazy golf; pitch'n'putt; outdoor pool; activity club for children on Saturday

CLARA-LARA FUN PARK*****
Vale of Clara, **Rathdrum**
Tel: (+353) 0404 46161

Open: April to September, daily, 11a.m.–6p.m.
Admission: A and C=££££ (free for children under 4); additional charges for certain activities; a 'Gold Bracelet' pay-once supplement is good value and gives unlimited access to all rides
Facilities: toilets; coffee shop; fast-food restaurant

There are 100 acres of fun here for the whole family on a fine day, but remember the water will be cold even in the middle of summer, so go well prepared. The attractions, both natural and man-made, are numerous, so allow plenty of time. The breathtaking Aqua Shuttle is the biggest water slide in Ireland, and you can go rafting, canoeing or boating on the 5 acres of shallow ponds and lakes. Kids can sail away on the pirate galleon, play Tarzan in the many tree-houses, woodland playgrounds and enormous water swings. There's a challenging assault course, go-karts for the under-12s, and remote-controlled power cruisers for parents and children alike. The park has lovely waterside picnic and barbecue areas, mini-golf, a junior playground with sandpits, seesaws and swings for toddlers, and a fast-food café. This is one attraction that my children insist on going to every time we come to Ireland. I guarantee that most adventurous kids will love this park, but I'm not sure if every parent will be brave enough! Remember to take towels, a full change of clothing and some trainers for the children to wear in the water – they're going to get wet here, and mums and dads will be lucky to stay dry!

INTERNATIONAL LEISURE BOWL**
*Quinsboro Road, **Bray***
Tel: (+353) 01 2864455
Open: all year round, daily, 10a.m.–11.30p.m.
Facilities: video games; children's activity centre; coffee bar and snacks
Has 20 world-class bowling lanes and computerised scoring.

Museums

ARKLOW MARITIME MUSEUM**
*St Mary's Road, **Arklow***
Open: 10a.m.–6p.m., Tuesday to Sunday, May/June to September; 7 days, July/August; Sundays only, October
Admission: A=££, C=£, F

The museum deals extensively with the maritime history of Arklow and includes an operational model of the wheelhouse controls of a trawler, which children will love. On display are many interesting photos of the port dating back to the 19th century, and models of vessels built in Arklow, including a model of *Gypsy Moth 111*.

GREENAN FARM MUSEUMS AND MAZE****
*Ballinanty, Greenan, **Rathdrum***
Tel: (+353) 0404 46000
Open: May/June, Tues–Sun, 10a.m.–6p.m.; July/Aug, daily, 10a.m.–6p.m.; Sept/Oct, Sun only, 10a.m.–6p.m.
Admission: A=£££, C=££, F; maze only, A=££, C=££
Facilities: toilets; farm walk; maze; museums; tea-rooms

A wonderful combination of interesting, educational and fun attractions, which will provide a knowledge and understanding of the different aspects of life on a traditional hill-farm. As well as a large barn displaying implements and tools (some of which were used at the time of the Famine), there's a farmhouse dating from the 1750s containing traditional furniture and utensils such as butter churns. There's a museum upstairs which has a large collection of antique bottles. The large maze beside the carpark is a considerable challenge but great fun. Water flows through it to a pond in the centre, which is surprisingly difficult to find. If you manage to find your way out, visit the traditional Irish cottage close to the old farmhouse where lunch, afternoon-tea and light refreshments are served.

MODEL WORLD****
*Ballinahinch Lower, **Newtownmountkennedy***
Tel/Fax: (+353) 01 2810877
Open: Easter to September, daily, 10.30a.m.–6p.m.; October to
Christmas, weekends, 10.30a.m.–dusk
Admission: A=£££, C=£, F
Facilities: toilets; baby-changing facilities; wheelchair access; shop; picnic area; coffee shop; barbecue area; playground
This is a unique exhibition looking at Ireland through the ages. Covering 6 acres and using scale models, it will intrigue visitors both young and old. From mesolithic settlements to working replicas of 19th-century canals and railways and an 8ft model of the Fastnet Lighthouse, every exhibit presents a miniature historical picture. Walk along winding paths planted with dwarf pine and oak and see the living development of Ireland's history. Remote-controlled boats can be hired by children (dads included) and the park has a number of water features, so parents with young children should take particular care. Children under 10 must be accompanied by an adult.

WICKLOW'S HISTORIC GAOL***
*Kilmantin Hill, **Wicklow Town***
Tel: (+353) 0404 61599
Fax: (+353) 0404 61612
Open: March to October, daily, 10a.m.–5p.m.,
Admission: A=££££, C=££, F
Facilities: toilets; Gaol café and shop
The Gaol gives visitors an absorbing overview of Irish social and political history.

Parks

PARNELL NATIONAL MEMORIAL PARK
Rathdrum
This recently created town park provides a restful haven from the hustle and bustle of everyday tourist attractions. Has some nice walks and water features, and a children's play area.

Swimming-Pools

ARKLOW SPORTS AND LEISURE CENTRE
*Seaview Avenue, **Arklow***
Tel: (+353) 0402 39016
Large open-air pool open during the summer from 9.30a.m.

BRAY SWIMMING-POOL
*Presentation College, Putland Road, **Bray***

Tel: (+353) 01 2867517
Very limited access for public swimming, but check locally for times.

SPORTS AND FITNESS CLINIC SWIMMING-POOL
Oldcourt Road, **Bray**
Tel: (+353) 01 2862972
Open to the public 7 days a week. Check locally for times.

• • • • •

PLACES TO EAT

Cafés and Restaurants

AVOCA HANDWEAVERS VISITOR CENTRE RESTAURANT
Kilmacanogue, near **Bray**
Tel: (+353) 01 2867466
Open: food served all day, Monday to Friday, 9.30a.m.–5.30p.m.,
weekends, 10a.m.–5.30p.m.
Situated in a 19th-century arboretum, the centre features the full
range of Avoca clothing and a wide range of the finest Irish crafts.
The restaurant has an excellent menu with a wide range of dishes
to suit all tastes.

AVOCA MILL STORES****
Avoca Village
Tel: (+353) 0402 35105
Open: all year round
The restaurant at the centre is very child friendly. It has a good
menu, serving homemade dishes suitable for the whole family, high
chairs and baby-changing facilities.

MITCHELL'S RESTAURANT
Glendalough, **Laragh**
Tel: (+353) 0402 45302
Rustic, country-style, family-run restaurant in a 200-year-old granite
building. Meals are served all day. Children can choose from their
own menu or have small portions from the main menu.

Fast-Food Restaurants and Take-Aways

THE JASMINE HOUSE
85 Main Street, **Bray**
Tel: (+353) 01 2860305
Open: every day
Chinese restaurant and take-away.

McDONALD'S
Bray Townhall, **Bray**
Te: (+353) 01 2761923

Hotels and Pubs

GLENDALOUGH HOTEL
Glendalough
Tel: (+353) 0404 45135; Fax: (+353) 0404 45142
The restaurant and bar have a child-friendly atmosphere. There are children's meals on the menu or they can have small portions of adult meals (**see WHERE TO STAY**).

LYNHAM'S LARAGH INN
Laragh
Tel: (+353) 0404 45345
Family-orientated traditional restaurant serving good food. Has a children's menu and high-chairs.

CARTOON INN
Rathdrum
Tel: (+353) 0404 46774
Meals are only served at lunchtimes on weekdays, but if you're in the area the children will enjoy seeing the walls of this inn – they're covered with the work of many famous cartoonists.

• • • • •

PLACES TO STAY

Country Houses and Hotels

CHERRYBROOK COUNTRY HOME
Avoca
Tel: (+353) 0402 35179
Open: all year round
Family-friendly country home with large garden. Free baby-sitting service until midnight.

BLAINROE HOTEL AND LEISURE RESORT
Blainroe
Tel: (+353) 0404 67500; Fax: (+353) 0404 69737
Luxury accommodation and leisure facilities that include a heated indoor swimming-pool, jacuzzi, steam baths, fitness area, sports bar and crèche.

ROYAL HOTEL AND LEISURE CENTRE
Main Street, **Bray**
Tel: (+353) 01 2862935; Fax: (+353) 01 2867373
Situated in the centre of Bray, this hotel has an indoor heated swimming-pool, sauna, steam room, and supervised crèche facilities.

GLENDALOUGH HOTEL
Glendalough
Tel: (+353) 0404 45135; Fax: (+353) 0404 45142

If you want to stay in this beautiful area, this family-friendly hotel is in the ideal location (**see** WHERE TO EAT).

AVONBRAE GUEST-HOUSE
Rathdrum
Tel/Fax: (+353) 0404 46198
Welcoming, friendly guest-house with an indoor heated swimming-pool, tennis court, gardens and games room. Baby-sitting available.

Farmhouse Accommodation

TYNTE HOUSE
Dunlavin
Tel: (+353) 045 401561; Fax: (+353) 045 401586 (or contact Irish Farm Holidays – see Directory)
Open: all year round (except Christmas and New Year)
Old-world farmhouse situated in the picturesque village of Dunlavin. Spacious rooms, tennis court and children's playground.

Holiday Parks and Villages

JOHNSON'S CARAVAN AND CAMPING PARK
*Redcross, **Ballintim***
Tel: (+353) 0404 48133
Open: mid-March to September
Quiet park, ideal for families. It has a modern fleet of mobile homes and first-class facilities for campers and tourers, a games room, TV room, outdoor swimming-pool, tennis court and playground. A shop is open in high season.

RIVER VALLEY CARAVAN AND CAMPING PARK
Redcross Village
Tel: (+353) 0404 41647
Open: mid-March to September
Well-maintained park with lots of excellent facilities, such as caravan and camping pitches, golf course, outdoor bowling green, tennis courts, crazy golf, coffee bar, shop, restaurant, take-away, games room, pets corner and adventure playground. A new sports complex with a range of indoor facilities is soon to be opened. The accommodation is in well-appointed mobile homes and special hire rates are available for families during low season.

Self-Catering Apartments and Houses

OLD CURT COACH-HOUSES
*Moneylands Farm, **Arklow***
Tel: (+353) 0402 32259; Fax: (+353) 0402 32438
Open: all year round
Luxury stone-built coach-houses on farm, sleeps 5 to 6 people.

BROOKVILLE FARMHOUSE
Redcross Village
Tel: (+353) 0404 41647
Open: all year round
Georgian-style farmhouse in country village with TV, wood-burning

stove and central heating. Facilities include tennis courts, bowling green, golf, children's play area and indoor games facilities.

Caravan and Camping Parks

MOAT FARM CARAVAN AND CAMPING PARK
Donard
Tel: (+353) 045 404727
Modern fully equipped and serviced park in a tranquil setting beside the village of Donard. Facilities include a tennis court, children's play area, reading room, TV room, laundry and campers' kitchen.

ROUNDWOOD CARAVAN AND CAMPING PARK
Roundwood
Tel: (+353) 01 2818163
Open: April to September
A mature, modern park with campers' kitchen/dining-room/TV room, bikes for hire, children's playground, and car hire. Shops, restaurants, pubs and entertainment are all close by.

Hostels

RATHCORAN HOUSE
Baltinglass
Tel: (+353) 0508 81073
Open: 1 May to 15 September

THE OLD PRESBYTERY
The Fairgreen, Rathdrum
Tel: (+353) 0404 46930; Fax: (+353) 0404 46604
Open: all year round

WICKLOW BAY HOSTEL
Marine House, Wicklow
Tel: (+353) 0404 69213
Families welcome.

Bicycle Hire

IRISH CYCLE HIRE – *see Directory*
RALEIGH RENT-A-BIKE – *see Directory*

BRAY SPORTS CENTRE
8 Main Street, Bray
Tel: (+353) 01 2863046; Fax: (+353) 01 2828387

Car Hire

MURRAYS EUROPCAR – *see Directory*

Bus Services

Bus Eireann travel information – Tel: (+353) 01 8366111
DART *(Dublin Bus)* – Tel: (+353) 01 8734222

Rail Services

Arklow – Tel: *(+353) 0402 32519*
Bray – Tel: *(+353) 01 2862236*
Greystones – Tel: *(+353) 01 2874160*
Rathdrum – Tel: *(+353) 0404 46426*
Wicklow – Tel: *(+353) 0404 67329*

THE PROVINCE OF

MUNSTER

The Province of Munster is made up of six counties: Clare, Cork, Kerry, Limerick, Tipperary and Waterford. The area has a temperate climate all year round thanks to the warmth provided by the Gulf Stream, and takes full advantage of its weather by providing a wide variety of indoor and outdoor attractions to satisfy visitors of all ages. The Atlantic rushes in along the coastline of four counties, creating a mixture of wonderful sandy beaches and rugged sea cliffs and caves, and forming a great natural playground for families. The two inland counties have the benefit of the great River Shannon and its estuary along one of their borders. The mixture of climatic conditions, terrain and diversity of attractions makes this province a perfect venue for families, so it is understandably one of the busiest areas in Ireland during the high season. If you plan to come here during the summer, be prepared for long queues for the major attractions, and the popular towns and cities will be very busy.

• • • • •

COUNTY CLARE

County Clare is sandwiched between the River Shannon and Lough Derg along its eastern boundary, and the Atlantic coastline with its rugged cliffs and golden beaches to the west.

We discovered some quiet secluded beaches along the coast such as Spanish Point, Doolin Cove, Quilty and White Strand, all ideal for picnics, where children can play safely on the sand or in the sea.

Lahinch is a very popular resort, and has a fine beach and sea-front, but beware of the surf and take careful notice of the lifeguards' safety flags. The town has the added attraction of the **Lahinch Seaworld and Leisure Centre** with an amazing aquarium and a 25m swimming-pool.

A Blue Flag award-winning beach makes Kilkee one of the county's leading resorts. A charming seaside town on the Loop Head Peninsula, it is fronted by a mile of golden sands. Nearby is Pollock Holes, a series of natural rockpools that are ideal for bathing with the water changing at every tide.

On the south of the peninsula is the village of Carrigaholt. It's here that Ireland's only resident group of bottlenose dolphins can be observed. About 70 of them live in the Shannon Estuary; **Dolphin-watch Carrigaholt** will take you on a 2-hour boat trip to observe them in their natural environment. The guide will tell you about the dolphins and marine life, and you will get the opportunity to use a hydrophone to listen to the dolphins as they communicate with each other. This is a great adventure for children and adults alike.

The **Burren National Park** is a fascinating place to learn about the area's spectacular limestone subterranean world. Children will enjoy the tour of the cave and the adventure of climbing over the Burren limestone. Parts of it are too dangerous to enter, however, but there is another opportunity to explore the Burren underworld in the safety and comfort of a developed **cave at Aillwee** near Ballyvaughan.

Just a few miles south-west of Ennis, County Clare's main town, is Ireland's original, award-winning prehistoric park, **Craggaunowen – The Living Past.** Situated in the grounds of a medieval Irish chieftain's castle, with guides in costume and in character, this is a wonderful place for a family visit.

Bunratty Castle and Folk Park has to be one of the top attractions in County Clare: Irish village life from a century ago is recreated in the grounds of this magnificently restored medieval castle. The Shannon Ceili provides excellent night-time entertainment in the park.

The 25-mile-long Lough Derg is the largest and most southerly of the Shannon lakes. On the southern shore is Killaloe. Once the ancient capital of Ireland, this regal town connects Clare and Tipperary with a distinctive 13-span bridge. Killahoe has a **watersports** playground, offering canoeing, boating, sailing, windsurfing and raft-building.

Public transport access to the county by rail and bus is via Limerick or Galway, and there are airports at Shannon and Galway. The road network is very good throughout the county

● ● ● ● ●

PLACES TO VISIT

Animals, Birds and Fish

FORTFIELD FARM ZOO**
*Donail, **Killimer***
Tel: (+353) 065 9051457/9052533
Open: May to September, daily, 10a.m.–6p.m., Sunday, 2p.m.–6p.m.
Admission: A=££, C=£, F
Facilities: toilets; tea-shop with home-baking; sweet shop
Fortfield Farm Zoo comprises a large selection of domesticated rare animals and birds including llamas, deer, goats, pot-bellied pigs, cattle, rabbits and an aviary. Visitors are welcome to stroll through the working farm. The owners also offer bed and breakfast accommodation (**see WHERE TO STAY**).

LAHINCH SEAWORLD – **see LEISURE CENTRES**

Boats and Boat Trips

DERG LINE CRUISERS
Killaloe
Tel: (+353) 061 376364; Fax: (+353) 061 376205
Hire a fully equipped cruiser with oil-fired heating, charts of the Shannon, compass, radio, stereo, bed linen and crockery.

DOLPHINWATCH CARRIGHOLT
Carrigholt
Tel: (+353) 065 9058156 or mobile 088 584711
Two-hour trips to see bottlenose dolphins swimming in the Shannon Estuary. It is advisable to book in advance.

KILLALOE BOAT HIRE
Killaloe
Tel: (+353) 061 376693/376670
Lake boats with outboard engines for hire. Hourly, daily and weekly rates; life-jackets and fishing-rods supplied.

SCATTERY ISLAND FERRIES***
Kilrush
Tel/Fax: (+353) 065 9051327
This company operates daily sailings from Kilrush Creek Marina to the beautiful Scattery Island in the Lower Shannon estuary. The un-inhabited island is a 6th-century monastic settlement with remains of 7 churches and a 10th-century, 120ft-high round tower. This is a great place to explore on a fine day; the island is home to a wide variety of wildlife and the lighthouse still plays a major part in the safe navigation of the Shannon today. The company also organises dolphin-watch trips during the summer months to see bottle-nosed dolphins at play in their natural habitat.

Castles

BUNRATTY CASTLE – *see* HERITAGE CENTRES

DYSERT O'DEA CASTLE AND ARCHAEOLOGY CENTRE**
Dysert O'Dea, Corofin
Tel: (+353) 065 6837722
Open: 1 May to 30 September, daily, 10a.m.–6p.m.
Admission: A=££, C=£
Facilities: museum; exhibitions; history trail; audio-visual show; tea-room; souvenir shop
The trail features 25 sites of historical and archaeological interest within a 2-mile radius of the castle. A detailed and illustrated guide is available from the souvenir shop. Children will enjoy locating and exploring all the sites on the trail.

KNAPPOGUE CASTLE***
Quin
Tel: (+353) 061 360788
Open: April to October, daily, 9.30a.m.–5p.m. (last admission 4.30p.m.)
Admission: A=££, C=£ F
Facilities: free parking; disabled access (one of the most accessible

castles in Ireland); toilets with disabled access and baby-changing facilities; picnic area; craft shop

The castle has been beautifully restored in 15th-century style. The history of Knappogue is told in an audio-visual display.

Caves

AILLWEE CAVE****
*Near **Ballyvaughan***
Tel: (+353) 065 7077036; Fax: (+353) 065 7077107
Open: mid-March to June, daily, 10a.m.–5.30p.m.; July to August, daily, 10a.m.–6.30p.m.;   September to November, daily, 10a.m.–5.30p.m.
Admission: A=££££, C=££, F
Facilities: free parking; toilets with disabled access and baby-changing room; craft centre; tea-shop

Highly trained expert guides to take you on a leisurely tour through a maze of spectacular underground caverns, over bridged chasms, past a thunderous waterfall and wonderful formations of stalagmites and stalactites. After passing the frozen waterfall there is a series of hibernation chambers, once home to the now extinct brown bear. Even if the weather is hot and sunny when you visit, it will be much colder in the cave, so take a sweater or light jacket to wear for the tour. Outside, children can climb freely over the typical Burren limestone pavements above the cave while parents sample the home-made delights on offer in the tea-room. Inside the award-winning building that guards the entrance to the cave are a number of distinctively different craft shops. You can watch cheese being made in the dairy, honey being extracted from combs in the apiary or jams and chutneys being made in the farm kitchen.

Equestrian Facilities

CARROWBAUN FARM
*Ogonnelloe, **Killaloe***
Tel: (+353) 061 376754
Accompanied rides amidst beautiful scenic countryside on a good selection of horses, cobs and ponies to suit everyone.

CASTLEFERGUS FARM RIDING STABLES
Quin
Tel: (+353) 065 6825914
The O'Brien family have a good range of horses and ponies to suit all levels, located on 100 acres of pleasant farmland in the heart of County Clare. There's also an all-weather floodlit arena.

Festivals and Events

FEILE BRIAN BORU***
Killaloe
Tel: (+353) 061 376866 for further information
Open: mid-July
A weekend of celebration of Brian Boru's reign as High King of Ireland. The town comes alive with music, song and pageantry. There's lots of fun for everybody, with fancy-dress parades, dancing and barbecues.

Forest and Amenity Walks

BALLYCUGGARAN
*Two miles (3.2km) north of **Killaloe** on route R463*
Facilities: parking; picnic site; activity centre; watersports centre; swimming; viewpoints; forest trails
There are many historic sites in this area and families can enjoy hill-walks to Slieve Bernagh. There are camping and caravan parks near by. Interesting fact: the oak beam supports in London's Westminster Abbey came from the great woods that once covered these hills.

BALLYALLA LAKE
*Near **Ennis** on the N18 Gort road*
Facilities: Toilets; car park; picnic facilities
Pleasant walk around the lake, where many wild lake birds can be seen.

DOON
*Two miles (3.2km) north-west of **Broadford** off route R466 to Tulla*
Facilities: parking; lakeshore picnic site; forest and lakeshore walks
Originally this was the site of Doon Mulvihill, a tower house built where an ancient fort once stood.

DROMOLAND
*Just north of **Newmarket-on-Fergus** on route N18 to Ennis*
Facilities: picnic site; carpark; access to Mooghaun Fort
There are prehistoric stone forts enclosing 6 hectares at Mooghaun, close to the carpark. Mooghaun Castle, with its lofty 3-storey square tower, adjoins the wood and has been well preserved.

ENNIS
Ennis Town
Facilities: River Walk, Sculpture Park and Mill Wheel
This is a pleasant stroll along part of the River Fergus, the river on which Ennis was built. The walk begins at the Maid of Erin roundabout, here is a scupture park and restored mill wheel, and ends at Wood Quay in the town centre.

GRAGAN'S WOOD
*Five miles (8km) north-east of **Lisdoonvarna** on N67 to Ballyvaughan*
This is a super place for the outdoor enthusiast and the Burren National Park is clearly visible from this site. The area is rich in ring forts, stone forts, cairns and megalithic tombs which are generally freely accessible to the visitor. In the surrounding areas there are good opportunities for hill-walking, fishing and swimming.

Heritage Centres

BUNRATTY CASTLE AND FOLK PARK****
Bunratty, *on route N18, Limerick to Ennis road*
Tel: (+353) 061 361511
Open: all year, daily
Folk park: *June to August, daily, 9.30a.m.–7p.m.; September to May, daily, 9.30a.m.–5.30p.m.;* **Castle:** *June to August, daily, 9.30a.m.–4.15p.m.; September to May, daily, 9.30a.m.–4.15p.m.*

Admission: A=££££, C=££, F
Facilities: toilets with disabled access and baby-changing facilities; disabled access to the park, and limited access to the castle; free parking; picnic area; children's play area; tea-shop; restaurant; craft shop

Bunratty Castle is the most complete and authentic medieval castle in Ireland. Built in 1425 and plundered on many occasions, it was restored to its former medieval splendour in 1954. Within the castle grounds is Bunratty Folk Park, where 19th-century Irish village life is recreated with a range of typical urban and rural dwellings, a blacksmith's forge and a village street complete with a hotel and shops. You can see people dressed in traditional costume engaged in crafts such as bread-making, knitting, weaving, pottery and photography. There is also a story exhibition, together with works by artists from around the world. Be moved to laughter and tears at the stories and memories of the special events and memorabilia of people's lives. Mac's Pub in the village street serves soup, sandwiches and lunches.

THE BURREN CENTRE***
Kilfenora
Tel: (+353) 065 7088030; Fax: (+353) 065 7088102
Open: March, April, May and October, daily, 10a.m.–5p.m.; June to September, daily, 9.30a.m.–6p.m.
Facilities: toilets with disabled access and baby-changing facilities; audio-visual presentations; landscape models and displays; tea-room; craft and book shops; garden

In the north of the county is an area known as the Burren, a limestone plateau so rich in natural beauty that it has been elevated to the status of a national park. It is a fascinating area: its terraced hills and pavements appear as giant helter-skelters on the horizon, and its hidden underworld is a labyrinth of tunnels and caves. These are definitely out of bounds, however, and not for exploration unless you are an experienced pot-holer. Should you wish to discover more about the Burren's geology and archaeology a visit to the Burren Centre in Kilfenora will help explain this enigma. The landscape models, displays and audio-visual presentations look back over the 350 million years that shaped the Burren. The centre also has craft and book shops, a tourist information point, tea-room and garden.

CRAGGAUNOWEN – THE LIVING PAST****
*Kilmurray; near the village of **Quin**, 6 miles (10km) north of Sixmilebridge; signposted from route N18, Limerick to Galway road*
Tel: (+353) 061 360788; Fax: (+353) 061 367097
Open: April to October, daily, 10a.m.–6p.m. (mid-May to August open at 9a.m.); last admission 5 p.m.
Admission: A=£££, C=££, F
Facilities: disabled access; toilets with disabled access and baby-changing facilities; tea-shop; picnic areas; craft shop; free parking

This original, award-winning prehistoric park features a ring fort, a reconstructed 5th-century farmer's house, an Iron Age roadway, an outdoor cooking site and a Bronze Age lake dwelling. Wild boar and Soay sheep are also to be seen in the grounds. During the main holiday season actors in costume help to bring the past to life, adding to the atmosphere of this interesting site. This is a great place for children as they can roam in freedom and safety, and learn about the historic events of the past.

ENNIS FRIARY**
Ennis
Tel: (+353) 065 6829100
Open: Mid-June to mid-September, daily, 9.30a.m.–6.30p.m.
Admission: A=£, C=£, F
Public parking nearby
Well-preserved ruins of a 13th-century Franciscan friary founded by the O'Briens, Kings of Thomond.

KILRUSH HERITAGE CENTRE**
*Town Hall, Market Square, **Kilrush***
Tel: (+353) 065 9051577
Open: June to September, Monday to Saturday, 10a.m.–6p.m.; Sundays, noon–4p.m.
Admission: A=££, C=£, F
Exhibition and audio-visual presentation depicting the history and heritage of the town. This is also the starting point for the Kilrush Heritage Trail, an interesting walk through the town.

Ireland at Work – Past and Present

THE SALMON OF KNOWLEDGE EXPERIENCE*
*The Burren Smokehouse, **Lisdoonvarna,** on route N67, 5 miles (8km) north from Doolin*
Tel: (+353) 065 7074432; Fax: (+353) 065 7074303
Open: all year round, daily, 10a.m.–7p.m.
Admission: free
Facilities: selection of Clare food products available from the visitor centre; audio-visual displays; exhibition
Experience the ancient Irish tradition of oak-smoking Atlantic salmon, King of the Sea, and hear the legend of 'An Bradan Feasa', the 'Salmon of Knowledge'.

Leisure Centres and Adventure Playgrounds

KILKEE DIVING AND WATERSPORTS CENTRE
*East End, **Kilkee***
Tel: (+353) 065 9056707; Fax: (+353) 065 9056020
The centre provides a selection of both water- and land-based activities such as scuba-diving, canoeing, windsurfing, waterskiing, boat rides, angling and dolphinwatch trips, golf, pitch'n'putt and walking. The Blue Flag beach here is excellent and a safe swimming area. Note: 12 is the minimum age required to participate in most of the water-based activities.

LAHINCH SEAWORLD AND LEISURE CENTRE***
Lahinch
Tel: (+353) 065 7081900; Fax: (+353) 065 7081901
Open: daily, 10a.m. until late (subject to seasonal variation)
Admission: pool A=£££, C=££, F; aquarium A=£££, C=££, F; visit to both A=£££££, C=£££, F
Facilities: spectator area; café; souvenir shop; children's pool; baby-

changing facilities; disabled toilets

Lahinch Seaworld gives visitors the opportunity to discover the world beneath the Atlantic Ocean. In addition to the aquarium containing conger eels, young sharks, rays and starfish, there's a unique blow-hole wave explosion that demonstrates the power of the Atlantic as it pounds against the Clare coastline, a Clare fisherman's cabin, and a children's touchpool. The swimming complex has a 25m indoor heated pool, a separate children's pool, a sauna and jacuzzi. Children under 10 must be accompanied by an adult.

SHANNONSIDE ACTIVITY CENTRE
Killaloe
Tel: (+353) 061 376622
Lots of fun and activities, including canoeing, windsurfing, sailing and raft-building.

Swimming-Pools

ENNIS SWIMMING-POOL
Ennis
Heated swimming-pool.

KILKEE WATERWORLD***
Kilkee
Tel: (+353) 065 9056855
Open: April, May, Sept, October, Tues–Sun, 12noon–8p.m.; June, July, August, daily, 12noon–8p.m.
Restaurant; toddlers pool; Lazy River, geysers and gushers, and lots of other fun things for the kids.

LAHINCH LEISURE CENTRE – *see* LEISURE CENTRES

• • • • •

PLACES TO EAT

Cafés and Restaurants

AVOCA HANDWEAVERS VISITOR CENTRE RESTAURANT****
Bunratty
TEL: (+353) 061 364029
Located near the famous Bunratty Castle the ricerside café is open 7 days and serves a delicious selection of home-made foods all day. They have chairs and baby changing facilities.

EVERGREENS RESTAURANT
Lough Derg Holiday Park, **Killaloe**
Tel: (+353) 061 376929
Beautifully located on the shores of Lough Derg.

MEGABITES FAST-FOOD RESTAURANT
*Ballina, **Killaloe***
Tel: (+353) 061 376987
A variety of the fast stuff served either in the restaurant or to take away.

SIMPLY DELICIOUS COFFEE SHOP
*Ballina, **Killaloe***
Tel: (+353) 061 376883
A wide variety of home-baked food served all day in a child-friendly, relaxing atmosphere.

SUPERMAC'S
*Town Centre, **Shannon***
Tel: (+353) 061 360450

*O'Connell Street, **Ennis***
Tel: (+353) 065 20914

Hotels and Pubs

PIPERS INN
*Ogonnolloe, **Killaloe***
Tel: (+353) 061 376885
Just over 3 miles (5km) from Killaloe, this country pub surrounded by hills and country walks has a children's menu and play area.

● ● ● ● ●

PLACES TO STAY

Country Houses and Hotels

GREAT SOUTHERN HOTEL***
Shannon Airport
Tel: (+353) 061 471122
Fax: (+353) 061 471982
This hotel offers a special room-only rate for family rooms accommodating two adults and two children.

CARRAIG MHUIRE
*Barefield, **Ennis***
Tel: (+353) 065 6827106; Fax: (+353) 065 6827375
Located on the Ennis–Galway road, route N18, this country home is family-friendly, has a games room and can arrange baby-sitting.

ANVIL GUEST-HOUSE
*Loophead, **Kilbaha***
Tel: (+353) 065 9058018

Facilities include a games room, baby-sitting by arrangement, safe sandy beaches and angling nearby. There is also a highly recommended restaurant.

CANTERS LODGE
Mrs Anne Balfe, Cloonfadda, **Killaloe**
Tel: (+353) 061 376954
Spacious rooms overlooking the River Shannon. Fishing available and facilities for children include a games room and baby-sitting.

LAKESIDE HOTEL AND LEISURE CENTRE
Killaloe
Tel: (+353) 061 376122; Fax: (+353) 061 376431
This modern 3-star family-friendly hotel on the River Shannon has an indoor leisure centre and pool with a 120ft water slide. There are also games and crèche rooms; baby-sitting can be arranged.

OLD PAROCHIAL HOUSE
Alyson and Sean O'Neill, Cooraclare, **Kilrush**
Tel: (+353) 065 9059059
Formerly the priest's residence, this restored 19th-century family home has a pitch'n'putt course in the grounds, and there are cycles and a boat available for guests.

BAY VIEW GUEST-HOUSE
Spanish Point, **Miltown Malbay**
Tel: (+353) 065 7084006
Facilities include a games room and baby-sitting. Sandy beaches, pubs, restaurants, golf, angling and watersports are all nearby.

LYNCH FAMILY HOTELS
Clare Inn Golf and Leisure Hotel, **Newmarket-on-Fergus**
Tel: (+353) 061 368161 Fax: (+353) 061 368622
and
West Country Conference and Leisure Hotel, **Ennis**
Tel: (+353) 065 6828421; Fax: (+353) 065 6828801
The Lynch Family Hotels are known for being particularly friendly. Both have excellent leisure facilities that include supervised games and playrooms, heated indoor swimming-pools, jacuzzis, saunas, steam rooms and solariums. Outdoor facilities at Newmarket-on-Fergus include crazy golf, pitch'n'putt, tennis, lawn bowls, croquet, outdoor draughts and chess. There are supervised crèche facilities at both hotels, and children's meals. Parents will feel at ease knowing that their children are also welcome and catered for. They have a good children's menu and will provide half portions of adult meals.

Farmhouse Accommodation

FORTFIELD FARM
Sean and Brid Cunningham, **Killimer**
Tel: (+353) 065 9051457/9052533
Working farm with farm zoo as an added attraction (see ANIMALS, BIRDS AND FISH). Child-friendly accommodation and the musical hosts entertain their visitors nightly.

HARBOUR SUNSET FARMHOUSE
*Bridget O'Gorman and Family, Cliffs of Moher, Rannagh, **Liscannor***
Tel/Fax: (+353) 065 7081039 (or contact Irish Farm Holidays – see
Directory)
Open: Easter to end November
Working farm with friendly owners and pet animals. There's a
friendly, homely atmosphere, especially during the evenings when
guests are invited to join the family as they play Irish music around
an open peat fire. Facilities include a putting green, pony rides, a
farm museum and a colourful garden.

FIONNUAIRE
*Theresa and Tim Donnellan and Family, Mullagh, **Quilty***
Tel/Fax: (+353) 065 7087179 (or contact Irish Farm Holidays – see
Directory)
Open: 1 March to 31 October
Guests are invited to experience life on a working dairy farm. There
are farm pets and a pony, a games/gym/leisure room and bicycles
for hire. A beautiful, well-appointed self-catering cottage is also
available to rent.

CLOHAUNINCHY HOUSE
*Sean and Anne O'Connor, Seafield, **Quilty***
Tel: (+353) 065 7087081 (or contact Irish Farm Holidays – see Directory)
Open: 1 June to 1 September
Beautiful, family-run horse farm near a sandy beach. Facilities include
a tennis court, games room, football pitch, riding and pony cart rides.

Holiday Parks and Villages

LOUGH DERG HOLIDAY PARK
Killaloe
Tel: (+353) 061 376929; Fax: (+353) 061 376777
Exclusive holiday cottages on the shore of Lough Derg with their
own individual boat berth. Guests will enjoy the excellent restau-
rant, take-away shop, games room and tennis court.

Self-Catering Apartments and Houses

CLONLARA GOLF AND LEISURE COMPLEX
Clonlara
Tel: (+353) 061 354141; Fax: (+353) 061 354143
Well-appointed apartments and cottages set in the grounds of a 9-
hole golf course. Facilities include a bar/restaurant, tennis, angling,
games room and baby-sitting by arrangement.

DERG MARINA VILLAGE
Killaloe
Tel: (+353) 061 376364; Fax: (+353) 061 376205
Fully appointed self-contained holiday cottages overlooking the
marina. Shops, pubs, restaurants and a leisure centre are nearby.

QUILTY HOLIDAY COTTAGES
*Caharush, **Quilty***
Tel: (+353) 065 7087095; Fax: (+353) 065 7087388

Situated on an elevated site overlooking the Atlantic, 2km from Quilty village. On-site facilities include an indoor swimming-pool, sauna, gym and tennis court.

Caravan and Camping Parks

CUNNINGHAM'S HOLIDAY PARK
Kilkee
Tel: (+353) 061 451009; Fax: (+353) 061 327877
Open: Easter weekend and from the end of April to end of September
Near the town and beach, this beautifully situated park has indoor and outdoor play areas for children as well as the popular Noddy Train to take visitors for a spin around the park. If it's wet, there's a games room, or television and videos to watch.

LOUGH DERG HOLIDAY PARK
Killaloe
Tel: (+353) 061 376329; Fax: (+353) 061 376777
Open: end of April to end of September.
This 4-star caravan and camping park is located 3 miles (5km) from Killaloe on the shores of Lough Derg. You'll find boats and bikes for hire, a sandy shore, shop, television and games rooms, take-away food and the excellent Evergreens Restaurant.

OCEAN VIEW CARAVAN AND CAMPING PARK
Milltown Road, **Lahinch**
Tel: (+353) 065 7081626; Fax: (+353) 065 6828476
The park's many amenities include a bar, restaurant, games room and 18-hole pitch'n'putt course. Baby-sitting can be arranged.

Hostels

COROFIN VILLAGE HOSTEL
Main Street, **Corofin**
Tel: (+353) 065 6837683; Fax: (+353) 065 6837239
Open: all year round

PADDY MOLONEY'S DOOLIN HOSTEL
Fisher Street, **Doolin**
Tel: (+353) 065 7074006
Open: all year round

RAINBOW HOSTEL
Doolin
Tel: (+353) 065 7074415
Open: all year round

ABBEY TOURIST HOSTEL
Harmony Row, **Ennis**
Tel: (+353) 065 6822620/6828974; Fax: (+353) 065 6821423
Open: all year round

LAHINCH HOSTEL
Church Street, **Lahinch**
Tel: (+353) 065 7081040; Fax: (+353) 065 7081704

Open: all year round

LISCANNOR VILLAGE HOSTEL
Liscannor
Tel: (+353) 065 7081385; Fax: (+353) 065 7081417
Open: all year round

KINCORA HOUSE AND THE BURREN HOSTEL
Lisdoonvarna
Tel: (+353) 065 7074300; Fax: (+353) 065 7074490

Bicycle Hire

IRISH CYCLE HIRE – see *Directory*
RALEIGH RENT-A-BIKE – see *Directory*

DAVID MONKS
*Burren Cycle tours, Monks Bar, **Ballyvaughan***
Tel: (+353) 065 7077059

JUDE NEYLON
*Corofin Village Hostel, Main Street, **Corofin***
Tel: (+353) 065 6837683; Fax: (+353) 065 6837239

M.F. TIERNEY CYCLES
*17 Abbey Street, **Ennis***
Tel/Fax: (+353) 065 6829433; after hours/Sunday, Tel: 065 6821293

WILLIAMS RENT-A-BIKE
*Circular Road, **Kilkee***
Tel: (+353) 065 9056141

GLEESON'S CYCLES
*Henry Street, **Kilrush***
Tel: (+353) 065 9051127; Fax: (+353) 065 9051733

Car Hire

TOM MANNION TRAVEL
*71 O'Connell Street, **Ennis***
Tel: (+353) 065 6824211; Fax: (+353) 065 6824166
Cars and luxury motor homes to rent.

Airports

SHANNON AIRPORT
Tel: (+353) 061 471444; Fax: (+353) 061 474420

Bus Services

BUS EIREANN
*Bus station, **Ennis***
Tel: (+353) 065 6824177

Bus depot, Shannon Airport

Tel: (+353) 061 361311

Rail Services

Ennis – *Tel: (+353) 065 6840444*

Ferry Services

KILLIMER–TARBERT FERRIES
Daily sailings from Killimer, Co. Clare to Tarbert, Co. Kerry, every hour on the half-hour. 20-minute crossing time.

COUNTY CORK

Cork is the largest county in Ireland and attracts visitors for many different reasons, such as the excellent **beaches** around the coast, the vibrant towns and the wonderful countryside.

The city of Cork is full of charm and character. Like Venice, it is built on water – the town centre stands on an island in the River Lee. The many bridges that span the river give the city a distinctive continental air. There are plenty of things for families to do here. The old **city gaol**, a castle-like building, is a fascinating place to visit. In the Blackrock area of the city is **Cork Heritage Park,** offering a fascinating insight to many aspects of the city's past, while on the outskirts are the **Royal Gunpowder Mills** at Ballincollig.

The **West Cork Model Railway Village** is a great favourite with children. Situated beside the picturesque Clonakilty Bay, the model village depicts life in West Cork. If you want to see how Irish whiskey is produced, it's worth visiting the **Jameson Heritage Centre** at Midleton, 12 miles east of Cork. Midleton is also a good shopping centre and has lots of shops, pubs, cafés and restaurants.

Fota Wildlife Park, 10 miles south-east of Cork near Cobh, is among the most modern wildlife parks in Europe. Fota is one of the three large islands in Cork Harbour (Cobh and Little Island are the others) which are now all joined by roads and bridges. This is a wildlife haven for children and a conservationist's dream. Endangered species such as cheetahs, oryx and white-tailed sea eagles are bred here. If you don't want to walk around the park, you can take the easy option and ride on the tour train. Fota even has its own railway station with a regular service from Cork, so you don't even have to drive here. Alongside the park is the internationally renowned **Fota Arboretum** with its wonderful collection of trees and shrubs from China, Japan, Australia and the Himalayas. The nearby town of Cobh (pronounced *Cove*), a popular health and seaside resort, is situated on the largest island in Cork Harbour, but is best known as Ireland's main emigration port – between 1845 and 1960 over 2.5 million adults and children emigrated from Ireland via Cobh.

In Shanagarry, overlooking Ballycotton Bay, is one of Ireland's leading **pottery and craft centres.** The original home of William Penn, the founder of Pennsylvania, is also located here and his story will be the theme for a major new visitor attraction in the area. Nearby is Garryvoe and its fine Blue Flag beach.

Youghal (pronounced *Yawl*) is one of the few places in Ireland where the medieval town walls are still standing. This historic port sits at the mouth of the River Blackwater. It has two sandy beaches (both Blue Flags) and scenes from the movie *Moby Dick* were filmed here in 1954. This quaint town has a fascinating **heritage centre** telling of the development of Youghal from the 9th century.

The southern coastline to the west of the city of Cork has many quaint fishing villages and harbours, with a good selection of coves to explore and secluded sandy beaches for quiet days on the beach away from it all. The fishing village of Baltimore has a **ruined castle** perched on a rock overlooking the harbour to remind visitors of the stormy history associated with this coastline. Further along is Mizen Head, Ireland's most south-westerly point. The **Mizen Head Signal Station Visitor Centre** was developed by local people to create rural employment, following the automation of the signal station in 1993.

No visit to County Cork would be complete without a visit to Blarney, one of the most picturesque spots in Ireland, known as 'the biggest little village in Ireland' – or is this just a load of old Blarney? **Blarney Castle,** one of Ireland's oldest and most historic castles, has the world-famous **Blarney Stone** embedded in its battlements.

Access to the county is excellent via road, rail, air or sea. There is an excellent network of major roads throughout the county and a mainline rail route. Cork Airport is serviced directly from many UK airports, and car ferries from Wales and France operate direct into Cork Harbour.

● ● ● ● ●

PLACES TO VISIT

Amusement Arcades and Funfairs

PERKS FUN FAIR AND AMUSEMENT ARCADE***
*Pleasure Beach, **Youghal***
Tel: (+353) 024 92438

Animals, Birds and Fish

DONERAILE WILDLIFE PARK*
*Turnpike Road, **Doneraile***
Tel: (+353) 022 24244
Open: mid-April to October, Monday to Friday, 8a.m.–8.30p.m., Saturday, 10a.m.–8.30p.m.; Sunday and public holidays, 11a.m.–7p.m.; November to mid-April, Monday to Friday, 8a.m.–4.30p.m., Saturday, Sunday and public holidays, 10a.m.–4.30p.m.
Admission: A=£, C=£, F
Facilities: free carpark; picnic areas; toilets; disabled access
The Doneraile Wildlife Park consists of 160 hectares of magnificent parklands with mature groves of deciduous trees, indigenous wildlife and herds of roaming deer. The grounds were designed in the early 18th century in the style of Capability Brown to give the impression that nature, not man, had shaped the landscape. The many water features, spanned by elegant stone bridges, are attractive and important elements at Doneraile.

FOTA WILDLIFE PARK *****
***Carrigtwohill,** near Cobh; route N25, approximately 10 miles (16km) east of Cork, signposted south; access by rail: Fota Station is beside the park entrance*
Tel: (+353) 021 812678/812736; Fax: (+353) 021 812744
Open: Daily, 1 April to 31 October, Mon to Sat, 10a.m.–6p.m.;Sundays,

11 a.m.–6p.m.
Admission: A=££££, C=££, F
Facilities: parking (there is a charge); coffee shop; souvenir shop; games park; tour train; toilets and baby-changing facilities; wheelchair access
Take a walk on the wild side as you wander on pathways through 40 acres of grassland and woods where a variety of animals roam freely in natural surroundings. Fota is among the most modern wildlife parks in Europe. The animals – giraffes, zebras, antelopes, kangaroos and monkeys among others – are not restrained by cages or obvious barriers, yet visitors walk through the park in complete safety. Many species have total freedom of the park; only the spacious cheetah breeding compound has a conventional fence. There is an excellent coffee shop overlooking the flamingo pool, or share a picnic bench with a lemur or macaw. The games park is full of safari-themed attractions to keep the kids amused, and there's a tour train to take you around the park in style if you're feeling lazy!

Beaches

There are many excellent beaches around the coast. In the **Kinsale** area there are beaches at Sandy Cove and Castlepark. At **Garretstown,** 8 miles (13kms) from Kinsale, there are a couple of fine beaches at Harbour View and Coolmain. Howe Strand and Burren are the main beaches in the area around **Kilbrittain.** The **Clonakilty** area, known as the 'beach centre' of West Cork, has many fine beaches such as Inchydoney, Dunnycove, Red Strand, Long Strand and Owenahincha. Also worth visiting are Broad Strand and Dunworly near **Courtmacsherry,** and the Warren at **Rosscarbery.** In the **Skibbereen** district there are fine beaches at Tragumna, Tralispean, Sandycove and Sherkin Island. Cuss Strand is 2 miles (3.2kms) from **Ballydehob,** and Toormore beach is near **Schull.** Further south between Crookhaven and Mizen Head, the **Barleycove** area has long been renowned for its beaches. **Bantry Bay** is one of the most beautiful along the Irish coast. Swimming is possible at Reenour Strand, whilst outside **Glengarriff** there are good bathing sites at Zeatland Pier, Seal Harbour, Tragleahan and Poulgorm. Further down the **Beara Peninsula** some of the best beaches include Ballydonegan, Garinish and Cathermore near Castletownbere. Also on the peninsula from Dursey Sound to Dursey Island, is one of the few cable-cars operating in Ireland.

Boats and Boat Trips

CORK HARBOUR
*Cobh Marine Services, **Cobh***

Cork Harbour Cruises
*Lower Aghada Pier, **Cork***
Both provide a daily cruise service from Cork Harbour.

ILNACULIN ISLAND (GARNISH)
Glengarriff
Operates: March to October
Boats depart from Glengarriff to this beautiful island in Glengarriff Harbour laid out in Italian gardens with rare and subtropical plants.

RIVER BLACKWATER

Cruises on the River Blackwater are available from the pier at Youghal.

Castles and Historic Houses

BARRYSCOURT CASTLE**
Carrigtwohill
Tel: (+353) 021 882218
Open: Daily, June to September, 10a.m.–6p.m.
Admission: A=£, C=£, F
Facilities: Car park, toilets, exhibition, restaurant/teashop, craft shop
Built in 1206, the castle has had a colourful history – Sir Walter Raleigh lived here for a short time. The complex includes a shop, tea-room and audio-visual area which are open to visitors.

BLARNEY CASTLE**
Blarney
Tel: (+353) 021 385252
Open: May, Monday to Saturday, 9a.m.–6p.m., Sunday, 9.30a.m.–5.30p.m.; June to August, Monday to Saturday, 9a.m.–7p.m., Sunday, 9.30a.m.–5.30p.m.; September, Monday to Saturday, 9a.m.–6.30p.m., Sunday, 9.30a.m.–5.30p.m.; October to April, Monday to Saturday, 9a.m.–dusk (or 6p.m.), Sunday, 9.30a.m.–dusk
Admission: A=£££, C=££, F
Facilities: free parking; disabled toilets and baby-changing facilities; gift and souvenir shop; parkland walks
Blarney Castle and its 1,000 acres of magnificent woodlands are an ideal place for walking, but you'll never be far from some of the 200,000 multinational visitors whose main priority is to kiss a stone! This is a wonderful Irish tradition that has captured the imagination of people all over the world, evidence of which can be seen in the long queues that wind up the narrow stone staircase to the battlements of Blarney Castle during the peak holiday period. When finally arriving at the battlements the views are outstanding; you will see people of all ages, sizes and shapes, lying on their backs supported by a trusty guide over a hole in the parapet walk 40m above the ground, and kissing a battlement stone on the very same spot that thousands have kissed before them! Tradition holds that 'There is a stone that whoever kisses never misses to grow eloquent, he may clamber to a lady's chamber or become a member of parliament'. The village, castle and grounds are very pretty and well worth seeing, but unless your kids really do wish to experience the age-old tradition, I would suggest just taking a look and then heading for the Blarney Woodland Farm Park.

DESMOND CASTLE (French Prison)**
Cork Street, Kinsale
Tel: (+353) 021 774855
Open: Daily, mid-June to mid-September, 9.30a.m.–6.30p.m.
Admission: A=£, C=£, F
Desmond Castle has had a colourful history, ranging from Spanish occupation in 1601 to use as a prison for captured American sailors during the American War of Independence. Note that access to the site is by a stone staircase.

MACROOM CASTLE***
Macroom
Tel: (+353) 026 41133
Open: the park and grounds are open all year round
Admission: free
This was one of the seats of the McCarthys of Muskerry, built in the 13th century by the O'Flynn family. The castle was burnt out though the entrance gateway was subsequently restored. A most attractive riverside park has been developed, and there's a pitch'n'putt course.

Country Parks

MILLSTREET COUNTRY PARK*
Millstreet; N22 west from Cork, then R583 north, shortly after **Macroom**
Tel: (+353) 029 70810; Fax: (+353) 029 70899
Open: March to October, daily
Admission: A=£££££, F
Facilities: visitor centre; reception/leisure area; shop; audio-visual theatre; ornamental gardens; sensory gardens; deer farm; open-air musical area; picnic areas; restaurant; disabled access and toilets; free parking
This is the deluxe version of country parks, so much so that it almost appears to be exclusively for adults. There are no children's admission tickets, and although there are family tickets available this is not what I would term a particularly child-friendly attraction. An excellent starting place to the 203-hectare grounds is the visitor centre in the heart of the park, an area in which to relax and where there are occasional piano recitals. Then head off to explore this haven of flora and fauna. You will need good walking shoes to circumnavigate the many walks and trails – there are over 70 points of interest listed on the map.

Craft Centres

STEPHEN PEARCE POTTERY**
Shanagarry; *route N25 Cork to Midleton, then route R629 south to Shanagarry*
Tel: (+353) 021 646807; Fax: (+353) 021 646706
Open: all year, daily, 9a.m.–6p.m.
Admission: free
Facilities: toilets with disabled access and baby-changing facilities; café
This state-of-the-art pottery houses a workshop and the Emporium of good quality international crafts, including the entire ranges of Stephen Pearce Pottery, the best-known range of hand-made pottery in Ireland. Visitors are welcome to see the 50 skilled craftspeople at work, and maybe even try making something themselves!

Crèches

COOGAN CHILDCARE CONSULTANTS
The Crèche, Paul Street Shopping Centre, **Cork**
Tel: (+353) 021 276888

The Crèche, Douglas Court Shopping Centre, **Cork**
Tel: (+353) 021 894766

*The Crèche, Wilton Shopping Centre, **Cork***
Tel: (+353) 021 345233

Equestrian Facilities

BLARNEY RIDING CENTRE**
*The Paddock, **Killowen***
Tel: (+353) 021 385854
Beginners and advanced riders welcome. Qualified instructors are available.

Farm Parks

BLARNEY WOODLAND FARM PARK***
*Waterloo Road, **Blarney***
Tel: (+353) 021 385733
Open: 1 June to 30 September, Monday to Saturday, noon–6p.m.;
Sunday, 2p.m.–6p.m.
Admission: A=££, C=£, F
Just 1km north of Blarney's village square on the Waterloo road is the Blarney Woodland Farm Park. Located in the picturesque River Martin valley, it has a pets corner, fairytale grove and a 2.5km wild woodland nature trail that meanders through fields and trees where deer and goats roam freely alongside other farm animals.

Festivals and Events

CAPE CLEAR INTERNATIONAL STORYTELLING FESTIVAL****
Cape Clear Island
Tel/Fax: (+353) 028 39157
For accommodation list and all festival details contact the event organisers, Chuck and Nell Kruger
On: end of August/beginning of September
This is a wonderful event for all the family on the island of Cape Clear, off the south-west coast (daily ferry service from Baltimore). The inhabitants retain the Irish language and traditions which add to the ambience of this 3-day event. Tales are told beside peat fires in island homes by storytellers from Ireland and many other countries. There are stories with music, a puppet theatre, storytelling concerts, boat trips around the Fastnet Rock, organised archaeological explorations and ornithological rambles. The organisers also have an excellent renovated holiday house on the island that is available to rent (**see WHERE TO STAY**).

CORK INTERNATIONAL CHORAL AND FOLK DANCE FESTIVAL
On: April–May
This is a major festival of music, song and dance.

CORK SUMMER SHOW
On: June
Major agriculture and craft show held in the Cork Showgrounds.

CORK FOLK FESTIVAL AND MUSIC FAIR
On: June
This is a must for those with an interest in traditional music.

CORK CITY SPORTS
On: July
This sports meeting attracts athletes from Ireland and overseas.

COBH INTERNATIONAL FOLK DANCE FESTIVAL
On: July
This well-established festival of music and dance features continental dance teams. During the festival many of the visiting groups can be seen providing free street entertainment.

COBH REGATTA
On: August
A major celebration of watersports in Cork Harbour.

Forest and Amenity Walks

BANDON
Duke's Wood is 3 miles (5km) north of **Bandon** on the R590. It has a picnic area, forest and riverside walks.

BANTRY
Three miles (5km) from **Bantry,** on route N17 to Ballydehob, is the Barnegeehy forest which is open to public.

CASTLETOWNBERE
Two miles (3.2km) south-west of the town, next to Dunboy Castle, is a wooded area with a picnic site and forest and seashore walks.

CLOGHEENMILCON SANCTUARY
Located on the outskirts of Blarney Village, on the Cork road, this 100-acre wetland area is a great place to visit. The footpaths are well maintained, there's a lake with 18 islands and the area has been designed to cater for the needs of waterfowl. Carparks have been provided at each end and there are seats and picnic facilities within the sanctuary.

CLONAKILTY
Castlefreke forest is 6 miles (9.6km) from **Clonakilty** on the coast road to Rosscarbery. The Carbery Folk Park near **Castlefreke** is being developed at the present time by a local co-operative. It is set in around 400 acres of forest, marsh and sand dunes.

DUNMANWAY
Five miles (8km) west of **Dunmanway** is the forest of Cullenagh, with forest and lakeside walks. Two miles north of the town is Cool-kellure forest, which is also open to the public. The Clashnacrona forest is 3 miles south-west of Dunmanway on the R586, and Aultagh Wood is on the R587, 4 miles north of the town.

FARRAN FOREST PARK***
Located 11 miles (18km) west of Cork on route N22 to Macroom
Tel: (+353) 026 42833
Open: All year
Admission: Free (note there is a small charge for parking)
Facilities: carpark, toilets, picnic areas, ecology centre, children's

playground, wildlife enclosure. An ideal place to let the kids go. They can play in the adventure playground, explore the forest trails, and visit the Woodland Ecology Display Centre, It's educational, fun and free!

GARRETTSTOWN

Garrettstown Wood, 1 mile (1.6km) south of **Ballinspittle** on the R604 to the Old Head of Kinsale, is open to the public. The nearby Ballinspittle/Kilmore Wood, which has extensive forest walks, may also be visited. The beach at Garrettstown is a major attraction. The nearby village of Ballinspittle has become well known in recent years for its Marian shrine, which attracts large numbers of pilgrims.

GLENGARRIFF

The wood at Glengarriff, on the N17 Kenmare road, is well worth visiting as it is one of the few remaining examples in Ireland of original oak and holly woodland that once covered the country. There are a number of enjoyable nature trails through the forest.

GOUGANe BARRA

Tel: (+353) 026 42833
Open: all year round
Admission: free (note there is a small charge for parking)
Facilities: carpark, toilets, picnic areas
Gougane Barra, between **Macroom** and Kenmare, is Ireland's first national park and was opened in 1966. It is possible to drive through the park following the one-way system, but to see this splendid area at its very best you should take to some of the many trails which have been waymarked through the woodlands. The source of the River Lee is marked within the national park. The patron saint of the city of Cork, St Finbarr, had his first monastery on the island in the lake at Gougane Barra. The present tiny church on the island was designed by Samuel F. Hynes in 1901. The island is linked to the mainland by a short causeway.

KILBRITTAIN

On route R603 to Bandon, adjacent to the village, is Kilbrittain Wood with a picnic area and forest walks.

MACROOM

The **Gearagh** is located on the Inchigeela road, a short distance outside Macroom. The forest and scrubland is of unique botanical and scientific interest. It is also an important wildlife area. At **Bealnamorrive**, 5 miles (8km) east of Macroom on the Coachford road, an attractive forest area has been opened to the public.

SKIBBEREEN

There are fine forest and seashore walks at **Rineen**, 4 miles (6.5km) from Skibbereen. At Lough Hyne, 2 miles (3.2km) south-west of the town, there are scenic forest walks. From the highest point at 200m there is a panoramic view over Carbury's Hundred Isles, down the length of the Mizen Peninsula, and eastwards towards Kinsale.

Gardens

ANNE'S GROVE
Castletownroche, *halfway between Malow and Fermoy*
Tel: (+353) 022 26145
Open: Seasonal, Monday to Friday, 10a.m.–5p.m.
Saturday to Sunday, 1p.m.–6p.m.
Admission: A=££, C=£
Three contrasting gardens within the 30 acres of grounds – the walled garden, the glen and the riverside gardens.

BANTRY HOUSE
Bantry
Tel: (+353) 027 50795
Open: daily, 9a.m.–6p.m.
Admission: to the gardens, free; to the house and grounds: A=££
Located near Bantry, the house and gardens are of both botanical and historical interest. There is a tea-room and craft shop in a wing of the house, and an exhibition in the grounds with many details of the 47-strong fleet of the French Armada which could well have changed the course of Irish history. The 16 French warships lying off Bantry Bay on a stormy Christmas Day in 1796 must have been a spectacular sight.

CREAGH
Near **Skibbereen,** *on the road to Baltimore*
Tel: (+353) 028 22121
Open: seasonal, daily, 10a.m.–6p.m. (out of season: by arrangement)
Admission: A=££
There are many things to see and discover at Creagh, including a pepper-pot mill and a jungle walk for the children.

FOTA ARBORETUM
Fota Island
Tel: (+353) 021 812678
Open: April to September, daily, 10a.m.–6p.m.; Sundays, 2p.m.–6p.m.
Admission: free
Facilities: parking; wheelchair access; fast-food restaurant
see ANIMALS, BIRDS AND FISH

MILLSTREET GARDENS – **see COUNTRY PARKS**

TIMOLEAGUE CASTLE GARDENS
Timoleague, *on the coast between Bandon and Clonakilty, route R602*
Tel: (+353) 023 46116 or (+353) 021 831512
Open: Easter weekend and mid-May to mid-September, daily, noon–6p.m.
Admission: A=£
Visitors have the pleasure of picking raspberries in the delightful garden on the shores of Courtmacsherry Bay. There is a soft-fruit-picking scheme in the walled kitchen garden during the season and a picnic and play area on the lawn in front of this Edwardian house.

Heritage Centres

CHARLES FORT**
Summer Cove, *Kinsale*
Tel: (+353) 021 772263
Open: Daily, mid-March to October, 10a.m.–6p.m.; Sat/Sun, November to mid-March, 10a.m.–5p.m.
Admission: A=££, C=£, F
Facilities: ample parking; restricted disabled access; disabled toilets; guided tours and exhibition centre
This star-shaped fort was built about 1677 on the site of an earlier Norman harbour fortification. Many alterations have been made to it since, and it continued to be garrisoned until 1922.

COBH – THE QUEENSTOWN STORY ****
Cobh Railway Station; **Cobh;** *on the southern shore of the Great Island, approximately 15 miles (24km) east from Cork; follow route N25, and look for the signpost south*
Tel: (+353) 021 813591
Open: March to December, daily, 10a.m.–6p.m. (last admission: 5p.m.)
Admission: A=£££, C=££, F
Facilities: incorporates Blarney Woollen Mills gift shop; toilets and baby-changing facilities; restaurant
From 1848 to 1960, over 6 million people emigrated from Ireland. About half of them left from Cobh, making it the single most important port of departure. Tall ships called to transport convicts to Australia and to carry Irish emigrants to North America, then early transatlantic steamers and latterly the great liners continued the role of shipping the Irish people in search of a new lives in new lands. The *Titanic* called here for her final port of call before setting sail on her ill-fated voyage across the Atlantic. The town was renamed Queenstown in honour of a visit by Queen Victoria in 1849, but in 1921 the local council reverted to the old name of Cove, using the Irish spelling Cobh. A multimedia exhibition at the restored Victorian railway station recalls the history and legacy of the town's origins in the **Queenstown Story**, a major new heritage centre. There are excellent restaurant facilities in the centre. Visitors can explore the conditions on board the early emigrant vessels, including the dreaded 'coffin ship'; learn about an 'Irish Wake', the special farewell for emigrating sons and daughters, many of whom never returned to Ireland; and experience life on board a convict ship leaving for Australia in 1801.

CORK CITY GAOL AND RADIO MUSEUM EXPERIENCE
Sunday's Well, **Cork**
Tel: (+353) 021 305022; Fax: (+353) 021 307230
Open: Daily, March to October, 9.30a.m.–6p.m.; November to February, 10a.m.–5p.m.
Admission: A=£££, C=££, F (joint Gaol and Radio Museum tickets available at discout prices)
Facilities: free on-site parking; toilets and baby-changing facilities; wheelchair access
Friendly staff, interesting displays and exhibits, and good facilities combine to make this well worth visiting. As you wander through this majestic building, it's difficult to imagine the wretched conditions

suffered here by 19th-century prisoners. Today, cells furnished with amazingly life-size figures, sound effects and fascinating exhibitions give visitors a glimpse into the day-to-day life once endured by prisoners. Also in the Gaol Centre is a spectacular sound and image presentation showing contrasting lifestyles in 19th-century Cork, and the Gaol House Stop, an entertaining refreshment area where diners can choose from either the Prisoners or Governors menus!

CORK HERITAGE PARK****
*Bessboro, Blackrock, **Cork***
Tel/Fax: (+353) 021 358854
Open: April, Sundays only, 12noon–5.30pm; May to September, Sat/Sun, 12noon–5.30pm; Monday to Friday, 10.03a.m.–5.30p.m.
Admission: A=£££, C=£, F; free for children under 3
Facilities: carpark; disabled toilets and access; baby-changing facilities; indoor and outdoor play area; picnic area; restaurant; pet farm
Cork Heritage Park is set in 6 acres of landscaped grounds and the restored 19th-century courtyard of the Bessboro Estate. In addition to having a variety of attractions specifically for children, the park offers the visitor a varied and fascinating introduction to the many aspects of Cork's rich heritage. The displays demonstrate the local ecology, and its archaeological and maritime heritage with photos of the area's seafaring exploits and tales of shipwrecks and plundering; the history of Cork's fire service and transport with the development of train, tram and bus services. There's also an environmental centre, restaurant and picnic area, plus a superb children's play area that includes a sand-pit, playhouse and indoor play area.

DUHALLOW FOLK PARK**
*Duhallow; the park is halfway **between Killarney and Mallow** on N72*
Tel: (+353) 029 79217
Open: April to September, daily, 10a.m.–6p.m.
Admission: A=££, C=£, F
Facilities: craft shop; toilets; pets corner; coffee shop; free parking
Thirty-four life-size figures are part of the display that shows the craft and skills of Duhallow during the years 1900 to 1950. In the indoor section, the harness-maker, tinsmith, dressmaker, poteen-maker etc are seen at work. Outdoors there are skilled workmen like the sawyer, turf-cutter etc. demonstrating their skills. There is an extensive display of hand-operated and horse-drawn machinery.

MIZEN HEAD SIGNAL STATION VISITOR CENTRE***
***Mizen Head**, south off route N71 between Skibbereen and Bantry*
Enquiries: Mizen Co-operative Society Ltd, Harbour Road, Goleen, West Cork, Tel: (+353) 028 35225/35253; summer enquiries: Tel: (+353) 028 35115, Fax: (+353) 028 35422 or Tel/Fax: (+353) 028 35255
Open: April, May and October, daily, 11a.m.–5p.m.; June to September, daily, 10a.m.–5.30p.m.; November to March, weekends, noon–4p.m.
Admission: A=££, C=£, F; free for children under 5
Facilities: toilets; tea-room
Ireland's most south-westerly point is also the furthest fringe of Europe; you cross the amazing suspension bridge from where there are splendid views of the wild Atlantic waves rushing in to pound the coastline, and climb the 99 steps to the peninsula and visitor centre which is a great place for children to explore. Here you will

see the keeper's house and the engine-room, an audio-visual room, a map and archive room, a bird- and sea-watch room, the under-water room, the storm room, the keeper's kitchen and bedroom and the Mizen environment cave.

THE ROYAL GUNPOWDER MILLS***
Ballincollig, 5 miles (8km) from **Cork** *on route N22*
Tel: (+353) 021 874430; Fax: (+353) 021 874836
Open: Easter to 30 September, daily, 10a.m.–6p.m.
Admission: A=£££, C=£, F
Facilities: restaurant; craft and souvenir shop; toilets and baby-changing facilities; guided tours; visitor centre
An interesting tour takes you through a tree-lined complex, along canal towpaths and the banks of the River Lee and leads to a fully operational incorporating mill, powered by a waterwheel. The many buildings used in the manufacture of gunpowder are still scattered along the main canal and millraces which stretched for over a mile along the banks of the Lee. The site is one of the largest of its type in Europe and supplied gunpowder to the armies of the British Empire. There is a cleverly designed visitor centre with a main display area, educational panels, models and audio-visual displays.

Ireland at Work – Past and Present

JAMESON HERITAGE CENTRE**
Midleton; *route N25 east from Cork*
Tel: (+353) 021 613594/6; Fax: (+353) 021 613642
Open: March to October, daily tours, 10a.m.–6p.m. (last tour starts at 4p.m.); November to February, Monday to Friday, 10a.m.–6p.m.
Admission: A=£££, C=£, F
Facilities: free parking; toilets; guided tours; videos; restaurant
On the guided tour you will discover how the Irish monks perfected the mystical spirit in the 6th century, and see how Irish whiskey was made in this magnificent old distillery. At the end of the tour there is the opportunity to sample the 'water of life' for yourself – with soft drinks for the children of course!

PRINCE AUGUST TOY SOLDIER FACTORY
VISITOR CENTRE****
Kilnamartyra, **Macroom**
Tel: (+353) 026 40222; Fax: (+353) 026 40004
Open: Monday to Friday, 9a.m.–5.30p.m.; Saturday, 10a.m.–4p.m. during June/July/August
Admission: Free
This is one of particular interest for the boys, both large and small! In the visitor centre you can discover how the artist designs the models and the craftspeople produce the finished moulds and figures, you can even try your own hand at casting a figure, or have the process demonstrated. You can see hundreds of collectable military figures crafted and painted by specialists, or buy a casting kit to craft your own figures.

Leisure Centres and Adventure Playgrounds

PIER LEISURE CENTRE
Kinsale
Tel: (+353) 021 772101

VICTORIA SPORTING CLUB
*St Patrick's Quay, **Cork***
Tel: (+353) 021 504749

GRAND CENTRAL LEISURE AND BOWLING CENTRE***
*Sheares Street, **Cork***
Tel: (+353) 021 273000

LEISUREPLEX COLISEUM***
*1 MacCurtain Street, **Cork***
Tel: (+353) 021 505155

Museums

CORK PUBLIC MUSEUM**
*Fitzgerald Park, **Cork***
Tel: (+353) 021 20679
Open: all year
Closed: lunchtimes, Sunday mornings, all day Saturday, public holidays
Admission: free
Housed in a Georgian building on the banks of the River Lee in
Fitzgerald's Park, about 1 mile (1.6km) from the city centre, the
Cork Public Museum offers some unique insights into this attractive
maritime city.

KINSALE REGIONAL MUSEUM***
*Old Courthouse, Market Square, **Kinsale***
Tel: (+353) 021 772044
The Market House, which was built around 1600, has now been
converted into the Kinsale Regional Museum. The enquiry into the
loss of the *Lusitania* liner was held in the courtroom. Also in the
museum you will learn of the famous Kinsale giant, and his shoes
are on display here!

Swimming-Pools

MATT TALBOT POOL
*Churchfield, **Cork***
Tel: (+353) 021 303931/303294
Admission: A=££, C=£
Note: the wearing of swimming caps is compulsory
Includes a swimming-pool, gymnasium, saunas, steam rooms and
sunbeds.

MAYFIELD SWIMMING-POOL
*Old Youghal Road, **Cork***
Tel: (+353) 021 505284; Fax: (+353) 021 506232
Admission: A=££, C=£

GUS HEALY POOL
*Douglas, **Cork***
Tel: (+353) 021 293073/295594
Admission: A=££, C=£
Note: the wearing of swimming caps is compulsory
Includes a swimming-pool, gymnasium, saunas, steam rooms and sunbeds.

DUNMANWAY
Tel: (+353) 023 45349
There is a modern heated indoor swimming-pool, which is part of an excellent sports complex, located at the town park.

Trains and Model Railways

WEST CORK MODEL RAILWAY VILLAGE★★★★
*The Station, Inchydoney Road, **Clonakilty***
Tel/Fax: (+353) 023 33224
Open: Daily, 11a.m.–5p.m. February to October
Admission: A=££, C=£, F
This is the type of attraction that will appeal to most children. The Model Village depicts in miniature life and industry in West Cork as they were 50 years ago. The whole scene is enhanced by the miniature working railway that winds its way through the village and depicts the long-closed West Cork Railway.

• • • • •

PLACES TO EAT

Cafés and Restaurants

BULLY'S
*Paul Street, **Cork***
Tel: (+353) 021 273555

CAFE MEXICANO
*1 Careys Lane, **Cork***
Tel: (+353) 021 273535

CLOUDS RESTAURANT
*Imperial Hotel, South Mall, **Cork***
(+353) 021 274040

THE FARMGATE CAFE
*Old English Market, Princes Street, **Cork***
(+353) 021 278134

FLEMINGS RESTAURANT
*Tivoli, near **Cork***
(+353) 021 821621

PADDY GARIBALDIS
*8 Careys Lane, **Cork***
Tel: (+353) 021 277915

PROBYS BISTRO
*Crosses Green, **Cork***
Tel: (+353) 021 316531

QUAY CO-OP***
*24 Sullivan's Quay, **Cork***
Tel/Fax: (+353) 021 317660
This wholefood store and bakery, with a take-away counter serving salads, rolls, juice and freshly made ice-cream, also has a vegetarian restaurant serving breakfast, lunch and dinner.

SCOOZI RESTAURANT
*3/4 Winthrop Lane, **Cork***
Tel: (+353) 021 275077

HERONS COVE RESTAURANT
*Goleen Harbour, **West Cork***
Tel: (+353) 028 35225; Fax: (+353) 028 35422

JIM EDWARDS
*Market Quay, **Kinsale***
Tel: (+353) 772541

MAN FRIDAY
*Scilly, **Kinsale***
Tel: (+353) 021 772260

SAVANNAH RESTAURANT
*Trident Hotel, **Kinsale***
Tel: (+353) 772301

THE VINTAGE RESTAURANT
*50 Main Street, **Kinsale***
Tel: (+353) 021 772502

BALLYMALOE HOUSE
*Shanagarry, **Midleton***
Tel: (+353) 021 652531

Fast-food Restaurants

McDONALD'S
*Daunt Square, **Cork***
Tel: (+353) 021 278233

*4–5 Winthrop Street, **Cork***
Tel: (+353) 021 270890

*Douglas Village, **Cork** (Drive-through)*
Tel: (+353) 021 364456

Davis Street, **Mallow**
Tel: (+353) 022 50520

SUPERMAC'S
Main Street, Charleville, **Cork**
Tel: (+353) 063 89113

Lower Cork Street, **Mitchelstown**
Tel: (+353) 025 89113

Hotels and Pubs

VINES RESTAURANT
Doughcloyne Hotel, Togher, **Cork**
Tel: (+353) 021 312535

• • • • •

PLACES TO STAY

Country Houses and Hotels

BALTIMORE HARBOUR RESORT HOTEL AND LEISURE
CENTRE
Baltimore
Tel: (+353) 028 20361; Fax: (+353) 021 20466
Open: All year
The hotel has family rooms and an excellent new leisure centre
with a swimming-pool and children's pool.

MUNSTER ARMS HOTEL
Oliver Plunkett Street, **Bandon**
Tel/Fax: (+353) 023 41562
Located in West Cork, this hotel is conveniently situated for touring
the county. Facilities include cycle hire and children's playroom.
Baby-sitting by arrangement.

ANNGROVE LODGE
Teresa Murray, Anngrove, **Carrigtwohill**
Tel: (+353) 021 883834
Set in scenic surroundings with landscaped gardens and play area.
Baby-sitting available.

LISCUBBA HOUSE
Mrs Phil Beechinor, Rossmore, **Clonakilty**
Tel: (+353) 023 38679
Friendly family home near Rossmore. Fresh farm produce and
home-baking. Children's facilities and baby-sitting available. Pottery
and craft tuition arranged.

TRAVARA LODGE
Mandy Guy, **Courtmacsherry**

Tel: (+353) 023 46493
Open: March to November
Georgian house overlooking Courtmacsherry Bay. Guests can walk,
fish, ride and hire bikes. Cots and bunk-beds available if required.

DOUGHCLOYNE HOTEL
Togher
Tel: (+353) 312535
Accommodation includes complimentary use of the hotel's nearby
leisure complex which has a swimming-pool, sauna, gym, crazy golf,
tennis courts, kiddies' pool and crèche. Baby-sitting by arrangement.

THE MILLS INN
*Donald and Mary Scannell, Ballyvourney, **Macroom***
Tel: (+353) 026 45237; Fax: (+353) 026 45454
Open: all year except Christmas
One of Ireland's oldest inns (established 1755), set in acres of
landscaped gardens. Facilities include luxury rooms, some with
jacuzzis; private river walks and fishing.

VICTORIA HOTEL
Macroom
Tel: (+353) 026 41082; Fax: (+353) 026 42148
This is a small family-run hotel where children are especially
welcome. Baby-sitting facilities are available.

Farmhouse Accommodation

HILLCREST FARM
*Mrs Agnes Hegarty, Ahakista, Durrus, **Bantry;** 7 miles (11km) west of
Durrus on the Sheep's Head Peninsula*
Tel: (+353) 027 67045
Open: 15 April to 1 November
Guests can fish and boat and will enjoy the farm's mature grounds,
games room and donkey rides. The beach is nearby.

SPRINGFIELD HOUSE
*John and Maureen Callanan, Kilkern, Castlefreke, **Clonakilty;** signposted
on route N71, Clonakilty to Skibbereen road*
*Tel: (+353) 023 40622 (or contact Irish Farm Holidays — see
Directory)*
Open: 1 March to 31 October
Working farm with excellent home-cooking, ideally located for
sandy beaches and touring West Cork.

KILKERN HOUSE
*Mrs Eleanor O'Donovan, Rathbarry, **Castlefreke;** signposted on route
N71 Clonakilty to Skibbereen road, 3 miles (5km) west of Clonakilty*
*Tel/Fax: (+353) 023 40643 (or contact Irish Farm Holidays — see
Directory)*
Open: all year round
Excellent child-friendly accommodation on a working farm, beautifully
situated on the shores of Kilkern Lake. Facilities include horseriding,
farm animals, bicycle hire, home-baking, fresh produce, children's
facilities, baby-sitting and free use of a boat.

Holiday Parks and Villages

KINSALE HOLIDAY VILLAGE
*Glanbeg, **Kinsale***
Tel: (+353) 023 33110 (agents); Fax: (+353) 023 33131
Fully appointed townhouses overlooking Kinsale. Facilities nearby include watersports, angling, equestrian sports and discounted access to a 4-star hotel leisure centre. Baby-sitting and bicycle hire available by arrangement.

THE OYSTERHAVEN CENTRE
*Oysterhaven, **Kinsale***
Tel: (+353) 021 770738; Fax: (+353) 021 770776
These spacious cottages in a village-style holiday and activity centre are ideal for family adventure holidays. Facilities include a children's play area and a games room. Baby-sitting is also available by arrangement.

TRABOLGAN HOLIDAY VILLAGE*****
***Midleton;** route N25 to Midleton bypass, follow signs south from roundabout*
Tel: (+353) 021 661551; Fax: (+353) 021 661698
Open: March to November
The park offers a wide choice of holiday homes in an attractive village-style layout over 140 acres of woodland and meadow. You can choose from a range of beautifully appointed terraced townhouses, semi-detached or detached houses and bungalows, or there's the 5-acre, fully serviced touring caravan and dormobile park. There are no camping facilities at Trabolgan. The Crocodile Club is Trabolgan's own children's club with trained and experienced leaders who organise a host of activities to keep the liveliest of youngsters content. All 4- to 10-year-olds are automatically enrolled for their entire stay, and the toddlers have their own fully supervised crèche. There's a brilliant adventure playground amid the trees, and an indoor adventure playground to ensure that there is plenty to keep the children occupied whatever the weather. The Wigwam Club is for 2- to 5-year-olds and is supervised at all times. The swimming-pool has a toddlers' pool, wavemaker and waterslide, and 11- to 16-year-olds can abseil and go quad-biking among many other activities. There is a variety of free evening entertainment and a wide choice of dining options on the site, including take-away food and a well-stocked mini-market. Experienced and reliable baby-sitters are available to look after the children in your own holiday home if required. The perfect venue to use as a base, children will be content and in a safe environment, and its location is ideal for visiting the many other attractions throughout the county.

CARBERY HOLIDAY HOMES
*Skibbereen Road, **Schull***
Tel: (+353) 023 33110 (agent); Fax: (+353) 023 33131
Traditional-style cottages overlooking Schull Harbour. Baby-sitting and bicycle hire by arrangement.

Self-Catering Houses and Apartments

SOUTHERNMOST HOUSE
Cape Clear Island

Tel/Fax: (+353) 028 39157
Fully renovated farmhouse overlooking the Atlantic, with panoramic views from every room. The house is fully equipped with a TV and an array of toys and books for kids of all ages, but it is situated on a remote part of an Island with no discos or amusement arcades.

GRENVILLE COURT APARTMENTS
*Grenville Place, **Cork** (3-minute walk from city centre)*
Tel: (+353) 021 272932; Fax: (+353) 021 271662
Activities include sailing, golf, cycling tours. Baby-sitting available.

SOUTHBROOK APARTMENTS
*21/22 South Terrace, **Cork***
Tel: (+353) 021 319249; Fax: (+353) 021 319196
Conveniently located in the heart of the city. Bicycle hire and baby-sitting by arrangement.

Camping and Caravan Parks

DOWLINGS CARAVAN AND CAMPING PARK
*On Castletownbere Road (R572), 1 mile (2km) from **Glengarriff***
Tel: (+353) 027 63154
Open: Easter to 31 October
Friendly, family-run park in wooded area just 400m from Glengarriff harbour. Offers a games room, play area, restaurant, take-away and traditional music and singing. Nearby are forest walks and places to fish, swim and sail. Baby-sitting available by arrangement.

O'RIORDAN'S CARAVAN PARK
***Rosscarbery;** 6 miles (9.6km) south of Clonakilty off the N71*
Tel: (+353) 021 541825; Fax: (+353) 023 48216
Open: all year
Family-run park beside beaches and Castlefreke Woods. Modern mobile homes fully equipped with showers, toilets and TV. Baby-sitting available by arrangement.

BARLEYCOVE HOLIDAY PARK
*Crookhaven, **Skibbereen;** on route R591 to Crookhaven (N71 from Cork to Bandon, R589 Bandon to Bantry)*
Tel: (+353) 021 35302, or off season: 021 542444; Fax: (+353) 021 307230
Open: Easter week then 11 May to 15 September
Family-run park with modern, fully serviced mobile homes. Facilities include a children's club, play area, tennis and pitch'n'putt. Nearby are restaurants, an indoor heated swimming-pool, horseriding, golf, windsurfing, fishing and boat trips. Baby-sitting and bicycles available.

Hostels

TIG BARRA
Ballingeary
Tel: (+353) 026 47016
Open: mid-March to end September

ROLF'S HOSTEL
*Baltimore Hill, **Baltimore***
Tel: (+353) 028 20289
Open: all year

BANTRY INDEPENDENT HOSTEL
*Bishop Lucy Place, **Bantry***
Tel: (+353) 027 51050
Open: mid-March to end October

THE VILLAGE HOSTEL (BONNIE BRAES)
*Allihies Village, **Beara***
Tel: (+353) 027 73107
Open: 20 March to 30 September

CAPE CLEAR ISLAND YOUTH HOSTEL
Cape Clear Island
Tel: (+353) 028 39144
Open: April to October

CAMPUS HOUSE HOSTEL
*3 Woodlands View, Western Road, **Cork***
Tel: (+353) 021 343531
Open: all year round

ISAAC'S CORK
*48 MacCurtain Street, **Cork***
Tel: (+353) 021 500011; Fax: (+353) 021 506355
Open: all year round

KINLAY HOUSE
*Shandon, **Cork***
Tel: (+353) 021 508966; Fax: (+353) 021 506927
Open: all year round

SHEILA'S BUDGET ACCOMMODATION CENTRE
*Belgrave Place, Wellington Road, **Cork***
Tel: (+353) 021 505562; Fax: (+353) 021 500940
Open: all year round

SHIPLAKE MOUNTAIN HOSTEL
Dunmanway
Tel/Fax: (+353) 023 45750
Open: all year round

DEMPSEY'S HOSTEL
*Eastern Road, **Kinsale***
Tel: (+353) 021 772124
Open: all year round

SCHULL BACKPACKERS' LODGE
*Colla Road, **Schull***
Tel/Fax: (+353) 028 28681
Open: all year round

LETTERCOLLUM HOUSE
Timoleague
Tel/Fax: (+353) 023 46251
Open: mid-March to end October

MARIA'S SCHOOLHOUSE
*Cahergal, **Union Hall***
Tel: (+353) 028 33002/33062
Open: 1 April to 1 October

Bicycle Hire

IRISH CYCLE HIRE – see *Directory*
RALEIGH RENT-A-BIKE – see *Directory*

J. O'DONOVAN
*4/5 South Main Street, **Bandon***
Tel: (+353) 023 41227; Fax: (+353) 023 42257

TONY McGRATH CYCLES
*Stoneview, **Blarney***
Tel/Fax: (+353) 021 385658

SUPER VALU SUPERMARKET
Castletownbere
Tel: (+353) 027 70020/70248; Fax: (+353) 027 70520

AIDAN QUINLAN
*2 Bandon Road, Barrack Street, **Cork***
Tel: (+353) 021 323233; Fax: (+353) 021 274143

CYCLE SCENE
*396 Blarney Street, **Cork***
Tel: (+353) 021 301183

KILGREW'S CYCLES
*6/7 Kyle Street, **Cork***
Tel/Fax: (+353) 021 276255

JEM CREATIONS
*Ladybird House, **Glengarriff***
Tel: (+353) 027 63113

ROYCROFT CYCLES
*Llen Street, **Skibbereen***
Tel: (+353) 028 21235; Fax: (+353) 028 22197

Car Hire

AVIS/JOHNSON AND PERROTT
*Emmet Place, **Cork***
Tel: (+353) 021 273295; Fax: (+353) 021 272202

BUDGET RENT-A-CAR
Cork

Tel: (+353) 021 314000

DEASY RENT-A-CAR
*Commons Road, **Cork***
Tel: (+353) 021 395024/5; Fax: (+353) 021 397658

MOTOR WORLD RENT-A-CAR
*Carrigrohane Road, **Cork***
Tel: (+353) 021 542344; Fax: (+353) 021 342696

Airports

CORK
Tel: (+353) 021 313131

Bus Services

BUS EIREANN
*Travel Centre, Parnell Place, **Cork***
Timetable enquiries: Tel: (+353) 021 508188
Other departments: Tel: (+353) 021 506066

Ferries

Timetable and other details for all services are available from Cork Tourist Information Office, Tel: (+353) 021 273251; Fax: (+353) 021 273504

CORK HARBOUR CROSSING
The car and passenger ferry operates between Carrigaloe and Glenbrook in Cork Harbour. Crossing takes 5 minutes.

CORK HARBOUR to SWANSEA
Tel: (+353) 021 271166
Car ferries operate from Swansea in Wales to Cork City direct.

CORK to LE HAVRE, ROSCOFF and CHERBOURG (Irish Ferries)
Tel: (+353) 01 661 0511

CORK to ROSCOFF (Brittany Ferries)
Tel: (+353) 021 277801

Rail Services

Banteer *– Tel: (+353) 029 56004*
Cobh *– Tel: (+353) 021 811655*
Cork *(Kent Station) – Tel: (+353) 021 504422/506766*
Little Island *– Tel: (+353) 021 354120*
Mallow *– Tel: (+353) 022 21120*
Millstreet *– Tel: (+353) 029 70096*

COUNTY KERRY

If you want to take your children to where the action is, head for Kerry. This is a place of pleasure, leisure and treasure which is noted for its great sense of fun, range of all-weather sporting attractions, extravagant festivals, breathtaking inland and coastal scenery and magnificent beaches. If you're looking to improve your health and cleanse your skin, you can even take a seaweed bath here!

The county offers a great diversity of scenery, culture and leisure activities: the sporting enthusiast can golf, cycle, pony-trek, walk and enjoy watersports from angling to diving. The culture vulture can take part in many great festivals, including a bachelor festival, a busking festival and the world-famous Rose of Tralee festival. The county has a number of major heritage centres, open farms, museums, castles and panoramic tours, such as the spectacular Ring of Kerry. For something really different, you can even tour in a **horse-drawn gypsy caravan** or **go rambling with a donkey.**

County Kerry is ideal for either touring or as a base because there are so many things here to amuse children. In Killarney, for example, there are opportunities for walking, cycling, sailing, nature trails and boat trips. Or there's the option of a tour in a 'jaunting car' (horse-drawn 'side car') with a storytelling 'jarvey' as a guide, or going on a pony-trekking tour. One of the world's largest **model railways** is in Killarney. A great favourite with children, it has over 50 trains running on a mile of track, covering a huge area. **Coolwood Wildlife Sanctuary** in Killarney has 50 acres of scenic walks, animals and birds, a playground, a pet shop, a coffee shop and a picnic area. Also in Killarney is the **National Museum of Irish Transport,** a fascinating collection of Irish vintage cars, bicycles, motorbikes, carriages and many other items of national historic interest.

Muckross House, Gardens and Traditional Farms are at the heart of the beautiful **Killarney National Park,** containing craft workshops and traditional working farms with animals and machinery that will give grandparents the opportunity to relive past times and children the chance to experience life from a bygone era. Another farm worth a visit is **Kennedy's Animal, Bird and Pet Farm** at Glenflesk. Children will have lots of fun here spotting the birds and animals and in the excellent playground with its tree-house, slides and swings.

In Castleisland, north of Killarney on the road to Limerick, is the magnificent **Crag Cave,** which has dramatic sound and lighting effects. Just 10 miles west of here is Tralee, the capital town of County Kerry, and its endless list of multi-million-pound visitor attractions that can transport you back to medieval times or at high speed down a giant water chute. It gets very busy during the high season. The enormous **Tralee Aqua Dome** provides fun for all ages, including mums and dads; the town's **Jungle Jim's** is Kerry's largest indoor adventure playground and has lots of fantastic fun attractions; older and more adventurous kids might like to take part in a race at **Karting Kingdom,** an indoor karting centre; and everyone will enjoy a ride on the **Tralee & Dingle Railway,** Ireland's only private railway. Steam trains leave Tralee from the new Ballyard Station for the 20-minute journey to Blennerville. The **Kerry County Museum** in Tralee is host to 'Kerry the Kingdom', a unique exhibition and interactive display area.

North of Tralee, nestling at the mouth of the Shannon, is Bally-bunion, another of Ireland's premier seaside resorts. There is a good **leisure complex** at Lisselton near Ballybunion. The **Ballyloughran Centre** has a swimming-pool, jacuzzi, tennis, crazy golf and canoeing. Alternatively, there's the **Seaweed Baths** at the North Beach in Ballybunion where you can take a warm seaweed bath or enjoy a snack in the tea-rooms – or even do both.

South-west of Tralee is **Dingle Oceanworld,** a spectacular aquarium overlooking Dingle Harbour. Come here to see many of the fascinating species that inhabit the waters around the magnificent Dingle Peninsula. One of the highlights is the undersea tunnel, where you come face to face with the sea creatures. You can also take a **boat trip** from the pier to see Fungi the famous dolphin swimming wild and free in his natural habitat. Why not hire a wetsuit and take an early morning **swimming trip** and have the most amazing experience of your life by swimming with Fungi in the peace and tranquillity of Dingle Harbour. Children over 9 years old, who are competent swimmers, can also hire a wetsuits and swim alongside this amazing creature.

Access throughout the county is excellent by road, via routes N21, N22, N23, N69 and N72, and public transport via mainline rail and Bus Eireann. Kerry Airport serves this region.

• • • • •

PLACES TO VISIT

Animals, Birds and Fish

COOLWOOD WILDLIFE SANCTUARY***
*Just out of **Killarney** off route N22 to Cork*
Tel: (+353) 064 36288
Open: April to October, daily, 10a.m.–6p.m.
Facilities: parking; toilets; children's playground; animals and birds; pet shop; craft area; picnic area; coffee shop
The 50 acres of wildlife sanctuary and 4 miles (6.5km) of scenic walks combine with the many other attractions on the site to make this an interesting and fun place to be.

DINGLE OCEANWORLD***
*Mara Beo, near **Dingle** Harbour*
Tel: (+353) 066 9152111; Fax: (+353) 066 9152155
Open: summer season, daily, 10a.m.–8p.m.
winter season, daily, 10a.m.–5p.m.
Admission: A=££££, C=££, F
Facilities: disabled access; toilets and baby-changing facilities
Dingle Oceanworld is a spectacular new aquarium revealing some of the fascinating species that live in the waters around the Dingle

Peninsula, and also introduces visitors to the area's ancient sea culture and its people's relationship with the sea from the pre-Christian era to the present time. The highlights of a visit to Ocean-world are the undersea tunnel (where you come face to face with the inhabitants of the seas) and the touch tank. There's also an audio-visual display and artefacts from the Spanish Armada on view.

FENIT SEAWORLD***
*The pier, **Fenit***
Tel: (+353) 066 7136544
Open: all year, daily, 10a.m.–6p.m. (July to August till 9p.m.)
Admission: A=££££, C=££, F
Facilities: disabled access and toilets with baby-changing facilities; café; gift and craft shop
Seaworld on Fenit pier offers a unique opportunity to observe closely the hundreds of species that inhabit the underwater world of Tralee Bay. Visitors can wander through an amazing submarine labyrinth and explore the haunted timbers of a shipwreck.

Beaches

There are many fine beaches throughout Kerry, many of which have won Blue Flags. These are located at **Ballybunion** in the north, **Banna Strand** on the north-western coastline, **Ventry** and **Inch** on the Dingle Peninsula, and **Rossbeigh, Kells, Waterville** and **Caherdaniel** on the Kerry Peninsula. Other peaceful retreats with fine sandy beaches are at **Castlecove, Westcove, Derrynane** and **Ballinskelligs** on the Ring of Kerry. Inch is one of the most notable and romantic beaches in Kerry. During the 1960s it was used as a location for the filming of *The Playboy of the Western World*, and in the 1970s it featured in *Ryan's Daughter*. It is a very good area for fishing, canoeing, windsurfing and, of course, swimming. North of Tralee at the mouth of the Shannon is Ballybunion, another of Ireland's premier seaside resorts. The golden sands, clifftop walks and spectacular seas are all beautiful, but remember this is the Atlantic Ocean here and although the surf is sensational and may be inviting, heed the beach signs and take note of the lifeguard's instructions.

Boats and Boat Trips

DINGLE BOATMEN'S ASSOCIATION TRIP TO SEE FUNGI*****
*The Pier, **Dingle***
Tel: (+353) 066 52626/51967
Take the boat trip of a lifetime to see Fungi the Bottlenose Dolphin swimming freely in Dingle Harbour. Boats leave Dingle pier all day, every day, all year round (weather permitting). The swimming trips are from 8a.m. to 10a.m., children must be over 9 years old and be competent swimmers. Wetsuits are essential and can be hired from Flannery's Wetsuit Hire, Cooleen, Dingle; Tel: (+353) 066 9151967.

BLASKET ISLAND GUIDED TOURS FROM CAHIRCIVEEN
*Hugh Maguire, The Anchor, **Cahirciveen***
Tel/Fax: (+353) 066 9479189
Full-day tours (weather permitting).

SEAFARI
Marine Activities Centre, Kenmare Pier, Kenmare
Tel: (+353) 064 83171
The Seafari cruises offer two-hour Eco-Nature and Wildlife trips on
Menmare Bay, and the Marine Activities Centre provides instruction
on windsurfing, canoeing, sailing, water-skiing and tube rides. Guided
sailing and canoeing discovery expeditions are also available. Free
use of equipment for all activities.

BLASKET ISLAND FERRY and ISLAND CRUISES
Dun Chaoin Quay
Tel: (+353) 066 9156455
Daily sailings on the half-hour from 10a.m. (weather permitting).

DESTINATION KILLARNEY
*Scotts Gardens, **Killarney***
Tel: (+353) 064 32638
Daily sailings from Ross Castle. Most children enjoy a boat trip and
this is a great way to see the area and its fantastic scenery with
knowledgeable guides to explain all.

KILLARNEY LAKES AND NATIONAL PARK
*Killarney Watercoach Cruises, 3 High Street, **Killarney***
Tel: (+353) 064 31068
Two water-buses offer trips beginning from Ross Castle. The tours
are about 1 hour long and include a full commentary on the history
of the area.

SKELLIGS ROCK
*Michael O'Sullivan, Lobster Bar and Restaurant, **Waterville***
Tel: (+353) 066 9474255; Fax: (+353) 066 9474676
Daily cruises from Portmagee pier to Skelligs Rock (weather
permitting).

Castles and Historic Houses

MUCKROSS HOUSE, GARDENS and TRADITIONAL FARMS****
*The National Park, **Killarney;** on route N71 Kenmare road, 3¹/₂ miles
(6km) from Killarney*
Tel: (+353) 064 31440; Fax: (+353) 064 33926
Muckross House and Gardens *open: daily, all year round*
Muckross Traditional Farms *open: mid-March to end April, weekends
and bank holidays; May to October, daily*
*Admission: no charge for Killarney National Park or Muckross Gardens;
for Muckross House and Traditional Farms, each attraction: A=£££, C=£,
F; joint ticket for both: A=££££, C=££, F*
*Facilities: nature trails; walking routes; lakeshore bathing area; audio-
visual presentation; folk museum; exhibitions; toilets and baby-changing
facilities; disabled toilets and access; restaurant*
Muckross House, Gardens and Traditional Farms are situated at the
heart of Killarney National Park (**see COUNTRY PARKS**). Muckross
House is a magnificent Victorian mansion and one of Ireland's leading stately homes. The elegantly furnished rooms show the lifestyle
of the landed gentry – a real contrast with the servants' working
rooms in the basement. A number of craft workers using traditional

skills in weaving, pottery and bookbinding can be seen in the house.
The 3 traditional farms recreate the lifestyles and farming traditions
of Kerry in the 1930s with animals, poultry and traditional farm
machinery. The gardens are renowned throughout the world for
their beauty, in particular the azaleas and rhododendrons.

ROSS CASTLE*
*On the shores of Lower Lake, **Killarney***
Tel: (+353) 064 35851/31947
*Open: April, daily, 11a.m.–6p.m.; May, daily, 9a.m.–6p.m.; June to August,
daily, 9a.m.–6.30p.m.; September, daily, 9a.m.–6p.m.; October, daily,
9a.m.–5p.m.* **Note: access is by guided tour only**
Admission: A=££, C=£, F
*Facilities: exhibitions; toilets; free parking; disabled access to the ground
floor only, by prior arrangement*
The restored castle now houses a fine collection of 16th- and 17th-
century oak furniture. There is a circular stone staircase in the
north-east corner which leads directly to all the chambers and
eventually to the parapets.

Caves

CRAG SHOWCAVE***
Castleisland
Tel: (+353) 066 7141244; Fax: (+353) 066 7142352
*Open: March to November, daily, 10a.m.–6p.m. (open until 6.30p.m.
during July and August)*
Admission: A=££££, C££, F
*Facilities: restaurant with home-cooking; souvenir shop; disabled toilets
and baby-changing facilities; free parking*
Most children enjoy the opportunity to explore these ancient
wonders of geology. This natural phenomenon with its beautiful
limestone formations of stalagmites and stalactites has been fitted
out with dramatic sound and lighting effects to present a colourful
wonderland that will enthral visitors of all ages.

Cinemas

PHEONIX
Dingle
Tel: (+353) 066 51222

CINEDROME
Tralee
Tel: (+353) 066 21055

CLASSIC
Listowel
Tel: (+353) 068 22796

CINEPLEX
East Avenue Road, Killarney
Tel: (+353) 064 37007

OISIN
Killorglin
Tel: (+353) 066 61144

Country Parks

KILLARNEY NATIONAL PARK*****
*On route N71 Kenmare road, 3 miles (6km) from **Killarney**
(alternatively, the park can be entered at Knockreer)*
Tel: (+353) 064 31440; Fax: (+353) 064 33926
*Open: daily, all year round; visitor centre open mid-March to June, daily,
9a.m.–6p.m.; July to August, daily, 9a.m.–7p.m.; September to October,
daily, 9 a.m.–6p.m.*
Admission: free
*Facilities: nature trails; walking routes; lakeshore bathing area; free audio-
visual presentation; folk museum; exhibitions; toilets and baby-changing
facilities; disabled toilets and access; restaurant*
Killarney National Park extends to over 10,000 hectares of natural
beauty, containing many points of interest that include Muckross
House and Gardens (**see CASTLES**), Muckross Abbey (a Franciscan
friary founded in 1448), a unique yew and oak woodland, the
amazing Torc Waterfall, Dinis Cottage and the only native herd of
red deer in Ireland. The park also encloses Killarney's 3 lakes and
surrounding mountains. An excellent way to tour the park is on a
traditional 'jaunting car' or lightweight horse-drawn 'side-cars'.
Alternatively, hire a bicycle, collect your maps and cycle guides
from the Centre, and spend a wonderful day cycling with the
whole family exploring this 26,000-acre haven of nature and
history. The official cycle tour is a comfortable 15-mile (24km)
route, but allow a full day to appreciate the area. You can either
take a picnic with you or there are snacks available on the
route.

Diving

DISCOVER SCUBA DIVING
*PADI Dive Centre, Harbour House, Scraggane pier, The Maharees,
Castlegregory*
Tel: (+353) 066 7139292; Fax: (+353) 066 7125032
Note: 12 is the minimum age for participating in this activity
The PADI Discover Scuba Diving programme allows beginners to
safely experience the thrill of scuba-diving.

Equestrian Facilities

EAGLE ROCK EQUESTRIAN CENTRE****
***Caherdaniel** (off the N70 main Ring of Kerry)*
Tel: (+353) 066 9475145
Open: all year round
They have horses and ponies here to suit all levels of experience.
There are woodland trails and brilliant beach rides along the shores
of Derrynane Bay.

EL RANCHO RIDING STABLES
*El Rancho Farmhouse, **Tralee***

Tel: (+353) 066 7121840
Hourly base trekking, or trail riding on the Dingle Peninsula for
week-long or 3-day trails.

MUCKROSS RIDING STABLES
Mangerton Road, Muckross, **Killarney**
Tel: (+353) 064 32238
Open: All year
The centre has horses and ponies to cater for riders of all ages and
capabilities. Hard hats and boots provided.

ROCKLANDS RIDING SCHOOL AND TREKKING CENTRE
Tralee Road (N22), **Killarney**
Tel: (+353) 064 32952; Fax: (+353) 064 34003
Escorted ride-outs for all ages. Tuition available in large indoor and
outdoor areas.

THOMPSON HORSERIDING
The Mountain Man, Strand Street, **Dingle**
Tel: (+353) 066 9152018
Instruction given. Riding hats and footwear supplied. Hourly and
daily rates.

Farm Parks

KENNEDY'S ANIMAL, BIRD AND PET FARM***
Glenfesk; *on route N22 east of Killarney*
Tel: (+353) 064 54054
Open: Easter to September, daily, 10a.m.–8p.m.
Plenty of traditional farm animals and pets such as ponies, rabbits,
chipmunks, donkeys and guinea pigs to amuse the children. A
superb adventure playground with a tree-house, wooden tunnel,
fort, sand play area, slides and swings. There's also a selection of
vintage farm machinery on view.

SCANLON'S PET FARM***
Baile an Locaigh, 5 miles west of **Dingle**
Tel: (+353) 066 9155135
Open: April to September, Monday to Saturday, 10a.m.–6p.m., Sunday,
12noon–6p.m.
Admission: A=££, C=£, F
Facilities: parking; toilets; refreshments; children's plaground, picnic area
Visitors can observe, watch and walk, or follow one of the guided
tours to see the wide variety of animals and birds.

MUCKROSS TRADITIONAL FARMS – **see** CASTLES

Festivals and Events

DINGLE RACES
Dingle *Racecourse*
Open: second week in August
Admission: A=££££, C=££, F
The carnival atmosphere at this annual horseracing event makes it a
great day out for all the family.

EASTER FOLK FESTIVAL
Killarney
Weekend of traditional and folk music with street entertainment.

GUINNESS ROARING 1920s FESTIVAL
Killarney
On: March (St Patrick's week)
Includes barbershop recitals, a fancy-dress vintage car rally, a boot-leggers' ball and many other fun events.

KERRY BOATING CARNIVAL
On: August
A festival of rowing events on the lakes of Killarney.

KILLORGLIN PUCK FAIR
Killorglin
On: August
The events and festivities of this fair make it a unique occasion, even by Irish standards. On the first day of the fair, 'Gathering Day', the Puck Goat is paraded through the town with great enthusiasm before being installed as 'king' on a lofty platform above the market square. The second day it's down to the business of selling livestock. Then on the third day, 'Scattering Day', the goat is released with great ceremony and celebration (or inebriation!) at sunset.

ROSE OF TRALEE FESTIVAL
Tralee
On: August
During late August/early September, Tralee plays host to the world in Ireland's biggest bash, the amazing Rose of Tralee festival. This is a week of gaiety, pageantry, fun and informality. The streets vibrate for 7 days with a festive atmosphere; music from folk singers and brass bands; free outdoor entertainment; parades and ceremonies; and the grand finale is the crowning of the 'Rose of Tralee'.

Forest and Amenity Walks

BALLAGHISHEEN
*Located off route N70, 13 miles (21km) north-east of **Waterville***
Facilities: carpark; picnic site; forest trails; viewing point

CARAGH LAKE
*Located 5 miles (8km) south of **Killorglin** off the Ring of Kerry*
Facilities: carpark; scenic views; forest walks; picnic site
Fishing on the river is preserved, but on the lake it is free.

GLENBEIGH WOOD
*Located just 1km from **Glenbeigh** on the Rossbeigh road*
Included in the walk is a stretch of the old railway line between Tralee and Cahirciveen. The Rossbeigh sand dunes are nearby.

GLENTEENASSIG FOREST PARK
*Located 16 miles (26km) west of **Tralee** on the Castlegregory road*
A good selection of scenic forest trails with waterfalls and lakeside walks. Picnic site.

PIKE WOOD

*Located 3 miles (3.5km) east of **Killarney** on route N22 to Cork*
Facilities: parking; picnic site; forest walks; access to the 'crooked tree'

ROSSACRUE

*Five miles (8km) north-east of **Kilgarvan** on route R569 to Killarney*
Facilities: parking; picnic site; forest walks

Gardens

DERREEN**

*Laragh, near **Kenmare**; off the Kenmare to Castletownbere road*
Tel: (+353) 064 83103
Open: May to September, daily, 11a.m.–6p.m.
Admission: A=££, C=£
Facilities: picnic areas; toilets; teas are served at weekends
The contrasting worlds of the wild Kerry scenery, the lushness of a subtropical garden and sea bathing blessed with the warming effect of the Gulf Stream, is all part of what makes Derreen so special.

DERRYNANE HOUSE GARDENS – see HERITAGE CENTRES

GLANLEAM HOUSE SUBTROPICAL GARDENS***

Valentia Island
Tel: (+353) 066 9476176; Fax: (+353) 066 9476108
Open: mid-June to September, daily, 11a.m.–7p.m.; October to mid-June, daily, 11a.m.–5p.m.
Admission: A=£££, C=£
Facilities: toilets; tea-room with home-baking (mid-April to September); pets corner with lots of small animals for children
Beautiful subtropical gardens with extensive collection of exotic plants from the southern hemisphere. Lovely walks through the gardens and safe beaches for the children nearby. There are also fully appointed self-catering cottages available here (**see WHERE TO STAY**).

MUCKROSS GARDENS – see CASTLES AND HISTORIC HOUSES

Heritage Centres

THE BLASKET CENTRE*

*Dun Chaoin, **Dingle Peninsula***
Tel: (+353) 066 9156444/9156371; Fax: (+353) 066 9156446
Open: Easter to June, daily, 10a.m.–6p.m.; July to August, daily, 10a.m.–7p.m.; September, daily, 10a.m.–6p.m. (last admission 45 minutes before closing)
Admission: A=££, C=£, F
Facilities: restaurant; disabled access and toilets; free parking
The Blasket Centre is a state-of-the-art visitor centre in Dun Chaoin, on the tip of the Dingle Peninsula overlooking Great Blasket Island. The modern centre celebrates the story of the Blasket Islanders, their language and the unique literary achievements of its writers. The island was sadly abandoned in 1953 as a result of the decline of its community. The Blasket Centre houses an audio-visual presentation, exhibitions and a research room.

CAHIRCIVEEN HERITAGE CENTRE*

*The Barracks, **Cahirciveen,** Ring of Kerry*
Tel: (+353) 066 9472777; Fax: (+353) 066 9472993
Open: daily, Monday to Saturday, 10a.m.–5p.m., Sunday, 10a.m.–4p.m.
Facilities: exhibitions; geology displays; elevator to lookout tower; tea-room

A unique building giving an insight into the life and times of Cahirciveen. The Barracks provides a focal point for tourist information for the far west of the Iveragh Peninsula.

DERRYNANE NATIONAL HISTORIC PARK**

*Derrynane, **Iveragh Peninsula***
Tel: (+353) 066 9475113
Open: January to March, weekends, 1p.m.–5p.m.; April and October, Tuesday to Sunday, 1p.m.–5p.m.; May to September, Monday to Saturday, 9a.m.–6p.m., Sunday, 11a.m.–7p.m.; November and December, weekends, 1p.m.–5p.m. (last admission 45 minutes before closing time)
Admission: A=££, C=£, F
Facilities: free parking; toilets; disabled access and toilets; audio-visual show; coffee shop

Derrynane Historic Park is made up of 120 hectares of plantations and garden walks, together with Derrynane House. Also included is nearly a mile (1.5km) of sandy and rocky shoreline.

KENMARE HERITAGE CENTRE*

*The Square, **Kenmare** (enter through the Tourist Information Office)*
Tel: (+353) 064 41233
Open: May to September, Monday to Saturday, 9.30a.m.–6p.m.; Sunday, 11a.m.–1p.m. and 2.15p.m.–5p.m.
Admission: A=££, C=£, F (free for accompanied children under 12)

The Heritage Centre has personal sound tours (Walkman headsets), covering themes such as Kenmare lace, famous visitors, the town's history and historical sites, and the effects of the Famine. A free heritage trail map enables you to find the sites in the town after visiting the centre (allow about 40 minutes to walk the trail). There is ample free parking outside the centre.

KERRY THE KINGDOM****

*Ashe Memorial Hall, **Tralee***
Tel: (+353) 066 7127777; Fax: (+353) 066 7127444
Open: mid-March to end October, 10a.m.–6p.m.; August, 10a.m.–7p.m.; November and December, 2p.m.–5p.m.
Closed: 24–26 December and January to February
Admission: A=££££, C=££, F
Facilities: café; craft shop; tourist information centre

Kerry the Kingdom at the Ashe Memorial Hall is made up of 3 superb attractions under one roof: **Audio-Visual Kerry in Colour** (a multi-image audio-visual presentation that takes visitors on a tour of County Kerry with its spectacular scenery, historic monuments, towns and traditions), the visitor-friendly **Kerry County Museum** (in which priceless archaeological treasures stand beside the most modern interpretative media to bring history to life with the use of slide presentations, scale models, audio and video displays and live link-ups with Radio Kerry and the Irish language station Radio Na Gaeltachta), and **Geraldine Tralee** (a unique experience of urban life in medieval Ireland in which visitors are taken back in time to the Middle Ages and ferried by time car through the reconstructed streets, houses and abbey of medieval Tralee with the aid of special lighting and sound effects).

MICHAEL J. QUILL VISITOR CENTRE***
Kilgarvan
Tel: (+353) 064 85511
Open: daily, Easter to end September, 10a.m.–5p.m.
This centre is a unique memorial to Michael J. Quill, a native son of Kilgarvan, who was founder and first president of the Transport Workers Union of America. The centre has a craft shop and excellent tearoom.

THE SKELLIG EXPERIENCE***
Valentia Island (where the road bridge meets the island), Ring of Kerry
Tel: (+353) 066 9476306
Open: mid-April to end September, daily, 10a.m.–7p.m.
Admission: A=£££, C=£, F
Facilities: free parking; disabled toilets and baby-changing facilities
The Skellig Experience Heritage Centre has exhibits on themes that include the life and work of the early Christian monks on Skellig, the men of Skellig Lighthouse, and the seabirds and underwater sealife of the Skelligs. The 16-minute audio-visual presentation in the purpose-built auditorium takes visitors on a personal guided tour of the Skellig Michael monastery. The Centre has a good range of craft items on sale, and an attractive refreshment area serving lunches and snacks overlooking the estuary to Portmagee.

STAIGUE FORT**
Castlecove, Killarney
Tel: (+353) 066 9475127; Fax: (+353) 066 9475288
Exhibition Centre open: Easter to end September, daily, 10a.m.–9p.m.
Fort open: all year round, dawn to dusk
Facilities: toilets; coffee shop
Exhibition centre with a complete model of the 2,000-year-old fort, and an audio-visual display with animation.

TARBERT BRIDEWELL VISITOR CENTRE*
Tarbert
Tel: (+353) 068 36500
Open: April to October, daily, 10a.m.–6p.m.
An exhibition on crime and punishment in the 19th century. Visitors can explore the courthouse, holding cells, exercise yard and keeper's quarters. The centre has a coffee shop and gift shop.

Horse-Drawn Gypsy Caravans

SLATTERY'S TRAVEL AGENCY – GYPSY CARAVAN HIRE***
1 Russell Street, Tralee
Tel: (+353) 066 7124088 or freephone: 1800 673 673; Fax: (+353) 066 7125981
To travel the wonderful countryside of Ireland in a horse-drawn gypsy caravan really is a unique experience. You are provided with a

horse and fully equipped caravan, plus instructions and a list of suggested routes and overnight stops. The charges of between £50 to £60 per day include the hire of horse and caravan, horse feed, insurance, gas for cooking, overnight parking fees, bed linen and blankets. The caravans accommodate up to 5 people in a double and 3 single beds. Most children will enjoy this adventure, but probably only for a couple of days or so before getting bored.

If you prefer to walk, why not take a donkey with you! Slattery's also organise 'Rambling with a Donkey' tours. They provide you with a donkey complete with saddle bags for your gear, a route map and instructions. For longer overnight treks, bed and breakfast with a packed lunch is arranged for you. If your kids enjoy walking, this will be an enjoyable experience for them, and they will love having the donkey along – but don't forget to take some carrots!

Ireland at Work – Past and Present

BLENNERVILLE WINDMILL AND VISITOR CENTRE***
*Blennerville, **Tralee***
Tel: (+353) 066 7121064
Open: March to October, daily, 10a.m.–6p.m.
Admission: A=£££, C=£, F
Facilities: toilets with disabled access; craft shop and workshops; restaurant
The 18th-century Blennerville Windmill is the focal point of a major visitor centre and craft complex on the shores of Tralee Bay. The windmill is the tallest of its kind in Europe. Visitors can take a guided tour of the 5-storey windmill and view the various stages of the grain milling process, watch the giant sails turn, and look around the exhibition gallery.

KERRY WOOLLEN MILLS*
*Ballymalis, **Beaufort**; 9 miles (14km) west of Killarney towards Killorglin off route R562*
Tel: (+353) 064 44122; Fax: (+353) 064 44556
Open: April to October, Monday to Saturday, 9a.m.–5p.m.; November to March, Monday to Friday, 9a.m.–5p.m.
Admission: A=££, C=£, F
Facilities: carpark; mill shop; tea-room
These 17th-century mill buildings have recently been refurbished to provide better facilities for visitors. Tours of the mill can be pre-booked and lots of information on the processes is available.

THE SKELLIGS CHOCOLATE FACTORY*****
*The Glen, **Ballinskelligs***
Tel: (+353) 066 9479119
Fax: (+353) 066 9479433
Open: all year round, Monday to Friday, 9.30a.m.–5.30p.m.; also Saturday and Sunday in July/August, 11a.m.–5p.m.
Admission: free
The kids will enjoy a visit here, especially the free samples. They can see the chocolate being made and gift boxes being hand-painted by artists in the factory. Everyone is made welcome at this informal little working factory to see the various flavours of chocolate being made to supply many top stores world wide. They even have a special fun website for kids at www.skelligschocolate.com.

Leisure Centres and Adventure Playgrounds

ROCKY RABBITS***
*Ross Road, **Killarney***
Tel: (+353) 064 36020
Open: Daily, 12noon–6p.m.
Admission: C=££
Enormous soft play arena for children of allages. Also Toddlers
World, cafeteria, and parents seating.

THE AQUA DOME*****
*Ballyard, **Tralee***
Tel: (+353) 066 7128899; Fax: (+353) 066 7129130
*Open: April to September, daily, 10a.m.–10p.m. (call the information
line, (+353) 066 7129150, for opening times out of high season)*
Admission: A=£££££, C=£££
The Aqua Dome at Tralee is one of Ireland's most exciting water-
worlds. It's wild, wet and wonderful, with fun to be had by all the
family. Children will love the giant water chutes, falling rapids, wave
pool, lazy river, gushers and geysers, raging rapids, whirlpools and
bubblers, medieval castle and water cannons. For the younger ones
there's a separate kiddies' pool with slides. The restaurant serves
children's meals and there's also a refreshment bar. There are baby-
changing facilities in both ladies and gents toilets. Parents can take
advantage of the sauna, steam rooms and cool pool.
*Note: all children under 8 years must be accompanied by an adult, and
child and weaker swimmers must wear buoyancy aids.*

JUNGLE JIM'S ADVENTURE WORLD***
*20 Pembroke Street, **Tralee***
Tel: (+353) 066 7128187
Open: daily, 10a.m. till late
Admission: C=££
Fully supervised indoor adventure playground with all the usual
attractions: ball pool, monster maze, haunted house, giant tube slide,
free-fall slides and large-screen video games – fantastic fun.

KARTING KINGDOM***
*Upper Rock Street, **Tralee***
Tel: (+353) 066 7129511
*Open: all year round, Monday to Saturday, noon–11p.m.; Sunday, noon–
10p.m.*
Charges: A=£££££, C=£££
Full tuition and protective equipment provided for racing sessions.
Junior karts and racing club available. This is one for the older
children – plenty of excitement in relatively safe conditions.

TRALEE SUPERBOWL***
*Godfrey Place, **Tralee***
Tel: (+353) 066 7122311; Fax: (+353) 066 7122120
*Open: Monday to Friday, 11a.m. till late; Saturday, Sunday and bank
holidays, 10a.m. till late*
Charges: A=££ per game; hourly rate available
Excellent 10-pin bowling centre where you can also play
snooker and pool and the latest action video games. The

restaurant overlooking the bowling lanes serves children's meals. Ball bumpers are provided for younger children, who can also join the fully supervised Dinosaur junior bowling club every Saturday morning.

Museums

DERRYNANE HOUSE
Derrynane – see HERITAGE CENTRES

KERRY BOG VILLAGE MUSEUM**
Glenbeigh, Ring of Kerry
Tel: (+353) 066 9769184
Open: I March to 30 November, daily, 8.30a.m.–7p.m.; November and December, open on request
Admission: A=££, C=£, F
The village consists of 6 dwellings, all restored and laid out to reflect the domestic lifestyles of the Irish in the early 1800s.

KERRY COUNTY MUSEUM
Tralee – see HERITAGE CENTRES

KILGARVAN MOTOR MUSEUM***
Kilgarvan (2 miles from Kilgarvan village on the Bantry road)
Tel: (+353) 064 85346
Fax: (+353) 064 85609
Open: all year round, daily, 9.30a.m.–6p.m.
Admission: A=££, C=£
Facilities: toilets; coffee shop with home baking
An interesting collection covering a wide range of cars.

MUSEUM OF IRISH TRANSPORT***
*Scott's Gardens, **Killarney***
Tel: (+353) 064 32638
Open: daily
Unique collection of vintage and classic cars, motorcycles, carriages and fire engines. The collection includes the rarest car in the world – the 1907 Silver Stream – and the entire history of bicycles.

Science and Technology

THE SCIENCE WORKS***
*Godfrey Place, **Tralee***
Tel: (+353) 066 7129855; Fax: (+353) 066 7123163
Open: May to September, daily, 9a.m.–9p.m.; October to April, daily, 11a.m.–5p.m.
Admission: A=£££, C=££, F
Facilities: toilets
Entertainment and education for all the family, with over 70 hands-on experiments and wonders of science in this interactive science centre, designed to help visitors get a better understanding of the scientific principles behind natural phenomena. There are no 'Do Not Touch' signs to frustrate children – here they can handle and make things work – and learn a lot at the same time. Dads quite enjoy it too!

Swimming-Pools

TRALEE SPORTS AND LEISURE CENTRE
Tralee
Tel: (+353) 066 7126442/7126983
Open: Call the public swimming times information line: 066 7123131
Admission: A=££, C=£, F
The centre has 2 pools – a learners' pool provides safe swimming
for younger and novice swimmers, and a main pool for experienced
swimmers. There's a summer swim school with a series of 2-week
intensive courses and a summer camp for 6- to 12-year-olds with
organised daily activities and lots of fun and games.

Theatres

SIAMSA TIRE – THE NATIONAL FOLK THEATRE OF IRELAND***
*Siamsa Tire Theatre, **Tralee***
Tel: (+353) 066 7123055; Fax: (+353) 066 7127276
Open: May to mid-October
Founded in 1974, the aim of Siamsa Tire is to present on stage a
dance/theatre entertainment based on a wealth of music, folklore
and dance which evolved from an age when Irish (Gaelic) was the
first language in the country. Regular performances explore traditional rural themes through song, dance, music and mime. The
training centre for Siamsa Tire is situated in Finuge, on the R557
Finuge road from Listowel. Folk theatre performances are held here
once a week during high season.

Trains and Model Railways

KILLARNEY MODEL RAILWAY****
*Beech Road, **Killarney***
Tel/Fax: (+353) 064 34000
Open: Mid-March to October, daily, 10.30a.m.–6p.m.
Admission: A=£££, C=£, F
Facilities: disabled access
This world-famous attraction is a great favourite with the children.
There are over 50 trains running on a mile of track, laid out with
magnificent attention to detail, and covering over 1,000 square feet.

TRALEE AND BLENNERVILLE STEAM RAILWAY***
*Ballyard, **Tralee***
Tel: (+353) 066 7128888/7121064; Fax: (+353) 066 7127444
Open: April to September
**Steam trains operate daily, 11a.m.–5p.m.; trains leave hourly on the
hour from Tralee, and hourly on the half-hour from Blennerville*
*Closed 2nd Sunday and Monday of each month for maintenance
The Tralee & Dingle Steam Railway (1891–1953) was one of the
world's most famous narrow-gauge lines. Now, a section of the
historic railway between Tralee and Blennerville has been restored
and visitors can experience the wonders of steam travel on board
traditional carriages pulled by the last surviving Tralee & Dingle
steam train. On arrival in Blennerville, a visit to the largest working
windmill in Ireland and Great Britain is well worth while (**see** IRELAND
AT WORK – PAST AND PRESENT).

Walks and Tours

ARTHUR YOUNG TRAIL
*National Park, **Killarney***
Named after an English journalist who visited here in 1776 and described it in his famous book, *Tour in Ireland*.

BLUE POOL WOOD
*Rear of Muckross Park Hotel, **Killarney***
Ideal family walks along woodland paths encircling a small lake, the sea-green colour of which is caused by copper deposits.

CASTLELOUGH TOURS****
*7 High Street, **Killarney***
Tel: (+353) 064 32496/31115; Fax: (+353) 064 35088
More of an adventure than a tour, this makes an exciting day out for all the family. Start with a bus trip to Kate Kearney's Cottage, then a 7-mile journey by either jaunting car, pony-trek or on foot to Lord Brandon's Cottage, where snacks are available. After lunch it's onto the water to travel by boat through the 3 lakes of Killarney to Ross Castle, where a bus will pick you up and return you to Killarney.

THE DINGLE WAY
The 112-mile (180km) route encompasses the Dingle Peninsula, beginning and ending in ***Tralee***.

GLENINCHAQUIN WATERFALL AMENITY AREA****
*Tuosist, **Kenmare**; route R571 from Kenmare to Castletownbere. Turn left after 8 miles (13km) at road sign to Inchaquin Lake, travel for 5 miles (8km) to the amenity area.*
Tel: (+353) 064 84235
Facilities: parking; picnic areas
This idyllic valley is perfectly suited for days out with the entire family. The picnic areas and walking routes around the waterfall, cascades, streams, woodlands and lakes are very accessible. There's a wide variety of farm animals to see on the site, and when you have enjoyed your walk and worked up an appetite, excellent home-baking, teas, coffee and refreshments are available. Also found here is the Kerry Slug – a shiny black creature with silver spots. Enjoy your picnic!

KNOCKREER HOUSE
*End of New Street, **Killarney***
Short walks to Knockreer House and Gardens, and a river walk to Ross Castle.

THE KERRY WAY
Described as the 'walkers' Ring of Kerry', the Kerry Way is a magnificent route beginning in the **Killarney National Park.** The 117-mile (188km) route takes in some of the most spectacular scenery in Kerry. It is a moderate route for experienced hill-walkers.

O'CONNOR AUTOTOURS
*Ardross, Ross Road, **Killarney***
Tel: (+353) 064 31052/34833; Fax: (+353) 064 31703
A selection of day tours to all areas of the county.

PLACES TO EAT

Cafés and Restaurants

AVOCA HANDWEAVERS VISITOR CENTRE
*Molls Gap, near **Killarney***
Tel: (+353) 064 34720
Situated onthe Ring of Kerry this restaurant with excellent views is open 7 days and serves a delicious selection of home-made foods all day. They have high chairs and baby changing facilities.

CARAGH RESTAURANT
*106 New Street, **Killarney***
Tel: (+353) 064 31846
Children's menu and high-chair available.

CLARETS RESTAURANT AND WINE BAR
*10 College Street, **Killarney***
Tel: (+353) 064 36467
Children's menu and vegetarian dishes.

MAC'S ICE-CREAM PARLOUR AND RESTAURANT
*Main Street, **Killarney***
Tel: (+353) 064 35213; Fax: (+353) 064 36673

SHERKAN INDIAN RESTAURANT****
*Milk Market, Glebe Lane, **Killarney***
Tel: (+353) 064 37228
Excellent family friendly restaurant with good food, high chairs and children's menu.

SWISS BARN SPECIALITY RESTAURANT
*17 High Street, **Killarney***
Tel: (+353) 064 36044
Children's menu and high-chair. Home-made ice-cream is a speciality.

Fast-food Restaurants

McDONALD'S
Park Road, Killarney (Drive-through)
Tel: (+353) 064 37188

Manor West, Tralee (Drive-through)
Tel: (+353) 066 28811

Hotels and Pubs

DINGLE SKELLIG HOTEL
Dingle
Tel: (+353) 066 9151144

Children's menu and special Sunday lunch – with a free swim for children in the hotel's indoor heated pool.

RED FOX INN
Ring of Kerry, **Glenbeigh**
Tel: (+353) 066 9769184
Adjacent to Kerry Bog Museum. Children's menu and snacks served all day.

THE MOORINGS GUEST HOUSE,
RESTAURANT AND PUB*****
Portmagee
Tel: (+353) 066 77108
Fax: (353) 066 77220
Excellent family friendly, traditional pub with high chairs, children's menus, great hospitality, good craic and the food is even better!

● ● ● ● ●

PLACES TO STAY

Country Houses, Pubs and Hotels

BUTLER ARMS HOTEL***
Waterville
Tel: (+353) 066 9474144
Fax: (+353) 066 9474520
Excellent hotel with family rooms.

DERRYNANE HOTEL***
Caherdaniel
Tel: (+353) 066 9475136
Fax: (+353) 066 9475160
Nicely located, family friendly hotel, with an outdoor swimming-pool and leisure facilities.

THE CLIMBERS INN***
Glencar
Tel: (+353) 066 60101
Fax: (+353) 066 60104
Open: Easter to October; weekends only in winter
Although they specialise in catering for walkers, this homely country inn welcomes families. Even the Siamese cat, Joe, has his own website.

THE GRAND HOTEL
Denny Street, **Tralee**
Tel: (+353) 066 21499
Open: all year
Children welcomed here and family rooms are available at discounted rates.

MOORINGS*****
Portmagee
Tel: (+353) 066 77108
Fax: (+353) 066 77220
Family friendly guest house with family rooms and excellent hospitality. Everyone is assured of a warm welcome from Gerry and Patricia Kennedy at their beautifully located guest house overlooking the harbour in Portmagee and Valentia Island bridge.

MUCKCROSS PARK HOTEL AND
MOLLY'S TRADITIONAL PUB AND RESTAURANT****
Muckcross Village, **Killarney**
Tel: (+353) 064 31938
Fax: (+353) 064 31965
Excellent family friendly hotel where the hospitality is brilliant and the food is even better.

TORC GREAT SOUTHERN***
Killarney
Tel: (+353) 064 31611
Fax: (+353) 064 31824
The hotel caters for families and children. They have family rooms, baby-sitting service, and free swimming lessons and play centre during July/August and bank holiday weekends.

SHANNON VIEW
David and Nuala Sowden, Ferry Road, **Ballyduff**
Tel: (+353) 066 7131324
Children's play area; baby-sitting available.

DROM HOUSE
Mrs Rita Brosnan, Coumgaugh, **Dingle**
Tel: (+353) 066 9151134; Fax: (+353) 066 9156348
Playground for children; baby-sitting available.

DROMQUINNA MANOR HOTEL
Blackwater, **Kenmare**
Tel: (+353) 064 41657; Fax: (+353) 064 41791
Situated on lovely wooded estate with a mile of sea front. Children welcome. Boats for hire. Play area with Tarzan and Jane tree-house.

THE GLENEAGLE HOTEL
Muckross Road, **Killarney**
Tel: (+353) 064 31870; Fax: (+353) 064 32646
Facilities: ice-cream parlour; heated indoor swimming-pool; jacuzzi; sauna; squash courts; bowls; snooker; table-tennis; crèche; activity centre
Excellent facilities here. Look out for the special deals for weekend/midweek breaks and special children's rates.

HOLLY GROVE
Mrs Peggy Coffey, Gap of Dunloe, **Killarney**
Tel: (+353) 064 44326
Facilities: children's playground; baby-sitting available

KILLARNEY RYAN HOTEL***
*Cork Road, **Killarney***
Tel: (+353) 064 31555; Fax: (+353) 064 32438
An excellent family-friendly hotel with plenty of facilities for children. The leisure centre is fully equipped with indoor heated swimming-pools, a jacuzzi and sports hall. The 15 acres of extensive grounds have tennis courts, crazy golf and children's play areas. The hotel has an award-winning crèche and a games room, and offers a full programme of organised activities for children of all ages.

KILTEELY HOUSE
*Dingle Road, Ballard, **Tralee***
Tel: (+353) 066 7123376; Fax: (+353) 066 7123461
Families will be sure to receive a friendly welcome here from Mike and Anne Lundon and their 6 children.

Bed and Breakfast

TRALEE TOWNHOUSE
*High Street, **Tralee***
Tel: (+353) 066 81111; Fax: (+353) 066 81112
Open: All year
Four-star luxury townhouse located in the heart of Tralee, where children are welcome.

Farmhouse Accommodation

OCEAN VIEW FARMHOUSE
*Claire O'Donoghue, Renard Road, **Cahirciveen***
Tel: (+353) 066 9472261
Children's play area, baby-sitting and horseriding available.

O'DOWD'S FARM BUNGALOW
*Catherine O'Dowd, Knockavrogeen West; just over 2 miles (4km) west of **Dingle** on the Ballyferriter road*
Tel: (+353) 066 9151307 (or contact Irish Farm Holidays – see Directory)
Open: April to October
With a heated, covered swimming-pool, tennis court, mini-golf and other facilities for children all on the premises, there are more facilities here than are available at many hotels.

FARMSTEAD LODGE
*John and Eileen O'Shea, Shanara Cross, Kilgobnet, Beaufort, **Killarney***
Tel: (+353) 066 9761968
Pony-trekking and beach nearby. Children's playroom and baby-sitting available.

INVERARAY
*Noel and Eileen Spillane, Beaufort; 6 miles (9km) west of **Killarney**, 1km off R562 at petrol station*
Tel: (+353) 064 44224; Fax: (+353) 064 44775 (or contact Irish Farm Holidays – see Directory)
Open: 1 March to 1 November
Horseriding, golf, nature walks. Games room, playground and a pony for the children.

Holiday Parks and Villages

WEST HOLIDAY PARK
Killarney Road, **Killorglin**
Tel: (+353) 066 9761240; Fax: (+353) 066 9761833
Free fishing, tennis, small indoor swimming-pool and playground.
Baby-sitting available.

Self-Catering Apartments and Houses

TRALEE TOWN CENTRE APARTMENTS
Maine Street, **Tralee**
Tel: (+353) 066 7123456; Fax: (+353) 066 7123285
Fully equipped apartments with baby-sitting by arrangement.

GLANLEAM HOUSE
Valentia Island
Tel: (+353) 066 9476176; Fax: (+353) 066 9476108
Fully appointed self-catering houses available. Tea-room with home-
baking (mid-April to September). Pets corner with lots of small
animals for children. Beautiful subtropical gardens and safe beaches
for the children nearby (see GARDENS).

Caravan and Camping Parks

FOSSA CARAVAN AND CAMPING PARK
Fossa; on route R562 Killorglin road, 3 miles (5km) west of **Killarney**
Tel: (+353) 064 31497; Fax: (+353) 064 34459
Open: 13 March to 31 October
*Facilities: shop; take-away food; restaurant; children's playground; games
room*
Ideally set in 6 acres of wooded area overlooking the
MacGillycuddy Reeks.

WATERVILLE CARAVAN AND CAMPING PARK
Waterville; *1km north of Waterville off route N70 Cahirciveen road*
Tel: (+353) 066 9474191; Fax: (+353) 066 9474538
Open: 1 April to 23 September
Small supervised swimming-pool, shop, children's playground and
games room. Baby-sitting by arrangement. Beach close by (1km).

WOODLANDS TOURING CARAVAN AND CAMPING PARK
Dingle Road, **Tralee**
Tel: (+353) 066 7121235; Fax: (+353) 066 7181199
Open: March to October
Ireland's newest four-star caravan/camping park located on 16 acres
alongside Tralee's Aquadrome. Facilities include shop, games room
and restaurant.

Hostels

FUCHSIA LODGE
Annascaul, **Dingle Peninsula**
Tel: (+353) 066 9157150; Fax: (+353) 066 9157402
Open: all year round

O'FLAHERTY'S HOSTEL
*East End, **Ballybunion***
Tel: (+353) 068 27684
Open: all year round

THE BREAKERS
*Cliff Road, **Ballyheigue***
Tel: (+353) 066 7133242
Open: all year round

SIVE HOSTEL
*15 East End, **Cahirciveen***
Tel: (+353) 066 9472717
Open: all year round

CARRIGBEG
Cahirdaniel
Tel: (+353) 066 9475229
Open: all year round

BALLINTAGGART HOSTEL AND EQUESTRIAN CENTRE
*Racecourse Road, **Dingle***
Tel: (+353) 066 9151454; Fax: (+353) 066 9151385
Open: all year round

FAILTE HOSTEL
*Shelbourne Street, **Kenmare***
Tel: (+353) 064 41083
Open: all year round

LAUNE VALLEY FARM HOSTEL
*Banshagh, **Killorglin***
Tel: (+353) 066 9761488
Open: all year round

COLLIS-SANDES HOUSE
*Oakpark, **Tralee***
Tel/Fax: (+353) 066 7128658
Open: all year round

LISNAGREE HOSTEL
*Ballinorig, Clash East, **Tralee***
Tel: (+353) 066 7127133
Open: all year round

Bicycle Hire

IRISH CYCLE HIRE – see *Directory*
RALEIGH RENT-A-BIKE – see *Directory*

CASEY CYCLES
*New Street, **Cahirciveen***
Tel: (+353) 066 9472474

FIOS FEASTA
*Holy Ground, **Dingle***
Tel: (+353) 066 9151937/911606

FOXY JOHN MORIARTY
*Main Street, **Dingle***
Tel: (+353) 066 9151316

JEREMY O'NEILL
*Plunkett Street, **Killarney***
Tel: (+353) 064 31970

TRALEE CYCLE SUPPLIES
*Strand Street, **Tralee***
Tel: (+353) 066 7122018; Fax: (+353) 066 7127960

Car Hire

KILLARNEY AUTOS LTD
*Park Road, **Killarney***
Tel: (+353) 064 31355; Fax: (+353) 064 32053

Airports

KERRY COUNTY AIRPORT
Farranfore
Tel: (+353) 066 9764399

Ferry Service

TARBERT–KILLIMER FERRIES
Daily sailings from Tarbert, Co Kerry to Killimer, Co Clare, every hour on the half hour. 20 minutes crossing time.

Bus Services

BUS EIREANN
*Travel Centre, Bus Station, **Killarney***
Tel: (+353) 064 34777

BUS EIREANN
*Travel Centre, Casement Station, **Tralee***
Tel: (+353) 066 7123566

Rail Services

Farranfore *– Tel: (+353) 066 9764101*
Killarney *– Tel: (+353) 064 31067*
Rathmore *– Tel: (+353) 064 58006*
Tralee *– Tel: (+353) 066 7123522*

COUNTY LIMERICK

County Limerick is the gateway to the south-west of Ireland. Its charming county town of the same name was founded by the Vikings on an island in the River Shannon that ends its long journey to the Atlantic Ocean here. This is a beautiful county and typifies many elements of Irish life with its pretty settlements such as Adare (Ireland's 'most picturesque village') and Askeaton (a fine medieval town); its excellent horseracing and golf courses; its festivals such as the **Adare Jazz Festival,** the **Adare Country Fair,** the **Foynes Irish Coffee Festival** and **sailing regattas** on the Shannon Estuary; its parks and gardens; and many other visitor attractions.

During our last visit to Ireland we were fortunate to discover **Fitzgerald's Guest-House,** a mile from the town centre of Abbey-feale on the N21, a farmhouse which is an exceptional example of the many child-friendly places to stay in Ireland. Ideally situated for visiting all the main attractions in the area, the farm itself has lots for youngsters to do; they can help feed the chickens, ducks, goats, rabbits, guinea pigs, lambs and birds, there's a nature trail, antique farm machinery and a small tea-room in a wonderful setting surrounded by farm animals, plus the opportunity to go pony-trekking.

Limerick is a very attractive city and has many fun things for kids to do. The **Peter Pan Fun World** in the Crescent Shopping Centre is a fully supervised indoor adventure playground for children of all ages. It has a special soft-play area for under-5s, and for the older children a couple of huge slides down into an enormous ball pond, plus a giant bouncy castle, a haunted cave, aerial glides, scrambling nets, log rolls and climbs, rope bridges and Captain Hook's hideout. The kids will be happy in here for hours while parents relax in the coffee bar or wander round the shopping centre. **Fun World** is a family entertainment centre on the Ennis road in Limerick. It has a bowling alley and a kiddies' adventure play area with soft-ball pool, slide and merry-go-round.

King John's Castle uses imaginative models and displays to interpret 800 years of history in Limerick and Ireland, while a most unusual attraction on the Shannon Estuary, 24 miles (39km) west of the city, is the **Foynes Flying Boat Museum,** which has some amazing souvenirs of the 1940s.

Access to the county is very good via mainline rail or bus. There is also a good network of main roads, plus airports near by at Shannon and Cork.

PLACES TO VISIT

Castles

GLIN CASTLE*
Glin
Tel: (+353) 068 34173/34112; Fax: (+353) 068 34364
Open: May and June, daily, 10a.m.–noon and 2p.m.–4p.m.
Admission: A=£££, C=£, F
Built in the 1780s, the castle has a unique collection of 18th-century furniture made by Irish craftsmen, together with beautiful formal gardens and a walled kitchen garden. The castle is guarded by 3 lodges, one of which is both a restaurant and craft shop.

KING JOHN'S CASTLE**
*Nicholas Street, King's Island, **Limerick***
Tel: (+353) 061 411201/361511; Fax: (+353) 061 472523
Open: mid-March to October, daily, 9.30a.m.–5.30p.m.; November to mid-March, Sunday, 11a.m.–4p.m.
Admission: A=£££, C=£, F
Facilities: toilets with disabled access; tea/coffee shop; shop
The restored King John's Castle in the heart of Limerick's medieval heritage precinct on King's Island attracts many visitors. Features include imaginative models and 3-D displays, an audio-visual show, excavated Norman houses and fortifications, copies of the war machines used before the advent of gunpowder or cannons, and battlement walkways along the castle's walls and towers.

Cathedrals

ST MARY'S CATHEDRAL***
*Bridge Street, **Limerick***
Tel: (+353) 061 416238/310393/413157; Fax: (+353) 061 315721
Open: summer, daily, 9a.m.–1p.m. and 2p.m.–5p.m.
The cathedral dominates a hill on King's Island, which was formerly the site of a palace for one of the Kings of Munster. It contains many fine antiques. Don't miss the fantastic sound and light show which takes place in the cathedral from mid-June to mid-September. The spectacular performance is held nightly from Monday to Friday at 9.15p.m. in this vast, historic building.

Cinemas

LIMERICK OMNIPLEX
*Beside the Crescent Shopping Centre, **Dooradoyle***
What's on: (+353) 061 305007;
Ticket office: (+353) 061 305405
Twelve-screen cinema complex.

SAVOY CINEMA COMPLEX
*Bedford Row, **Limerick***
Tel: (+353) 061 311900
Five screens plus 10-pin bowling.

Crèches

ARTHUR'S QUAY SHOPPING CENTRE
*Arthur's Quay, **Limerick***
Tel: (+353) 061 419888
Crèche and baby-care facilities.

CRESCENT SHOPPING CENTRE
*Dooradoyle, **Limerick***
Tel: (+353) 061 228560
Crèche and baby-care facilities.

Equestrian Facilities

ADARE EQUESTRIAN CENTRE
*Clongownagh, **Kildimo***
Tel: (+353) 061 396373
Offers trekking and tuition.

ASHROE RIDING CENTRE
*Ashroe House, **Murroe***
Tel: (+353) 061 378271
Trail rides and trekking along country lanes and forest tracks.

FITZGERALD'S HORSE AND PONY-TREKKING CENTRE
*Fitzgerald's Farm, **Abbeyfeale***
Tel: (+353) 068 31217
Open: Monday to Friday, noon–8.30p.m.; weekends, 9a.m.– 8.30p.m.
Accompanied trekking for all ages into the unspoilt countryside of
the Abbeyfeale hills (**see FARM PARKS *and* WHERE TO STAY**).

Farm Parks

BALLYNEETY PHEASANT FARM***
*Ballyneety; off route R512, 4 miles (6.5km) south of **Limerick***
Tel: (+353) 061 351607
Open: 1 April to 15 October, daily, 10a.m.–6p.m.
The farm is renowned for its collection of rare and colourful
pheasants from all over the world. Visitors can see chicks being
hatched and look into the incubators. The aviary is home to
many colourful birds. Children can feed and handle a range of
animals in the pets corner, or they can run freely in the safe
secure play area.

BUTTERCUP FARM***
*Ballygrennan, **Croom***
Tel: (+353) 061 397556
Open: seasonal, Monday to Saturday, 10a.m.–6p.m., Sunday, noon– 6p.m.
Admission: A=££, C=£, F
Facilities: disabled access; toilets with baby-changing facilities; pets

corner; children's play area; tree trail and nature quiz; picnic area; farmhouse refreshments

Lots of farm and domestic animals, birds and exotic breeds to amuse the children.

FITZGERALD'S FARM PETLAND***
Fitzgerald's Farm, **Abbeyfeale**
Tel: (+353) 068 31217
Open: daily, noon–8.30p.m.
Facilities: tea-room; nature trail
Bring your children here to see ducks, lambs, goats, chickens, birds, fish and rabbits. There's also an exhibition of antique farm machinery, and you can try pony-trekking on trails into the unspoilt countryside of the surrounding Abbeyfeale Hills (see EQUESTRIAN FACILITIES *and* WHERE TO STAY).

RYAN'S HONEY FARM***
Pallasgreen
Tel: (+353) 062 57147
Open: Easter to September (check direct for times)
A unique working honey farm with its own specially planted bee garden. Visitors can view the fascinating work of the honey bee and the various stages of honey production in the safety of an observatory. There's a shop selling honey and beeswax products.

SPRINGFIELD CASTLE DEER CENTRE****
Jonathan and Betty Sykes, Springfield, **Drumcollogher**
Tel: (+353) 063 83162; Fax: (+353) 063 83255
Open: June to August, daily, noon–6p.m.; September, Saturday and Sunday only, 1p.m.–6p.m.
Admission: A=££, C=£, F (includes a tractor tour to feed the deer)
Facilities: toilets with disabled access; baby-changing facilities; nature walks; children's playground; coffee shop (excellent); gift shop
The children will love the tractor trailer tour through herds of deer which are not afraid to come up close and feed from their hands. The farm also has lots of pet animals and birds.

Festivals and Events

ADARE GAME FAIR
Clonshire Equestrian Centre, **Adare**
On: first Sunday in May
The Game Fair has something for all the family, including a hound show, archery, art and craft exhibitions, Irish dancing and a funfair.

CHILDREN'S MUSIC FEST
University of Limerick Concert Hall, **Limerick** (see THEATRES AND MUSIC)

KILFINANE AUTUMN FESTIVAL
On: September
Tel: (+353) 063 91300; Fax: (+353) 063 91330

LOUGH GUR HALLOWEEN FESTIVAL***
Lough Gur
Tel: (+353) 061 385386

On: last weekend in October
Three days of storytelling, traditional music, song, dance, drama workshops, concerts, theatre, exhibitions and folklore. An excellent array of events in a wonderful setting.

POWERS IRISH COFFEE FESTIVAL
Foynes
On: August
Tel: (+353) 069 65416
Street entertainers, music, dance and exhibitions, plus water-based activities.

Forest and Amenity Walks

AUGHINISH ALUMINA NATURE TRAIL
*Aughinish Island, **Askeaton***
Tel: (+353) 061 604000
Open: all year round
A nature trail through some very interesting flora and fauna.

BALLYHOURA MOUNTAIN PARK
Ballyhoura Country Holidays; signposted from the R512
Tel: (+353) 063 91300
A natural park of woodland, rugged mountains, grouse moor and peat bog, with waymarked walks and nature trails.

CURRAGHCHASE FOREST PARK
***Kilcornan**; 14 miles (22km) west of Limerick on route N69 to Askeaton*
Tel: (+353) 061 337322; Fax: (+353) 061 338271
Open: all year round, daily, 9a.m.–dusk
The park has a choice of excellent forest walks and a nature trail around the wildlife lake. Has a carpark, picnic site, caravan and camping site, arboretum and gardens.

GALTEE CASTLE WOOD
*North of **Cork**, off the main Cork to Dublin road (N8)*
The Galtee Castle Wood has a series of interesting woodland and riverside walks. The castle is a preserved site and can be viewed together with the farm buildings and estate houses. There is a carpark and picnic site with seats on the riverside.

GREENWOOD
*On route R512, south-west of **Kilfinane***
The area has a lot of historic interest and a fine forest trail. There is a carpark, picnic site and viewing point.

Heritage Centres

ADARE HERITAGE CENTRE***
Adare
Tel: (+353) 061 396666; Fax: (+353) 061 396932
***Centre** open: September to May, daily, 9a.m.–6p.m.; June to August, daily, 9a.m.–10p.m.; **exhibition** open: March to October, daily*
Admission: A=££, C=£, F
Facilities: free parking; toilets with disabled access and baby-changing

facilities; restaurant; coffee shop; craft shop; tourist information office
The rich and varied history of Adare is told in a multimedia display which shows the development of the town from the 13th century and traces the significance of the Earls of Dunraven in shaping Ireland's most picturesque village.

CELTIC PARK AND GARDENS***
Kilcornan; on route N69, 10 miles (16km) from Limerick on the road to Tralee
Tel: (+353) 061 394243
Open: March to November, daily, 9a.m.–7p.m.
Admission: A=££, C=£, F (free for children under 12)
Facilities: disabled toilets; limited disabled access to park and gardens; souvenir shop; coffee shop
Celtic Park and Gardens are situated on what was once an original Celtic settlement and historically one of the most important Cromwellian plantations in the south-west of Ireland. The park has reconstructions of a dolmen, lake dwelling, ring fort, cooking site etc, all of which are associated with ancient Ireland.

CROOM MILLS WATERWHEEL AND HERITAGE CENTRE***
Croom
Tel: (+353) 061 397130; Fax: (+353) 061 397199
Open: all year round, daily, 8a.m.–6p.m. (till 5p.m. in winter)
Admission: A=££, C=£, F
Facilities: free parking; toilets with disabled access and baby-changing facilities; restaurant; craft and gift shop; picnic area and riverside walks
A visit to Croom Mills is a journey through country life in Ireland. The heritage centre recalls the history of flour milling and its impact on rural life in Croom and the surrounding area. The restaurant has a selection of home-cooked food and a children's menu.

LOUGH GUR INTERPRETATIVE CENTRE***
Holycross; off Kilmallock Road (R512), 16 miles (26km) south of Limerick
Tel: (+353) 061 360788
Open: May to September, daily, 10a.m.–6p.m.
Lough Gur introduces visitors to the habitat of Neolithic Man on one of Ireland's most important archaeological sites. Near the lake is an interpretative centre which, through an audio-visual presentation, models of stone circles, burial chambers and facsimiles of weapons, tools and pottery found in the area, tells the story of 5,000 years of human presence at the lough. You can also go on many interesting walking tours around the archaeological features of the area.

PLUNKETT HERITAGE CENTRE*
Dromcollogher
Tel: (+353) 063 83113
Open: May to September, daily, 10a.m.–6p.m. (open the rest of the year by appointment)
Facilities: free parking; audio-visual show; coffee shop
The first co-operative creamery was established here in 1889 by Sir Horace Plunkett. It has now been restored and is equipped with a working boiler, steam engine and other equipment of the era.

Leisure Centres and Adventure Playgrounds

FUNWORLD FAMILY ENTERTAINMENT CENTRE****
*Ennis Road, **Limerick***
Tel: (+353) 061 325088
You'll find all the latest state-of-the-art computer games here, along with 10 lanes of computerised bowling, and an adventure play area with a ball pool, merry-go-round and slides.

PETER PAN FUNWORLD****
*Crescent Shopping Centre, Dooradoyle, **Limerick***
Tel: (+353) 061 301033
Open: daily, 10a.m.–7p.m. (till 9p.m. on Thursday and Friday)
Admission: C=££
Facilities: toilets with baby-changing facilities; coffee bar
Soft-play area for under-5s with a ball pool, bouncy castle, playhouses, slides etc. Older children enter the maze of activity and adventure with tunnel slides, the snake slide, the haunted cave, Captain Hook's hideout, aerial glides, rope bridges and scramble nets, log climbs, crazy cubes etc. A great way for kids to get rid of surplus energy in a safe, supervised environment – I get tired just watching!

Museums and Galleries

ANNE FITZGERALD'S STUDIO AND GALLERY
*Mungret College, **Mungret***
Tel: (+353) 061 303022; Fax: (+353) 061 339995
Open: Monday to Saturday, 10.30a.m.–5.30p.m.
Anne Fitzgerald is internationally known for her illustrated series of 'Dear God Kids'. She is often available at the studio to do original 'Dear God' sketches for special occasions.

DOLMEN ART AND CRAFT GALLERY
*Honan's Quay, **Limerick***
Tel: (+353) 061 417929
Open: all year round
Paintings, sculpture, prints, drawings, ceramics etc, in a number of Irish and international exhibitions throughout the year. Large restaurant on site.

FOYNES FLYING BOAT MUSEUM****
Foynes
Tel/Fax: (+353) 069 65416
Open: daily, March to 31 October, 10a.m.–6p.m.
Facilities: toilets with disabled access and baby-changing facilities; parking; tea-room; souvenir shop; tourist information point
The famous flying boats frequented the port of Foynes during the 1930s and early 1940s, carrying passengers between America and Europe. The museum recalls this era with a good range of exhibits, illustrations and an audio-visual show. The main features are a '40s-style cinema, radio and weather room with original transmitters, receivers and Morse code equipment, and a '40s-style tea-room.

LIMERICK CITY MUSEUM*
*John's Square, **Limerick***

Tel: (+353) 061 417826
Open: all year round but phone to check for seasonal time changes
The museum, housed in 2 elegant stone buildings, boasts a comprehensive display illustrating the long and varied history of the city of Limerick and the surrounding area from the Stone Age to the present century.

Shopping Centres

ARTHUR'S QUAY CENTRE
Arthur's Quay, **Limerick**
Tel: (+353) 061 419888
Late opening on Thursday and Friday till 7p.m.
Secure multistorey parking. Crèche and baby-care facilities.

CRESCENT SHOPPING CENTRE
Dooradoyle, **Limerick**
Tel: (+353) 061 228560
Crèche and baby-care facilities.

PARKWAY SHOPPING CENTRE
Dublin Road, **Limerick**
Tel: (+353) 061 416144
Baby-changing facilities.

Swimming-Pools

ROXBORO SWIMMING-POOL
Roxboro, **Limerick**
Tel: (+353) 061 415799

MOYLISH LEISURE CENTRE
Beside the Thomond Park, **Limerick**
Tel: (+353) 061 415799

ST ENDA'S SPORTS CENTRE
Kilmallock Road, **Limerick**
Tel: (+353) 061 410310

Theatres and Music

BELLTABLE ARTS THEATRE***
69 O'Connell Street, **Limerick**
Tel: (+353) 061 319866; Fax: (+353) 061418552
Reputed to be the most active, alive and vital arts centre in the country, this 315-seat theatre hosts 48 weeks of performances a year. Shows include traditional Irish and classical concerts, contemporary dance, lunchtime recitals, poetry readings and, for children, drama workshops, pantomimes and magic shows. The centre also houses 2 exhibition areas and a restaurant.

UNIVERSITY OF LIMERICK CONCERT HALL***
Plassey
Tel: (+353) 061 331549; Fax: (+353) 061 331585
The largest purpose-built hall in Ireland hosts a wide range of

entertainment. The Limerick Summer Fest is held here in June with a variety of concerts including the Children's Music Fest.

Walks and Tours

BALLYHOURA WAY
This route is part of the O'Sullivan Beara trail and stretches 56 miles (90km) from John's Bridge in west Limerick to Limerick Junction in Co. Tipperary. An attractive and varied route, mostly on 'green roads', forest trails, droving paths, along riverbanks, across the wooded Ballyhoura mountains and through the Glen of Aherlow. Best suited to experienced hill-walkers and older children.

LIMERICK CITY TOURS
Tel: (+353) 061 311935
Guided walking tours of Limerick's medieval quarter start from the tourist office. Long-distance scenic walks and weekend walks by arrangement.

• • • • •

PLACES TO EAT

Cafés and Restaurants

SCRUMMY'S FOOD EMPORIUM
*St Nessan's Road, **Dooradoyle***
Tel: (+353) 061 228852
Wholesome, home-cooked food, reasonably prices and served in a family-friendlysetting.

THE ABBOT'S REST
*The Heritage Centre, **Adare***
Tel: (+353) 061 396449
A choice of charcoal grills and pizzas, served in the superb surroundings of the Adare Heritage Centre.

KRANKS KORNER
*Thomas Street, **Limerick***
Tel: (+353) 061 410023
Family restaurant serving burgers, pizzas, milk-shakes and ice-cream. Hot/cold deli.

JASMINE PALACE CHINESE RESTAURANT
*O'Connell Street, **Limerick***
Tel: (+353) 061 412484

MOLL DARBY'S RESTAURANT
*8 George's Quay, **Limerick***
Tel: (+353) 061 411511
An excellent menu with vegetarian options and home-made ice-creams. Children's menu and high-chair available. Families welcome.

O'GRADY'S CELLAR RESTAURANT
118 O'Connell Street, **Limerick**
Tel: (+353) 061 418286
Family-run traditional-style restaurant in the centre of the city. Extensive menu including children's meals. High-chair available. Families welcome.

SAILS RESTAURANT
Arthur's Quay Centre, **Limerick**
Tel: (+353) 061 416622
Meals and snacks to eat in or take away.

Fast-Food Restaurants

THE PINK POTATO
Main Street, **Adare**
Tel: (+353) 061 396723
Open: daily, 10.30a.m.–12.30am

McDONALD'S
Cruises Street, **Limerick**
Tel: (+353) 061 417111
and
Crescent Shopping Centre, **Limerick**
Tel: (+353) 061 303133

SUPERMAC'S
O'Connell Street, **Limerick**
Tel: (+353) 061 411449
Open: daily 7.30a.m.–4a.m.
and
Ennis Road, **Limerick** (Drive Thru)
Tel: (+353) 061 325100
Open: daily, 10a.m.–midnight

Hotels and Pubs

CASTLE LANE TAVERN
Nicholas Street, **Limerick**
Tel: (+353) 061 318044
Traditional riverside tavern with a friendly atmosphere and a good children's menu.

SEAN COLLINS'S BAR
Adare
Tel: (+353) 061 396400
A traditional bar with Irish music on Tuesday and Saturday nights. Excellent food served daily in the family restaurant.

PATRICK PUNCH'S BAR AND RESTAURANT
Punch's Cross, **Limerick**
Tel: (+353) 061 229588

WOODFIELD HOUSE HOTEL
Ennis Road, **Limerick**
Tel: (+353) 061 453022

Bar food and full range of traditional dishes. Children's menu and beer garden.

• • • • •

PLACES TO STAY

Country Houses and Hotels

CASTLE OAKS HOUSE HOTEL
Castleconnell
Tel: (+353) 061 377666; Fax: (+353) 061 377717
Superb Georgian mansion house with a country club and indoor heated swimming-pool. This is a family-friendly hotel set in a 25-acre estate on the banks of the River Shannon.

DEEBERT HOUSE
Kilmallock
Tel: (+353) 063 98106; Fax: (+353) 063 82002 (or contact Bally-houra Country Holidays – see Directory)
Delightful Georgian house with award-winning gardens. There is a games room, small playground and facilities for children. Baby-sitting and child-minding service available. Family-run restaurant on site. Self-catering accommodation also available.

FITZGERALD'S WOODLANDS HOUSE HOTEL
Knockane, Adare
Tel: (+353) 061 396118
Open: All year
Hotel and leisure centre with excellent facilities including supervised children's activities during peak times, creche, playroom and playgroound. Baby-sitting service available for an extra charge.

JURY'S HOTEL AND LEISURE CLUB***
Ennis Road, Limerick
Tel: (+353) 061327777; Fax: (+353) 061 326400
Open: All year
Hotel and leisure centre with family rooms, children's menus, swimming-pool and tennis court.

Farmhouse Accommodation

FITZGERALD'S FARMHOUSE AND EQUESTRIAN CENTRE*****
*Hill Road, **Abbeyfeale***
Tel/Fax: (+353) 068 31217 (or contact Irish Farm Holidays – see Directory)
Open: All year
Facilities: nature trail; Petland; display of old farm machinery; baby-sitting service; pony trekking and riding lessons
Luxury farmhouse on working farm just 1 mile from Abbeyfeale. An ideal place for families to stay, with pony-trekking and pet animals, a child-minding service and a coffee shop. The Fitzgerald

family are very welcoming, and children especially will enjoy staying here.

HILLGARE
Bruff *(contact Ballyhoura Country Holidays – see Directory)*
Dairy farm with organic produce, a pony for the children and a free child-minding service.

BALLYTEIGUE HOUSE
Bruree *(contact Ballyhoura Country Holidays – see Directory)*
Working farm with a garden for visitors, facilities for children and a baby-sitting service.

Self-Catering Apartments and Houses

DEEBERT HOUSE
Kilmallock
Tel: (+353) 063 98106; Fax: (+353) 063 82002 (or contact Bally-houra Country Holidays – see Directory)
Beautifully restored apartments on the ground floor of a delightful Georgian house. There is a games room, small playground, award-winning gardens and facilities for children. Baby-sitting and child-minding services available. Family-run restaurant on site.

SHANNONSIDE TOWN HOMES
*14 Rosehill, O'Callaghans Strand, **Limerick***
Tel: (+353) 061 326566; Fax: (+353) 061 326377
Award-winning luxury homes just 5 minutes' walk from the heart of Limerick. They are fully appointed and family-friendly. Baby-sitting by arrangement.

Caravan and Camping Parks

CURRAGHCHASE CARAVAN AND CAMPING PARK
*Curraghchase Forest Park, Kilcornan, **Pallaskenry;** 14 miles (22km) west of Limerick on route N69 to Askeaton*
Tel: (+353) 061 396349
Open: Easter to 31 October
Wonderful setting in the Curraghchase Forest Park (see FOREST PARKS).

Hostels

BARRINGTON LODGE
*George's Quay, **Limerick***
Tel: (+353) 061 415222; Fax: (+353) 061 416611
Open: all year round
Facilities: carpark; restaurant; launderette

CLYDE HOUSE
*St Alphonsus Street, **Limerick***
Tel: (+353) 061 314727/314357; Fax: (+353) 061 314234
Facilities: carpark; disabled facilities; breakfast room/coffee shop; games room; launderette

KILKREE LODGE
Clare Street, off Dublin Road, **Limerick**
Tel: (+353) 061 401288/401364; Fax: (+353) 061 401290
Open: all year round
Facilities: carpark; disabled facilities; coffee shop; games room; laundry

Bicycle Hire

IRISH CYCLE HIRE – *see Directory*
RALEIGH RENT-A-BIKE – *see Directory*

EMERALD CYCLES
1 Patrick Street, **Limerick**
Tel/Fax: (+353) 061 416983

McMAHONS CYCLEWORLD
25 Roches Street, **Limerick**
Tel/Fax: (+353) 061 415202; after 6p.m. Tel: (+353) 061 341353

THE BIKE SHOP
O'Connell Avenue, **Limerick**
Tel: (+353) 061 315900

Car Hire

DAN DOOLEY/KENNING RENT-A-CAR
Knocklong
Tel: (+353) 062 53103; Fax: (+353) 062 53392

CARA RENT-A-CAR
Coonagh Cross, Ennis Road, **Limerick**
Tel: (+353) 061 55811; Fax: (+353) 061 55369

TREATY RENT-A-CAR
37 William Street, **Limerick**
Tel: (+353) 061 416512; Fax: (+353) 061 412266

Bus Services

BUS EIREANN
Colbert Station, Parnell Street, **Limerick**
Bus Office – Tel: (+353) 061 418855
Travel Info – Tel: (+353) 061 313333
24-hour talking timetable – Tel: (+353) 061 319911

Rail Services

Colbert Station, Parnell St, **Limerick** *– Tel: (+353) 061 315555/418666*

COUNTY TIPPERARY

It is no wonder that people have long been singing the praises of Tipperary. The beautiful landscape makes it one of the most picturesque counties in Ireland. It has to be said, however, that apart from the scenery, most of the county's visitor attractions (either outdoor activities such as golfing, horseriding, walking and angling, or of historical interest such as the **Rock of Cashel**) are of little interest to children. But the largest inland county in Ireland is an ideal quiet base if you want to be free from crowds and travel on uncongested roads. The major attractions and beaches in adjacent counties are within easy reach and, contrary to the famous song associated with the county, it's not a long way to Tipperary!

The 12th-century town of Tipperary is very much as you would expect in this sleepy part of the country, but there are some good shops, pubs and restaurants here as well as the excellent **Canon Hayes Recreation Centre** and the recently refurbished **Sean Tracy Memorial Swimming-Pool.**

The route along the Tipperary side of Lough Derg travels through many delightful villages, each with its own atmosphere and charm. Ballina has a fine amenity area along the riverbank; Castlelough is one of the most charming places on the lakeshore and has a small sandy beach; and Dromineer is where watersports enthusiasts can windsurf, boat and swim. The **Charlie Swan Equestrian Centre** in Cloughjordan caters for riders of all levels of ability, and offers daily or residential sessions. At the **Bru Boru Heritage Centre,** adjacent to the Rock of Cashel, you will find folk theatre, music and art and craft exhibitions. Traditional Irish music and dance is provided for visitors in the summer by the famous resident group of musicians and artists.

Also near the Rock is the **Cashel Folk Village,** which gives the visitor a good perspective on Irish life in bygone days. West of Cashel is the **Dundrum Plantarum.** Set in 8 acres of trees and shrubs, the site has lakes and a waterfall. South-east of the town of Tipperary is **Cahir Castle,** one of Ireland's largest and best preserved castles. South-west of here is the **Mitchelstown Cave,** which has almost half a mile of underground caverns and chambers to explore.

To the east is **Fethard Folk, Farm and Transport Museum** with a wide range of exhibits to interest all ages, while in Ballynoran is the **Tipperary Crystal Craft** factory, a very interesting place to visit. The **Sean Kelly Sports Centre** in Carrick-on-Suir has a swimming-pool and indoor sports and leisure facilities.

Clonmel, Ireland's largest inland town, is situated on the banks of the River Suir, and has much to support its claim of being the best shopping town in the south-east. There's a large swimming-pool here plus an indoor adventure centre called **Jumpin' Jacks.** In the south of the county at Clogheen is the **Parsons Green Park and Pet Farm.**

The county is serviced by mainline rail and has an excellent network of good roads. Cork, Waterford and Shannon Airports are all within easy reach of the county.

PLACES TO VISIT

Boats and Boat Trips

SHANNON SAILING
New Harbour, Dromineer, **Nenagh**
Tel: (+353) 067 24499/24295; Fax: (+353) 067 33488
Waterbus cruises daily on Lough Derg, one of Ireland's pleasure lakes. Cruisers and yachts are also available for charter and hire.

Castles

CAHIR CASTLE***
Cahir
Tel: (+353) 052 41011
Open: April to mid-June, daily, 10a.m.–6p.m.; mid-June to mid-September, daily, 9a.m.–7.30p.m.; mid-September to mid-October, daily, 10a.m.–6p.m.; mid-October to March, daily, 10a.m.–1p.m. and 2p.m.–4.30p.m.
Admission: A=££, C=£, F
Facilities: toilets; shop; public parking close to the site
Set on a rocky island in the River Suir, Cahir Castle was one of the major strongholds of medieval Ireland. The impressive keep and tower and much of its original defensive structure are still standing. An excellent audio-visual show of the area can be seen.

ORMOND CASTLE*
Carrick-on-Suir
Tel: (+353) 051 640787
Open: mid-June to September, daily, 9.30a.m.–6.30p.m.
Admission: A=££, C=£, F
Facilities: free parking; shop; toilets
This 15th-century castle is fronted by an elegant 16th-century Elizabethan manor-house.

Caves

MITCHELSTOWN CAVE***
Burncourt; 10 miles (16km) south of **Cahir** *off the N8, Cahir to Mitchelstown road*
Tel: (+353) 052 67246
Open: all year round, daily, 10a.m.–6p.m.
Admission: A=££, C=£
Children will enjoy exploring the many caverns and 3 large chambers in this limestone show cave. Discovered in 1833, the caverns were named the 'House of Commons' by their former owner who used to show visitors around with a tilly lamp. Today the many features and huge calcite columns are dramatically lit and well worth seeing. The range of dripstone formations includes one of Europe's finest, the magnificent Tower of Babel. Remember that although it may be hot and sunny outside, the temperature

will be much lower in the cave so take a jacket or sweater with you.

Craft Centres

TIPPERARY CRYSTAL CRAFT***
*Parnell Street, **Clonmel**; on the N24 Clonmel to Carrick-on-Suir road*
Tel: (+353) 052 21399; Fax: (+353) 052 24355
Open: all year round, Monday to Saturday, 9a.m.–6p.m., Sunday (showroom only), 11a.m.–6p.m.
Admission: free
Facilities: free parking; toilets with baby-changing facilities; restaurant/café; shop; audio-visual display
Housed in 2 thatched cottages. Visitors to the display area and factory can watch glass being created by the age-old hand-crafted method of skilful blowing.

Equestrian Facilities

BANSHA HOUSE STABLES
*Bansha House, Bansha; 5 miles (8km) south from **Tipperary** off N24*
Tel: (+353) 062 54194/54533; Fax: (+353) 062 54215
Treks by the hour or by the day for both novices and experienced riders. Half-mile all-weather track for on-farm riding.

CAHIR EQUESTRIAN CENTRE***
*Grangemore, Ardfinnan Road, **Cahir***
Tel: (+353) 052 41426; Fax: (+ 353) 052 41428
Residential riding holiday offering pony-trekking through Cahir Park wildlife sanctuary to the famous 18th-century Swiss Cottage. All the trekking is supervised and tuition is available for beginners. Full-board residential riding is a speciality of the Hyland family and they welcome unaccompanied children (**see WHERE TO STAY**).

THE CHARLIE SWAN EQUESTRIAN CENTRE***
*Modreeny, **Cloughjordan***
Tel: (+353) 0505 42221
The centre caters for riders of all levels of ability on its all-weather track and cross-country course set in 200 acres of private parkland. Daily sessions ranging from individual lessons, cross-country riding, show jumping, schooling and horsemanship classes are available with the emphasis being on entertainment, fun and good riding. Accommodation is available (**see WHERE TO STAY**).

Farm Parks

PARSONS GREEN PARK AND PET FARM
Clogheen
Tel: (+353) 052 65290
Open: April to September, daily, 10a.m.–8p.m.
Admission: A=££, C=£, F
Facilities: toilets; garden and river walks; picnic area
Well-laid-out farm park with plenty to see and do. Children will love the many attractions set in beautiful countryside such as the garden and river walks, the farm museum, pet field, pony and trap

rides, boat rides, 18-hole crazy golf course, tennis and basketball courts and picnic area. There's also a caravan and camping park, and self-catering apartments available.

Forest and Amenity Walks

BANSHA WOODS
Four miles (6.5km) from **Tipperary** *on route N24 to Cahir*
Facilities: carpark; picnic site; viewing point; forest walks

BISHOP'S WOOD
On the Thurles road, just north of **Dundrum**
Facilities: carpark; picnic area

CAHIR PARK
Near **Cahir**
Facilities: carpark; picnic site; river walks; fishing
There is a nice walk to Swiss Cottage here and pony-trekking in the woods (**see** EQUESTRIAN FACILITIES).

CASTLELOUGH
Near Portroe; 3 miles (5km) west of **Nenagh** *off route R494*
Facilities: carpark; picnic site
Come here to enjoy excellent lakeside and forest walks, cruises and watersports on the nearby River Shannon.

GLENGARRA WOOD
Nine miles (15km) west of **Cahir** *on route N8 to Mitchelstown*
Facilities: carpark; picnic sites; forest and riverside walks

GORTAVOHER
Three miles (5km) south of **Tipperary** *on route R664*
Facilities: carpark; picnic site
Wild pigs used to roam through this area, which was once completely covered in oak woods. Good viewpoints.

KILBALLYBOY WOOD
Just south-east of **Clogheen** *on route R668 to Lismore*
Facilities: carpark and an excellent picnic site with seats on the riverside

MARL BOG
On route R661, Tipperary to Thurles road, just south of **Dundrum**
Facilities: carpark; forest and lakeside trails

STEP FOREST
Three miles (5km) from **Nenagh** *off R499 through Silvermines village*
Facilities: carpark; picnic site; fishing
The walks here are along mountain trails.

Gardens

DUNDRUM PLANTARUM***
Dundrum, *west of Cashel on the R505*
Tel/Fax: (+353) 062 71526
Open: All year round, daily, 9a.m.–dusk

Admission: A=££, C=free
Facilities: free parking; disabled access; toilets with disabled access and baby-changing facilities; shop; café; picnic area; play area
With over 60,000 trees and shrubs, historic artefacts, a dolmen, crannog and a fort, excellent walks, a lake, waterfall and a play area this is a super place to visit on a sunny day with the family.

Heritage Centres

BRU BORU HERITAGE CENTRE****
Cashel
Tel: (+353) 062 61122; Fax: (+353) 062 62700
Open: April to mid-June, Monday to Friday, 9a.m.–6p.m.; mid-June to mid-September, daily, 9a.m.–11p.m.; mid-September to March, Monday to Friday, 9a.m.–5p.m.
Shows: mid-June to mid-September, Tuesday and Saturday, 9p.m.
Admission to theatre show: A and C=£££££
Facilities: parking; disabled access; toilets; baby-changing facilities; craft centre; folk theatre; information centre; restaurant
Bru Boru is a national heritage centre at the foot of the Rock of Cashel. This cultural village is a place to study Irish music, dance, song, theatre and Celtic studies. The famous Bru Boru group provide visitors with a display of traditional Irish music, song and dance during the summer months which is well worth seeing. All the family will enjoy this theatre presentation.

CARRICK-ON-SUIR HERITAGE CENTRE*
*Main Street, **Carrick-on-Suir***
Tel: (+353) 051 40200
Open: January to April and October to December, Monday to Friday, 2p.m.–4p.m.; May to September, Monday to Saturday, 10a.m.–5p.m.
Admission: A=£, C=free
Housed in a former church, the centre has a series of displays, photographs and posters depicting the colourful past of Carrick-on Suir and the surrounding area

CASHEL FOLK VILLAGE***
*Dominic Street, **Cashel***
Tel: (+353) 052 61947
Open: March to April, daily, 10a.m.–6p.m.; May to October, daily, 9.30a.m.–7.30p.m.
Admission: A=££, C=£, F
Facilities: toilets with disabled access; parking
Gives the visitor a good perspective on Irish life in bygone days. The village consists of thatched 18th-, 19th- and 20th-century dwellings including a pub, kitchen, butcher's shop, blacksmith's forge, tool and trades exhibition and museum looking at penal times, the Great Famine, the 1916 rising and the War of Independence.

NENAGH HERITAGE CENTRE***
*Governor's House, **Nenagh***
Tel: (+353) 067 32633
Open: April to September, Monday to Friday, 9.30a.m.–5p.m., Sunday, 2.30p.m.–5p.m.; guided tours at 11.30a.m. and 2.30p.m.
Admission: A=££, C=£, F

This interesting centre is in the governor's house and gatehouse of the former county gaol. Exhibits take a look at life in the gaol, while the museum of rural and prison life has hands-on displays in the shop, schoolroom, kitchen, dairy and forge. There are 3-D models of the gaol. The building also houses a family history research centre which conducts research on a fee basis.

ROSCREA HERITAGE CENTRE*
Roscrea
Tel: (+353) 0505 21850
Open: June to September, daily, 9.30a.m.–6p.m.
Admission: A=££, C=£, F
The 13th-century castle consists of a gate tower and 2 corner towers. In the courtyard is the 18th-century Damer House.

THE ROCK OF CASHEL***
Cashel
Tel: (+353) 062 61437
Open: mid-March to June, daily, 9.30a.m.–5.30p.m.; June to September, daily, 9.00a.m.–7.30p.m.; September to March, daily, 9.30a.m.–4.30p.m.
Admission: A=££, C=£
Facilities: free parking; toilets; shop; audio-visual show
This is one of Ireland's great historic sites: a remarkable crop of limestone rising 200ft and capped with a spectacular group of medieval buildings. The ruins include a round tower, a romanesque chapel and a cathedral. Well worth visiting along with the nearby Bru Boru Heritage Centre.

Leisure Centres and Adventure Playgrounds

CANON HAYES RECREATION CENTRE**
Tipperary
Tel: (+353) 062 52022; Fax: (+353) 062 33140
Open: Monday to Thursday, 10a.m.–11p.m., Friday and Saturday, 10a.m.–10p.m., Sunday, 10a.m.–6p.m.
Facilities: coffee lounge; baby-changing facilities; crèche facilities, Monday to Friday, 10a.m.–12.30p.m.
Lots of sporty things to do – outdoor floodlit tennis courts, multi-purpose main hall, squash courts, gymnasium and table-tennis.

JUMPIN' JACKS****
Ormond Court, Prior Park, **Clonmel**
Tel: (+353) 052 25015
Open: Monday to Thursday, 10a.m.–6p.m., Friday to Sunday, 10a.m.–7p.m.
Admission: ££ per hour
Facilities: fully supervised; soft-play area for under-5s; tea/coffee area and mineral bar; toilets; crèche and baby-changing facilities
This is a fully supervised play area with a separate soft-play section for the under-5s. Older kids have an aerial glide, giant ball pool, tube slide, net climb and bridge etc. There's also a video room with children's films and cartoons showing all day.

Museums

FETHARD FOLK, FARM AND TRANSPORT MUSEUM***
*On the Cashel road (R892) near **Fethard***
Tel: (+353) 052 31516
Open: June to August, daily, 10a.m.–6p.m., September to November and
February to May, Sunday, 1.30p.m.–6p.m.
Admission: A=£, C=£
Facilities: disabled access; free parking; toilets with disabled access;
tea/coffee shop; children's play area and picnic areas
Located in an 1879 railway goods store near the historic walled
town of Fethard, this museum has over 2,000 exhibits ranging from
folk life to farm life, plus transport from bygone days. The kids will
particularly enjoy the play area.

TIPPERARY COUNTY MUSEUM*
*Parnell Street, **Clonmel***
Tel: (+353) 052 21399
Open: Tuesday to Saturday
Admission: free
The museum has a collection of over 10,000 items and a
permanent art display. No wheelchair access.

Parks

TEMPLEMORE TOWN PARK***
Templemore
In the 70-acre town park are the remains of Templemore Abbey
and Black Castle as well as a swimming-pool and a large lake
providing good fishing.

Swimming-Pools

Clonmel *Swimming-Pool – Tel: (+353) 052 21972*
Open: daily, 10a.m.–7p.m.; baby-changing facilities

Nenagh *indoor heated swimming-pool – Tel: (+353) 067 31788*

SEAN KELLY SPORTS CENTRE AND SWIMMING-POOL
Carrick-on-Suir
Tel: (+353) 051 640955
Open: Monday to Friday, 10a.m.–10p.m., weekends, 10a.m.–8p.m.
Swimming-pool and full indoor sports and leisure facilities.

SEAN TRACY MEMORIAL SWIMMING-POOL
*Adjacent to the Canon Hayes Recreation Centre, **Tipperary,** Tel: (+353)*
062 52022

There is an excellent open-air swimming-pool in ***Ballina**.– Tel:*
(+353) 096 70506

Templemore *Swimming-Pool, Templemore Town Park – Tel: (+353)*
0504 31138

PLACES TO EAT

Cafés and Restaurants

THE GALTEE INN
Cahir
Tel: (+353) 052 41247
Children's menu and high-chair available.

ROMA CAFE AND TAKE-AWAY
*Church Street, **Cahir***
Tel: (+353) 052 41504
Open: daily, noon–1 a.m.

CRANLEYS RESTAURANT
*7 St Michael's Street, **Tipperary***
Tel: (+353) 062 33917
Open: daily, noon–3p.m., and 5.30p.m.–10.30p.m.

MANDARINE PALACE CHINESE RESTAURANT
*3 Blind Street, **Tipperary***
Tel: (+353) 062 33168
Open: daily, 5.30p.m.–12.30a.m.
Eat-in or take-away service.

Fast-food Restaurants
SUPERMAC'S
*The Square, **Thurles***
Tel: (+353) 0504 21825

*Main Street, **Rosecrea***
Tel: (+353) 0505 22746

*Pearse Street, **Nenagh***
Tel: (+353) 067 31833

McDONALD'S
*8–9 Gladstone Street, **Clonmel***
Tel: (+353) 052 28181

*Carrig Roundabout, **Rosecrea** (Drive-through)*
Tel: (+353) 0505 23681

Hotels and Pubs

ABBEY TAVERN
Cahir
Tel: (+353) 052 41326/42085
A good selection of soups and sandwiches are served here. Traditional Irish music is played on Wednesday and Saturday, and there's a pool room and video games.

SHAMROCK LOUNGE
*Castle Street, **Cahir***
Tel: (+353) 052 41423
Home-made soups, sandwiches, snacks and all-day lunches.

MULCAHY'S
*Market Street, **Clonmel***
Tel: (+353) 052 25054; Fax: (+353) 052 24544
Self-service carvery serving hot and cold dishes from 10.30a.m. to
6p.m.; Irish dishes and *à la carte* menu in the restaurant from 6p.m.

● ● ● ● ●

PLACES TO STAY

Country Houses and Hotels

ASHLEY PARK HOUSE
Nenagh
Tel: (+353) 067 38223
Open: all year round
Country house overlooking the lake, with a children's playground
and playroom. Baby-sitting available (extra charge for this service).

GRANGEMORE HOUSE AND CAHIR EQUESTRIAN CENTRE
*The Hyland family, Ardfinnan Road, **Cahir***
*Tel: (+353) 052 41426; Fax: (+353) 052 41428 (or contact Irish
Farm Holidays – see Directory)*
Open: all year round
Facilities for children plus pony-trekking through Cahir Park, residen-
tial riding holidays and bicycle hire.

CHARLIE SWAN EQUESTRIAN CENTRE
*Captain and Mrs Donald Swan, Modreeny, **Cloughjordan***
*Tel: (+353) 0505 42221; Fax: (+353) 0505 42128 (or contact Irish
Farm Holidays – see Directory)*
Open: all year round
This Georgian family home (complete with the ruins of a 16th-
century castle) is an ideal holiday base for families. Facilities include
horseriding and instruction, residential riding holidays, a children's
games room, garden and swimming-pool.

BALLINACOURTY HOUSE
*C. and M. Stanley, **Glen of Aherlow***
Tel/Fax: (+353) 062 56230
Family-friendly house with many facilities including a children's play-
room, tennis and pitch'n'putt. Baby-sitting by arrangement.

THE GLEN HOTEL
***Glen of Aherlow** (contact Ballyhoura Country Holidays – see
Directory)*
The hotel has facilities for children and has a baby-sitting service.

Farmhouse Accommodation

DUALLA HOUSE
*Mrs Mairead Power, **Cashel***
Tel/Fax: (+353) 062 61487
Family-friendly accommodation. Baby-sitting available.

TIR NA FIUISE
*Niall and Inez Heenan, Borrisokane, **Terryglass***
Tel/Fax: (+353) 067 22041 (or contact Irish Farm Holidays – see Directory)
Open: Easter to end September
There's a farm museum, walks on the farm and bog, and bicycles and boats to be hired.

Self-Catering Apartments and Houses

BANSHA
*Mrs Walsh, **Glen of Aherlow** (contact Ballyhoura Country Holidays – see Directory)*
Country cottage set in its own grounds. Children welcome; baby-sitting service available.

WATERSIDE COTTAGES
*Dromineer Bay, **Nenagh***
Tel: (+353) 067 24432
Open: All year
Holiday homes set in fabulous grounds on the lake shore in the village of Dromineer. Boats and bikes for hire.

ARDMAYLE HOUSE
*Annette V. Hunt, Ardmayle, **Cashel***
Tel: (+353) 0504 42399; Fax: (+353) 0504 42420
Luxury self-catering accommodation in an attractive old limestone house. Golf, horseriding, pitch'n'putt and fishing on the River Suir all available to guests.

Caravan and Camping Parks

BALLINACOURTY HOUSE CARAVAN AND CAMPING PARK
Glen of Aherlow
Tel/Fax: (+353) 062 56230 (or contact Ballyhoura Country Holidays – see Directory)
Scenic location in mature gardens with pets corner, games room, tennis court, shop and crazy golf. Baby-sitting by arrangement.

Hostels

LISAKYLE HOSTEL
*Lisakyle, **Cahir***
Tel: (+353) 052 41963
Open: all year round

KILCORAN FARM HOSTEL
*Kilcoran, **Cahir***

Tel: (+353) 052 41906; Fax: (+353) 052 36141
Open: all year round

CASHEL HOLIDAY HOSTEL
*6 John Street, **Cashel***
Tel: (+353) 062 62330; Fax: (+353) 062 62445
Open: all year round

O'BRIEN'S FARM HOSTEL
*St Patrick's Rock, Dundrum Road, **Cashel***
Tel: (+353) 062 61003
Open: all year round

Bicycle Hire

IRISH CYCLE HIRE – see *Directory*
RALEIGH RENT-A-BIKE – see *Directory*

OK SPORTS
*New Street, **Carrick-on-Suir***
Tel: (+353) 051 640626

J. MOYNAN & CO LTD
*61 Pearse Street, **Nenagh***
Tel/Fax: (+353) 067 31293

Car Hire

WOODVIEW CAR AND VAN RENTALS
*Mitchelstown Road, **Cahir***
Tel: (+353) 052 41529

Bus Services

BUS EIREANN
*Rafferty Travel, **Tipperary***
Tel: (+353) 062 51555

Rail Services

***Cahir** – Tel: (+353) 052 41578*
***Carrick-on-Suir** – Tel: (+353) 051 640044*
***Clonmel** – Tel: (+353) 052 21982*
***Nenagh** – Tel: (+353) 067 31232*
***Roscrea** – Tel: (+353) 0505 21823*
***Templemore** – Tel: (+353) 0504 31342*
***Thurles** – Tel: (+353) 0504 21733*
***Tipperary** – Tel: (+353) 062 51206*

COUNTY WATERFORD

Attractive fishing villages, Blue Flag resorts and a scenic coastline all mean County Waterford has much to offer visitors of all ages. Nestling in the south-east of Ireland, the county is surrounded by water, stretching between the rivers Barrow, Suir and Nore at its eastern boundary, to the famous River Blackwater in the west. A long coastline – golden beaches, sheltered coves, rocky peninsulas, towering cliffs and deep caves – washed by the Atlantic forms its southern boundary. Inland, gentle grassland plains and scenic river valleys, landscaped with castles, cathedrals and steeped in history, are framed by the rugged mountain ranges of the Knockmealdowns, Monavullagh and the Comeraghs, full of spectacular corries and waterfalls. Waterford's Blue Flag beaches are located at Dunmore near Tramore, Clonea near Dungarvan and the historic seaside village of Ardmore.

The historic city of Waterford is a bustling maritime place, full of colour and excitement. Its busy streets and small lanes have plenty of fascinating shops, museums and heritage centres. This is a wonderful place to spend a day just browsing around the shops, visiting historic attractions, and sampling lots of traditional Irish food and culture. One of the best ways of seeing the city and the major tourist attractions is to take a **guided walking tour.**

No visit to Waterford would be complete without a trip to the **Waterford Crystal** factory. The workers have a long tradition of extending a warm welcome to visitors of all ages. The factory tour is interesting and educational, and the audio-visual presentation shows the history of the ancient craft of glassmaking.

Just 9 miles (14.5km) south of the city is Tramore, the main seaside resort in the county for children's attractions. This is the place most youngsters will want to be – it has 3 miles of golden sandy beach. If you prefer to swim indoors, there's the magnificent **Splashworld** aqua leisure centre with its water slides, wave machine and bubble pools. **Celtworld** is an exciting multimedia experience of magic, mystery and mythology that will take you on a fascinating journey back through the ages to a time when legends lived. And for the ultimate in special effects and high technology set in a unique Celtic maze, **Laserworld** is the place to be. If it's white-knuckle rides that you're looking for, Tramore's 50-acre amusement park is the place to visit. North of Dungarvan on the way to Clonmel is the **Touraneena Heritage Centre,** while west of Dungarvan is the beautiful town of Lismore. Standing on the Blackwater River, Lismore is a historic seat of learning, rich in natural beauty and architectural splendour. The **Old Courthouse** has an interesting multimedia presentation which will allow you to experience the rich history of the town and its surroundings. South of Dungarvan is the historic seaside village of Ardmore, which offers the best of all worlds for both parents and children; its beautiful bay and sandy shore are overlooked by a 12th-century round tower, one of the best examples in Ireland. Ardmore is the oldest Christian settlement in Ireland, founded by St Declan in AD416, before the arrival of St Patrick. According to legend, a stone was miraculously carried on the waves across the sea from Wales following St Declan's visit there. Bridged by two supporting stones, St Declan's Stone is now visited by devotees who drag themselves beneath it in prayer on Pattern Day (24 July) every year, believing they will receive health or spiritual benefits.

Access throughout the county is excellent by road (via routes N9, N24 and N25) and public transport via mainline rail, Bus Eireann and Waterford Airport.

• • • • •

PLACES TO VISIT

Amusement Arcades and Funfairs

TRAMORE AMUSEMENT PARK****
Tramore
Fifty acres of fun and carnival atmosphere for all the family. Spectacular white-knuckle rides plus arcades and a boating lake.

Boats and Boat Trips

PASSAGE EAST CAR FERRY
Tel: (+353) 051 382480
Continuous service operating every 10 minutes, linking Passage East with Ballyhack in County Wexford.

Craft Centres

WATERFORD CRYSTAL****
*Kilbarry, Cork Road, **Waterford***
Tel: (+353) 051 373311; Fax: (+353) 051 378539
Open: April to October, daily tours, 8.30a.m.–4p.m. (showrooms, 8.30a.m.–6p.m.); November to March, Monday to Friday, tours, 9a.m.– 3.15p.m. (showrooms, 9a.m.–5p.m.)
Charges for tour: A=£££, free for children under 12
Facilities: disabled access and toilets; toilets with baby-changing facilities; coffee shop; audio-visual theatre
Visitors from all over the world come here to marvel at the skills of Waterford's peerless craftsmen using modern technology plus the traditional skills of master blowers, cutters and engravers. The factory tour is an amazing experience, and one that both adults and children will enjoy. Each manufacturing process is clearly shown as you watch. It is a great credit to these workers that they can be so friendly and work to such a high standard while constantly under the gaze of the many visitors – over 250,000 annually – that pass so close to their work stations.

Equestrian Facilities

COLLIGAN EQUESTRIAN CENTRE
*Crough, Colligan; 3 miles (5km) from **Dungarvan***
Tel: (+353) 058 68261
Open: all year round
Outdoor and indoor arenas. Daily or hourly treks for all ages.

FINISK VALLEY RIDING CENTRE
Kilmolash Bridge Farmhouse, Kilmolash Bridge; 4 miles (6.5km) south of
Cappoquin
Tel: (+353) 024 96257
Open: all year round
Residential riding centre with excellent facilities. Free refreshments
are provided after the pony-treks and ride-outs.

KILOTTERAN EQUESTRIAN CENTRE
*Kilotteran; 4 miles (6.4km) from **Waterford***
Tel: (+353) 051 384158; Fax: (+353) 051 384712
Open: all year round
Treks and rides for all ages and standards. Tuition available.

LAKE TOUR STABLES
*Carrigavantry; 2 miles (3.2km) from **Tramore***
Tel: (+353) 051 381958
Open: all year round
The centre offers 1- or 2-hour treks for riders of all standards and
age groups, through scenic countryside and along the shores of
Ballyscanlan Lakes. During the off season they offer beach trekking
along 3 miles (4.8km) of sandy beach.

MELODY'S NIRE VALLEY EQUESTRIAN CENTRE
*Nire View, **Ballymacarbry;** on route R671/R672 Dungarvan to Clonmel*
Tel: (+353) 052 36147
Open: all year round
The centre caters for both novices and experienced riders, offering
short forest treks and half-week and full-week programmes over
well-chosen, scenic trails.

Forest and Amenity Walks

BALLYSCANLAN
*Four miles (6.5km) west of **Tramore** off route R675 to Dungarvan*
Facilities: carpark; picnic site; forest and lakeside walks
Coniferous woodland overlooking Ballyscanlan Lake.

CAREY'S CASTLE
*Two miles (3.2km) south of **Clonmel** off route R671 to Dungarvan*
Picnic site close to carpark, riverside walks and a walk through
mixed woodland to Carey's Castle.

GLENSHELANE
*Near **Cappoquin***
Facilities: carpark; picnic site; river and forest walks

KILCLOONEY WOOD

*Nine miles (15km) south of **Carrick-on-Suir** on route R676*
Facilities: picnic site; forest and lakeside walks
Nearby in the Comeragh mountains are the popular attractions of Coumshingaun Lake, Crotty's Lake and Crotty's Rock.

KNOCKAUN VALLEY

*Eight miles (13km) south from **Clonmel** off route R671 to Dungarvan*
Picnic site and forest walks deep in the heart of the Comeragh mountains, in whose famous caves Crotty the Robber lived.

Gardens

CARRIGAHILLA HOUSE AND GARDENS
Stradbally
Tel: (+353) 051 93127
Open: all year round (during daylight hours)
Refreshments available all day.

CURRAGHMORE**
Portlaw
Tel: (+353) 051 87101
Open: Easter to October, Thursdays and bank holidays only, 2p.m.–5p.m.
Admission: Grounds only, ££
Acres of beautiful grounds of parkland and gardens with the impressive Curraghmore House set amidst ancient oak woodlands. Hidden among the shrubbery is a most enchanting shellhouse created by Catherine, Countess of Tyrone, in 1754.

LISMORE CASTLE GARDENS
Lismore
Tel: (+353) 058 54424
Open: mid-May to mid-September, daily
Admission: A=££, C=£
Lismore Castle is the birthplace of the eminent scientist Robert Boyle and was once home to Sir Walter Raleigh. You can wander through the enchanting castle gardens in the footsteps of famous poets such as Spencer, Thackeray and Betjeman.

Heritage Centres

CELTWORLD****
Tramore
Tel: (+353) 051 386166; Fax: (+353) 051 390146
Open: mid-April to end May, Monday to Friday, 10a.m.–5p.m., weekends, 11a.m.–6p.m.; June, daily, 10a.m.–8p.m.; July and August, daily, 10a.m.–10p.m.; September, daily, 10a.m.–6p.m.
Admission: A=££££, C=£££, F
Facilities: disabled access; free parking; toilets; baby-changing facilities
Stunning audio-visual and special-effects technology are used to introduce visitors to the Celtic myths and legends of early Ireland. This hi-tech wizardry is a magical experience for children.

LISMORE HERITAGE CENTRE**
*The Courthouse, **Lismore***
Tel: (+ 353) 058 54975
Open: April, May and September, Monday to Friday, 10a.m.–5p.m.,
Sunday, 2p.m.–5.30p.m.; June to August, Monday to Friday, 9.30a.m.–
5.30p.m., Sunday, 12.30p.m.–5.30p.m.; October, Sunday only, 2p.m.–
5.30p.m.
Admission: A=££, C=£, F
Facilities: disabled access and toilets; shop
The story of Lismore since AD636 is told in an award-winning
audio-visual presentation.

TOURANEENA HERITAGE CENTRE****
*Touraneena, **Ballinamult**; 12 miles (19km) from Dungarvan on route*
R672 to Clonmel
Tel/Fax: (+353) 058 47353
Open: May to October, daily, 10a.m.–7p.m.
Admission: A=£££, C=£, F
Facilities: toilets with baby-changing facilities; gift shop; tea-room; picnic
area; adventure playground; pet farm, pony and tractor rides
This is a 300-year-old thatched farm, depicting traditional Irish life in
the 1890s. Visitors can take part in demonstrations of bread- and
scone-baking over a turf fire, using original pots in the farmhouse
kitchen, or try butter-making in the dairy. There's a blacksmith's
forge, gypsy wagon, stable loft, hatchery and pet farm. All in all, lots
of interesting and fun things to see and do here for all the family –
including Irish dancing on Sunday afternoons in July and August.

Leisure Centres and Adventure Playgrounds

FUNDERWORLD***
*Cork Road, **Waterford***
Tel: (+353) 051 71117
Open: daily
Fully supervised adventureland with 10 full-size bowling alleys, video
games and a coffee bar.

LASERWORLD***
Tramore
Tel: (+353) 051 386565
Open: mid-April to end May, Monday to Friday, 10a.m.–5p.m.,
weekends, 11a.m.–6p.m.; June, daily, 10a.m.–8p.m.; July and August,
daily, 10a.m.–10p.m.; September, daily, 10a.m.–6p.m.
The ultimate in special effects and high-technology laser games.

Museums

REGINALD'S TOWER AND WATERFORD HERITAGE MUSEUM**
*The Quay, **Waterford***
Tel: (+353) 051 73501; Fax: (+353) 051 79124
Open: April to May and September to October, daily, 10a.m.–5p.m.;
June to August, daily, 8.30a.m.–8.30p.m.
Admission charges combined: A=££, C=£, F
Facilities: shop; toilets
A tower on this site has protected the quays of Waterford for over

1,000 years. The present tower, dating from the 12th century, is the oldest urban civic building in the country. The museum houses 2 fascinating collections showing artefacts from the Viking and medieval periods and decorated royal charters and civic regalia.

Parks

PEOPLE'S PARK
Waterford
Over 16 acres of well-established parkland with play areas for kids.

Shopping Centres

CITY SQUARE SHOPPING CENTRE
Waterford
Tel: (+353) 051 53528; Fax: (+353) 051 53554
Facilities: toilets with baby-changing facilities
Department stores, supermarkets and restaurants, with late-night shopping on Thursday and Friday.

Swimming Pools

SPLASHWORLD****
Tramore
Tel: (+353) 051 390176; Fax: (+353) 051 390214
Open: seasonal, 10a.m.–10p.m.
Admission: A=£££, C=££, F
Facilities: disabled access; toilets with baby-changing facilities; café with children's menu
This aqua adventure playground is a must for all the family. There are waterslides, a wave machine, bubble pools and a river ride to enjoy, followed by refreshments in Bluebeard's cafe which overlooks all the action. **Note: children under 10 must be accompanied by an adult, and swimming hats must be worn in the pool.**

Walks and Tours

ARDMORE HERITAGE TRAIL
Ardmore
A 3-mile (5km) waymarked walk around the many heritage sites surrounding this picturesque fishing village. The walk includes a cliff path – extra care will need to be taken of younger children.

WATERFORD WALKING TOURS***
*Jenkins Lane, **Waterford***
Tel: (+353) 051 73711; Fax: (+353) 051 50645
Open: March to October, daily tours, noon and 2p.m.
Charges: A=£££
A 1-hour walking tour around the city, taking in historical monuments, cathedrals and a gallery of rogues and rascals. Walks start from the foyer of the Granville Hotel.

PLACES TO EAT

Cafés and Restaurants

MAXIM HOUSE CHINESE RESTAURANT
8 O'Connell Street, Waterford
Tel: (+353) 051 75820
Children's menu and take-away service available.

Fast-Food Restaurants

ABRAKABABRA
41 Michael Street, Waterford
Tel: (+353) 051 850220
Open: daily, noon–3.30a.m.
Just say the magic word for a selection of fast food!

McDONALD'S
Cork Road, Waterford (Drive-through)
Tel: (+353) 051 350202
Open: daily, 8a.m.–12.30a.m., Sunday, 9a.m.–12.30a.m.

Barronstrand Street, Waterford
Tel: (+353) 051 843939

SUPERMAC'S
Barronstrand Street, Waterford
Tel: (353) 051 54521
Open: daily, 10a.m.–midnight

Hotels and Pubs

THE GRANARY
73 O'Connell Street, Waterford
Tel: (+353) 051 75043
Excellent selection of home-cooked food served all day in a
welcoming, traditional Irish pub with a wonderful atmosphere.
Traditional music can be heard most nights during the main season.

THE OLDE STAND
45 Michael Street, Waterford
Tel: (+353) 051 79488
Excellent selection of food including a lunchtime carvery, a salad bar
and home-made soup and sandwiches.

JACK MEADES PUB***
Under the Bridge, Cheekpoint Road, 4 miles (6.4km) from Waterford
Tel: (+353) 051 73187/50950
The scenic surrounds have been tastefully converted into natural
beer gardens, walks and a play area making this an excellent place

to visit with the children. Outdoor music and a barbecue on Sunday afternoons in summer add to the atmosphere (weather permitting).

• • • • •

PLACES TO STAY

Country Houses and Hotels

THE OLD SCHOOL HOUSE
Ballymacarbry
Tel: (+353) 052 36217
Homely guest-house where guests can go walking and horseriding; and there's a children's playroom and a baby-sitting service.

ASHGROVE
Dunmore East
Tel: (+353) 051 383195
Country home in a scenic setting. There's a children's playroom, and a baby-sitting service.

CANDLELIGHT INN HOTEL
Dunmore East
Tel: (+353) 051 383215; Fax: (+353) 051 383289
Family-run hotel overlooking the bay at Dunmore East. There's an outdoor heated swimming-pool and a tennis court.

WATERFORD MANOR HOTEL
*Kilotteran, 4 miles (6.4km) from **Waterford***
Tel: (+353) 051 77814; Fax: (+353) 051 54545
Guests can use the tennis courts, snooker room, golf driving-range and indoor heated swimming-pool.

TOWER HOTEL
*The Mall, **Waterford***
Tel: (+353) 051 75801; Fax: (+353) 051 70129
Facilities include a leisure centre complete with heated swimming-pool.

Farmhouse Accommodation

NEWTOWN VIEW
*Mrs Teresa O'Connor, Grange, **Ardmore;** off route N25, Dungarvan to Youghal road*
Tel/Fax: (+353) 024 94143 (or contact Irish Farm Holidays – see Directory)
Open: Easter to mid-October
A working dairy farm which has a tennis court, large gardens, a games room and a pony.

SUMMERHILL FARMHOUSE
*Mrs Sheila Budds, Kinsalebeg, **Ardmore;** on route N25 between*

Dungarvan and Youghal
Tel: (+353) 024 92682 (or contact Irish Farm Holidays – see Directory)
Open: 1 April to 30 September
Modern farm bungalow with sea views. There's a games room, crazy golf and a pony for the children.

THE CASTLE FARM
*Mrs Joan Nugent, Modeligo, Cappagh, **Dungarvan;** off route N72, Dungarvan to Cappoquin road*
Tel/Fax: (+353) 058 68049 (or contact Irish Farm Holidays – see Directory)
Open: 1 April to 31 October
Excellent rooms in the restored wing of a 15th-century castle. Facilities include children's pony rides and playground, tennis court and trout fishing.

Self-Catering Apartments and Houses

DUNMORE HOLIDAY COTTAGES
*Killea Road, **Dunmore East***
Tel: (+353) 051 383424; Fax: (+353) 051 383665
A great opportunity to stay in a traditional, fully equipped thatched cottage. Located on an elevated site overlooking Dungarvan East, the facilities include tennis and a children's playroom. Baby-sitting service available by arrangement.

DUNMORE HOLIDAY VILLAS
*Killea Road, **Dunmore East***
Tel: (+353) 051 383699; Fax: (+353) 051 383787
Luxury villas on a secluded site with a tennis court, play area and weekly barbecue for children.

Caravan and Camping Parks

CASEY'S CARAVAN AND CAMPING PARK
*Cloneen, **Dungarvan***
Tel: (+353) 058 41919
Has direct access to the beach, a games room and crazy golf.

Hostels

DUNGARVAN HOLIDAY HOSTEL
*Youghal Road, **Dungarvan***
Tel: (+353) 058 44340; Fax: (+353) 052 36141
Open: all year round

DUNMORE HARBOUR HOUSE
Dunmore East
Tel: (+353) 051 383218; Fax: (+353) 051 383728
Open: all year round

THE MONKEY PUZZLE
*Upper Branch Road, **Tramore***
Tel: (+353) 051 386754
Open: all year round

VIKING HOUSE
Coffee House Lane, The Quay, **Waterford**
Tel: (+353) 051 53827; Fax: (+353) 051 71730

Bicycle Hire

IRISH CYCLE HIRE – *see Directory*
RALEIGH RENT-A-BIKE – *see Directory*

HOLIDAY HOSTEL
Youghal Road, **Dungarvan**
Tel/Fax: (+353) 052 36141

MURPHY'S TOYS AND CYCLES
68 Main Street, **Dungarvan**
Tel: (+353) 058 41376

WRIGHT'S CYCLE DEPOT
19/20 Henrietta Street, **Waterford**
Tel: (+353) 051 874411; Fax: (+353) 051 873440

Car Hire

AVIS RENT-A-CAR
Waterford Airport
Tel: (+353) 051 70170

AUTOBOLAND
Newrath, **Waterford**
Tel: (+353) 051 78990

Airports

WATERFORD AIRPORT
Tel: (+353) 051 75589

Bus Services

SUIRWAY BUS AND COACH SERVICES
Knockroe, **Passage East**
Tel: (+353) 051 382209

BUS EIREANN
Bus Depot, Plunkett Station, The Bridge, **Waterford**
Tel: (+353) 051 73401; travel information – Tel: (+353) 051 79000

Rail Services

Plunkett Station, The Bridge, **Waterford** *– Tel: (+353) 051 73401*

THE PROVINCE OF

ULSTER

The Troubles of Northern Ireland in recent years have done much to deflect attention away from the true character of this part of Ireland. The historic province of Ulster is made up of nine counties, six of which are in Northern Ireland (Antrim, Armagh, Derry, Down, Fermanagh and Tyrone) and three of which are in the Republic (Cavan, Donegal and Monaghan). Five of the northern counties fit neatly around the shores of Lough Neagh, the largest lake in the British Isles, and three of these have coastal boundaries. Covering an area of 5,500 square miles, Ulster has much to offer all ages. The six counties of Northern Ireland amount to a sixth of the total area of Ireland, yet is home to a third of the population.

• • • • •

COUNTY ANTRIM

Stretching from the world-famous Giant's Causeway to the capital city Belfast and the southern shores of Lough Neagh, County Antrim boasts an unrivalled mix of attractions to suit all tastes, and the north-west coast is spectacular, with many beaches boasting the prestigious European Blue Flag awards.

Portrush, on the Causeway Coast, is an ideal gateway to the north, with all of Ulster's other counties within a 2-hour drive. Its facilities are excellent, especially the magnificent **Dunluce Centre,** a sensational new entertainment complex with shops, a restaurant, and a viewing tower. Other attractions in the town include **Waterworld,** one of the largest indoor aqua leisure centres in Ireland; **Fantasy Island,** a state-of-the-art indoor adventure playground; and **Barry's,** a huge amusement park with all the very latest rides. Portrush really is a children's paradise, and for those of us who never grow up, it has to be as near to Never Never Land as you can get.

Just along the coast is the spectacular **Giant's Causeway,** often dubbed the Eighth Wonder of the World. Children can run freely and explore the honeycomb of six-sided basalt columns and rocks that make up Ireland's most famous landmark. Youngsters will love to hear about the legendary giant, Finn MacCool, at the **Causeway Visitor Centre.**

Two miles south of the Causeway is Bushmills, home to the world's oldest **whiskey distillery,** which has been in operation since 1609. A few miles east of Bushmills is the infamous **Carrick-A-Rede rope bridge,** spanning a 60ft chasm, 80ft above the sea between the coast and a small island used by salmon fishermen. This is a dangerous crossing and not recommended for children of any age. It is a spectacular sight and most children would enjoy the challenge, but it's not worth the risk – and there are so many other things to do safely near by.

One of the oldest fairs in Ireland, the **Ould Lammas Fair,** is held annually on the last Monday and Tuesday in August at Ballycastle. Look out for the **Marconi Memorial,** an inviting picnic site near Ballycastle harbour with stone tables and pillars shaped to symbolise radio waves and aerials as a memorial to Marconi, who sent the world's first wireless message across the sea, from Ballycastle to Rathlin, in 1898.

Why not take a 50-minute **boat journey to Rathlin Island,** a great place to explore; it has an RSPB reserve which is home to the largest seabird colony in Northern Ireland. Pirates and smugglers had bases on Rathlin, and in the ruined **Smuggler's House** you can see cavities in the walls used for hiding booty.

Take the alternative coastal route south from here to join up with the famous Antrim Coast Road that winds its way precariously between sea and cliff along the east coast, one of the most scenic coastal drives to be enjoyed anywhere in Ireland. You will find lots of safe, clean, uncrowded, fine sandy beaches along the route at Waterfoot, Ballygally and Brown's Bay – all great places for a day at the seaside.

Providing a majestic backdrop to the coastline are the world-famous nine **Glens of Antrim,** rich in myth and legend. Cushendall is the 'Capital of the Glens', while Glenariff is the 'Queen of the Glens' and has a series of waterfalls cascading down through a gorge criss-crossed by a series of rustic bridges. Further south is the pretty village of Carnlough with its bustling little white limestone harbour. Another popular visitor point is the **Carnfunnock Country Park.** There's plenty to amuse children here, with a visitor centre and café, a maze in the shape of Northern Ireland, a time garden and an adventure playground.

Carrickfergus is a good base for visitors to the area. There are many things to see and do, such as walking the town walls or visiting **Carrickfergus Castle,** magnificently sited on a rocky outcrop and one of Europe's best preserved examples of a Norman castle. Children can try a bow and arrow or play medieval games, while the **Knight Ride** takes time travellers by monorail on a theme ride in which they are transported back through the centuries of Carrickfergus's turbulent history.

Access throughout the county is excellent. Motorways take you out of Belfast in all directions on to a network of first-class roads, leading to every part of the county. There is a good road and rail public transport system giving access throughout the area.

PLACES TO VISIT

Amusement Arcades and Funfairs

BARRY'S AMUSEMENTS AND FAIRGROUND****
Portrush
Tel: 028 7082 2340
Open: Easter to June, weekends and bank holidays; July to September, daily
This is the largest amusement park in Ireland and has the very latest in rides for indoor and outdoor entertainment.

Animals, Birds and Fish

BELFAST ZOO***
*Antrim Road; 4 miles (6.4km) north of **Belfast***
Tel: 028 9077 6277
Open: April to September, daily, 10a.m.–5p.m.; October to March, daily, 10a.m.–3.30p.m.
Admission: A=££££, C=££, F
Facilities: toilets with baby-changing room; disabled access; picnic areas; snack shop; souvenir shop; restaurant; tea-room
Located in a picturesque park above the city, the zoo has some fascinating attractions such as a children's farm with a collection of rare breeds; Spider Monkey Island; an award-winning primate enclosure; the African enclosure and the Polar Bear Canyon; a free-flight aviary and bird house; and the penguin and sealion pools with underwater viewing areas. If your kids become especially attached to any of the creatures they see here, there is a scheme that allows them to adopt an animal!

RATHLIN ISLAND BIRD SANCTUARY
*Kebble National Nature Reserve, **Rathlin Island***
Tel: 028 2076 2024
Open: all year round (check times to avoid nesting season)
The reserve is home to the island's main breeding colonies of kittiwakes, razorbills and puffins.

Boats and Boat Trips

ANTRIM
Maid of Antrim, *Sixmilewater* Marina
Tel: 028 9446 3113
On: May to September
Trips on Lough Neagh lasting from 1 to 3 hours.

Castles and Historic Houses

CARRICKFERGUS CASTLE****
Carrickfergus
Tel: 028 9335 1273
Open: April to September, Monday to Saturday, 10a.m.–6p.m., Sunday, 2p.m.–6p.m.; October to March, Monday to Saturday, 10a.m.–4p.m., Sunday, 2p.m.–4p.m.
Admission: A=£££, C=£, F
Facilities: toilets with baby-changing room; disabled access; shops; audio-visual presentations; visitor centre; café; activity room
You'll find something of interest for all the family in one of the best preserved Norman castles in Ireland. It has exhibitions, demonstrations and audio-visual presentations that detail the history of this 12th-century castle built by John de Courcy. Visitors are invited to try their hand at medieval writing, put on some armour or play a medieval game. Every month there is a special exhibition or demonstration at the castle such as archery, military tattoos, pageants, fairs and children's medieval games

DUNLUCE CASTLE
On route A2 between Bushmills and Portrush
Tel: 028 2073 1938
Open: April to September, Monday to Saturday, 10a.m.–7p.m., Sunday, 2p.m.–7p.m.; October to March, Tuesday to Saturday, 10a.m.–4p.m., Sunday, 2p.m.–4p.m.
Admission: A=£, C=£
Facilities: visitor centre and shop; audio-visual presentation; displays
Dramatic 16th/17th-century ruins sited on a rocky headland beside the A2 coast road.

MALONE HOUSE*
Barnett Park, Upper Malone Road, Belfast
Tel: 028 9068 1246
Open: all year round, Monday to Saturday, 10a.m.–4.30p.m.
Admission: free
Facilities: toilets; wheelchair access to ground floor only; parkland walks (park open daily, dawn to dusk); coffee shop serving lunches and teas
Early 19th-century house set in beautiful parkland. There's an art gallery and a permanent exhibition on Belfast parks.

Cinemas

ANTRIM CINEPLEX
Fountain Hill, Antrim
Tel: 028 9446 9500
Four screens.

CINEWORLD
Kennedy Centre, Falls Road, Belfast
Tel: 028 9060 0988
Five screens.

MGM MULTIPLEX CENTRE
Dublin Road, Belfast

Tel: 028 9024 5700
Ten screens.

THE MOVIE HOUSE
*Yorkgate, York Street, **Belfast***
Tel: 028 9075 5000
Eight screens.

REGAL
*Curran Road, **Larne***
Tel: 028 2827 7711
Four screens.

Country Parks

CARNFUNNOCK COUNTRY PARK***
*Carnfunnock, on route A2, just over 3 miles (5.5km) north of **Larne***
Tel: 028 2826 0088
*Open: October and Easter to June, daily, 11.30a.m.–6p.m.; July to
September, daily, 11.30a.m.–8p.m.; November to Easter, weekends,
11.30a.m.–dusk*
Admission: free; maze: A=£, C=£
*Facilities: toilets; disabled access; café serving tea, coffee, snacks and
lunches; barbecue and picnic sites*
Lots of fun things to do here for all. There's a walled garden, a
visitor centre, golf and putting and an adventure playground.

CAVE HILL COUNTRY PARK**
Belfast
Tel: 028 9077 6925
Centre open: daily, 9a.m.–6p.m.
Admission: free
The park has many interesting archaeological and natural features.
There's an excellent waymarked trail up Cave Hill, past neolithic
caves to MacArt's Fort. The Heritage Centre inside Belfast Castle
interprets the life and times of this area.

COLIN GLEN WOODLAND PARK**
*Stewartstown Road, **Belfast***
Tel: 028 9061 4115
***Park** open: daily, dawn to dusk; **centre** open: Monday to Thursday,
9a.m.–4.30p.m., Friday, 9a.m.–1p.m.*
A beautiful 200-acre natural park located at the foot of Black
Mountain, with a wide variety of flora and fauna, nature trails,
wildlife ponds and a mill race. The heritage centre has exhibitions
and an audio-visual presentation.

Crèches

ABBEY CENTRE
*Longwood Road, **Newtownabbey***
Tel: 028 9086 8018

KINDER KARE DAY NURSERY
*80 Crankill Road, **Ballymena***

Tel: 028 2588 0178
Open: 7.30a.m.–6p.m.

TOWER SHOPPING CENTRE
Wellington Street, **Ballymena**
Tel: 028 2564 6049

Environment and Ecology Centres

LAGAN LOOKOUT VISITOR CENTRE****
Donegal Quay, **Belfast**
Tel: 028 9031 5444
*Open: March to September, Monday to Friday, 11a.m.–5p.m., Saturday,
noon–5p.m., Sunday, 2p.m.–5p.m.; October to February, Monday to
Friday, 11.30a.m.–3.30p.m., Saturday, 1p.m.–4.30p.m., Sunday, 2p.m.–
4.30p.m.*
Admission: A=££, C=£, F
Facilities: toilets; disabled access
This fascinating centre uses videos and hi-tech, hands-on computer
systems to explain the background to the weir with industrial and
folk history of the area. There is a Time Tunnel under the Lagan
River and a platform to view activities on the river. You can also take
river cruises from here.

PORTRUSH COUNTRYSIDE CENTRE***
8 Bath Road, **Portrush**
Tel: 028 7082 3600
Open: summer months only, daily, noon–8p.m.
A fascinating trip into the past with the aid of an audio-visual
presentation. You can also dabble in a living rockpool and find
anything from a limpet to a lobster, and take the opportunity to
look at present-day environmental issues such as the problem of
litter on our beaches.

Equestrian Facilities

MADDYBENNY RIDING CENTRE***
Maddybenny Park, **Portrush**
Tel: 028 7082 3394
Open: All year
They cater for all ages and levels of experience. There's an indoor
arena or plenty of quiet routes for hacking.

CONNELL HILL RIDING CENTRE
48 Drumsrough Road, **Randalstown**
Tel: 028 4947 2632
Lessons available.

Farm Parks

LESLEY HILL HERITAGE FARM PARK**
Ballymoney
Tel: 028 2766 6803
*Open: September and Easter to May, Sunday and bank holidays,
2p.m.–6p.m.; June, weekends, 2p.m.–6p.m.; July and August, Monday to*

Saturday, 11a.m.–6p.m., Sunday, 2p.m.–6p.m.
Admission: A=££, C=£, F
Facilities: picnic area; shop; café; nature trails, gardens and lakes
Lots of interesting things to do and see here. There's a threshing barn, granary and a comprehensive collection of horse-drawn machines and vehicles, a museum of hand tools, costumes and household items; horse-trap and donkey rides through an 18th-century estate teeming with rare breeds, deer and ornamental fowl, and a children's adventure playground.

LOUGHSIDE OPEN DAIRY FARM***
Ballycarry
Tel: 028 9335 3312
Open: March to October, daily, noon–7p.m.; November to February, weekends, noon–dusk
Admission: A=££, C=£, F
Facilities: toilets; disabled access; refreshments
Plenty for the youngsters here: a pets corner, bird sanctuary, adventure playground, miniature train rides, farm animals, fallow deer, Highland cattle, ponies and donkeys are all on view.

STREAMVALE OPEN DAIRY FARM***
*38 Ballyhanwood Road, Dundonald, **Belfast***
Tel: 028 9048 3244
Open: February to May and September to October, Wedneday and weekends, 2p.m.–6p.m.; June, daily, noon–6p.m.; July and August, daily, 10.30a.m.–6p.m.; animal feeding times: 11.30a.m. and 3.30p.m.; milking times: 4p.m.–5.30p.m.
Admission: A=££, C=£, F
Facilities: toilets; disabled access; picnic areas; shop; café
Visitors can watch the milking from a viewing gallery, or get involved with bottle-feeding lambs and hand-milking goats. There are plenty of other things to do as well: try the nature trail, straw bounce, pets corner, outdoor play area, tractor and trailer rides and pony rides.

WATERTOP OPEN FARM***
*Cushendall Road, on A2 6 miles (9.6km) south-east of **Ballycastle***
Tel: 028 2076 2576
Open: Easter, May and June, Monday to Friday, 10a.m.–5.30p.m.; July and August, daily, 10a.m.–5.30p.m.; September, weekends, 10a.m.–5.30p.m.
Admission: A=£, C=£
Excellent family activity centre with lots of fun things to do. There's a museum, a shop, a lakeside tea-house, barbecues, pony-trekking, fishing, boating, a camping and caravan park, and farm tours.

Festivals and Events

OULD LAMMAS FAIR***
Ballycastle
Tel: 028 2076 2024
On: last Monday and Tuesday in August
One of the oldest fairs in Ireland, the Ould Lammas fair has taken place in Ballycastle since 1606. The 2-day event features everything from sheep and horse trading to hundreds of stalls, some of which

sell local specialities such as 'dulse' (dried edible seaweed) and 'yellowman' (hard crunchy toffee).

BALLYCLARE MAY FAIR***
Ballyclare
Tel: 028 9086 8751
On: third week in May
A week-long festival with something for everyone. Festivities include a funfair, band parades, street traders, concerts, sports tournaments, treasure hunts and the mayor's parade.

PORT SUMMER FESTIVAL***
Portrush
Tel: 028 7082 2855
On: first week in July
Daily events include music, dancing, a kids' disco, treasure hunts, children's parties and entertainment, Ulster's biggest barbecue, parades, grand finale party and a fireworks display

PORTSTEWART COMMUNITY FESTIVAL***
Portstewart
Tel: 028 7083 3767
On: last week in July
Festivities include a funfair, fancy dress and carnival parade, barbecue, clown show and open-air disco, fireworks display and family entertainment.

RATHLIN FESTIVAL WEEK
Rathlin Island
Tel: 028 2076 2024
On: second week in July
A week of festivities that include theatre, ceilidhs, sports and model yacht races.

Football Clubs

LINFIELD FOOTBALL CLUB
Windsor Park, **Belfast**
Tel: 028 9024 4198
If you would like to visit the club, just telephone the marketing manager to make an appointment. Visitors can see the trophy room, boardroom and dressing-rooms, and go to the trackside.

Forest and Amenity Walks

GLENARIFF FOREST PARK****
Glenariff
Tel: 028 2175 8232
Open: all year round, daily, 10a.m.–dusk
Admission: ££ per car, A=£, C=£
Facilities: toilets; disabled access; visitor centre; shop; restaurant; forest walks and trails to mountain viewpoints; picnic and barbecue areas
This magnificent park is situated amid the world-famous Glens of Antrim and covers an area of 1185 hectares. There are 4 way-marked circular trails of varying length that wind their way through

beautiful woodland and scenic glens. The waterfall trail (3 miles) is probably the most spectacular. It follows the Glenariff River with its famous waterfalls and rustic bridges, through the National Nature Reserve's colourful display of mosses and ferns.

MINNOWBURN BEECHES
*Shaw's Bridge, just over 3 miles (5.5km) south of **Belfast** on B205*
Trails and woodland walks in the Lagan Valley with routes to Giant's Ring and Edenderry village.

Gardens

BELFAST BOTANIC GARDEN**
*Stranmills Road, **Belfast***
Tel: 028 9032 4902
Open: all year round, daily, dawn to dusk
Open: April to September, Monday to Friday, 10a.m.–5p.m., weekends, 2p.m.–5p.m.; October to March, Monday to Friday, 10a.m.–4p.m., weekends, 2p.m.–4p.m.
Admission: free
Two of the most notable early greenhouses in Europe are to be found here. The Palm House has a variety of tropical plants including palms, cycads and flowering plants, as well as economic plants such as coffee, sugar and bananas. You can sweat it out in the luxuriant tropical glen and get some great views from a high walkway.

O'HARABROOK
Ballymoney
Tel: 028 7066 6273
Open: seasonal
Admission: ££ per person
An interesting flower and wild garden and woodland walks. The gardens are particularly colourful in spring when the azaleas and rhododendrons are in bloom and the grounds are carpeted with bluebells, daffodils and primroses.

Heritage Centres

CAUSEWAY VISITORS' CENTRE****
Giant's Causeway
Tel: 028 2073 1855
Open: summer, daily, 10a.m.–7p.m.; winter, daily, 10a.m.–5p.m.
Admission: exhibition and audio-visual presentation, A=£, C=£, F
Facilities: toilets; disabled access; shops; cafeteria
The modern visitor centre has excellent exhibitions and presentations telling the history of the Causeway and the fascinating story of Finn MacCool. Children will enjoy the story and spending some of their pocket money on one of the many causeway mementoes available in the shop. A bus service runs from here to the Giant's Causeway, but unless the weather is poor I would recommend taking the scenic route – the walk down to the coastline is stunning.

KNIGHT RIDE AND HERITAGE PLAZA*****
*Antrim Street, **Carrickfergus***
Tel: 028 9336 6455; Fax: 028 9335 0350

Open: April to September, Monday to Saturday, 10a.m.–6p.m., Sunday, noon–6p.m.; October to March, Monday to Saturday, 10a.m.–5p.m., Sunday, noon–5p.m.

Admission: A=££, C=£, F; joint ticket with Carrickfergus Castle: A=££££, C=£, F

Facilities: toilets; disabled access (special car available for wheelchair users); shops; café

Exhibitions and a fascinating monorail themed ride through the history of Carrickfergus. Step aboard one of the specially designed cars and experience over 1,000 years of exciting history. After the ride, visitors can walk through an exhibition that includes a scale model of the town, with audio-visual descriptions of how it developed through the centuries.

STATION 597

*Langford Lodge, Gortnagallon Road, **Crumlin***

Tel: 028 9065 0451

Open: Easter to November, weekends, noon–6p.m.

Admission: A=££, C=£, F

Facilities: toilets, disabled access; shop; café; picnic area

Among the memorabilia from this Second World War US Air Force base are medals, posters, maps and photographs.

Ireland at Work – Past and Present

DUNDONALD OLD MILL

*Belfast Road, Quarry Corner, **Dundonald***

Tel: 028 9048 0117

Open: Monday to Saturday, 10a.m.–5.15p.m., Sunday, 11a.m.–5.15p.m.

Admission: free

Facilities: toilets; disabled access; craft shop; displays; restaurant

The Old Mill, dating from 1752, has Ireland's largest waterwheel. The millstones can be seen in the restaurant.

LISBURN MUSEUM AND IRISH LINEN CENTRE***

*Market Square, **Lisburn***

Tel: 028 9266 3377

Open: April to September, Monday to Saturday, 9.30a.m.–5.30p.m., Sunday, 2p.m.–5.30p.m.; October to March, Monday to Saturday, 9.30a.m.–5p.m.

Admission: A=££, C=£, F

Facilities: toilets; restaurant; audio-visual shows; shop; activities gallery

The museum exhibition tells the story of how the Famine affected Lisburn and the Lagan Valley. The Irish Linen Centre re-creates Ulster's greatest industry with a spinners' cottage, weaving workshops and exhibitions. The centre is very child-friendly and youngsters are encouraged to participate in the educational activities.

MAUD'S ICE-CREAM FACTORY****

Gleno

Tel: 028 2827 2387

Open: Monday to Friday, 8a.m.–4p.m.

Admission: free

This is the home of Northern Ireland's favourite ice-cream

producer. A fascinating opportunity to see all the processes involved in making this wonderful ice-cream (including the kids' favourite, Pooh Bear flavour). There's a shop and café where all the flavours are available to choose from, but I suggest you limit the intake on-site and take the cool box to take some away with you for later.

OLD BUSHMILLS DISTILLERY
Bushmills
Tel: 028 2073 1521
Open: April to October, Mon–Sat, 9.30a.m.–5.30p.m.; Sun 12noon–5.30p.m.; November to March, Mon–Fri, 9.30a.m.–3.30p.m.
Admission: A=£££, C=£, F
This is the world's oldest whisky distillery and has been in business since the 1600s. A guide will lead you through the many stages in the age-old art of whisky-making, completing the tour with a sample of the product – parents only, of course!

PATTERSON'S SPADE MILL
*Antrim Road, **Templepatrick***
Tel: 028 9443 3619
Open: April, May and September, weekends, 2p.m.–6p.m.; June to August, daily (except Tuesday), 2p.m.–6p.m.
Admission: A=££, C=£, F
This is the last surviving water-driven spade mill in Ireland. All the original equipment has been fully restored and there are demonstrations of spade-making.

Leisure Centres and Adventure Playgrounds

COKE BEACH CLUB****
*Landsdowne Crescent, **Portrush***
Open: July and August
Admission: free
Two sessions a day of fun and capers for the kids. Activities include puppet shows, sand designing, competitions and fun sports.

CRAZY CAPERS****
*Loughshore Marina, **Sixmilewater***
Tel: 028 9083 3681
Fun for all the family: jet-skiing, windsurfing, canoeing, crazy golf, fun buggies, boat trips, kiddies' karts, mini-train and a bouncy castle.

DUNDONALD INTERNATIONAL ICE BOWL***
*Old Dundonald Road, **Belfast***
Tel: 028 9048 2611
Excellent entertainment complex with an Olympic-sized ice-rink, 10-pin bowling centre, and 'Indiana Land' – a play paradise on a jungle theme for children.

DUNLUCE family entertainment CENTRE*****
*Sandhill Drive, **Portrush***
Tel: 028 7082 4444
Open: March to October, Sat–Sun, 12noon–5p.m.; April/May/June/Sept, daily 10a.m.–7p.m.
Admission: Inclusive tickets=£££££ pp; family tickets available

Facilities: toilets with baby-changing facilities; disabled access; shop; tourist information; restaurant

This is a wonderful, hands-on attraction with lots of exciting things to do. **Turbo Tours** lets you be part of the movie by synchronising seat movement with on-screen action adventures – if you have not yet sampled virtual reality theatre, now is the time to do so: it's an amazing experience. The **Earth Quest Nature Trail** is a fascinating interactive display area with quizzes and touch computers that portray the local wildlife in both town and country environments. Don't miss the exceptional **Myths and Legends** multimedia show, bringing the folklore of the North Antrim coast vividly to life. And climb the viewing tower for a dramatic panoramic view of Portrush and the surrounding area. The themed restaurant is particularly good for parents with young kids. There's also a great children's playground in the surrounding parkland (free access at any time).

FANTASY ISLAND***
*Kerr Street, **Portrush***
Tel: 028 7082 3595
Open: Easter to September, Mon–Sat, 10a.m.–8p.m.; Sun, 12noon–8p.m.
Admission: C=£££ (over 4), ££ (under 4)
Facilities: toilets with baby-changing facilities; restaurant; coffee bar
Fully supervised adventure play centre with toddlers' soft-play areas, and specially organised summer clubs for the over-5s. The restaurant has a full kiddies' menu.

SPORTSBOWL***
*Wakehurst Road, **Ballymena***
Tel: 028 2564 8122
Open: daily, 10a.m.–10p.m.
Fun centre with 10-pin bowling (including special lanes for kids), amusement games and simulators, snooker and pool tables, a restaurant and a play area.

VALLEY LEISURE CENTRE***
Newtownabbey
Tel: 028 9086 1211
Facilities: crèche and children's activities
The largest leisure centre in the province has 10-pin bowling, squash courts and a swimming-pool.

Museums

BALLYCASTLE MUSEUM
*59 Castle Street, **Ballycastle***
Tel: 028 2076 2024
Open: July and August, Monday to Saturday, noon–6p.m.
Admission: free
Located in Ballycastle's 18th-century courthouse, the museum has displays on the folklife and social history of the Glens of Antrim.

CAUSEWAY SCHOOL MUSEUM***
Causeway Head *(next to Giant's Causeway Centre)*
Tel: 028 2073 1777

Open: July and August, daily, 11 a.m.–5p.m.
Admission: A=£, C=£, F
The place to experience life in a 1920s school classroom. The desks are complete with inkwells and splodgy pens, and you'll see playground toys such as whip peeries, yoyos, marbles and skipping ropes.

FORD FARM PARK AND MUSEUM*
Low Road, Islandmagee (on route B90)
Tel: 028 9335 3264
Open: March to October, daily, 2p.m.–6p.m.
Admission: A=£, C=£
Small country museum in a former farm outbuilding with a folk collection, fishing nets, lobster pots, farming implements and demonstrations of butter-making and wool-spinning.

ULSTER MUSEUM**
Botanic Gardens, Belfast
Tel: 028 9038 1251; Fax: 028 9066 5510
Open: all year round, Monday to Friday, 10a.m.–5p.m., Saturday, 1p.m.–5p.m., Sunday, 2p.m.–5p.m.
Admission: free
Facilities: toilets; disabled access; shop; café
The museum's permanent collection looks at dinosaurs, the making of Irish linen, medieval Ireland, treasures from wrecks of Spanish Armada ships, geology and flora and fauna of Ireland, and British and Irish paintings and sculptures – truly something for everyone! The museum organises many interesting temporary exhibitions throughout the year – check directly for a programme of events.

Parks

ARTS COUNCIL SCULPTURE PARK**
185 Stranmills Road, Belfast
Tel: 028 9038 1591
Open: all year round
Admission: free
A fascinating walk amongst works in bronze, steel, wood, iron and ceramics made by local sculptors.

DIXON PARK**
Malone Road, Belfast
Tel: 028 9032 0202
Open: daily, dawn to dusk
The City of Belfast International Rose Trials are held here. There's a Japanese garden, children's play area and restaurant.

RAMORE HEAD***
Portrush
Tel: 028 7082 3378
Lots of fun things to do such as bowling, tennis, putting, crazy golf, adventure play park and a giant slippery dip. Refreshments available.

RIVERSIDE PARK***
Ballymoney
Tel: 028 2766 4962
Open: all year round, dawn to dusk
Twenty acres of parkland with toilets, riverside walks, a boating lake, picnic areas, and a children's play area.

Shopping Centres

ABBEY CENTRE
*Longwood Road, **Newtownabbey***
Tel: 028 9086 8018
One of the largest shopping centres in Northern Ireland, it has a crèche and good parking facilities.

FAIRHILL CENTRE
*Fairhill Lane, **Ballymena***
Tel: 028 2565 1199
Large shopping centre with many top stores.

TOWER SHOPPING CENTRE
*Wellington Street, **Ballymena***
Tel: 028 2564 6049
Lots of shops, easy parking and a children's crèche, all in the centre of town.

Swimming-Pools

CARRICKFERGUS LEISURE CENTRE***
*Prince William Way, **Carrickfergus***
Tel: 028 9335 1711; Fax: 028 9336 0504
Facilities: disabled facilities; restaurant
Has a play area and bouncy castle, table football and table-tennis, badminton and squash courts, plus adult and junior pools.

GROVE LEISURE CENTRE***
*York Road, **Belfast***
Tel: 028 9035 1599; Fax: 028 9074 8594
This designated swimming centre of excellence for Northern Ireland offers swimming lessons, a junior pool, Funtasia play area, cafeteria, aquafit, canoeing and diving.

RIADA CENTRE
*33 Garryduff Road, **Ballymoney***
Tel: 028 2766 5792
This centre has swimming-pools, a hi-tech fitness centre, squash courts and a cafeteria.

SEVEN TOWERS LEISURE CENTRE**
*Trostan Avenue, **Ballymena***
Tel: 028 2564 1427
Open: Monday to Friday, 10a.m.–9p.m., Saturday, 10a.m.–4p.m., Sunday noon–4p.m.
Facilities: baby-changing room; crèche; disabled facilities; restaurant
The centre has learner and adult swimming-pools, and a diving

pool. Special sessions are arranged for young children and people with disabilities – check with the centre for times.

SHANKHILL LEISURE CENTRE***
*100 Shankhill Road, **Belfast***
Tel: 028 9024 1434; Fax: 028 9032 1647
Unique leisure pool with high pool and air temperatures to give a Mediterranean atmosphere. Kids will love the 'Zoom Flume', whirl-pool and wave-maker.

WATERWORLD****
*The Harbour, **Portrush***
Tel: 028 7082 2001
Open: June to August, Monday to Saturday, 10a.m.–9p.m., Sunday, noon–9p.m.; September, Friday, 3p.m.–9p.m., Saturday, 10a.m.–9p.m., Sunday, noon–9p.m.
Indoor holiday aqua-paradise with thrilling giant flumes, water cannon, whirlpools, a kiddies' pool, sprays and jacuzzis. Inflatable and soft-play sessions for children under 10 are regularly staged in the Piazza's Play Korner.

Theatres

THE COURTYARD THEATRE**
*Ballyearl Arts and Leisure Complex, **Newtownabbey***
Tel: 028 9084 8287
Children's craft and drama activities. Check locally for details.

Walks and Tours

CARRICKFERGUS TOWN WALL TRAIL****
Carrickfergus
A fascinating tour around the walls of this historic town.

• • • • •

PLACES TO EAT

Cafés and Restaurants

DESPARATE DAN'S
*12 Ballymoney Street, **Ballymena***
Tel: 028 2564 9677

SOLOMON GRUNDY
*Wellington Street, **Ballymena***
Tel: 028 2565 9602

THE CHICAGO PIZZA PIE FACTORY
*MGM Cinema Centre, Dublin Road, **Belfast***
Tel: 028 9023 3555
Open: all year round, Monday to Wednesday, noon–11p.m., Thursday to Saturday, noon–midnight, Sunday, noon–10.30p.m. (Sunday is a family

day with balloons and entertainment laid on between noon and 3p.m.)

SUN KEE
*38 Donegal Pass, **Belfast***
Tel: 028 9031 2016
*Open: Sunday to Thursday, 5p.m.–1a.m., Saturday, 5p.m.–11.30p.m.
(closed Friday)*
Child-friendly Chinese restaurant serving excellent food.

MORELLI'S
*7 Eglinton Street, **Portrush***
Tel: 028 7082 4848
Open: daily, 11a.m.–10p.m.
Pizza, toasties and home-made ice-cream.

Fast-Food Restaurants

HARRY RAMSDEN'S
Yorkgate Shopping Centre, York Road, Belfast
Tel: 028 9074 9222

BURGER KING
*Thomas Street, **Ballymena***
Tel: 028 2564 2733

GOOD FOOD INN – CHINESE TAKE-AWAY
*65 Ballymoney Street, **Ballymena***
Tel: 028 2565 6553

KENTUCKY FRIED CHICKEN
*27–33 Queen Street, **Ballymena***
Tel: 028 2564 6335

McDONALD'S
*24/28 Bradbury Place, **Belfast***
Tel: 028 9033 3400

*Westwood Shopping Centre, **Belfast***
Tel: 028 9022 1151

*Donegal Place, **Belfast***
Tel: 028 9031 1600

*The Arches Retail Park, Conswater, **Belfast***
Tel: 028 9045 7599

*290 Antrim Road, **Glengormley***
Tel: 028 9083 8900

*Sprucefield Shopping Centre, **Lisburn***
Tel: 028 9266 1900

*GalgormRoad, **Ballymena***
Tel: 028 3563 2330

Upper Newtownards Road, **Dundonald**
Tel: 028 9048 0100

Bow Street, **Lisburn**
Tel: 028 9266 0222

Abbeycentre, **Newtownabbey**
Tel: 028 9086 8877

TERRY'S FAST-FOOD BAR
Tower Centre, **Ballymena**
Tel: 028 2564 0940

KENTUCKY FRIED CHICKEN
54 Main Street, **Portrush**
Tel: 028 7082 4689

Hotels and Pubs

THE BUSHMILLS INN*****
25 Main Street, **Bushmills**
Tel: 028 2073 2339
The food is excellent and the restaurant very child-friendly. Children
can choose from their own menu or have half portions from the
main menu.

HARBOUR BAR AND RESTAURANT
The Harbour, **Portrush**
Tel: 028 70822430
Open: All year
Family-friendly bar and restaurant, children's menu available.

LONDONDERRY ARMS HOTEL*****
Harbour Road, **Carnlough**
Tel: 028 2888 5255
This child-friendly restaurant has a good choice of meals for youngsters. They are well catered for here and made to feel very
welcome. The Londonderry Arms Hotel was originally built in 1848
as a coaching inn and once owned by Winston Churchill. This is still
a good place to stop to feed and water the children – they can't be
tethered but there is a good, reasonably priced children's menu, and
a child-friendly atmosphere with 'things to do' provided to keep
them content.

PLACES TO STAY

Guest-Houses and B&Bs

GLENHAVEN
10 Beechwood Avenue, **Ballycastle**
Tel: 028 2076 3612

TORR BRAE
77 Torr Road, Torr Head, **Ballycastle**
Tel: 028 2076 9625

THE COTTAGE
377 Comber Road, Dundonald, **Belfast**
Tel: 028 9187 8189

BEECHGROVE
412 Upper Road, Trooperslane, **Carrickfergus**
Tel: 028 9336 3304

PARKLANDS
Trooperslane, **Carrickfergus**
Tel: 028 9336 2528

AVAREST
64 Mark Street, **Portrush**
Tel: 028 7082 3121

Country Houses and Hotels

THE BUSHMILLS INN*****
25 Main Street, **Bushmills**
Tel: 028 2073 2339
Dating back to the 1600s, the award-winning Bushmills Inn is a
tastefully modernised coaching inn with turf fires and gas lamps that
give it wonderful character, richly evocative of bygone days. The
hotel has 2 unique open-plan family rooms, where children's beds
have been built into the roof space – you can only get to them by
ladder. As the owner explained on our visit, the novelty is such that
it isn't always the children who get to sleep in the upper beds!

BEACH HOUSE HOTEL
Beach Road, **Portballintrae**
Tel: 028 2073 1214; Fax: 028 2073 31664
Open: all year round
Hotel with lots of large family rooms and located on the seafront
overlooking a sandy beach. The hotel is renowned for its bar meals
and suppers.

CAUSEWAY COAST HOTEL***
*Ballyreagh Road, **Portrush***
Tel: 028 7082 2435
Open: all year round
Modern hotel with family rooms and children's menu. An excellent place to stay or just to stop and eat.

JURY'S BELFAST INN
*Great Victoria Street, **Belfast***
Tel: 028 9053 3500; Fax: 028 9053 3511
Open: all year round
Conveniently located in the city, this hotel has family rooms but no leisure facilities.

LONDONDERRY ARMS HOTEL*****
*Harbour Road, **Carnlough***
Tel: 028 2888 5255
Welcoming, family-friendly hotel. The hotel organises many special deals with good rates for children. Enquire direct for details.

WHITE PARK HOUSE
*Antrim Coast Road, **White Park Bay***
Tel: 028 2073 1842

Room-only Hotels

HOLIDAY INN EXPRESS
*106 University Street, **Belfast***
Tel: 01232 311909; Fax: 01232 232999
Open: all year

JURY'S BELFAST INN
*Great Victoria Street, **Belfast***
Tel: 028 9053 3500
Fax: 028 9053 3511
Open: all year round
Conveniently located in the city, this hotel has family rooms but no leisure facilities.

TRAVELODGE BELFAST CITY
*15 Brunswick Street, **Belfast***
Tel: 028 9033 3555; Fax: 028 9023 2999
Open: all year round
Ideal family accommodation for a stay in the city.

Farmhouse Accommodation

SPRING FARM
*15 Isle Road, Dunseverick, **Bushmills***
Tel: 028 2073 1780

MADDYBENNY FARMHOUSE****
*18 Maddybenny Park, **Portrush***
Tel: 028 7082 3394
Open: all year round

This award-winning farmhouse accommodation is a great place to stay with the children. The food and hospitality are excellent and if you like horses there are riding and trekking facilities available. The farm also has excellent self-catering accommodation.

Holiday Parks and Villages

SILVERCLIFFS HOLIDAY VILLAGE
Ballycastle
Tel: 028 2076 2550; Fax: 028 2076 2259
Open: all year round; facilities open daily, 10a.m.–8p.m.
Modern holiday village with choice of lodges, apartments and cottages, situated on a mature 28-acre park overlooking Ballycastle Bay. Facilities include free entertainment, a bar, café/snack bar, tropical leisure pool complex with an indoor heated swimming-pool, and a children's adventure playground.

Self-Catering Apartments and Houses

ASHLEA COTTAGES
*39 Magheraboy Road, **Portrush***
Tel: 028 7082 2779

Caravan and Camping Parks

JORDANSTOWN LOUGH SHORE PARK
*Shore Road, **Newtownabbey***
Tel: 028 9086 8751; Fax: 028 9036 5407

CARRICK DHU CARAVAN AND CAMPING PARK
*12 Ballyreagh Road, **Portrush***
Tel: 028 7082 3712

Hostels

CASTLE HOSTEL
*62 Quay Road, **Ballycastle***
Tel: 028 2076 2337
Open: all year round

ARNIE'S BACKPACKERS
*63 Fitzwilliam Street, **Belfast***
Tel: 028 9024 2867
Open: all year round

Bicycle Hire

IRISH CYCLE HIRE – see *Directory*
RALEIGH RENT-A-BIKE – see *Directory*

Car Hire

HERTZ CAR HIRE
Belfast City Airport
Tel: 028 9073 2451

and
Belfast International Airport
Tel: 028 9041 932533
and
Larne
Tel: 028 2827 8111

McCAUSLAND CAR HIRE
21–31 Grosvenor Road, **Belfast**
Tel: 028 9033 3777
and
Belfast City Airport
Tel: 028 9045 4141
and
Belfast International Airport
Tel: 028 9041 932022

Airports

BELFAST CITY AIRPORT
Tel: 028 9045 7745; Fax: 028 9073 8455

BELFAST INTERNATIONAL AIRPORT
Aldergrove
Tel: 028 9442 2888

Bus Services

Ulsterbus, **Ballymena** *Bus Station – Tel: 028 2565 2214*
Europa Bus Centre, Glengall Street, **Belfast** *– Tel: 028 9032 0011*
CITYBUS – *Tel: 028 9024 6485*
ULSTERBUS – *Tel: 028 9033 3000*

Ferry Services

BALLYCASTLE to RATHLIN ISLAND
Ballycastle
Tel: 028 2076 2024
Daily sailings all year from Ballycastle at 10.30a.m., returning from
Rathlin Harbour at 4p.m. Additional sailings from June to August at
11.45a.m., returning at 5.30p.m. Crossing time takes 40 minutes.

BELFAST to STRANRAER (SeaCat)
Tel: 0345 523523

BELFAST to STRANRAER (Stenna Sealink)
Tel: 028 2827 3616

BELFAST to LIVERPOOL (Norse Irish Ferries)
Tel: 028 9077 9090
LARNE to CAIRNRYAN (P&O)
Tel: 028 2827 4321

Rail Services

NORTHERN IRELAND RAILWAYS (NIR) — *Tel: 028 9089 9411*
Ballymena *Station, Galgorm Road* — *Tel: 028 2565 2277*
Belfast *Central* — *Tel: 028 9089 9400*
Lisburn — *Tel: 028 9266 2294*

COUNTY ARMAGH

The fertile county of Armagh is known as the 'Orchard of Ireland', and in May and June has a signposted blossom trail to guide you through the apple orchards. The city of Armagh has two cathedrals and is considered the ecclesiastical capital of Ireland. **Saint Patrick's Trian** is an exciting, innovative visitor complex in the heart of the city. As well as the Land of Lilliput, where children can dress up as Little People and go on a magical, enchanting journey through the world created by Jonathan Swift in *Gulliver's Travels*, the complex offers a stimulating approach to the historical and literary aspects of the city.

A fascinating new attraction in the city is the **Garden of Sensory Delights at the Palace Stables Heritage Centre.** This is no ordinary garden, but has been carefully designed to appeal to both able-bodied and special needs people. It's also worth visiting the **Armagh Planetarium,** where video technology allows you to fly through space and experience the wonders of the universe in a fun, interesting and entertaining way. Outside is the Astropark and the Eartharium, both of which give children and parents a wonderful opportunity to learn more about this fascinating subject.

Two miles west of Armagh is Navan, the ancient capital of Ulster. **Navan Fort** is steeped in mystery and mythology and is Ulster's most important historical site. From the innovative **Navan Visitor Centre** you can walk up to the Navan Fort and view the mound, where recent excavations have revealed the remains of one of the most impressive Iron Age structures in Europe: a temple dating from 94BC.

There are many other places to go around this attractive county. One is **Gosford Forest Park,** with its arboretum, walled garden, a deer park and nature trails. Close to the southern shores of Lough Neagh in the north of the county is Craigavon and its **Centrepoint Family Leisure Complex:** a bowling alley, cinema and soft-play area. **Tannaghmore Animal Farm and Gardens** are very popular for family visits. Here you'll find an adventure playground, guided nature walks and tours of the rare breeds farm, treasure hunts and a bouncy castle. The **Leisure Complex** at Lurgan and **Cascades** at Portadown have exceptional family facilities: wave pools, fun pools, flumes, adventure play areas, soft-play areas for under-8s and a crèche.

Lough Neagh Discovery Centre in the **Oxford Island National Nature Reserve** has an exciting exhibition telling the story of the Lough, plus an Ecolab, an interactive hands-on games room. You can take a boat trip, have a picnic or take part in the special activities such as family fun days that are held throughout the year.

Tandragee Castle is a castle but it is also the home of Tayto, one of the most modern crisp manufactures in Europe! Visitors can see all the stages of crisp production, and youngsters will be pleased to know they can sample any new products.

Access throughout Armagh is excellent. There's a network of first-class roads leading to every part of the county. There is also a good public transport system and the two Belfast airports are close by.

PLACES TO VISIT

Activity Centres

CRAIGAVON WATERSPORTS CENTRE**
Craigavon Lakes
Tel: 028 3834 2669; Fax: 028 3834 6018
Open: summer, dawn to dusk; winter, check directly for times
Situated beside a lake and surrounded by attractive open parkland,
the centre has a wide range of activities to suit all the family and
beginners as well as experts. Activities include sailing, windsurfing,
canoeing, water and jet skiing, banana boat, orienteering and
treasure hunts. There is a café and changing facilities on the site.

Castles and Historic Houses

ARDRESS HOUSE**
Annaghmore
Tel: 028 3885 1236
*Open: April, May and September, weekends and bank holidays, 2p.m.–
6p.m.; June to August, daily (except Tuesday), 2p.m.–6p.m.; farmyard
also open May and September, weekdays (except Tuesday), noon–4p.m.*
Admission: A=££, C=£, F
Facilities: toilets; disabled access; picnic area
A 17th-century farmhouse with interesting furniture and paintings.
There's a display of farm implements and livestock in the farmyard
plus a playground and woodland walks.

THE ARGORY**
Moy, Dungannon
Tel: 028 8778 4753
*Open: April, May and September, weekends, 2p.m.–6p.m.; June to
August, daily (except Tuesday), 2p.m.–6p.m.*
Admission: A=££, C=£, F
Facilities: toilets; disabled access; shop; tea-room
The Argory, built in 1824, is like a time capsule: no electricity and
everything just as it was at the turn of the century. The courtyards
have fascinating displays such as the oxyacetylene plant which pro-
duced the gas with which the house was lit. There's an old laundry
and mangle room, and the coach-house and stables are now converted to a shop and tea-room. Special events are held throughout
the season, including a children's fun day. Check directly for times.

Cinemas

CENTREPOINT
Portadown Road, Lurgan
Tel: 028 3832 1997
Four screens plus a licensed bar and restaurant.

Country Parks

MAGHERY COUNTRY PARK*
*Eight miles (12.8km) east of **Dungannon***
Tel: 028 3832 2205
Open: all year round, daily, 9a.m.–5p.m.
Admission: free
A good place to come for bird hides, nature walks, fishing on the Maghery canal, excellent views of Lough Neagh and boat trips to Coney Island.

Environment and Ecology Centres

LOUGH NEAGH DISCOVERY CENTRE***
*Oxford Island Nature Reserve, **Craigavon***
Tel: 028 3832 2205
Open: April to September, daily, 10a.m.–7p.m.; October to March,
Wednesday to Sunday 10a.m.–5p.m. (closed Monday and Tuesday)
Admission: A=£££, C=£, F
Facilities: toilets with baby-changing room; disabled access; craft shop;
café with a children's menu and high-chairs; picnic areas
You'll find lots of hands-on, exciting and interesting things to do at this innovative Discovery Centre where natural history and geography of Lough Neagh and Oxford Island are interpreted with the aid of audio-visual presentations and interactive exhibitions. Look out for the special activities and family fun days that are held throughout the year and try out the computer simulations where you can 'manage the lough'; visit the Ecolab, which is full of interactive games and displays; and don't miss the birdwatching hides, nature reserve, boat trips; walks; play areas and paddling-pool.

Farm Parks

TANNAGHMORE ANIMAL FARM***
*Silverwood, **Craigavon***
Tel: 028 3834 3244
*Open: all year round, daily; **gardens** open: dawn till 1 hour before dusk;*
***farm** open: 10a.m. till 2 hours before dusk*
Admission: free
The farm park was opened in 1991 with the aim of stocking as many of the traditional breeds of farm livestock and poultry found in Ulster at the turn of the century. Many of these are now rare and include Irish Moiled, Kerry and Dexter cattle, Soay and Galway sheep, Saddleback pigs, goats and a wide range of poultry, ducks and geese. There's also an adventure playground, a picnic area with tables, nature walks, a bouncy castle (small charge), organised treasure hunts, and Victorian and rose gardens (see GARDENS).

Forest and Amenity Walks

GOSFORD FOREST PARK***
Markethill
Tel: 028 3755 1277
Open: all year round, daily, 10a.m.–dusk
Admission: ££ per car, A=£, C=£
Facilities: toilets; barbecue site; café

This is a nice park for a family visit; see one of the largest collection of traditional breeds of poultry in Ireland wander around in open paddocks, as well as wildfowl, deer roaming in parkland and ornamental pigeons nesting in the dovecote. There's also an arboretum and nature trails.

PEATLANDS PARK**
Lough Neagh, 7 miles (11.2km) east of **Dungannon**
Tel: 028 3885 1102
Visitor centre *open: Easter and September, weekends and bank holidays, 2p.m.–6p.m.; June to August, daily, 2p.m.–6p.m.;* **park** *open: daily, 9am to dusk*
Admission: free
Facilities: toilets; disabled access; visitor centre; shop
Visitors can see peat faces and small lakes in this south-west corner of Lough Neagh basin. There are outdoor exhibits on peat ecology and you can take a 1-mile trip on a narrow-gauge railway.

SLIEVE GULLION FOREST PARK**
Off route B113, 5 miles (8km) south-west of **Newry**
Tel: 028 3073 8284
Open: Easter to September, daily, 10a.m.–dusk
Admission: £ per car
Facilities: toilets; visitor centre; coffee shop; gallery; craft shop
There's an 8-mile (12.8km) drive up and round this thickly wooded park and a series of excellent walks, including a mountain-top trail (1,880ft) to megalithic cairns and lake, with wondrous views of the Ring of Gullion and the Mourne Mountains.

Gardens

GARDEN OF SENSORY DELIGHTS*****
Friary Road, **Armagh**
Tel: 028 3752 9629
Open: April to September, Monday to Saturday, 10a.m.–5.30p.m., Sunday, 1p.m.–6p.m.; October to March, Monday to Saturday, 10a.m.–5p.m., Sunday, 2p.m.–5p.m.
Admission and facilities – see HERITAGE CENTRES
Situated in the historic woodland that surrounds the 18th-century palace stables, this is a garden to stimulate all the senses: hanging wind-chimes and percussion instruments for the sense of sound; herbs and delicately scented plants for the sense of smell; fruit and vegetables for the sense of taste; beautiful flowers, sculptures and patterned paving for the sense of sight; and textured plants and paving for the sense of touch. The adventure playground, with its climbing frames and assault course, caters for youngsters with plenty of energy, and is designed to provide hours of safe fun in a forest setting.

TANNAGHMORE GARDENS***
Silverwood, **Craigavon**
Tel: 028 3834 3244
Open: all year round, daily; gardens: 7.30a.m.–dusk; farm, 9.30a.m.– 1 hour before dusk
Admission: free
The gardens are an ideal venue for family visits and have something

to interest everyone, whether it's floral bedding schemes, rose gardens, nature walks, pools, picnic areas or the adventure playground. Kids will enjoy the bouncy castle (small charge), the organised treasure hunts and the farm park (see FARM PARKS).

Heritage Centres

NAVAN FORT AND VISITOR CENTRE****
*Killylea Road, **Armagh***
Tel: 028 3752 5550
Open: April, May, June and September, Monday to Saturday, 10a.m.–6p.m., Sunday, 11a.m.–6p.m.; July and August, Monday to Saturday, 10a.m.–7p.m., Sunday, 11a.m.–7p.m.; October to March, Monday to Friday, 10a.m.–5p.m., weekends, noon–5p.m.
Admission: free to the fort; A=£££, C=££, F for the centre
Facilities: toilets with baby-changing facilities; disabled access; visitor centre; shop; restaurant
This is the old and the new in direct contrast: Navan Hill Fort, capital of the Kings of Ulster from 600BC; and the innovative Navan Visitor Centre, an ultra-modern centre with a host of activities, exhibitions and presentations to please all the family.

PALACE STABLES HERITAGE CENTRE****
*Friary Road, **Armagh***
Tel: 028 3752 9629
Open: April to September, Monday to Saturday, 10a.m.–6p.m., Sunday, 1p.m.–6p.m.; October to March, Monday to Saturday, 10a.m.–5p.m., Sunday, 2p.m.–5p.m.
Admission: A=££, C=£, F
Facilities: toilets; picnic area, craft shop; gallery; restaurant
Housed in a picturesque Georgian stable block which encloses a cobbled courtyard, this restored building has been brought back to life as a heritage centre where you can experience stable life in the 18th century. Guided tours recreate the atmosphere of events which occurred in July 1776 when the agricultural improver Arthur Young visited the Archbishop of the Church of Ireland, while other features include the Primate's Chapel, Franciscan Friary, ice-house, eco-trail, exhibitions, horse-drawn carriage rides, an adventure playground and the Garden of the Senses (see GARDENS).

ST PATRICK'S TRIAN and 'THE LAND OF LILLIPUT'*****
*40 English Street, **Armagh***
Tel: 028 3751 0180
Open: July to August, Mon–Sat, 10a.m.–5.30p.m.; Sun, 1p.m.–6p.m.; September to June, Mon–Sat, 10a.m.–5p.m.; Sun, 2p.m.–5p.m.
Admission: A=£££, C=£, F
Facilities: toilets with baby-changing room; disabled access; craft shops; audio-visual presentation; exhibitions; craft workshops; restaurant
The development of Armagh from prehistoric times to the present, together with the city's importance as a world ecclesiastical centre, is illustrated with the aid of excellent audio-visual presentations and exhibitions. Also featured is 'The Land of Lilliput', a child-centred fantasy based on *Gulliver's Travels*. Children are invited to join Lemuel Gulliver on a voyage to Lilliput, where he is shipwrecked in a land where everything is a fraction of its normal size. This innovative

complex is an excellent place to visit with children, and the whole family will enjoy spending time here.

Ireland at Work – Past and Present

TAYTO CRISP FACTORY – TANDRAGEE CASTLE****
Tandragee
Tel: 028 3884 0249
Factory tours by arrangement (Monday to Thursday, 10.30a.m. and 1.30p.m., Friday, 10.30a.m.)
Facilities: shop
The factory produces an amazing one million packets of crisps and snacks each day in the 300-year-old castle. Visitors are taken on a castle/factory tour to see potatoes at all stages of production, the ultra-modern computerised potato storage system, frying and flavouring techniques and packaging. The children will be pleased to learn that there's also the opportunity to sample many of the flavours and any new products.

Leisure Centres and Adventure Playgrounds

CENTREPOINT FAMILY LEISURE COMPLEX***
*Portadown Road, **Lurgan***
Tel: 028 3832 5174
Ten-pin bowling alley, 4-screen cinema and soft-play area.

Museums

ARMAGH COUNTY MUSEUM**
*The Mall, **Armagh***
Tel: 028 3752 3070
Open: all year round, Monday to Friday, 10a.m.–5p.m., Saturday, 10a.m.–1p.m. and 2p.m.–5p.m.
Admission: free
The museum explains the prehistory of the city and county, and has a costumes room and natural history room, a library, art gallery and an extensive map collection. It organises a series of interesting special exhibitions throughout the year, including a children's art show – check directly for timetable of events.

MULLAGHBAWN FOLK MUSEUM
Mullaghbawn
Tel: 028 3088 8108
Open: May to September, Monday to Saturday, 11a.m.–7p.m., Sunday, 2p.m.–7p.m.; October to April, Sunday only, 2p.m.–7p.m.
Admission: A=£, C=free
This unusual thatched roadside museum is furnished as a traditional farmhouse. Visitors will enjoy looking at the exhibitions and crafts, and the coffee shop.

Swimming-Pools

CASCADES LEISURE COMPLEX***
*51 Thomas Street, **Portadown***
Tel: 028 3833 2802; Fax: 028 3833 9666
Open: summer, Monday to Saturday, 10a.m.–9p.m.; winter, Monday and

Wednesday, 3.30p.m.–7p.m., Tuesday and Thursday, 3.30p.m.–9p.m.,
Friday, 5p.m.–9p.m., Saturday, 10a.m.–9p.m.; times vary for minor pool
and flumes – check directly for timetable
A friendly and modern leisure facility with 2 swimming-pools, 2
giant flumes, diving-boards, spa baths, a party room, café, soft-play
centre for the under-8s and a crèche.

WAVES LEISURE COMPLEX***
*Robert Street, **Lurgan***
Tel: 028 3832 2906; Fax: 028 3834 7313
Open: July and August, Monday to Saturday, 10a.m.–9p.m.; September
to June, Monday to Friday, 10a.m.–8.30p.m. (Thursday till 6p.m.),
Saturday, 10a.m.–9p.m.
Excellent leisure complex with a wave pool, children's fun pool,
adventure play area, squash courts, restaurant and a crèche
(available Monday to Friday, 10a.m.–1p.m.).

Science and Technology

ARMAGH PLANETARIUM*****
*College Hill, **Armagh***
Tel: 028 3752 3689; Fax: 028 3752 6187
Open: All year, Mon–Fri, 10a.m.–4.45p.m.; Sat/Sun, 1.15p.m.–4.45p.m.
(check for times of shows which vary seasonally)
Admission: A=£££, C=££, F
Facilities: toilets; disabled access; gift shop; café
The highlight of a visit here is the show in the star theatre. Regardless of
the time of day or the weather, the stars can always be seen under the
Planetarium's silver dome. Interactive technology enables you to see the
very latest pictures from NASA's space telescope, or to look back
through time to the 'big bang' that was responsible for the creation of
our universe many millions of years ago. The solar system gallery
explains the beautiful rings of Saturn, or you can go on a 'flight' over the
surface of Venus. Combined with a visit to the Astropark and the
Eartharium (an earth science centre which allows you to work your
way up from the centre of the earth through volcanic vents, measure
earthquake activity, examine man's impact on the environment, study
atmosphere and see ozone depletion), this is a place guaranteed to
enthral the whole family. After a tiring journey through space, astronauts
can relax in the Voyager Café and choose from a range of out-of-this-
world snacks, at prices that are not astronomical!

● ● ● ● ●

PLACES TO EAT

Cafés and Restaurants

MR PICKWICK'S
*Craigavon Shopping Centre, **Craigavon***
Tel: 028 3834 1025
Disabled access. High-chairs and children's menu available.

PIZZA PASTA HUT
*42 Church Place, **Lurgan***
Tel: 028 3832 6444
Disabled access. High-chairs, family specials and children's menu available.

McCANN'S CAFE
*248 Obins Street, **Portadown***
Tel: 028 3833 2668
Disabled access. High-chairs and children's menu available.

Fast-food Restaurants

McDONALD'S
*Edwards Street, **Lurgan***
Tel: 01762 328000

*Meadows Shopping Centre, Meadow Lane, **Portadown***
Tel: 01762 335700

Hotels and Pubs

ASHBURN HOTEL
*81 William Street, **Lurgan***
Tel: 028 3832 5711
High-chairs and children's menu available.

CASTLE PARK INN
*Robert Street, **Lurgan***
Tel: 028 3832 2726
High-chairs and children's menu available.

LOUGH NEAGH LODGE
*Dungannon Road, **Maghery***
Tel: 028 3885 1901
Disabled access. High-chairs and children's menu available.

CARNGROVE HOTEL
*2 Charlestown Road, **Portadown***
Tel: 028 3833 9222
Disabled access. High-chairs and children's menu available.

PLANTERS TAVERN
*4 Banbridge Road, **Waringstown***
Tel: 028 3888 1510
Disabled access. High-chairs and children's menu available.

• • • • •

PLACES TO STAY

Guest-Houses and B&Bs

ST MICHAEL'S
*1 Mullinure Lane, **Armagh***
Tel: 028 3752 7958

THE CURATAGE
*6 Banbridge Road, **Waringstown***
Tel: 028 3888 2285

Country Houses and Hotels

CHARLEMONT ARMS HOTEL
*63 Lower English Street, **Armagh***
Tel: 028 3752 2028

LIMA COUNTRY HOUSE
*16 Drumalt Road, Silverbridge, **Crossmaglen***
Tel: 028 3086 1944

SILVERWOOD HOTEL
*Kiln Road, **Lurgan***
Tel: 028 3832 7722

REDBRICK COUNTRY HOUSE
*Corbrackey Lane, **Portadown***
Tel: 028 3833 5268

Caravan and Camping Parks

KINNEGO CARAVAN PARK
*Oxford Island, **Lurgan***
Tel: 028 3832 7573
Offers a laundry, children's playground, nature walks and fishing.

Bicycle Hire

IRISH CYCLE HIRE – *see Directory*
RALEIGH RENT-A-BIKE – *see Directory*

Bus Services

CITYBUS – *Tel: 028 9024 6485*
ULSTERBUS – *Tel: 028 9033 3000*

Rail Services

NORTHERN IRELAND RAILWAYS (NIR) – *Tel: 028 9089 9411*
Lurgan *– Tel: 028 3822 2052*

COUNTY CAVAN

Cavan is the most southerly of Ulster's counties, and is part of the Republic. Noted for its lakes and many islands offering excellent **fishing,** and for being the source of the Shannon, Ireland's longest river, it can be difficult to find many family visitor attractions in Cavan unless you happen to be a family of anglers – you get the impression that wherever you stop the car in this county, you will be within casting distance of a fish!

The town of Cavan is renowned for its crystal glass, produced in the traditional mouth-blown and hand-cut method. **Cavan Irish Crystal** is Ireland's second-oldest glassmaking factory and you can experience the wonders of this ancient craft as you watch master blowers breathe life into their creations. It's great to be able to see these completed works of art in the factory shop, but it's not really the place to take young children as you'll be on tenterhooks all the time. There is a coffee shop offering light refreshments, so it may be a good idea if one parent stays here with the children, while the other browses and spends the money!

One of the most unusual tourist attractions in Cavan is the **Lifeforce Watermill.** Built in 1846, the mill is now running again with all the original machinery restored. On arrival you are invited to mix a loaf of bread using Lifeforce stoneground wholemeal flour and natural ingredients such as buttermilk. This is then baked for you in the exquisite coffee shop and bakery while you go on a guided tour of the mill.

In the south of the county near Lough Sheelin is the pretty village of Mount Nugent. Nearby is the **Carraig Craft Visitor Centre** which has craft workshops, lectures and demonstrations, and a museum with audio-visual presentations. There is also a coffee shop and a local tour guide service.

There is a reasonable road network throughout the county, but public transport is very limited.

• • • • •

PLACES TO VISIT

Boats and Boat Trips

TURBET TOURS
*Deanery Banks, **Belturbet***
Tel: (+353) 049 9522360
Open: Easter to September
Cruising on the River Erne and the Shannon–Erne Waterway. The trip includes a 45-minute stop at the Crom Estate visitor centre.

The fully serviced *Erne Dawn* has catering facilities, a bar service and a commentary on places of interest.

Craft Centres

CARRAIG CRAFT VISITOR CENTRE**
Mountnugent
Tel: (+353) 049 40179
Open: all year round, Monday to Saturday, 10a.m.–6p.m., Sunday, 2p.m.–6p.m.
Facilities include a natural craft museum with audio-visual presentation, craft workshops and demonstrations, and a coffee shop (seasonal opening).

CAVAN CRYSTAL**
Cavan
Tel: (+353) 049 4331800
Open: June to September, Monday to Friday, 9.30a.m.–5.30p.m., Saturday, 10a.m.–5p.m., Sunday, 2p.m.–5p.m.
Admission: free
Facilities: factory tours (weekdays only); restaurant (May to September); factory shop
Visitors can tour Ireland's second-oldest lead crystal factory to see glass-blowing and crystal-cutting, and experience the magic of this ancient craft as master blowers breathe life into crystal creations.

Equestrian Facilities

KILLYKEEN EQUESTRIAN CENTRE
Killykeen Forest Park
Tel: (+353) 049 61707
Open: All year
Hacking, trekking, trail riding facilities and instruction. Unaccompanied children can attend. Self-catering chalet accommodation available.

REDHILLS EQUESTRIAN CENTRE
*Killynure, **Redhills***
Tel: (+353) 047 55042
Riders come here for the indoor and outdoor arenas, trekking in Killykeen Forest Park, tuition and residential courses.

Farm Parks

MILL VALLEY FARM**
*Moneyhall, Ballinagh Road, **Cavan***
Tel: (+353) 049 4361409
Open: April to September, daily, 10a.m.–7p.m.; October to March, weekends, 10a.m.–dusk
Admission: A=££, C=£, F
The Mill Valley farm has many interesting things to see and do for all the family, among them an old forge which is now a museum, an old farm mill, unusual poultry and ducks and a wide variety of livestock. Make sure everyone is appropriately dressed for a farm visit.

Festivals and Events

ARVA FESTIVAL***
Arva
Tel: (+353) 049 4335336
On: July
Fun-packed agenda with entertainment to suit everybody.

BALLYCONNELL COMMUNITY FESTIVAL***
Ballyconnell
Tel: (+353) 049 9526159
On: August
The people of Ballyconnell invite visitors and locals to join in the
fun and games and festival activities for all the family.

FESTIVAL OF THE LAKES***
Killeshandra
Tel: (+353) 049 4334316
On: June
A weekend of festive fun including music and dance, sports events,
powerboat racing, angling competitions and children's entertainment.

KILLINKERE WHIT JAMBOREE***
Killinkere
Tel: (+353) 042 9665684
On: June
Busking competitions, pony show and nightly entertainment.

Forest and Amenity Walks

DUN-AN-RI NATIONAL FOREST PARK***
*One mile (1.6km) north of **Kingscourt** on route R179 to Carrickmacross*
Open: all year round
Admission: free
Excellent scenic walks with points of interest. Marker posts point
out the Wishing Well, Cromwell's Bridge, Cabra Cottage, the Lady's
Lake and an ice-house, among other interesting features.

KILLYKEEN FOREST PARK AND CHALETS***
Killykeen; just over 7 miles (12km) west of Cavan town off route R201
Tel: (+353) 049 4332541; Fax: (+353) 049 4361044
Open: all year round, but some facilities (e.g. café/shop) are seasonal
A number of guided trails taking in the main points of interest are
laid out in this superb park on the shores of Lough Oughter (*see*
WHERE TO STAY).

Heritage Centres

ST KILIAN'S HERITAGE CENTRE***
Mullagh
Tel/Fax: (+353) 046 42433
Open: Easter to October, Monday to Saturday, 10a.m.–6p.m., Sunday,
12.30p.m.–6p.m.
Admission: A=££, C=£
Facilities: toilets; visitor centre; craft shop; coffee shop

This unique centre charts the life of St Kilian, the Apostle of Franconia, through audio-visual presentations and an exhibition.

Ireland at Work – Past and Present

LIFEFORCE MILL****
The Mill Rock, **Cavan**
Tel: (+353) 049 4362722; Fax: (+353) 049 4362923
Open: May to September
Admission: A=££, C=£, F (includes instruction and ingredients for making your own bread)
Facilities: toilets; guided tours; excellent coffee shop with home-baking
This unique restored mill allows visitors both to see and participate in the whole process of bread-making. The interesting and relaxed workings of bread production are shared with young and old alike, making this 'hands-*in*' attraction an excellent place to visit.

Museums

CAVAN FOLK MUSEUM**
Cornafean, **Cavan**
Tel: (+353) 049 4337248
Open: March to October (check direct for seasonal opening hours)
Admission: ££
You'll find over 3,000 items here reflecting rural life from the 1700s to the present day.

Swimming-Pools

COUNTY CAVAN SWIMMING AND LEISURE COMPLEX***
Drumalee
Tel: (+353) 049 4362888; Fax: (+353) 049 4362974
Open: Monday to Friday, 8a.m.–10p.m., Saturday, 9a.m.–6p.m., Sunday, 11a.m.–6p.m.
Offers a steam room, jacuzzi, sports hall, children's summer camps, restaurant and crèche.

• • • • •

PLACES TO STAY

Country Houses and Hotels

STAG HALL
Belturbet
Tel: (+353) 049 9522373
Has a children's playroom and a babysitting service.

MACNEAN BISTRO
Blacklion
Tel: (+353) 072 53022
All rooms are en-suite and there's a children's playroom.

RIVERSIDE HOUSE
Cootehill
Tel/Fax: (+353) 049 555552150 (or contact Irish Farm Holidays – see Directory)
Open: all year round (except Christmas and New Year)
Beautifully located family-friendly Victorian house set among mature trees overlooking the River Annalee. Facilities for children, plus bicycles and fishing available.

Farmhouse Accommodation

ROSS HOUSE
Mountnugent
Tel/Fax: (+353) 049 40218 (or contact Irish Farm Holidays – see Directory)
Open: March to October
Charming old manor house on a 360-acre working farm on the shores of Lough Sheelin. Has a tennis court, fishing, horseriding and facilities for children. Self-catering accommodation is also available.

Holiday Parks and Villages

KILLYKEEN FOREST CHALET PARK
*Lough Oughter; 7 miles (12km) west of **Cavan** off route R201*
Tel: (+353) 049 4332541
Killykeen incorporates a complex of 28 self-catering log cabins set amidst 600 acres of woodland, overlooking Lough Oughter. Has a recreation centre and games room, equestrian centre, tennis courts, children's play area, boat and bicycle hire, fishing, restaurant, shop, laundry, walks and trails.

Caravan and Camping Parks

LAKELANDS CARAVAN AND CAMPING PARK
Shercock
Tel: (+353) 042 9669488
Open: Easter to mid-September
Fishing, boating, windsurfing, waterskiing and canoeing from the lake shore of the park

Bicycle Hire

IRISH CYCLE HIRE – *see Directory*
RALEIGH RENT-A-BIKE – *see Directory*

ON YOUR BIKE RENTAL
Cavan
Tel: (+353) 049 9522219

Bus Services

National travel information, BUS EIREANN – *Tel: (+353) 01 8366111*
Cavan – *Tel: (+353) 049 4331353*

COUNTY DERRY

Dotted with small villages and rural towns, County Derry's farming traditions are still evident today. During the early part of the 20th century, children from all over Ireland came to hiring fairs here to find work on the rich, fertile land. Nowadays they still come to Derry – but this time to enjoy themselves at the county's many attractions.

The **beaches** are outstanding: Magilligan Strand is Ireland's longest beach, and the nearby Benone's golden sands were the first in the North to be given a European Blue Flag award. The high standards of safety, water quality and cleanliness here mean Benone is recognised as being Northern Ireland's first 'Premier' resort. Adjacent to the beach is the award-winning **Benone Tourist Complex** with its many attractions: a unique, ultra-modern children's adventure play area; two heated outdoor splash pools; a nature reserve; tennis and badminton courts; putting and bowling greens and a golf course. If the kids just want to play on the magnificent beach, they'll have fun collecting some of the many thousands of sea-shells there.

South of Benone is the town of Limavady, the name of which comes from the Gaelic meaning 'leap of the dog'. Legend has it that a dog owned by one of the O'Cahan chiefs jumped a gorge on the River Roe to bring warning of an unexpected enemy attack. The **Roe Valley Recreation Centre** in Limavady hosts activities for children during the summer holidays, offering trampolining, archery, lifeguard training, canoeing, and rafting. Further south is the **Roe Valley Country Park** in an area still known as Dogleap. Here you can venture deep into the woods to visit the site of the O'Cahan Castle and listen to legends about that brave dog. Carpeted with wildflowers, full of interesting wildlife and majestic trees, this is a wonderful place to roam – it's easy to see why this area is believed to have provided the inspiration for the beautiful melody 'Londonderry Air'. The surrounding area is very attractive, and the road through **Glenshane Pass** is one of the best scenic routes in Northern Ireland. There is also a drive with superb views up to the summit of Benbraddagh mountain.

The historic walled city of Derry is the regional capital of the North-west. Architecturally splendid, this is a great place to linger. There are magnificent views of the city and surrounding countryside from the great 17th-century walls, which are 18ft thick. Cannon still point their black noses over the ramparts. There are many places to visit, including the award-winning **Tower Museum** which tells the story of Derry, and the **craft village**. Kids will love **Banana's Fun Park, Brunswick Superbowl and Quaser Laserdrome,** and the **Lisnagelvin Leisure Centre** has a wave machine and poolside cafeteria.

The county is very accessible by either road, rail or air. There are now direct flights to Derry Airport, which has recently undergone a multi-million-pound development, from most UK airports.

PLACES TO VISIT

Castles and Historic Houses

SPRINGHILL***
*Moneymore, **Magherafelt***
Tel: 028 8674 8210
Open: April, May and September, weekends, 2p.m.–6p.m.; June to
August, daily (except Thursday), 1p.m.–6p.m.
Admission: A=££, C=£, F
Facilities: toilets; disabled access; woodland walks; gardens
A 17th-century manor house with a costume museum. Special
events for children are arranged throughout the season and include
Easter Eggcentricities, a Teddy Bears' Picnic, and a children's
challenge. Check directly for a timetable of events.

Cathedrals

ST COLUMB'S CATHEDRAL
Derry
Tel: 028 7126 7313
Open: April to October, Monday to Saturday, 9a.m.–5p.m.; November to
March, Monday to Saturday, 9a.m.–4p.m.
Admission: A=£, C=free
Stained glass depicts heroic scenes from the great siege of 1688–
89, and the keys of the gates closed against the Jacobites are dis-
played in the chapterhouse. Audio-visual shows give a presentation
of the siege and the history of the cathedral.

Cinemas

JET CENTRE
*Riverside Park, **Coleraine***
Tel: 028 7035 8011
Four-screen cineplex.

STRAND MULTIPLEX
*Quayside Centre, Strand Road, **Derry***
Tel: 028 7137 3900
Seven screens.

Country Parks

NESS WOOD COUNTRY PARK**
*Seven miles (11.2km) south-east of **Derry** off route A6*
Tel: 028 7772 2074
Open: all year round, dawn to dusk
Admission: free
Facilities: carpark; waymarked woodland walks; picnic areas
A path from the carpark leads to Ulster's highest waterfall, the Ness
waterfall on the Burntollet river.

ROE VALLEY COUNTRY PARK****
*Dogleap Road, **Limavady***
Tel: 028 7772 2074
***Park** open: all year round, daily, dawn to dusk; **visitor centre** open: Easter to September, daily, 10a.m.–5p.m.; October to Easter, Monday to Friday, 10a.m.–4p.m.*
Admission: free
Facilities: toilets; disabled access (including a disabled anglers' jetty); café (summer only)
This is a wonderful place to come for a family outing and spend a quiet, relaxing day away from the hustle and bustle of modern technology, in the company of a majestic display of flora and fauna, enhanced by an interesting array of local history and sporting activities. The story of the valley is told at the Dogleap Centre, and there are exhibitions, audio-visual theatre, riverside and woodland walks, a history trail and fishing.

Craft Centres

DERRY CRAFT VILLAGE***
*Shipquay Street, **Derry***
Tel: 028 7126 0329; Fax: 028 7136 0921
Open: all year round, Monday to Saturday, 9a.m.–5.30p.m.
Admission: free
Facilities:, toilets; craft shops; coffee shop; restaurant
Take a step back in time in this interesting craft village with many distinctive features (including a 15th-century thatched cottage). Informal music sessions are held throughout the summer.

Crèches

SPRINGTOWN DAY NURSERY
*Unit 5, Ballinska Road, Springtown Industrial Estate, **Derry***
Tel: 028 7136 7642

Equestrian Facilities

HILL FARM RIDING AND TREKKING CENTRE
*47 Altikeeragh Road, **Castlerock***
Tel: 028 7084 8629
Open: all year round
Offers outdoor arena, tuition, refreshments, beach trekking for experienced riders, and children's summer camps.

Farm Parks

HILLTOP OPEN FARM
*Dunn's Farm, 51 Beragh Hill Road, **Ballyarnet***
Tel: 028 7135 4556
Open: March to August, daily, 1p.m.–6p.m.
Admission: A=£, C=£
Facilities: toilets; disabled access; shop; picnic area
You can bottle-feed lambs and see a range of exotic game birds and poultry, rare breeds of sheep and pigs, as well as enjoy pony and cart rides.

Gardens

DOWNHILL CASTLE GARDENS***
Downhill
Tel: 028 7084 8728
Grounds open: all year round, daily, dawn to dusk; *temple* open: April,
June and September, weekends, 2p.m.–6p.m.; July and August, daily,
noon–6p.m.
Admission: free
A choice of wonderful themed gardens and glen walks to see and
explore. The Mussenden Temple, built by the eccentric Bishop of
Derry in 1783 as his library, is perched spectacularly on the edge of
sea cliffs overlooking the magnificent Downhill Strand.

Heritage Centres

KNOCKCLOGHRIM WINDMILL***
Maghera
Tel: 028 7963 3691
Open: Easter to September, Monday to Saturday, 10.30a.m.–4.30p.m.
Admission: A=£, C=£, F
This restored windmill was fully operational until the Great Storm
of 1895 blew the sails off. Today it houses local history exhibits and
a viewing gallery, together with a tea-room and a play area.

Leisure Centres and Adventure Playgrounds

BANANAS***
Pennyburn Industrial Estate, **Derry**
Tel: 028 7137 3731
*Open: all year round, Monday to Friday, 1p.m.–8p.m., Saturday and
bank holidays, 11a.m.–8p.m.*
Charges: ££ per hour
Children's fully supervised indoor action centre with soft-play areas
for toddlers.

BENONE TOURIST COMPLEX****
Magilligan, **Benone**
Tel: 028 7775 0555
*Open: July to August, daily, 10a.m.–8.30p.m. (Note: times vary through-
out the year for golf course and courts)*
This modern activity play park has a bowling green, 9-hole golf
course and tennis and badminton courts. All equipment is available
to hire. There's also a nature reserve, a unique modern children's
adventure play area and heated outdoor splash pools. In July and
August special events are organised such as shell painting, sandcastle
competitions, magic shows, junior discos, fancy dress competitions
and beach games. This is the ideal venue for a fun-packed holiday.

BRUNSWICK SUPERBOWL***
Brunswick Lane, Pennyburn, **Derry**
Tel: 028 7137 1999
*Open: all year round, Monday to Friday, 9a.m.–12.30a.m., weekends,
9a.m.–1a.m.*
Ten-pin bowling alley with adapted lanes for children.

JET CENTRE***
Riverside Park, **Coleraine**
Tel: 028 7035 8011
Open: all year round, daily
This exciting leisure centre has an ice-rink, a 4-screen cinema and
the Amazon Adventure Park.

KART KRAZY
Lower Newmills Road, **Coleraine**
Tel: 028 7035 5088
Indoor karting centre.

THE CRESCENT**
Portstewart
Tel: 028 7083 2847
Super children's play area with bumper boats, paddling-pools, an
electric car circuit, a café and a shop.

Museums

EARHART CENTRE AND WILDLIFE SANCTUARY**
Ballyarnet, **Derry**
Tel: 028 7135 4040
Centre *open: June to September, daily, 9a.m.–7p.m.; October to May,
Monday to Thursday, 9a.m.–4.30p.m., Friday, 9a.m.–1p.m.;* **wildlife
sanctuary** *open: all year round, daily, 9a.m.–dusk*
Admission: free
Amelia Earhart was the first woman to fly solo across the Atlantic. This
cottage exhibition looks at her achievements and you'll see a
commemorative sculpture at the landing site. There's also a wildlife
sanctuary here.

HARBOUR MUSEUM
Harbour Square, **Derry**
Tel: 028 7136 5151
Open: all year round, Monday to Friday, 10a.m.–1p.m. and 2p.m.–5p.m.
Admission: free
An exhibition of the maritime history of Derry, including a replica of
the 30ft curragh in which St Columba sailed to Iona in AD563.

TOWER MUSEUM
Union Hall Place, **Derry**
Tel: 028 7137 2411
*Open: September to June, Tuesday to Saturday, 10a.m.–5p.m.; July and
August, Monday to Saturday, 10a.m.–5p.m., Sunday, 2p.m.–5p.m.*
Admission: A=££, C=£, F
Located just inside the 17th-century walls of Derry, the Tower
Museum tells the history of the city from ancient times to the
present with the aid of audio-visual presentations and photos.

Shopping Centres

FOYLESIDE SHOPPING CENTRE
Foyle Street, **Derry**
Tel: 028 7137 7575

Open: daily (late-night shopping, Wednesday to Friday, till 9p.m.)
The city's newest major shopping complex.

Swimming-Pools

CASTLEROCK RECREATION GROUNDS
Castlerock *beach*
Tel: 028 7084 8258
Outdoor heated swimming-pool open July and August.

COLERAINE LEISURE CENTRE***
Railway Road, **Coleraine**
Tel: 028 7035 6432
This excellent modern leisure complex has a junior pool for families
with young children and a senior pool with 2 giant flumes. Also in
the complex are sports halls, gyms and a restaurant.

LISNAGELVIN LEISURE CENTRE***
Richill Park, **Derry**
Tel: 028 7147 695
Open: all year round, Monday, 2p.m.–10p.m., Tuesday to Friday,
10a.m.–9p.m., Saturday, 10a.m.–5p.m., Sunday, noon–4p.m.
Super slides, a wave pool, water cannon, gymnasium, sauna, jacuzzi
and poolside cafeteria.

ROE VALLEY RECREATION CENTRE***
Limavady
Tel: 028 7776 4009
Facilities include: indoor heated swimming-pool and squash courts.
Holiday fun times in July and August include inflatables, canoeing,
tuition, bouncy castle, trampoline sessions, games, quizzes, craft, art
and drama classes (check directly for timetable).

Theatres

PLAY HOUSE
Artillery Street, **Derry**
Tel: 028 7137 3538
Open: all year round, Monday to Saturday, 10a.m.–5.30p.m.
Productions and workshops. Phone for a programme of events.

RIVERSIDE THEATRE
University of Ulster, **Coleraine**
Tel: 028 7032 4459
Facilities: bar; coffee shop; sweet shop; art gallery and exhibitions
Amateur and professional companies put on a variety of produc-
tions that include educational projects and children's shows.

Trains and Model Railways

FOYLE VALLEY RAILWAY CENTRE***
Foyle Road, **Derry**
Tel: 028 7126 5234
Open: all year round, Tuesday to Saturday, 10a.m.–5p.m., Sunday,
(summer only), 2p.m.–6p.m.

Admission: free
Charges: A=££, C=£ (under-5s free)
A museum created around narrow-gauge railways. Trains operate (April to September) on a mile of scenic track alongside the River Foyle, and there are lots of original steam trains on view. Models, a large-scale map of the rail system and an audio-visual programme make the centre an interesting place to visit.

• • • • •

PLACES TO EAT

Cafés and Restaurants

CHARLY'S
34 Newbridge Road, Coleraine
Tel: 028 7035 2020
Open: daily, noon–10p.m.

FLORENTINI'S
67–69 Strand Road, Derry
Tel: 028 7126 0653
Home-made food, sandwiches and rolls. Ice-cream specialists.

GRAN'MA SMYTH'S
Railway Road, Coleraine
Tel: 028 7035 1150
Open: Monday ot Saturday, 7.30a.m. to 6p.m.
Good choice of meals and kiddies menu.

PIZZA HUT
Quayside shopping Centre, Derry
Tel: 028 7126 9696

MORELLI'S
57 The Promenade, Portstewart
Tel: 028 7083 2150
Open: summer, daily, 10a.m.–11pm.; winter, 10a.m.–6p.m.
Baked potatoes, pizza, pasta and home-made ice-cream.

Fast-Food Restaurants

McDONALD'S
Riverside Centre, Coleraine
Tel: 028 7032 1500
and
Foyleside Shopping Centre, Derry
Tel: 028 7137 7800

• • • • •

PLACES TO STAY

Guest-Houses and B&Bs

CASHEL
21 Knockaduff Road, Aghadowey
Tel: 028 70868606

BALLYSCULLION LODGE
Ballyscullion Park, Bellaghy
Tel: 028 7938 6235; Fax: 028 7938 6416

PORTNEAL LODGE
75 Bann Road, Kilrea
Tel: 028 2954 1444

THE POPLARS
352 Seacoast Road, Limavady
Tel: 028 7775 0360

ARDOWEN HOUSE
13 Northland Road, Derry
Tel: 028 7126 4950

Country Houses and Hotels

HEATHFIELD HOUSE
31 Drumcroon Road, Killykergan, Coleraine
Tel: 028 2955 8245

GORTEEN HOUSE HOTEL
187 Roe Mill Road, Limavady
Tel/Fax: 028 7772 2333

WATERFOOT HOTEL
Caw Roundabout, 14 Clooney Road, Derry
Tel: 028 7145 500; Fax: 028 7131 1006

ASHLEIGH HOUSE
164 Station Road, Portstewart
Tel: 028 7083 4452

Farmhouse Accommodation

BEARDIVILLE FARMHOUSE
8 Ballyhome Road, Coleraine
Tel: 028 2073 1323

Caravan and Camping Parks

BENONE TOURIST COMPLEX
*Benone, **Limavady***
Tel: 028 7775 0555
Open: all year round
Caravan and camping park with a host of facilities (see LEISURE
CENTRES AND ADVENTURE PLAYGROUNDS).

Hostels

FLAX-MILL HOSTEL
*Mill Lane, Derry Lane, **Dungiven***
Tel: 028 7774 2655
Open: all year round

OAK GROVE MANOR
*4-6 Magazine Street, **Derry***
Tel: 028 7137 2273
Family rooms, all en-suite, restaurant and city-centre location.

CAUSEWAY COAST HOSTEL
*4 Victoria Terrace, Atlantic Circle, **Portstewart***
Tel: 028 7083 3789
Open: all year round

Bicycle Hire

IRISH CYCLE HIRE – see *Directory*
RALEIGH RENT-A-BIKE – see *Directory*

BICYCLE DOCTOR
Portrush
Tel: 028 7082 4340
Seasonal

Car Hire

FORD RENT-A-CAR
*Desmond Motors Ltd, 173 Strand Road, **Derry***
Tel: 028 7136 0420

Airports

Derry Airport
Tel: 028 7181 0784

Bus Services

CITYBUS – *Tel: 028 9024 6485*
ULSTERBUS – *Tel: 028 9033 3000*

Rail Services

NORTHERN IRELAND RAILWAYS (NIR) – *Tel: 028 9089 9411*

COUNTY DONEGAL

As well as being one of the least polluted places in Europe *and* one of the most unexplored areas of Ireland, the north-western county of Donegal has many Blue Flag beaches and spectacular mountain scenery. It's definitely one of Ireland's best-kept secrets, and is a perfect place to spend a quiet holiday with children.

The main towns are Letterkenny and Donegal. Letterkenny is a bustling market town with a lot to offer visitors. It has a **bowling centre,** an **indoor adventure play centre** and an **aqua leisure centre.** The historic town of Donegal has done much to preserve its heritage and culture. The recently renovated **Donegal Castle** in the town centre is a joy to visit and explore. The name Donegal (*Dun na nGall*) means 'Fortress of the Foreigners' and refers to its history as a Viking stronghold.

Active youngsters will find a lot to do in this county. In the north there's **Leisure Land** at Redcastle and the **Vintage Car and Carriage Museum** at Buncrana. For outdoor enthusiasts the enormous **Glenveagh National Park** and **Glenveagh Castle and Gardens** are well worth a visit. Further south, railway buffs will love a 3-mile return trip along the shores of Lough Finn being pulled by a Simplex 102T loco. There is also an excellent **Railway Heritage Centre** in the town of Donegal.

The county's premier holiday resort is Bundoran in the south; **Water World** is an aqua adventure playground, and the town has modern amusements, pitch'n'putt and, for hardy types, excellent surfing.

Road access is good from north to south down the east and west of the county, but there's a maze of minor roads to explore in the central area that has the largest Irish-speaking community in the country. *Destination Donegal*, a comprehensive guidebook to the county, is available free from tourist offices. It has lots of useful information and a map of the county showing where various attractions can be found. There are airports at Derry and Donegal.

● ● ● ● ●

PLACES TO VISIT

Adventure Centres

DONEGAL ADVENTURE CENTRE
Bundoran
Tel: (+353) 072 42412
Open: all year round

A host of activities available for all ages including surfing, canoeing, diving, horseriding, mountain biking, fishing, golfing, etc.

Castles and Historic Houses

DONEGAL CASTLE***
Donegal
Tel: (+353) 073 22405
Open: June to September, daily, 10a.m.–6.30p.m.
Admission: A=££, C=£, F
The castle stands on an outcrop of rock beside the River Eask in the town of Donegal and is one of the most interesting and picturesque castles in Ireland.

GLENVEAGH CASTLE
Church Hill, **Letterkenny**
Tel: (+353) 074 37088
Open: April to October, daily (closed Friday in October), 10a.m.–6.30p.m.
Admission: A=££, C=£, F
Facilities: toilets; disabled access; visitor centre with audio-visual show; restaurant; tea-rooms (open Easter and May to October)
Built in 1870–73, the castle consists of a 4-storey rectangular keep. Access is by guided tour only (see COUNTRY PARKS and GARDENS).

Country Parks

GLENVEAGH NATIONAL PARK****
Church Hill, **Letterkenny**
Tel: (+353) 074 37088
Open: April to October, daily (closed Friday in October), 10a.m.–6.30p.m.
Admission: A=££, C=£, F
Facilities: see CASTLES
There are 10,000 hectares of glens and mountains waiting to be explored in the company of one of the largest herds of red deer in Ireland. Visitors can take a nature trail or a guided walk through woods of Scots pine and oak to an area of blanket bog, and there's a free minibus service to the CASTLE and GARDENS.

Craft Centres

CROLLY DOLLS***
Meenacrieve, **Annagry**
Tel: (+353) 075 48466
Open: all year round, Monday to Friday, 9.30a.m.–5p.m., Saturday, 2p.m.–5p.m.
This company has introduced a new generation of the world-famous Crolly Doll, first made in Donegal in 1939. It is worth paying a visit to the showroom to see these interesting creations.

DONEGAL CRAFT VILLAGE**
Donegal
Tel: (+353) 073 22053
Open: Monday to Saturday, 9a.m.–7p.m., Sunday, 9a.m.–6p.m. (phone to check for seasonal variations)
Admission: free

Facilities: toilets; coffee shop; picnic area
See traditional crafts expertly finished by skilled craftspeople in workshops grouped around a common courtyard.

Equestrian Facilities

DEANE'S EQUESTRIAN CENTRE
*Darney, **Bruckless***
Tel: (+353) 073 37160
Open: All year
Equestrian centre with indoor arena. Riding instruction for all ages, hacking, trekking, unaccompanied children. Coffee shop

LITTLE ACORN FARM***
*Coast Road, **Carrick***
Tel: (+353) 073 39386
Open: All year
Excellent centre with all facilities and instruction.

VILLAGE STABLES
*Malin, **Inishowen***
Tel: (+353) 077 70606; Fax: (+353) 077 70770
Open: all year round
Indoor riding schools, beach riding and tuition.

Festivals and Events

DONEGAL INTERNATIONAL ARTS FESTIVAL***
Donegal
Tel: (+353) 073 22312
On: end of June
This festival of fun for all the family features street performers, music, dancing, magic, storytelling, discos and kids' entertainment.

LETTERKENNY FOLK FESTIVAL***
Letterkenny
Tel: (+353) 074 27856
On: mid-August
A programme of events for all the family to enjoy, including street performers, music, dancing and concerts.

MARY FROM DUNGLOE FESTIVAL***
Dungloe
Tel: (+353) 075 21254
On: end July to early August
Ten days of fun with plenty of entertainment for young and old, including puppet shows, art workshops, games, sports, music, street entertainment, song and dance.

Forest and Amenity Walks

ARDS FOREST PARK
*Three miles (5km) north of **Creeslough** off route N56 to Dunfangahy*
Facilities: carpark; toilets
The park is situated on the shores of Sheephaven Bay. The area ha

a wide diversity of habitat and woodland, sand dunes, sea and lake shores, plus many features of historical and archaeological interest. There are numerous viewing points on the walks and trails with spectacular vistas of the surrounding countryside.

DRUMBOE
Stranorlar
Facilities: carpark; picnic site; forest and riverside walks; shelters

LOUGH ESKE
*Four miles (7km) north-east of **Donegal** on route N15 to Ballybofey*
Facilities: carpark; picnic area with outstanding views of Lough Eske

Gardens

ARDNAMONA
Lough Eske
Tel: (+353) 073 22650
Open: January to August, 10a.m.–5p.m. (by appointment only)
Admission: A=££, C=£ (under-12s free)
No facilities at the moment, but if you're in the area it's well worth making an appointment to visit. There is nothing else in Ireland to match this spectacular jungle of rhododendrons and conifers set in a forgotten paradise. Ardnamona, a designated National Heritage Garden, is rich in folklore, trails and waterfalls, and overlooks the beautiful Lough Eske.

GLENVEAGH GARDENS***
Churchill
Tel: (+353) 074 37088
Open: Easter to October, daily, 10.30a.m.–6.30p.m.
Admission: A=££, C=£, F
Facilities: see CASTLES
Glenveagh is a garden of outstanding beauty in a breathtaking setting that includes woodland gardens and pleasure grounds. Access is possible via the shuttle bus from the National Park vsitor centre (see COUNTRY PARKS *and* CASTLES).

Heritage Centres

BAILE CHONAILL
Falcarragh
Tel: (+353) 074 35363
Open: Easter to October, Monday to Friday, 9a.m.–5p.m.
Admission: A=£, C=£
Facilities: toilets
This cultural and heritage centre has displays, local history and art exhibitions, Japanese gardens and nature trails.

GLENCOLMCILLE FOLK MUSEUM***
Glencolumbkille
Tel/Fax: (+353) 073 30017
Open: Easter to September, Monday to Saturday, 10a.m.–6p.m., Sunday, noon–6p.m.
Admission: A=£, C=£

Facilities: toilets; craft shop; nature trails; tea-room
This wonderful example of a folk village museum has maintained the traditional culture in the area over 3 centuries.

GRIANAN OF AILEACH***
*Burt, **Inishowen;** off route N13, 4 miles (6.4km) west of Derry*
Tel: (+353) 077 68512; Fax: (+353) 077 68530
Fort *open: free access anytime; **visitor centre** open: summer, daily, 10a.m–6p.m.; winter, daily, noon–6p.m.; **restaurant** open: summer, daily, 10a.m.–10p.m.; winter, daily, noon–10p.m. (although winter times may vary)*
Admission to centre: A=££, C=£, F
Facilities: toilets; interpretative area; craft shop; restaurant
The Grianán of Aileach ('stone palace of the sun'), an ancient fort dating back to the time of the Tuatha Dé Danann, is built of dry stones and looks over 7 counties. The ancient site's long and interesting history is told in the visitor centre.

IONAD COIS LOCHA***
*Lakeside Centre, **Dunlewey***
Tel: (+353) 075 31699
Open: Easter to September, daily, 11a.m.–6p.m.
Admission: A=££, C=£, F
Facilities: craft shop; tea-room; restaurant
Interesting guided tours of a restored house and farm, plus boat trips, pet animals and an adventure play area.

LURGYVALE THATCHED COTTAGE**
*Kilmacrennan, **Letterkenny***
Tel: (+353) 074 39216
Open: May to September, Monday to Saturday, 10a.m.–7p.m., Sunday, 11a.m.–7p.m.
Admission: A=£, C=£
Restored white-washed cottage with many interesting features. There are demonstrations of traditional crafts on the first Sunday of each month, play facilities for children, a picnic area and a tea-shop.

TULLYARVAN MILL AND CULTURAL EXHIBITION*
*Buncrana, **Inishowen***
Tel: (+353) 077 61613
Open: June to September, Monday to Saturday, 10a.m.–6p.m., Sunday, 2p.m.–6p.m.
Admission: A=£, C=£
Facilities: toilets; coffee shop; craft shop; picnic park
This restored 19th-century corn mill has an informative visitor centre and a concert room, art and drama workshops, information on local wildlife and riverside walks.

ULSTER CULTURAL INSTITUTE
Glencolumbkille
Tel: (+353) 073 30213
Open: April to September, daily, 11a.m.–7p.m.
Admission: free
Facilities include an archaeological exhibition, archive art gallery, traditional music and an excellent restaurant specialising in seafood.

Leisure Centres and Adventure Playgrounds

BANANAS***
Pearse Road, **Letterkenny**
Tel: (+353) 074 26644
*Open: all year round, Monday to Friday, 1p.m.–7p.m., weekends and
bank holidays, 11a.m.–7p.m.*
Charges: ££ per hour
Indoor fully supervised children's play centre with a coffee shop and
a soft-play area for the under-3s.

LEISURELAND***
Redcastle Hotel Complex
Tel: (+353) 077 82073/82306
*Open: July and August, Mon–Sat, 12noon–6p.m.; every Sunday,
1p.m.–7p.m.*
*Facilities: toilets; tuck shop; souvenir shop; restaurant; picnic areas; baby-
changing area*
One of Ireland's leading indoor and outdoor leisure centres, offering
a wide variety of entertainment for children of all ages. The centre
is ideally situated in an enclosed area, which means that youngsters
are free to play in safety. Indoor activities include dodgems, a small
car track, a ball pool and video games. Outdoors there's a multi-
lane slide, thunder jets and a bouncy castle.

Museums

DOAGH VISITOR CENTRE
Doagh Island, **Innishowen**
Tel: (+353) 077 76493
Open: Easter to September, daily, 10a.m.–4p.m.
Admission: A=££, C=£, F
This outdoor museum tells the story of life in this area from the
time of the famine to the 1970s. There are lots of interesting
exhibits and displays, a teahouse and craft shop, and a children's play
area.

DONEGAL COUNTY MUSEUM
High Road, **Letterkenny**
Tel: (+353) 074 21160
*Open: all year round, Monday to Friday, 11a.m.–4.30p.m., Saturday,
1p.m.–4.30p.m.*
This museum has a permanent exhibition covering the archaeology,
railway, history and folk traditions of the county. You'll also find
exhibition galleries, workshops and a conservation service here.

FORT DUNREE MILITARY MUSEUM**
Fort Dunree, **Buncrana**
Tel: (+353) 074 24613
*Open: mid-June to mid-September, Monday to Saturday, 10.30a.m.–
6p.m., Sunday, 2p.m.–6p.m.*
Admission: A=£, C=£
A magnificently situated military museum, which uses historic docu-
ments, photographs, weapons and equipment to relate the history
of Lough Swilly in the context of Ireland's coastal defences. There is

a tea-room and an audio-visual theatre, and guides are available to conduct visitors around this impressive coastal fortification.

VINTAGE CAR MUSEUM
Buncrana
Tel: (+353) 077 61130
Open: June to October, daily, 10a.m.–8p.m.
Admission: A=££, C=£
Collection of vintage and classic cars, horse-drawn carriages, Victorian bicycles and motorcycles, a model car and railway collection.

Shopping Centres

THE COURTYARD SHOPPING CENTRE
Letterkenny
Variety and quality shopping with a wide range of shops and fast-food restaurants.

Swimming-Pools

BUNCRANA LEISURE CENTRE*
*Shore Road, **Buncrana***
Tel: (+353) 077 61000
Open: all year round, Monday to Friday, 9a.m.–10p.m., weekends, 10a.m.–9p.m.
Swimming-pool, jacuzzi, sauna, children's fun sessions and outdoor facilities.

LETTERKENNY LEISURE CENTRE**
*High Road, **Letterkenny***
Tel: (+353) 074 25251
Open: all year round, daily, 9.30a.m.–10p.m., weekends, 10a.m.–7p.m.
Public swimming-pool with sauna, steam room, jacuzzi, tennis court and play area.

WATER WORLD****
Bundoran
Tel: (+353) 072 41172
Open: Easter to September, daily, 11a.m.–8p.m.
Admission: A=££££, C=£££
Facilities: disabled access; fast-food restaurant; snack shop
This is an aqua-fun centre rather than a swimming-pool. The centre has lots of exciting things to do, including flumes, aqua volcano, tornado slide, water rapids and a tidal-wave pool. There are also outdoor facilities with a putting-green, tennis courts and an adventure playground.

Trains and Model Railways

FINTOWN RAILWAY***
Fintown
Tel: (+353) 075 46280
Open: June, Monday to Friday, 1p.m.–4p.m., Sunday, 1p.m.–5p.m.; July to September, Monday to Friday, 11a.m.–5p.m., weekends, 11a.m.–6p.m.
Charges: A=££, C=£, F

A unique 3-mile trip on a narrow-gauge railway along the scenic shores of Lough Finn.

• • • • •

PLACES TO EAT

Cafés and Restaurants

THE RIVERSIDE BISTRO
Main Street, Dungloe
Tel: (+353) 075 21062
A restaurant that has rapidly gained a reputation for its menu to suit all tastes and its special children's menu.

BAKERSVILLE
Church Lane, Letterkenny
Tel: (+353) 074 21887
Fresh home-baking.

CHARLY'S CAFE
Pearse Road, Letterkenny
Tel: (+353) 074 25961
Excellent fish and chips.

THE GRANARY RESTAURANT AND COFFEE SHOP
I Academy Court, Letterkenny
Tel: (+353) 074 24451
Tasty meals cooked fresh on the premises.

Hotels and Pubs

UBIQUITOUS RESTAURANT AND BAR
47 Upper Main Street, Buncrana
Tel: (+353) 077 62530
This is one of the most popular eating spots in town and is ideal for families.

HYLAND CENTRAL HOTEL***
The Diamond, Donegal
Tel: (+353) 073 21027; Fax: (+353) 073 22295
This hotel has a family friendly restaurant with an excellent children's menu. They serve an exceptionally good Sunday lunch.

PLACES TO STAY

Country Houses and Hotels

HYLAND CENTRAL HOTEL
The Diamond, **Donegal**
Tel: (+353) 073 21027; Fax: (+353) 073 22295
The hotel has family rooms and a leisure centre with a swimming-pool for residents only.

MOORLAND GUEST-HOUSE
Laghey
Tel/Fax: (+353) 073 34319
Family-friendly guest-house with facilities for children.

HOTEL CARRIGART
Letterkenny
Tel: (+353) 074 55114; Fax: (+353) 074 55250
Open: Easter to October
The hotel has an indoor heated swimming-pool, a squash court and a children's playground.

SHANDON HOTEL
Marble Hill Strand, **Sheephaven Bay**
Tel: (+353) 074 36137; Fax: (+353) 074 36430
Family-friendly hotel with an indoor heated swimming-pool and children's activity centre.

THE GREAT NORTHERN HOTEL
AND LEISURE CENTRE
Bundoran
Tel: (+353) 072 41204
Open: All year
The leisure centre has a swimming-pool and kiddies pool, and there's a playroom and KO Children's club to keep the kids amused.

Farmhouse Accommodation

THE HALL GREENE
Porthall, **Lifford**
Tel: (+353) 074 411318 (or contact Irish Farm Holidays – see Directory)
Open: all year round (except Christmas and New Year)
Family friendly 17th-century farmhouse with facilities for children.

Holiday Parks and Villages

MOORE'S HOLIDAY PARK
Dunfanaghy, **Letterkenny**
Tel: (+353) 074 36171

A choice of fully equipped bungalows or chalets. Facilities include a children's playground.

Self-Catering Apartments and Houses

ATLANTIC APARTOTEL
Bundoran
Tel: (+353) 072 41205
A modern self-catering holiday apartment complex with its own indoor heated water centre, bar and entertainment room, games room, teenagers' coffee shop, crazy golf and play garden.

THE RECTORY HOLIDAY COTTAGES
*Maghery, **Dungloe***
Tel: (+353) 075 21286; Fax: (+353) 075 21682
A complex of 8 fully appointed holiday cottages situated in the seaside village of Maghery.

Caravan and Camping Parks

LAKESIDE CENTRE
*Belleek Road, **Ballyshannon***
Tel/Fax: (+353) 072 52436
Open: all year round
Facilities include watersports, scenic walks, an adventure playground and a restaurant. A waterbus sails during the summer months on Assaroe Lake.

KNOCKALLA CARAVAN AND CAMPING PARK
*Knockalla, **Portsalon***
Tel: (+353) 074 59108
Open: Easter to September
Located near miles of safe golden beautiful beach. Facilities include a laundry, campers' kitchen, shop, TV and games rooms, and an outdoor play area. Mobile homes are available for hire on site.

Hostels

HOMEFIELD HOSTEL
*Bayview Avenue, **Bundoran***
Tel: (+353) 072 41288; Fax: (+353) 072 41049
Open: all year round

DONEGAL TOWN INDEPENDENT HOSTEL
*Doonan, **Donegal***
Tel: (+353) 073 22805; Fax: (+353) 073 22030
Open: all year round

THE MANSE HOSTEL
*High Road, **Letterkenny***
Tel: (+353) 074 25238
Open: all year round

MOVILLE HOLIDAY HOSTEL
*Malin Road, Moville, **Innishowen***

Tel: (+353) 077 82378
Open: all year round

Bicycle Hire

IRISH CYCLE HIRE – *see Directory*
RALEIGH RENT-A-BIKE – *see Directory*

Airports

DONEGAL INTERNATIONAL AIRPORT
Letterkenny
Tel: (+353) 075 48284; Fax: (+353) 075 48483

Bus Services

Stranorlar – *Tel: (+353) 074 31089*
Letterkenny – *Tel: (+353) 074 21309*

COUNTY DOWN

From the majestic summits of the Mountains of Mourne and Sleive Croob to the sea loughs of Strangford, Belfast and Carlingford and award-winning beaches, the diverse terrain of County Down is an ideal venue for family holidays. The resorts of Bangor, Newcastle and Warrenpoint have aqua leisure centres, soft-play areas, adventure playgrounds and parks, as well as offering plenty of opportunities for walking, cycling, climbing, riding, diving and sailing.

Just a short drive from the bustling streets of Belfast city centre is North Down, one of Northern Ireland's most popular holiday destinations; on the south shore of Belfast Lough, it has a mild climate with less rain and more sunshine than anywhere else in the North.

Bangor's **Pickie Family Fun Park** has a boating lagoon, paddling-pool, sand-pits, adventure playground and café all linked by the Pickie Puffer miniature train. There's a wonderful **amphitheatre** where children's entertainment, concerts and variety shows are held during the summer. **Bangor Cineplex** has a cinema, 10-pin bowling and an adventure playground, and the fascinating **Museum of Childhood** has an impressive collection of dolls'-houses, teddy bears, games and books.

The **Ark Rare Breeds farm** is a paradise for anyone who enjoys seeing and handling animals, and has a horse-drawn covered wagonette to take you on a guided tour. The **Ulster Folk and Transport Museum** at Cultra, near Holywood, is one of Northern Ireland's most popular tourist attractions. One part is a 60-acre outdoor museum consisting of a completely reconstructed small village showing how people lived in the north of Ireland at the turn of the century. The transport section has locomotives, motorcycles and lots to see.

On the north-west shore of Strangford Lough, just outside the pretty village of Comber, is the **Castle Espie Wildfowl and Wetlands Centre,** an outdoor paradise. Many of the birds are very tame and enjoy being hand-fed by children. With special children's events and a faimily-friendly restaurant, the whole place has been designed with youngsters in mind.

Following the coast road south brings you to Portaferry, home to **Exploris,** a fine aquarium. Children can handle sea creatures in the touch tank and go on a voyage under the Irish Sea (actually, below massive tanks full of sharks, conger eels and wrasse). The complex also has a good café and a park with a duckpond and playground.

Downpatrick has a wonderful **steam railway and museum**, as well as a magnificent **cathedral**: its organ is one of the finest in Ireland, and in the churchyard is a stone to commemorate the grave of St Patrick, who is buried on this hill. Near by, behind the high walls of the former county gaol, is the **Down County Museum**. Here you can visit 18th-century cells and discover the past through displays telling the story of St Patrick and the human and natural history of the region.

The **Seaforde Tropical Butterfly House** is set in beautiful grounds 20 miles south of Belfast. It has hundreds of free-flying exotic butterflies, as well as reptiles and insects (safely behind glass!). The surrounding ornamental garden has a maze, nursery, playground and tea-room.

The seaside resort of Newcastle, a popular venue for festivals, circuses and funfairs, has the **Tropicana Pleasure Beach** with a heated outdoor swimming-pool, giant water-slides and an adventure playground, as well as a supervised crèche. There are some superb parks in the town, including the **Downs Road Playpark,** a secure, supervised playground. **Coco's Indoor Adventure Playground** has snake slides, ball pools, an assault course, soft-play area and snack bar. Newcastle is the gateway to the Mourne Mountains and no stay here would be complete without a trip to **Silent Valley.** Take the shuttle bus (high season only) from the visitor centre to the top reservoir, a spectacular drive deep in the heart of the mountains. The dramatic parklands have good, safe woodland walks suitable for children.

The bustling town of Newry has a reputation for being one of the best shopping towns in Ireland. It has a colourful **market** on Thursday and Saturday, and the **Buttercrane Centre** is also a favourite with shoppers. Near by is Warrenpoint, a resort which is also the seaport for Newry. There's a good indoor adventure playground and soft-play area here called **Thrills and Spills,** a perfect spot for kids to get rid of excess energy while parents relax over a cup of coffee in the café overlooking the harbour.

There is an excellent network of roads throughout the county, including the motorway routes from Belfast. Rail and bus services run regularly from Belfast to most of the area, and Belfast Airport is very easy to get to.

• • • • •

PLACES TO VISIT

Animals, Birds and Fish

CASTLE ESPIE WILDFOWL AND WETLANDS CENTRE****
Ballydrain Road, **Comber**
Tel: 028 9187 4146
Open: March to October, Monday to Saturday, 10.30a.m.–5p.m.,
Sunday, 11.30a.m.–6p.m.; November to February, Monday to Saturday,
11.30a.m.–4p.m., Sunday, 11.30a.m.–5p.m.
Admission: A=£££, C=£, F
Facilities: toilets; disabled access; nature centre; gift shop; visitor centre;
café/restaurant with children's menu and high-chairs; picnic areas
Did you know that some migrating swans fly as high as Mount Everest? This is just one of the many interesting facts visitors to Castle Espie will learn at the centre. Children will enjoy handfeeding the birds from the largest collection of ducks, swans and geese in Ireland and participating in the many events the centre organises throughout the year, including Downy Duckling days, a festival to celebrate the arrival of ducklings, goslings, cygnets and chicks. In August they are invited to join the 'Wetland Wizard' to follow a magical watery trail (check directly with the centre for a timetable of events). There's a newly refurbished visitor centre and

restaurant on site which has a children's menu and high-chairs. The whole layout of the centre is very child-friendly and even the main bird hides have low windows specially for children.

SEAFORDE TROPICAL BUTTERFLY HOUSE AND GARDENS***
Seaforde
Tel: 028 4481 1225; Fax: 028 4481 1370
Butterfly house *open: April to September, Monday to Saturday, 10a.m.–5p.m., Sunday, 2p.m.–6p.m.;* **gardens and maze** *open: March to October, Monday to Saturday, 10a.m.–5p.m., Sunday, 2p.m.–6p.m.; November to February, Monday to Friday, 10a.m.–5p.m.*
Admission: butterfly house and gardens, A=£££, C=££; gardens only, A=££, C=£
Facilities: toilets; disabled access; gift shop; tea-room; playground
This is an excellent place for a relaxing family visit. The attractive gardens are a joy to wander through; children will enjoy navigating the hornbeam maze and having fun in the playground; look out for the insects and reptiles from Africa, Asia, Australasia and the Americas, all safely kept behind glass; and the whole family will love the sight of free-flying exotic butterflies in the Tropical House – which include Atlas moths with a 12-inch wing-span!

ULSTER WILDLIFE CENTRE***
3 New Line, Killyleagh Road, **Crossgar**
Tel: 028 4483 0282
Open: all year round, Monday to Friday, 10a.m.–4p.m. (also open April to September, Sunday, 2p.m.–5p.m.)
Admission: A=£, C=£
Facilities: toilets; disabled access; shop; tea-room; guided walks
Visitors can learn about wildlife on the wetlands, raised bogs, meadowland and woodland.

Boats and Boat Trips

CARLINGFORD LOUGH CRUISES
Warrenpoint
Tel: 028 3084 8916
Cruising tours on Carlingford Lough aboard the *Maiden of Mourne*.

Castles and Historic Houses

CASTLE WARD**
Strangford
Tel: 028 4488 1204
Castle *open: April, September and October, weekends, 1p.m.–6p.m.; May to August, daily (except Thursday), 1p.m.–6p.m.;* **estate and grounds** *open: all year round, dawn to dusk*
Admission: A=££, C=£, F
Facilities: toilets; baby-changing room; disabled access; shop; restaurant
Unique 18th-century house with classical and gothic façades. Other features include a Victorian laundry, a fortified tower house and a sawmill. Here you will also find a wildfowl collection, an exhibition, a theatre in the stableyard, an interpretative centre, craft fairs and beautiful gardens (**see GARDENS**).

MOUNT STEWART HOUSE AND GARDENS***
Newtownards
Tel: 028 9178 8387; Fax: 028 9178 8569
House *open: April and October, weekends, 1p.m.–6p.m.; May to September, daily (except Tuesday) 1p.m.–6p.m.;* **gardens** *open: March, Sunday, 2p.m.–5p.m.; April to September, daily, 10.30a.m.–6p.m.; October, weekends, 10.30a.m.–6p.m.*
Admission: A=£££, C=£, F; temple only: £
Facilities: toilets with baby-changing room; disabled access; tea-room
Fascinating 18th-century house and one of the greatest gardens in Ireland with an unrivalled collection of rare and unusual plants. The Temple of the Winds, James 'Athenian' Stuart's banqueting hall of 1785, overlooks Strangford Lough.

Cathedrals

DOWN CATHEDRAL***
Downpatrick
Tel: 028 4461 4922
Open: all year round, Monday to Friday, 10a.m.–5p.m., weekends, 2p.m.–5p.m. (except during services)
There are many interesting things to see in this magnificent cathedral. The Hill of Down has been a place of Christian worship since the time of St Patrick in the fifth century. The Apostle of Ireland was buried here and a stone was placed in the graveyard to commemorate the fact that Patrick's burial place is on this hill.

Cinemas

BANGOR CINEPLEX
Valentine Road, Castle Park, **Bangor**
Tel: 028 9145 4729
Four screens plus a bistro, 10-pin bowling and an adventure play area.

SAVOY CINEMA
Merchants Quay, **Newry**
Tel: 028 3026 7549
Two screens.

Country Parks

CRAWFORDSBURN COUNTRY PARK***
Helen's Bay, **Belfast Lough**
Tel: 028 9185 3621
Park *open: all year round, daily, dawn to dusk;* **visitor centre** *open: April to September, daily, 10a.m.–6p.m.; October to March, daily, 9a.m.–5p.m.;* **fort** *open: April to September, daily (except Tuesday), 2p.m.–5p.m.; October to March, Sunday, 2p.m.–4.45p.m.*
Admission: free
Facilities: toilets; nature trails; exhibitions; restaurant
The park is full of variety and is an ideal place for a family outing. It features over 2 miles (3.5km) of coastline which includes the best beaches in the Belfast area; a deep wooded glen with an attractive waterfall at its head; a series of waymarked trails; Grey Point Fort

(an old wartime coastal battery); and an excellent countryside centre with an informative exhibition ('Choices in the Environment'), which features interactive displays and a 3-D film show on bees and wasps. Take the coastal and riverside walks and see the waterfall.

DELAMONT COUNTRY PARK****
Mullagh, nr Downpatrick
Tel: 028 4482 8333
Open: daily, winter 9a.m.–5p.m.; summer 9a.m.–dusk
Admission: ££ per car
Facilities: Toilets with baby-changing facilities, disabled access, gift shop, tea-room, licensed restaurant, picnic facilities, children's adventure playground and a new miniature railway.
In the park are many interesting features including restored walled gardens, woodland walks, picnic sites and a children's play area. Among the summer events held in the park are Punch and Judy shows, magic shows, face painting and concerts.

Environment and Ecology Centres

EXPLORIS****
Castle Street, Portaferry
Tel: 028 9172 8062; Fax: 028 9172 8396
Open: all year round, Monday to Friday, 10a.m.–5p.m., Saturday 11a.m.–5p.m., Sunday, 1p.m.–5p.m. (till 6p.m. from April to August)
Admission: A=£££, C=££, F
Facilities: toilets with baby-changing facilities; disabled access; shop; café; picnic area; park with children's playground
A showcase for the rich diversity of life in the Irish Sea and Strangford Lough. Visitors can watch majestic rays and circling sharks in one of the largest open sea tanks in the UK. An interesting and educational attraction that all the family will enjoy.

QUOILE COUNTRYSIDE CENTRE***
Off A25 north of Downpatrick
Tel: 028 4461 5520
Open: April to September, daily, 11a.m.–5p.m.; October to March, weekends, 1p.m.–5p.m.
Admission: free
Facilities: visitor centre; guided walks; picnic area; fishing jetty
Exhibits show how flood-control barriers have changed the salt-water estuary to fresh water, resulting in interesting vegetation, fish and insect life in the Quoile pondage. The ruins of the 16th-century Quoile Castle are also here.

Equestrian Facilities

DRUMGOOLAND HOUSE EQUESTRIAN CENTRE
29 Dunnanew Road, Seaforde
Tel: 028 4481 1956; Fax: 028 4481 1265
Horseriding and pony-trekking to suit all levels of ability. Supervised hourly and half-day treks available for forest and beach rides. Residential packages can be arranged.

MOUNT PLEASANT HORSE RIDING AND
TREKKING CENTRE
Bannonstown Road, **Castlewellan**
Tel: 013967 78651; Fax: 013967 70030
Open: All year
*Facilities: picnic and barbecue areas; toilets, self-catering
accommodation*
Horse and ponies to suit all ages and levels of rider. Hourly and
daily sessions arranged along tracks through the Castlewellan Forest
Park.

ROSTREVOR EQUESTRIAN CENTRE
Greenpark Road, **Rostrevor**
Tel: 028 3073 9777
Quality riding and trekking for all the family. Tuition available.

Farm Parks

ARK OPEN FARM***
Bangor Road, **Newtownards**
Tel: 028 9182 0445
*Open: all year round, Monday to Saturday, 10a.m.–6p.m., Sunday,
2p.m.–6p.m.*
Admission: A=££, C=£, F
Facilities: toilets; disabled access; picnic and barbecue area; coffee shop
The farm has a wide variety of interesting livestock to interest all
the family, such as Vietnamese pot-bellied and Berkshire pigs,
Nigerian pygmy goats, llamas and guanacos, Chinese and pilgrim
geese, and Irish moiled cattle. There's also a pets corner, pony rides
and tours by horse-drawn wagonette.

BALLYWISKIN OPEN FARM***
216 Ballywalter Road, **Millisle**
Tel: 028 9186 2267
*Open: March to October, daily, dawn to dusk; November to February,
weekends, dawn to dusk*
Admission: free
See rabbits, ducks, sheep and fowl in a natural environment.

SHEEPLAND OPEN FARM***
Tollumgrange Road, Chapeltown, **Ardglass**
Tel: 028 4484 2268
Open: February to November, daily, noon–5p.m.
Admission: A=£, C=£, F
Facilities: toilets; disabled access; picnic area; shop; craft shop; tea-room
Lots to see and do, including bottle-feeding pet lambs and goats.
There's a display of farm machinery, plus sheep-shearing, hay-making
and potato-picking (all seasonal).

Forest and Amenity Walks

SILENT VALLEY MOUNTAIN PARK***
Mourne Mountains, *signposted off the A2, Newcastle to Kilkeel road*
Tel: 028 9074 6581
Open: Easter to September, daily, 10a.m.–6.30p.m.; October to Easter,

daily, 10a.m.–4.30p.m.
Charges: ££ per car; by bus: A=£, C=£
Facilities: toilets; disabled access; coffee shop; craft shop; visitor centre; picnic areas (note: some facilities are seasonal)
Excellent safe walking amidst beautiful woodlands and mountain scenery, suitable for all the family. The shuttle bus ride (high season only) alongside the reservoirs to the dams is spectacular.

TOLLYMORE FOREST PARK***
*Tullybrannigan Road, **Newcastle***
Tel: 028 4372 2428
Open: all year round, 10a.m.–dusk
Admission: £££ per car
Facilities: carpark; toilets; disabled access; restaurant
This is a super place to visit and explore. Interesting features include a series of bridges crossing the Shimna and Spinkwee Rivers (the Old Bridge was built in 1726), an obelisk, a grotto, and a rath known as the White Fort dating back to somewhere between AD500 and 1000. In spring the arboretum is carpeted with daffodils, narcissi and snowdrops. Look out for the strawberry tree – exclusive to Ireland. Visitors can also try pony-trekking and fishing.

Gardens

CASTLE WARD GARDENS***
Strangford
Tel: 028 4488 1204
Open: all year round, dawn to dusk
Admission: £££ per car
Facilities: toilets; baby-changing room; disabled access; shop; restaurant
An excellent 700-acre country estate providing an insight into the history of gardening. There's formal and landscaped gardens with fine shrubs and trees amidst woodland, lakes and seashore. Here you will also find Castle Ward House, a wildfowl collection, an exhibition, a theatre in the stableyard, an interpretative centre, craft fairs and beautiful gardens (**see CASTLES**).

CASTLEWELLAN GARDENS and ARBORETUM
Castlewellan
Tel: 028 4477 8664
Open: all year round, dawn to dusk
Admission: ££ per car
Facilities: toilets; disabled access; restaurant; caravan and camping park
The main features of this beautiful garden are a 12-acre walled garden, themed gardens, fountains, an arboretum, glasshouses with tropical birds and plants, forest walks and trails.

MOUNT STEWART GARDENS
Newtownards – see CASTLES AND HISTORIC HOUSES

ROWALLANE***
*Saintfield, **Ballynahinch***
Tel: 028 9751 0131
Open: April to October, Monday to Friday, 10.30a.m.–6p.m., weekends, 2p.m.–6p.m.; November to March, Monday to Friday, 10.30a.m.–5p.m.

Admission: A=££, C=£, F (reduced rates from November to March)
Facilities: toilets; disabled access; shop; tea-room
Rowallane is a garden that appeals both to keen gardeners and people who just enjoy a family stroll in a pleasant setting. This is a garden for all seasons; the spring displays of daffodils, azaleas and rhododendrons are spectacular; summer's flowering trees and shrubs continue the colourful display; autumn brings a spectacular display of colour in foliage and berries; and winter attracts many interesting birds to feed in the grounds. Special events arranged throughout the season include a Teddy Bears' Picnic – check directly for a timetable of events.

Heritage Centres

BURREN HERITAGE CENTRE**
*Bridge Road, **Burren***
Tel: 028 3077 3378
Open: April to September, Tuesday to Saturday, 11a.m.–6p.m., Sunday, 2p.m.–6p.m.; October to March, Monday to Friday, 10a.m.–5p.m.
Admission: A=£, C=£, F
Facilities: toilets; disabled access; coffee/craft shop; picnic area
The Burren Heritage Centre is housed in a converted school in the picturesque Drumlin area above Strangford Lough. Visitors can learn of a historic past through a series of interpretative models, exhibitions and audio-visual aids, which illustrate the development of the Burren area from prehistoric times to the present day. Special events such as folk nights, music and storytelling are organised at the centre.

NORTH DOWN HERITAGE CENTRE***
*Castle Park Avenue, **Bangor***
Tel: 028 9127 1200
Open: all year round, Tuesday to Saturday, 10.30a.m.–4.30p.m., Sunday, 2p.m.–4.30p.m. (also till 5.30p.m. and on Monday in July and August)
Admission: free
Facilities: toilets; disabled access; craft shop; restaurant
The heritage centre is beautifully situated in wooded surroundings, occupying former outbuildings of Bangor Castle. Permanent historical exhibitions look at the important early Christian monastery and at the coming of the Scottish settlers. There are lots of interesting things to see and do: discovery quiz sheets for children, an observation beehive in summer, audio-visual presentations, vintage films, toys and railway displays. Fun days, events and festivals are arranged throughout the year – check directly for details.

SOMME HERITAGE CENTRE
*Whitespots, Bangor Road, **Newtownards***
Tel: 028 9182 3202
Open: June and September, Tuesday to Sunday, noon–5p.m.; July and August, Monday to Saturday, 11a.m.–6p.m., Sunday, noon–5p.m.
Admission: A=£££, C=£, F
Facilities: toilets; shop; coffee shop; audio-visual displays
Commemorates Ireland's involvement in the First World War. Staff dressed in period military uniform take visitors back in time to a reconstructed front-line trench of the Battle of the Somme in 1916.

Ireland at Work – Past and Present

VICTORIA BAKERY***
*Castle Street, **Newry***
Tel: 028 3026 2076
Open: Tuesday to Friday, 9a.m.–6p.m.
Admission: free; tours by arrangement
Just follow your nose along Castle Street on a Friday morning and the smell of fresh bread will lead you to the Victoria Bakery. Friday is the day when traditional Ulster breads are baked, while on other days visitors can watch as yeast breads, fruit loaves, pastries, Porter Cake and barmbrack are being baked. This must be one of the 'yummiest' attractions in Ulster!

Leisure Centres and Adventure Playgrounds

COCO'S ADVENTURE PLAYGROUND****
*Central Promenade, **Newcastle***
Tel: 028 4372 6226
Open: summer, daily, 10a.m.–9p.m.; winter, Monday to Friday, 2p.m.–8p.m., weekends, 10a.m.–9p.m.
Admission: £££ per hour
Lots of fun for children from 2 to 14. Has all the usual slides and ball pools, plus a bouncy castle, soft-play area and a snack bar.

NEWCASTLE CENTRE***
*Central Promenade, **Newcastle***
Tel: 028 4372 5034; Fax: 028 4372 2400
Open: April to September, Monday to Saturday, 10a.m.–10p.m., Sunday, 2p.m.–9p.m.; October to March, Monday to Friday, 10a.m.–10p.m., Saturday, 10a.m.–6p.m., Sunday, 2p.m.–6p.m.
Facilities: coffee bar; crèche
This cinema, show and exhibition centre also has a fitness centre and gymnasium and a kiddies' fun club

NEWRY KARTING CENTRE
*Greenbank, **Warrenpoint***
Tel: 028 3026 6220; Fax: 028 3026 3360
Open: all year round, Monday to Friday, 10a.m.–10p.m., weekends, 2p.m.–10p.m.
Admission: varies according to age and session times
Fully supervised indoor karting centre. All equipment supplied for organised races. The minimum age for participants is 12.

PICKIE FAMILY FUN PARK****
*The Promenade, **Bangor***
Tel: 028 9127 4430
Open: Easter to September, daily, 10a.m.–10p.m.; October to March, weekends, 10a.m.–5p.m.
Admission: free to park; charges per individual ride
Facilities: toilets
All you need to have great day out: pedal boats, paddling-pools, sand-pits, an adventure playground, a café and a miniature railway – lots of fun for all the family.

THRILLS AND SPILLS***
Dock Street, **Warrenpoint**
Tel: 028 3075 2852
Open: summer, daily, 10a.m.–8p.m.; winter, Monday to Friday, 2p.m.–
8p.m., weekends, 10a.m.–8p.m.
Admission: ££ per hour
Fully supervised adventure playground with slides, ball pools, an
assault course and a café serving special children's meals and snacks.

TROPICANA PLEASURE BEACH****
Central Promenade, **Newcastle**
Tel: 028 4372 5034
Open: June, weekends, 2p.m.–8p.m.; July and August, daily, 10a.m.–8p.m.
Admission: separate charges for each attraction
Lots of outdoor fun to be had on a fine summer's day: heated out-
door fun pool, flumes, a bouncy castle and an adventure playground.

Museums

DOWN COUNTY MUSEUM***
The Mall, **Downpatrick**
Tel: 028 4461 5218
Open: October to June, Tuesday to Friday, 11a.m.–5p.m., Saturday, 2p.m.–
5p.m.; July to September, Monday to Friday, 11a.m.–5p.m., weekends,
2p.m.–5p.m.
Admission: free
This community museum explains the history and environment of
County Down. The museum occupies the restored buildings of the
old Down County Gaol and has special displays about the prison,
incorporating some of the original cells, and about St Patrick who
had close links with Downpatrick. This is a large complex with lots
of interesting things to see and visit, including an excellent tea-
room.

MUSEUM OF CHILDHOOD***
Central Avenue, **Bangor**
Tel: 028 9147 1915
Open: Monday, Tuesday, Wednesday, Friday and Saturday, 10a.m.–5p.m.
Admission: A=£, C=£
The museum has a large collection of toys, books, prams, games,
dolls and clothes from the Victorian era to the 1960s.

ULSTER FOLK AND TRANSPORT MUSEUM****
Cultra, **Holywood**
Tel: 028 9042 8428
Open: summer, Monday to Saturday, 10.30a.m.–6p.m., Sunday, noon–
6p.m.; spring and autumn, Monday to Friday, 9.30a.m.–5p.m., Saturday,
10.30a.m.–6p.m., Sunday, noon–6p.m.; winter, Monday to Friday,
9.30a.m.–4p.m., weekends, 12.30p.m.–4.30p.m.
Admission: A=££££, C=££, F
Facilities: toilets; mother and baby facilities; disabled access; tea-rooms;
Sunday carvery; craft and gift shops; exhibitions
This outdoor museum consists of a number of reconstructed build-
ings such as farmhouses and watermills – in fact an entire village
with shops, a school and church – all recovered from the Ulster

countryside and re-erected at Cultra. This is a wonderful opportunity to experience the traditional lifestyle of local people at the turn of the century. A pleasant stroll becomes an adventure as you wander through 176 acres overlooking Belfast Lough. The transport section features aircraft, horse-drawn vehicles, cars, buses, trams, motorcycles and the award-winning Irish Railway Collection, regarded as the best in Europe. Visitors can also take horse-and-carriage rides. The centre organises many events throughout the year, including a storytelling festival in June, craft fairs and Halloween celebrations (check directly for a timetable of events).

Parks

CASTLE PARK***
Bangor
Open: free access at all times
A walk through this wooded wonderland is an exhilarating experience throughout the seasons. To enjoy it to the full, collect a copy of the 'Castle Park Nature Trail' guide from the heritage centre and follow the waymarked routes.

DOWNS ROAD PLAYPARK***
Newcastle
Supervised playground for hours of safe fun for the kids.

SEAPARK***
*Seapark Road, **Holywood***
Tel: 028 9142 2894
Open: free access at all times
Has tennis courts, a bowling green, a putting course and a beautifully landscaped children's play area on the seafront.

WARD PARK***
*Castle Street, **Bangor***
Open: free access at all times
The whole family will enjoy a visit here. You can feed the ducks and geese on the many attractive ponds, and the park has a mini-pets corner, tennis courts, a bowling green and putting course, and a children's playground.

Swimming-Pools

BANGOR CASTLE LEISURE CENTRE****
*Castle Park Avenue, **Bangor***
Tel: 028 9127 0271
Open: all year round, daily
Excellent swimming centre with a choice of pools to cater for all the family and all levels of ability. There's a 25m swimming-pool, a diving pool, a learners' pool and a toddlers' pool. The centre also has squash courts, a fitness centre and a restaurant.

TROPICANA**
*Central Promenade, **Newcastle***
Tel: 028 4372 5034
Open: June to August

Freeform outdoor heated fun pool with slide, and toddlers' pools with elephant slide and water fountain (see LEISURE CENTRES).

Trains and Model Railways

DOWNPATRICK STEAM RAILWAY***
Market Street, **Downpatrick**
Tel: 028 4461 5779
Open: July to mid-September, 2p.m.–5p.m.
The steam locomotive *Guinness* takes visitors on a comfortable journey across the Downpatrick marshes to the restored Loop Station. Look out for the seasonal Santa Claus, Easter Egg and Halloween Specials – great fun for the kids.

Walks and Tours

MOURNE COUNTRYSIDE CENTRE
91 Central Promenade, **Newcastle**
Tel: 028 4372 4059
Open: June to September, daily, 9a.m.–5p.m.
Admission: free
All your questions about Mourne country will be answered here. Talks about the area and guided walks are arranged in the summer.

• • • • •

PLACES TO EAT

Cafés and Restaurants

PIZZA HUT
115 Main Street, **Bangor**
Tel: 028 9127 1272

LITTLE CHEF
Town and Country Shopping Centre, **Carryduff**
Tel: 028 9081 2097

THE COBBLER RESTAURANT
29 Church Street, **Warrenpoint**
Tel: 028 3077 2714

Fast-Food Restaurants

McDONALD'S
Bloomfield Shopping Centre, **Bangor**
Tel: 028 9127 3300

Ballyduggan Road, **Downpatrick**
Tel: 028 4461 9567

KENTUCKY FRIED CHICKEN
*1 Main Street, **Bangor***
Tel: 028 9145 2686

Hotels and Pubs

BRASS MONKEY STEAK HOUSE***
*Trevor Hill, **Newry***
Tel: 028 3026 3176; Fax: 028 3026 6013
During our stay in Newry we found this family-friendly pub to be
an excellent place to eat. Don't be put off by it being called a Steak
House – the menu has dishes to suit all tastes and ages. What is not
on the menu they will attempt to find, going so far as to boast that
'Whatever your needs, we will endeavour to satisfy'.

THE AYLESFORTE HOUSE
*Newry Road, **Warrenpoint***
Tel: 028 3077 2255
Family-friendly pub serving a range of meals including bar snacks,
lunches and evening meals to suit all ages.

• • • • •

PLACES TO STAY

Guest-Houses and B&Bs

BRAMBLE LODGE
*1 Bryansburn Road, **Bangor***
Tel: 028 9145 7924

HILLHOUSE
*53 Killyleagh Road, Crossgar, **Downpatrick***
Tel: 028 4483 0792

Country Houses and Hotels

CHESTNUT INN
*28–34 Lower Square, **Castlewellan***
Tel: 028 4377 8247

DRUMGOOLAND HOUSE
*29 Dunnanew Road, Seaforde, **Downpatrick***
Tel: 028 4481 1956
Set in 60 acres, it has its own trout-stocked lake and an equestrian
centre.

KILMOREY ARMS HOTEL
*41–43 Greencastle Street, **Kilkeel***
Tel: 028 3076 2220

HARBOUR HOUSE INN
*4 South Promenade, **Newcastle***
Tel: 028 4372 3445

SLIEVE DONARD HOTEL****
*Downs Road, **Newcastle***
Tel: 028 43723681; Fax: 028 4372 4830
Open: all year round
Child-friendly hotel with excellent family rooms and facilities that
include a crèche, children's club and leisure centre. The hotel is
set in wonderful grounds with a play area adjacent to the beach.
They also organise a very special Christmas programme with a
host of activities and fun for all the family to enjoy.

FIDDLERS GREEN
*10–14 Church Street, **Portaferry***
Tel: 028 9172 8136

Farmhouse Accommodation

DAIRY FARM
*52A Majors Hill, **Annalong***
Tel: 028 4376 8433

STRAND FARM
*231 Ardglass Road, **Ardglass***
Tel: 028 4484 1446

BRIDGE HOUSE FARM
*93 Windmill Road, **Donaghadee***
Tel: 028 9188 3348

FORTVIEW FARM
*16 Desert Road, Mayobridge, **Newry***
Tel: 028 3085 1310

Self-Catering Apartments and Houses

SEECONNELL CENTRE
*119 Clanvaraghan Road, **Castlewellan***
Tel: 028 4377 1412

CASTLE ESPIE COTTAGES
*11 Ballyglighorn Road, **Comber***
Tel: 028 9187 3011
Two fully appointed cottages situated on a working farm. Guests
have access to a barbecue area and a play garden for children.

CRANFIELD CHALETS
*c/o 125 Harbour Road, **Kilkeel***
Tel: 028 3076 2745

NEWCASTLE SELF-CATERING
*83–85 Central Promenade, **Newcastle***
Tel: 028 4372 4647
Fully equipped self-catering apartments.

Caravan and Camping Parks

ANNALONG MARINE PARK
*Main Street, **Annalong***
Tel: 028 4376 8736

SANDILANDS CARAVAN AND CAMPING PARK
*Cranfield Road, Cranfield East, **Kilkeel***
Tel: 028 3076 3634
Facilities include a children's playground, games room and private sandy beach.

Hostels

BARHOLM HOSTEL
*11 The Strand, **Portaferry***
Tel: 028 9172 9598

Bicycle Hire

IRISH CYCLE HIRE – see *Directory*
RALEIGH RENT-A-BIKE – see *Directory*

Bus Services

CITYBUS – *Tel: 028 9024 6485*
ULSTERBUS – *Tel: 028 9033 3000*

Ferry Services

STRANGFORD LOUGH FERRY SERVICE
Tel: 028 4488 1637
Open: all year round
Sailings: Every 30 minutes from each port; check locally for times
Car and passenger service between Strangford and Portaferry. This short sailing is one of Northern Ireland's most picturesque ferry crossings.

Rail Services

NORTHERN IRELAND RAILWAYS (NIR) – *Tel: 028 9089 9411*
Newry – *Tel: 028 3026 9271*

COUNTY FERMANAGH

With its vast stretches of water, Fermanagh is known as Northern Ireland's Lake District, and probably the best way to explore it is by boat. Considered by many to be the most attractive inland waterway in Europe, the beautiful **Shannon–Erne Waterway** is also the largest navigable inland water system in Europe. The centre of attraction in this tourist's mecca is the magnificent **Lough Erne,** an island-studded paradise covering over 300 square miles. You can don the cow-horns and sail the lough in a replica **Viking longship,** or hire a modern, well-equipped cabin cruiser from the many companies on the shore. So if you fancy skippering your own vessel and playing Captain Birdseye for a week, Fermanagh is the place for you.

For landlubbers, there's a wide range of tourist attractions to suit all tastes. You can experience Lough Erne without getting your feet wet by visiting the **Explore Erne Exhibition Centre** in Belleek, which tells the story of how the 50 miles of lough and surrounding land-scape were formed. Travel through time along the shores of Lough Erne and experience the changes from mythological beginnings to the age of hydro-electric power. These, and many more fascinating stories are told, all using the latest technology.

Florence Court, an 18th-century mansion with pleasure gardens, an ice-house and water-powered sawmill, is just one of the many historic sites, castle ruins and stately homes to visit. **Enniskillen Castle** has a regimental museum and a history and heritage centre. Now a craft and design centre where you can see local craftspeople at work, the **Buttermarket** in Enniskillen is also well worth a visit.

There are plenty of 20th-century attractions on offer too: leisure centres at **Fermanagh Lakeland Forum** and the **Castle Entertainment Centre** in Enniskillen, **Castle Park Centre** in Lisnaskea and **Bawnacre Centre** in Irvinestown. There are also lots of **activity centres and forest parks** scattered throughout the county.

Don't miss the spectacular **Marble Arch Caves** at Florencecourt, recognised as one of Europe's finest systems. A tour of these caves is a truly memorable experience: spectacular walkways allow easy access through a bewildering array of cave formations. Electric boats carry visitors gracefully along a subterranean river through a natural underworld of huge caverns and rock formations. This is a must for all ages, but the tour lasts 75 minutes, so be sure to wear comfortable shoes and warm clothing.

You need to choose your route carefully to explore Fermanagh because the county is virtually divided in half by Lough Erne. Enniskillen is a good base as it sits between Upper and Lower Lough Erne in the centre of the county.

PLACES TO VISIT

Activity Centres

ERNE AQUA JETS AND WATERSPORTS CENTRE***
*Tudor Farm guest-house, Boa Island Road, **Kesh***
Tel: 028 6663 1943
The centre operates from the private beach, slipway and jetty of
Tudor Farm guest-house on the shores of Lough Erne near the
village of Kesh. A range of accommodation and activity packages is
on offer including parascending and waterskiing.

LAKELAND CANOE CENTRE***
*Castle Island, **Enniskillen***
Tel: 028 6632 4250; Fax: 028 6632 3319
The centre has a wide range of land- and water-based activities for
all the family.

MELVIN OUTDOOR ADVENTURE CENTRE***
*Knockashangan, **Garrison***
Tel: 028 6665 8095; Fax: 028 6665 8033
Open: seasonal – check direct for timetable of activities
Lots of family activities, including windsurfing and canoeing on Lough
Erne and Lough Melvin, cycle tours, hill-walking and kite-flying.

Boats and Boat Trips

SHANNON–ERNE WATERWAYS***
*Erne Base, Blaney, **Enniskillen***
Tel: 028 6664 1507; Fax: 028 6664 1734
Peaceful cruising in an unspoilt landscape, linking together the Erne
and Shannon waterways.

VIKING VOYAGER****
*Share Holiday Village, **Lisnaskea***
Tel: 028 6772 2122
*Sailings: April, May, June and September, weekends and bank holidays,
3p.m.; July and August daily (except Tuesday), 3p.m.*
Fares: A=££££, C=£££
Visitors can enjoy the natural beauty of Upper Lough Erne with a
1-hour cruise aboard a powered replica of a Viking longship.

Castles and Historic Houses

CASTLE BALFOUR*
*Main Street, **Lisnaskea***
Open: all year round
Admission: free
Impressive castle ruins to see and explore. There is also an
interesting folklife display located in the nearby Lisnaskea library.

CASTLE COOLE***
Enniskillen
Tel: 028 6632 2690
Open: April and September, weekends and bank holidays, 1p.m.–6p.m.;
May to August, daily (except Thursday), 1p.m.–6p.m.
Admission: A=££, C=£, F
Facilities: toilets; disabled access; guided tours; shop; tea-room
Superb late 18th-century neoclassical house with fine interior
furnishings and plasterwork, stables, and the original Belmore private
coach in its original coach-house. The landscaped parklands have
many woodland walks and nature trails, and an ice-house.

ENNISKILLEN CASTLE AND REGIMENTAL MUSEUM***
Castle Barracks, Enniskillen
Tel: 028 6632 5000
Open: October to April, Monday, 2p.m.–5p.m., Tuesday to Friday, 10a.m.–
5p.m.; May to September, Saturday and Monday, 2p.m.–5p.m., Tuesday
to Friday, 10a.m.–5p.m.; July and August, weekends and Monday, 2p.m.–
5p.m., Tuesday to Friday, 10a.m.–5p.m.
Admission: A=££, C=£, F
Facilities: toilets; disabled access; visitor centre; shop; café
This early 15th-century castle, with turrets and barracks, is an
impressive feature of the scenic island town of Enniskillen. The
recently renovated castle keep incorporates a museum that traces
the history of the Enniskillen regiment, featuring uniforms, weapons,
regimental memorabilia, exhibitions about rural Fermanagh and an
audio-visual presentation. The new heritage centre, recommended
for its visitor care and education service, has special exhibitions and
permanent museum collections showing the unspoilt landscapes,
rich archaeology and history of the county.

FLORENCE COURT**
Enniskillen
Tel: 028 6634 8249
Open: April and September, weekends, 1p.m.–6p.m.; May to August,
daily (except Tuesday), 1p.m.–6p.m.
Admission: A=££, C=£, F
Facilities: toilets with baby-changing room; disabled access; shop; tea-room
One of the most important houses in Ulster, this impressive 18th-
century Palladian-style house set in spectacular grounds was built by
John Cole, father of the 1st Earl of Enniskillen. Visitors particularly
enjoy the gardens and pleasure grounds (see GARDENS).

TULLY CASTLE
Off route A46, 3 miles (4.8km) north of Derrygonnelly
Open: summer, Tuesday to Saturday, 10a.m.–7p.m., Sunday, 2p.m.–
7p.m.; winter, Tuesday to Saturday, 10a.m.–4p.m., Sunday, 2p.m.–4p.m.
Admission: A=£, C=£
Fortified house built in 1613, it has a visitor centre and a herb garden.

Caves

MARBLE ARCH CAVES****
Enniskillen
Tel: 028 6634 8855

Open: mid-March to September, daily, 10a.m.–4.30p.m.
Admission: A=£££££, C=££, F
Facilities: toilets; shop; café
The 1¼-hour tour begins with an underground boat trip past an array of fascinating stalactites and stalagmites, and through a labyrinth of huge underworld caverns. Spectacular walkways allow easy access for visitors to explore a maze of winding passages and lofty chambers. Remember to wear good walking shoes and a warm sweater when you come here. Look out, too, for the nature reserve, geology exhibition and audio-visual show.

Cinemas

CASTLE CINEPLEX
*Race View, Factory Road, **Enniskillen***
Tel: 028 6632 4172
Three screens.

Country Parks

CASTLE ARCHDALE COUNTRY PARK***
*On B82, 3 miles (4.8km) south of **Kesh***
Tel: 028 6862 1588
***Park** open: all year round, daily, dawn to dusk; **centre** open: Easter to May, weekends, noon–4p.m.; June to September, daily (except Monday), 11a.m.–7p.m.*
Admission: free
Facilities: toilets; limited wheelchair access; tea-room
A superb park with interesting exhibitions on natural history and the Battle of the Atlantic, scenic walks and nature trails. Visitors can go pony-trekking or hire bicycles.

CROM***
Newtownbutler
Tel: 028 6773 8174
Open: April to September, Monday to Saturday, 10a.m.–6p.m., Sunday, noon–6p.m.
Admission: £££ per car
Facilities: toilets; disabled access; visitor centre; shop; tea-room
With its mixture of woodland, water, parkland and old buildings, Crom is a wonderful place to visit. The estate woodlands consist of fine stands of ancient oak, providing a rich and diverse habitat, while the shorelines support many rare plants and the landscape is enhanced by a selection of interesting buildings that include Crom Old Castle, Crichton Tower and Crom Church.

Craft Centres

BUTTERMARKET CRAFT AND DESIGN CENTRE**
Enniskillen
Tel: 028 6632 4499
Open: all year round
Admission: free
See local craftspeople, artists and street performers at work in this modern centre. Has a gallery and a coffee shop.

Equestrian Facilities

CASTLE ARCHDALE PONY-TREKKING CENTRE
Lisnarick
Tel: 028 6862 1892
The centre offers a wide range of riding opportunities for all the family. Non-riders can travel in a horse-drawn vehicle while other members of the family hack or trek.

NECARNE CASTLE EQUESTRIAN PARK***
Irvinestown
Tel: 028 6862 1919; Fax: 028 6862 8382
Open: All year
Excellent facilities for both the novice and experienced rider in magnificent surroundings. The centre has indoor and outdoor arenas, a restaurant and accommodation.

Festivals and Events

LADY OF THE LAKE FESTIVAL***
Irvinestown
Tel: 028 6632 3110
On: mid-July
Ten days of fun and activities for all the family.

UPPER ERNE WATER FESTIVAL***
Lisnaskea
Tel: 028 6632 3110
On: early July
A wide range of activities, including powerboat racing and children's events.

Forest and Amenity Walks

CASTLE CALDWELL FOREST*
Belleek
Tel: 028 6632 5004
Open: free access all year round
Facilities: toilets; parking; exhibitions; woodland and loughside walks; nature trail; picnic areas

LOUGH NAVAR FOREST**
*Off route A46, 5 miles (8km) north-west of **Derrygonnelly***
Tel: 028 6864 1256
Open: all year round, daily, dawn to dusk
Admission: ££ per car
Visitors can take a 7-mile (11.2km) drive through this forest to a magnificent panorama over Lower Lough Erne. The forest has way-marked trails for walkers, disabled access, picnic sites, toilets, view-points, fishing and herds of red deer and wild goats.

Gardens

FLORENCE COURT***
Enniskillen
Tel: 028 6634 8249
Open: all year round, daily, 10a.m.–7pm (till 4p.m. in winter)
Admission: free to gardens
Facilities (seasonal): toilets with baby-changing facilities; disabled access; shop; tea-room; house (Easter to September – see CASTLES AND HISTORIC HOUSES)
The parklands and pleasure grounds are a joy to visit. The water-driven sawmill has been restored and the ice-house has been renovated. A little thatched tea-house is a feature of the pleasure grounds, as is the walled garden. Special events arranged throughout the season include an Easter Eggstravaganza and an Earthwalk (children's woodland walk). Check directly for a timetable of events.

Heritage Centres

EXPLORE ERNE EXHIBITION**
Corry, Belleek
Tel: 028 6865 8866; Fax: 028 6865 8833
Open: October to Easter, Monday to Friday, 9a.m.–5p.m.; Easter to September, Monday to Friday, 9a.m.–5p.m., Saturday, 10a.m.–6p.m., Sunday, 11a.m.–5p.m.
Admission: A=£, C=£, F
Facilities: toilets; disabled access; shop
The story of the formation of the lough and its effects on the people who live in the area is told through a series of excellent audio-visual presentations and exhibits.

ROSLEA HERITAGE CENTRE*
Monaghan Road, Roslea
Tel: 028 6775 1750
Open: April to September, Monday to Friday, 9a.m.–5p.m.
Admission: A=£, C=£
Facilities: disabled access; shop; tea-room
The centre is housed in an 1874 schoolhouse with old school desks. Also displayed are a variety of traditional farming implements.

Ireland at Work

BELLEEK POTTERY VISITORS CENTRE***
Belleek
Tel: 028 6865 9300
Open: April/May/June/September/October, Monday–Friday, 9a.m.–6p.m., Saturday, 10a.m.–6p.m., Sunday, 2p.m.–6p.m.; July to August, Monday–Friday, 9.am.–8p.m., Sat, 10a.m.–6p.m., Sun, 11a.m.–8p.m.; November to March, Monday–Friday, 9a.m.–5.30p.m.
Admission: free to visitor centre, shop, restaurant; charge for guided pottery tours
Facilities: toilets with baby-changing facilities; restaurant; shop; museum, audio-visual theatre
Excellent modern visitor centre with good facilities. Older children will enjoy the guided tour of Ireland's oldest and most historic pottery.

Leisure Centres and Adventure Playgrounds

CASTLE ENTERTAINMENT CENTRE***
Enniskillen
Tel: 028 6632 4172
Has a 10-pin bowling alley, cinema complex, adventure world for kids and a fast-food restaurant.

Swimming-Pools

CASTLE PARK CENTRE***
Lisnaskea
Tel: 028 6772 1299
The centre organises a series of events and craft workshops during the summer school holidays.

FERMANAGH LAKELAND FORUM***
Enniskillen
Tel: 028 6632 4121
Facilities include an indoor heated swimming-pool, sauna, squash and badminton courts, play centre for kids under 10, a crèche and a restaurant.

• • • • •

PLACES TO EAT

Cafés and Restaurants

MAUD'S PARLOUR
*Wellington Road, **Enniskillen***
Tel: 028 6632 6208
A great choice of ice-creams here as well as snacks.

THE MOORINGS
Bellanaleck
Tel: 028 6634 8328
A good choice of menus.

Hotels and Pubs
LANESBOROUGH ARMS***
*High Street, **Newtownbutler***
Tel: 028 6773 8488
The hotel's restaurant and bars are very family friendly and they have a good choice of menus and children's food.

THE HOTEL CARLTON****
Belleek
Tel: 028 6865 8282; Fax: 028 686559005
Open: All year
Good choice of reasonably priced menus in the restaurant and bar, both with children's menus.

Fast-food Restaurants

KENTUCKY FRIED CHICKEN
*Wellington Road, **Enniskillen***
Tel: 028 6632 7143

McDONALD'S
*Cathcart Square, **Enniskillen***
Tel: 028 66329329

• • • • •

PLACES TO STAY

Guest-Houses and B&Bs

CORRIGAN'S GUEST HOUSE
*Clonatrig, **Bellanaleck***
Tel: 028 6634 9572
Open: All year
Family friendly guest house located on the shores of Upper Lough
Erne.

DRUMCOO GUEST-HOUSE
*32 Cherryville, Cornagrade Road, **Enniskillen***
Tel: 028 6632 6672

WILLOWBANK GUEST-HOUSE
*60 Bellview Road, Dolan's Ring, **Enniskillen***
Tel: 028 6632 8582

Country Houses and Hotels

BELMORE COURT MOTEL
*Tempo Road, **Enniskillen***
Tel: 028 6632 6633; Fax: 028 6632 6362

MAHON'S HOTEL
*Mill Street, **Irvinestown***
Tel: 028 6862 1656; Fax: 028 6862 8344

MULLYNAVAL LODGE
*Boa Island, **Kesh***
Tel: 028 6863 1995

THE HOTEL CARLTON****
Belleek
Tel: 028 6865 8282; Fax: 028 6865 9005
Open: All year
Excellent family friendly hotel lcoated in the centre of Belleek
overlooking the River Erne. They have family rooms and will arrange
baby-sitting if required.

TUDOR FARM GUEST-HOUSE
619 Boa Island Road, **Kesh**
Tel: 028 6863 1943
Children's play area, watersports and private beach on shore of
Lower Lough Erne.

MANOR HOUSE HOTEL AND LEISURE COMPLEX
Killadeas
Tel: 028 6862 1561; Fax: 028 6862 1545

Farmhouse Accommodation

ABOCURRAGH FARM GUEST-HOUSE
Abocurragh, Letterbreen, **Enniskillen**
Tel: 028 6634 8484

TULLYHONA FARM GUEST-HOUSE
Marble Arch Road, **Florencecourt**
Tel: 028 6634 8452

TATNAMALLAGHT FARM GUEST-HOUSE
Farnamullan Road, **Lisbellaw**
Tel: 028 6638 7174

Holiday Parks and Villages

CORRALEA ACTIVITY CENTRE AND HOLIDAY COTTAGES
Corralea, **Belcoo**
Tel/Fax: 028 6638 6668
Well-appointed self-catering cottages in 15 acres of woodland
situated on the shores of Upper Lough McNean. Facilities include a
barbecue area, boat and bicycle hire, and family activity weekends.

LOUGH MELVIN HOLIDAY CENTRE
Garrison
Tel: 028 6865 8142; Fax: 028 6865 8719
Luxury residential centre with a restaurant and take-away service,
caravan and camping sites, and a range of weekend and 5-day
activity programmes that include pony-trekking, canoeing, fishing, hill
walking, cycling and archery.

SHARE HOLIDAY VILLAGE
Smith's Strand, **Lisnaskea**
Tel: 028 6772 2122; Fax: 028 6772 1893
The village has a range of accommodation in fully equipped self-
catering chalets or the village guest-house. Facilities include an
indoor leisure pool, children's pool, tennis court, playroom and soft
play area and a children's playschool. There are many activities
available for all the family to enjoy on this 30-acre site beautifully
located on the shores of Upper Lough Erne – why not try sailing,
canoeing, windsurfing, banana-ski rides, archery, mountain biking or
adventure games? The site has facilities for camping and caravans.

Self-Catering Apartments and Houses

CORRALEA ACTIVITY CENTRE AND COTTAGES
Corralea, **Belcoo**
Tel: 028 6638 6668

CROM HOLIDAY COTTAGES – NATIONAL TRUST****
Crom Estate, **Newtownbutler**
Tel: 0870 458 4422
Open: All year
Beautifully furbished and located cottages on the shores of Lough
Erne on the Crom estate (see page 347, Country Parks).

LOUGH ERNE HOLIDAY COTTAGES
Bolustymore, Roscor, **Belleek**
Tel: 028 6632 2608

RATHMORE COTTAGES
Belleek
Tel: 028 6865 8181

KILLYHEVLIN CHALETS
Killyhevlin, **Enniskillen**
Tel: 028 6632 3481

FERMANAGH LAKELAND LODGES
Near Boa Island, **Letter**
Tel: 028 6863 1957

MANOR HOUSE MARINE AND COUNTRY COTTAGES
Killadeas
Tel: 028 6862 8100

Caravan and Camping Parks

BLANEY CARAVAN AND CAMPING SITE
Blaney
Tel: 028 6864 1634

LOUGH MELVIN HOLIDAY CENTRE
Garrison
Tel: 028 6865 8142

LOANEDEN CARAVAN PARK
Muckross Bay, **Kesh**
Tel: 028 6863 1603

CASTLE ARCHDALE CARAVAN AND CAMPING PARK
Lisnarick
Tel: 028 6862 1333

MULLYNASCARTHY CARAVAN PARK
Lisnaskea
Tel: 028 6772 1040

Hostels

LOUGH MELVIN HOLIDAY CENTRE
Garrison
Tel: 028 6865 8142

Bicycle Hire

IRISH CYCLE HIRE – see *Directory*
RALEIGH RENT-A-BIKE – see *Directory*

CYCLE-OPS
Castle Archdale Country Park, near Kesh
Tel: 028 6863 1850

Bus Services

CITYBUS – *Tel: 028 9024 6485*
ULSTERBUS – *Tel: 028 9033 3000*

Rail Services

NORTHERN IRELAND RAILWAYS (NIR) – *Tel: 028 9089 9411*

COUNTY MONAGHAN

The county of Monaghan, which is part of the Republic, reminds me of a giant rollercoaster – not a place to bring bikes unless you're a keen and very fit cyclist! It has masses of little hills, though few rise above 1,000ft, and is a county rapidly gaining a reputation for the increasing number of activity holidays on offer. The town of Monaghan has a very fine **museum;** the unique 14th-century Cross of Clogher and a collection of artefacts from medieval crannogs (lake dwellings) are among its most treasured items. A few miles north is Glaslough, where the famous **Castle Leslie** boasts an ancestor whose godfather defeated Napoleon. Apparently, one of the castle's most frequent visitors is a ghost, so it's not a place to linger! It does, however, have pleasant tea-rooms in which to refresh your spirits.

The **Hope Castle and Lough Muckno Leisure Park** is set in 900 acres of parkland and is one of Ireland's best. It has a complete programme of outdoor and indoor activities for day guests as well as residents, and instruction and equipment hire is available. Excellent budget accommodation can be had in the **Coach House.** On the edge of the beautiful forest park is a fully serviced caravan and camping site. This is an ideal venue for a fun-packed, low-budget holiday.

Access to the county is limited to road transport, but there is a good network of roads throughout.

• • • • •

PLACES TO VISIT

Activity Centres

HOPE CASTLE AND LOUGH MUCKNO LEISURE PARK***
Castleblaney
Tel: (+353) 042 9746356; Fax: (+353) 042 9746610
Open: May to September, Tuesday to Friday, 2p.m.–7p.m., weekends and bank holidays, noon–7p.m.
Facilities: bar and restaurant; games room
A complete programme of residential weekend, 3- and 4-day outdoor and indoor activities. You can try watersports, cycling, orienteering, nature walks, tennis, golf, riding and fishing. Events for day visitors, plus instruction and equipment hire, are also available. Guests can stay in a residential centre, hostel or caravan and camping park.

TANAGH OUTDOOR EDUCATION CENTRE**
*Dartrey Forest, **Rockcorry***
Tel: (+353) 049 5552988; Fax: (+353) 049 5556004

Open: all year round
Activities for adults and children (minimum age 8) include canoeing, mountain-biking, rock-climbing, hill-walking, forest walks, swimming, camping and pony-trekking. Accommodation available.

Castles and Historic Houses

CASTLE LESLIE***
Glaslough
Tel: (+353) 047 88109; Fax: (+353) 047 88256
Open: May to August, Sunday to Thursday, 2p.m.–6p.m.
Admission: A=£££, C=£; reduced rate for garden only
Facilities: toilets; disabled access; shop; tea-rooms; guided tours
The castle's history dating back to the 1660s is vividly described during daily tours. Afternoon-tea is served in the pleasant tea-rooms. For the adventurous, there's a Ghost Tour at 6p.m.

Equestrian Facilities

CASTLEBLANEY EQUITATION CENTRE
Casstleblaney
Tel: (+353) 042 9740418
Open: all year round
The centre caters for riders of all levels of ability, with woodland trails and trekking in the Lough Muckno Leisure Park.

GREYSTONES EQUESTRIAN CENTRE
Castle Leslie, **Glaslough**
Tel: (+353) 047 88100; Fax: (+353) 047 88330
Open: all year round
Indoor and outdoor facilities, tuition and accommodation available.

Festivals and Events

FESTIVAL OF THE LAKES***
Ballybay
Tel: (+353) 047 81122
On: August
A week-long community festival of fun for all ages.

Forest and Amenity Walks

BELLAMONT***
One mile (1.5km) north of **Cootehill** *on route R188 to Monaghan*
This scenic site is located on the banks of the Dromore river where it emerges from Dromore Lake. Facilities include carparking, fishing, a picnic site and a play area.

ROSSMORE FOREST PARK**
Two miles (3.5km) south-west of **Monaghan** *on route R189 to Newbliss*
There are some excellent walks here. A special feature of the park is the colourful rhododendron and azalea displays in early summer. The ruins of Rossmore Castle are also an interesting feature to discover and explore. Facilities include a carpark, toilets, picnic sites, forest and lakeside walks, nature trails and viewing points.

Gardens

HILTON PARK GARDENS
Clones
Tel: (+353) 047 56007
Open: May to September, Sunday and bank holidays, 2p.m.–6p.m.
Admission: A=£££, C=£
Facilities: toilets; picnic area; seasonal produce available
An 18th-century recreational park which includes extensive tree plantations of oak, beech, scots pine, chestnut, open lawns and 2 lakes. Produce from the walled kitchen garden is grown organically.

Museums

MONAGHAN COUNTY MUSEUM
*Hill Street, **Monaghan***
Tel: (+353) 047 82928
Open: all year round, Tuesday to Saturday, 11a.m.–1p.m. and 2p.m.–5p.m.
Admission: free
Facilities: wheelchair access to most of the museum
The museum contains new displays of the history and archaeology of County Monaghan since the earliest times.

THE ULSTER CANAL STORES
Cara Street, Clones
Tel: (+353) 047 52125
Open: June/July/August, daily, 10a.m.–4p.m.
Admission: free
Facilities: toilets; tourist information point; cycle hire
This interesting building houses a unique exhibition of the world-famous Clones lace.

Swimming-Pools

MONAGHAN SWIMMING-POOL
*Clones Road, **Monaghan***
Tel: (+353) 047 81325

• • • • •

PLACES TO EAT

Cafés and Restaurants

TOMMIES RESTAURANT
*7 Glaslough Street, **Monaghan***
Tel: (+353) 047 81772
Open: Monday to Saturday, 10.30a.m.–8p.m., Sunday, 11a.m.–7p.m.

Fast-food Restaurants

McDONALD'S
Monaghan Shopping Centre, **Monaghan**
Tel: (+353) 047 71909

SUPERMAC'S
Main Street, **Carrickmacross**
Tel: (+353) 042 21850

• • • • •

PLACES TO STAY

Country Houses and Hotels

GLYNCH HOUSE***
Newbliss
Tel:(+353) 047 54045
Open: March to October
Family friendly accommodation in beautiful country house.

NUREBEG HOUSE
Ardee Road, **Carrickmacross**
Tel: (+353) 042 9661044
Open: all year round
Newly extended modern bungalow with ideal facilities for a family
stay. The spacious gardens have a play area, and donkey-and-cart
rides are available free to guests' children. There's also a 2-acre
paddock with a variety of farmyard animals and birds.

GLENCARN HOTEL AND LEISURE CENTRE
Castleblaney
Tel: (+353) 042 9746666; Fax: (+353) 042 9746521
Luxury hotel with family rooms and a leisure centre with a
swimming-pool, children's pool, plunge pool and jacuzzi.

THE FOUR SEASONS HOTEL AND LEISURE CLUB
Coolshannagh, **Monaghan**
Tel: (+353) 047 81888; Fax: (+353) 047 83131
Family-run hotel with excellent facilities including a leisure centre
with a swimming-pool and a children's playroom.

Holiday Parks and Villages

LOUGH MUCKNO LEISURE PARK
Castleblaney
Tel: (+353) 042 9746356; Fax: (+353) 042 9746610
Open: May to September
Complete programme of outdoor and indoor activities. Budget
accommodation in the Coach House which has family rooms.
Visitors can relax and enjoy the comfort and hospitality of the

Hope Castle Bar and Restaurant, overlooking the lake and its islands. Also has a camping and caravan park.

Caravan and Camping Parks

LOUGH MUCKNO LEISURE PARK – see ACTIVITY CENTRES and HOLIDAY PARKS AND VILLAGES

Hostels

LOUGH MUCKNO ADVENTURE CENTRE AND HOSTEL
Castleblaney
Tel: (+353) 042 9746356; Fax: (+353) 042 9746610
Open: April to September

Bicycle Hire

IRISH CYCLE HIRE – see *Directory*
RALEIGH RENT-A-BIKE – see *Directory*

M. & M. CYCLES
Monaghan
Tel: (+353) 047 83015

Bus Services

BUS EIREANN, *National travel information – Tel: (+353) 01 8366111*
Monaghan – Tel: (+353) 047 82377

COUNTY TYRONE

Tyrone is the largest county in Ulster and one of Ireland's most beautiful inland counties. There is an abundance of natural beauty, historic treasures and popular tourist attractions awaiting visitors. Located in the scenic Gortin Glens 7 miles north of Omagh is the 35-acre **Ulster History Park,** where children can explore a trail through time into the distant past. Full-scale models of houses and monuments illustrate how living conditions have changed from the skin-covered shelters built by the Stone Age people about 10,000 years ago.

Aspects of more recent times are graphically recounted in the **Ulster-American Folk Park,** an outdoor museum which tells the story of over 200 years of emigration from Ireland to North America. This is a wonderful example of how history can be made fun and exciting, as witnessed by the wide-eyed youngsters exploring the park. You'll see a replica of an 19th-century sailing ship which carried immigrants to the New World and there's a full programme of special events and demonstrations, so allow plenty of time for a visit.

Near by is **Gortin Glen Forest Park,** a large area of coniferous woodland. There are breathtaking views to be had here if you follow the forest and nature trails.

Tyrone Crystal is another place that will intrigue children. Here they can witness the art of glass-blowing as craftspeople demonstrate their skills to produce wonderful pieces of crystal. This is an ultra-modern factory and the viewing areas are excellent.

There is a good network of roads throughout Tyrone, the majority of which appear to emanate from Omagh like spider's legs sprawled across a map of the county.

• • • • •

PLACES TO VISIT

Cinemas

OMAGH STUDIOS
*Drumquin Road, **Omagh***
Tel: 028 8224 2034
Four screens.

RITZ CINEMA
*Burn Road, **Cookstown***
Tel: 028 8676 5182
Two screens.

Craft Centres

TYRONE CRYSTAL*
*Killybrackey, **Dungannon***
Tel: 028 8772 5335
Open: all year round, Monday to Saturday, 9a.m.–5p.m.
Admission: A=££ (redeemable against crystal purchases made during visit), C (under 12) = free
Facilities: toilets; craft centre; guided factory tours; coffee shop
Children will love this fascinating introduction to the art of producing mouth-blown, hand-cut Tyrone Crystal. They can follow the glass-making process from the raw, molten state through to the blower, cutter, engraver and finisher.

Environment and Ecology Centres

AN CREAGAN VISITOR CENTRE***
Creggan, Omagh
Tel: 028 8076 1112; Fax: 028 8076 1116
Open: April to September,, daily, 11a.m.–6.30p.m.; October to March, Monday to Friday, 11a.m.–4.30p.m.
Admission: A=£££, C=£, F
Facilities: toilets; interpretative exhibition; craft shop; licensed restaurant; adventure play area; bicycle hire
The interpretative centre offers a key to a region of great scientific interest. Visitors can take the bog and forest trails and stay in self-catering cottages.

Equestrian Facilities

TULLYWHISKER RIDING SCHOOL
*51 Brocklis Road, **Strabane***
Tel: 028 8265 8267
Trekking, hacking and riding lessons available.

Farm Parks

ALTMORE OPEN FARM**
*Altmore Road, **Pomeroy***
Tel: 028 8775 8977
Open: 9a.m.–dusk
Admission: A=£, C=£
Facilities: toilets; café;
This 175-acre sheep farm has 2 working waterwheels and a variety of rare breeds and domestic fowl. Visitors can go pony-trekking or fishing on a boat, take a farm tour or play pitch'n'putt.

Festivals and Events

FESTIVAL OF FUN***
Fivemiletown
On: early July
Four days of fun and madness for all the family. Festivities include a fun run, barrel rolling, music, dancing, clowns, a funfair, pet show, raft race and a barbecue.

Forest and Amenity Walks

DRUM MANOR FOREST PARK**

*Four miles (6.4km) west of **Cookstown** on route A505 Omagh road*
Tel: 028 8775 9664
Open: all year round, daily, 8a.m. to dusk
Admission: ££ per car
Facilities: picnic and barbecue areas; visitor centre; toilets; tea-room
Children will enjoy the butterfly garden, waymarked trails, wildlife
ponds and arboretum. There's also a caravan and camping park here.

GORTIN GLEN FOREST PARK**

*Six miles (9.6km) from **Omagh***
Tel: 028 8164 8217
Open: all year round, daily, 9am to dusk
Admission: ££ per car
Facilities: toilets; shop; picnic and barbecue areas
There's a lot to see and do here: forest trails, exhibitions, nature
trails, a children's play area, deer and wildlife enclosures, a camping
area and a 5-mile tarmac drive with parking areas at viewpoints.

Heritage Centres

CASTLEDERG VISITOR CENTRE**

*26 Lower Strabane Road, **Castlederg***
Tel: 028 8167 0795
Open: March to October, Tuesday to Friday, 11a.m.–4p.m., Saturday,
11a.m.–5p.m., Sunday, 1.30p.m.–5.30p.m.
Admission: A=£, C=£
Facilities: toilets; disabled access; shop; exhibitions
Stories from the area are told on a hi-tech video wall. Visitors can also
see a model of the Alamo Fort, Texas, where Davy Crockett (whose
family came from the Castlederg area) made his last stand. Most
children will enjoy seeing this, although I suspect the majority will ask,
'Davy who?'

SPERRIN HERITAGE CENTRE***

*Glenelly Road, **Cranagh***
Tel: 028 8164 8142
Open: Easter to October, Monday to Saturday, 11a.m.–6p.m., Sunday,
2p.m.–6p.m.
Admission: A=££, C=£, F
Facilities: toilets; disabled access; craft shop; café
A great opportunity to hire a Klondike-style gold pan and try gold
panning for yourself in the stream at the heritage centre. You can
also view the exhibition 'Treasures of the Sperrins', and learn about
the history of making poteen.

ULSTER-AMERICAN FOLK PARK****

*Camphill, Castletown, **Omagh***
Tel: 028 8224 3292
Open: Easter to September, Monday to Saturday, 11a.m.–6.30p.m., Sun-
day and bank holidays, 11.30a.m.–7p.m.; October to Easter, Monday to
Friday, 10.30a.m.–5p.m.
Admission: A=£££, C=£, F

Facilities: toilets; disabled access

The park gives visitors the opportunity to experience what it was like to leave behind the thatched cottages of rural Ulster and sail away on an emigrant ship to the New World. Costumed guides re-enact everyday life of the 1700s and 1800s in Ireland and America. Traditional thatched cottages, farm buildings and American log-cabins can be seen, as well as craft demonstrations, a ship and dock-side gallery, and a Victorian chemist shop. The park hosts many special events during the season, so check locally for a timetable.

ULSTER HISTORY PARK***
*Cullion, **Omagh***
Tel: 028 8164 8188; Fax: 028 8164 8011
Open: April to September, Monday to Saturday, 10.30a.m.–6.30p.m., Sunday, 11.30a.m.–7p.m.; October to March, Monday to Friday, 10.30a.m.–5p.m.
Admission: A=£££, C=£, F
Facilities: toilets; limited access for people with disabilities; shop; picnic areas; cafeteria

At the park, full-scale models of homes and monuments bring to life 10,000 years of the settlement history of Ireland, stretching from the Stone Age to the plantations of the 17th century. The whole family will enjoy exploring this trail into the past. There's an exhibition gallery and audio-visual show, demonstrations and events.

Leisure Centres and Adventure Playgrounds

MOURNE CHALLENGE FAMILY PARK***
Sion Mills
Tel: 028 8165 8414
Fun and entertainment for all the family: target golf, pitch'n'putt, quad fun-track, a supervised play area and tea-rooms.

Museums

NEWTOWNSTEWART GATEWAY CENTRE*
*Grange Court Complex, 21 Moyle Road, **Newtownstewart***
Tel: 028 8166 2414
Open: March to October, Monday to Friday, 11a.m.–4p.m., Saturday, 11a.m.–5p.m., Sunday, 1.30p.m.–5.30p.m.
Admission: A=£, C=£
Facilities: toilets; disabled access; café
Exhibition of militaria, old toys, Victoriana, and photographic and agricultural equipment dating from the 19th-century.

Swimming-Pools

CAMPSIE SWIMMING-POOL
*Crevenagh Road, **Omagh***
Tel: 028 8224 3850

RIVERSDALE LEISURE CENTRE
*Urney Road, **Strabane***
Tel: 028 7138 2672
Has a 25m swimming-pool, toddlers' pool, gym, squash and snooker.

PLACES TO EAT

Hotels and Pubs

MELLON COUNTRY INN
134 Beltany Road, **Omagh**
Tel: 028 8166 1224; Fax: 028 8166 2245
A wide variety of food served all day will satisfy all tastes.

• • • • •

PLACES TO STAY

Guest-Houses and B&Bs

CUL-LE-LOC
59 Killycoply Road, **Ardboe**
Tel: 028 8773 8343

EDERGOLE
70 Moneymore Road, **Cookstown**
Tel: 028 8676 2924

MULCANY HOUSE
86 Gorestown Road, Moy, **Dungannon**
Tel: 028 8778 4183

ARDELA
90 Shore Road, Ballyronan, **Magherafelt**
Tel: 028 7941 8444

AFTON HOUSE
32 Tattykeel Road, Clanabogan, **Omagh**
Tel/Fax: 028 8225 1257

Country Houses and Hotels

GLENAVON HOUSE HOTEL AND LEISURE CENTRE
52 Drum Road, **Cookstown**
Tel: 028 8676 4949

FOUR WAYS HOTEL
41–45 Main Street, **Fivemiletown**
Tel: 028 6652 1260

ROYAL ARMS HOTEL
51–53 High Street, **Omagh**
Tel: 028 8224 3262; Fax: 028 8224 5011

Travel Lodges

THE COHANNON INN AUTOLODGE
*212 Ballynakelly Road, **Dungannon***
Tel: 028 8772 4488
Family rooms available.

Farmhouse Accommodation

GARVEY LODGE
*62 Favour Royal Road, **Aughnacloy***
Tel: 028 8555 7239

GREENMOUNT LODGE
*58 Greenmount Road, **Gortaclare***
Tel: 028 8284 1325; Fax: 028 8284 0019

WATERSIDE HOUSE
*10 Drumott Road, **Moneymore***
Tel: 028 8676 2451

WOODVIEW FARM
*51 Cookstown Road, **Moneymore***
Tel: 028 8674 8417

Self-Catering Apartments and Houses

CLOGHER VALLEY SELF-CATERING
*Ashfield Park, **Clogher***
Tel: 028 8554 8684

ERIN DENE
*Tullyweary, Ardtrea, **Stewartstown***
Tel: 028 8676 2606

Caravan and Camping Parks

CLOGHER VALLEY COUNTRY CARAVAN PARK
*9 Fardross Road, **Clogher***
Tel: 028 8554 8932

GORTIN GLEN CARAVAN AND CAMPING PARK
*1 Lisnaharney Road, Lislap, **Omagh***
Tel: 028 8164 8108

Hostels

OMAGH HOSTEL
*9a Waterworks Road, Glenhordial, **Omagh***
Tel: 028 8224 1973

Bicycle Hire

IRISH CYCLE HIRE – see *Directory*
RALEIGH RENT-A-BIKE – see *Directory*

Bus Services

CITYBUS – *Tel: 028 9024 6485*
ULSTERBUS – *Tel: 028 9033 3000*

Rail Services

NORTHERN IRELAND RAILWAYS (NIR) – *Tel: 028 9089 9411*

DIRECTORY

Bicycle Hire

IRISH CYCLE HIRE
Central booking service: Tel: (+353) 041 9841067
This national network of bicycles for hire is based at mainline railway stations. You can hire from one depot and return to another if necessary.

RALEIGH RENT-A-BIKE
Central booking service: Tel: (+353) 01 8733622
This nationwide service is available mainly through appointed cycle agents. Again, you can hire from one place and drop off at another.

Most places hire out bikes for around £7 per day or £35 per week. A refundable deposit will be required.

Note: bicycles are not carried on city buses or on the DART (surface rapid rail service linking Dublin city centre with coastal suburbs). They can be taken on mainline trains and, at the discretion of the driver, on Expressway buses.
(Regional information can be found at end of each county)

Car Hire

MURRAYS EUROPCAR
Tel: (+353) 01 6681777; Fax: (+353) 01 6602958
Cars available from 15 rental locations throughout Ireland.
(Regional information can be found at end of each county)

Bus Travel

Central information:
Bus Eireann: Tel: (+353) 01 8366111
Dublin Bus: Tel: (+353) 01 8734222
Ulsterbus: Tel: 028 9033 3000
Belfast Citybus: Tel: 028 9024 6485
(Regional information can be found at end of each county)

Rail Travel

Central information:
Irish Rail: Tel: (+353) 01 8366222
Northern Ireland Railways (NIR): Tel: 028 9089 9411
(Regional information can be found at end of each county)

Accommodation

There is an excellent range of accommodation available in Ireland. Below is a list of recommended contacts:

IRISH FARM HOLIDAYS ASSOCIATION
2 Michael Street, Limerick
Tel: (+353) 061 400700, Fax: (+353) 061 400707
The Irish Farm Holidays Association have an excellent range of child-friendly accommodation on their books. Many of their choices are working farms and family homes, and children are made very welcome and are kept well entertained with such attractions as farm pets and pony-trekking. The Association produce a very good guidebook to their properties, which is available direct or from tourist information centres.

BALLYHOURA COUNTRY HOLIDAYS
Kilfinane, Co. Limerick
Tel: (+353) 063 91300, Fax: (+353) 063 91330
Ballyhoura Country Holidays have a wide range of child-friendly accommodation packages and rural-based activities to suit all ages, interests and pockets. They have activity centres, farmhouses, country homes and small family-run hotels on their books. Contact the above address for a brochure.

ENJOY IRELAND HOLIDAYS
Glenfield Park, Site 2, Blakewater Road, Blackburn, Lancashire, BB2 5QH
Tel: 01254 692899; Fax: 01254 693075
Enjoy Ireland Holidays have a full range of accommodation packages ranging from B&Bs, hotels and self-catering apartments to boating holidays. They will advise on the best child-friendly accommodation deal to suit your needs. Contact the above address for a brochure.

GREAT SOUTHERN HOTEL GROUP
Central reservation office: Tel: (+353) 01 2808031; Fax: (+353) 01 2808039
Great Southern has a chain of hotels throughout Ireland. Some, such as the one in Rosslare, Co. Wexford, are particularly child-friendly. Some also have a limited number of family rooms available on a room-only basis which accommodate 2 adults and 2 children. Contact the above number for details.

LAKELAND COUNTRY BREAKS
Tourist Information Centre, Wellington Road, Enniskillen, Co. Fermanagh, BT74 7ER
Tel: 028 6632 7205
It's the people that make Ireland unique, and the 13 participating villages in Fermanagh and Leitrim recognise that the beauty of their regions, the access to activities and culture, and the people themselves all add up to make a wonderful tourist area.

TOURIST INFORMATION OFFICES

BORD FAILTE – IRISH TOURIST BOARD
Head Office, Baggot Street Bridge, Dublin 2
Tel: (+353) 1 765871/616500 Fax: (+353) 01 764764

DUBLIN TOURISM CENTRE
Suffolk Street, Dublin 2
Tel: (+353) 1 6057755

NORTHERN IRELAND TOURIST BOARD
53 Castle Street, Belfast BT1 1GH
Tel: 028 9032 7888; Fax: 028 9024 0201

Republic of Ireland

Location	Tel (+353)	Open
The Sound, **Achill Island,** Co. Mayo	098 45384	July–Aug
Heritage Centre, **Adare,** Co. Limerick	061 396255	March–Oct
Kilronan, Inishmore, **Aran Islands,** Co. Galway	099 61263	May–Sept
The Parade Ground, **Arklow,** Co. Wicklow	0402 32484	all year
The Castle, Market Square, **Athlone,** Co. Westmeath	0902 94630	May–Oct
Town Hall, **Athy,** Co. Kildare	0507 31859	all year
Cathedral Road, **Ballina,** Co. Mayo	096 70848	April–Sept
Keller's Travel Agency, **Ballinasloe,** Co. Galway	0905 42131	July–Aug
The Square, **Bantry,** Co. Cork	027 50229	June–Sept
Rosse Row, **Birr,** Co. Offaly	0509 20110	May–Sept
Blarney, Co. Cork	021 381624	all year
Market Street, **Boyle,** Co. Roscommon	079 62145	May–Sept
Unit 2, Florence Road, **Bray,** Co. Wicklow	01 2867128	June–Aug
Main Street, **Bundoran,** Co. Donegal	072 41350	June–Sept
Folk Park, **Bunratty,** Co. Clare	061 360133	April–Sept
Castle Street, **Cahir,** Co. Tipperary	052 41453	May–Sept
Traynor House, College Street, **Carlow**	0503 31554	all year
The Marina, **Carrick-on-Shannon,** Co. Leitrim	078 20170	all year
The Clock Tower, **Carrick-on-Suir,** Co. Tipperary	051 40726	May–Sept
Town Hall, **Cashel,** Co. Tipperary	062 61333	May–Sept
Linen Hall Street, **Castlebar,** Co. Mayo	094 21207	April–Sept
Farnham Street, **Cavan**	049 4331942	all year
Market Street, **Clifden,** Co. Galway	095 21163	April–Sept
Liscannor, **Cliffs of Moher,** Co. Clare	065 7081171	April–Oct
9 Rossa Street, **Clonakilty,** Co. Cork	023 33226	June–Sept
Shannon Bridge, **Clonmacnois,** Co. Offaly	0905 74134	April–Sept
Chamber Buildings, **Clonmel,** Co. Tipperary	052 22960	all year
Grand Parade, **Cork**	021 273251	all year
Main Street, **Dingle,** Co. Kerry	066 9151188	April–Oct
Quay Street, **Donegal** Town	073 21148	all year
West Street, **Drogheda,** Co. Louth	041 9837070	June–Sept
Dublin Airport	01 376387	all year
Upper O'Connell Street, **Dublin**	01 747733	all year

Baggott Street Bridge, **Dublin**	01 765871	all year
Jocelyn Street, **Dundalk,** Co. Louth	042 9335484	all year
Mary Street, **Dungarvan,** Co. Waterford	058 41741	June–Aug
Main Street, **Dungloe,** Co. Donegal	075 21297	June–Aug
Michael's Wharf, **Dun Laoghaire,** Co. Dublin	01 2806984	all year
Road, **Ennis,** Co. Clare	065 6828366	all year
County Museum, The Castle, **Enniscorthy,** Co. Wexford	054 34699	June–Aug
Victoria Place, Eyre Square, **Galway**	091 563081	all year
Main Street, **Glengarriff,** Co. Cork	027 63084	July–Aug
Main Street, **Gorey,** Co. Wexford	055 21248	all year
The Heritage Centre, **Kenmare,** Co. Kerry	064 41233	April–Oct
Kildare Town	045 22696	June–Aug
Main Street, **Kilkee,** Co. Clare	065 9056112	June–Sept
Shee Alms House, Rose Inn Street, **Kilkenny**	056 51500	all year
The Heritage Centre, **Killaloe,** Co. Clare	061 376866	June–Sept
Town Hall, **Killarney,** Co. Kerry	064 31633	all year
Town Hall, **Kilrush,** Co. Clare	065 9051577	June–Sept
Pier Road, **Kinsale,** Co. Cork	021 772234	Mar–Nov
Knock, Co. Mayo	094 88193	May–Sept
Knock Airport, Co. Mayo	094 67247	all year
Main Street, **Lahinch,** Co. Clare	065 7081474	May–Sept
Derry Road, **Letterkenny,** Co. Donegal	074 21160	all year
Arthur's Quay, **Limerick**	061 317522	all year
St John's Church, **Listowel,** Co. Kerry	068 22590	June–Sept
Main Street, **Longford**	043 46566	June–Aug
Jameson Heritage Centre, **Midleton,** Co. Cork	021 613702	April–Sept
Market House, **Monaghan**	047 81122	all year
Dublin Road, **Mullingar,** Co. Westmeath	044 48650	all year
Connolly Street, **Nenagh,** Co. Tipperary	067 31610	May–Sept
Main Street, **Newbridge,** Co. Kildare	045 33835	June–Aug
Newgrange, via Slane, Co. Meath	041 9824274	April–Oct
The Quay, **New Ross,** Co. Wexford	051 21857	June–Sept
James Fintan Lawlor Avenue, **Portlaoise,** Co. Laois	0502 21178	all year
Harrison Hall, **Roscommon**	0903 26342	June–Sept
Rosslare Harbour, Co. Wexford	053 33232	June–Sept
Rosslare Terminal, Co. Wexford	053 33622	all year
The Promenade, **Salthill,** Co. Galway	091 63081	June–Sept
Shannon Airport, Co. Clare	061 471664	all year
Community Office, **Skerries,** Co. Dublin	01 490888	all year
Town Hall, **Skibbereen,** Co. Cork	028 21766	all year
Aras Reddan, John's Street, **Sligo**	071 61201	all year
Yeats Tower, Gort, **Thoorballylee,** Co. Galway	091 31436	June–Sept
Community Office, James Street, **Tipperary**	062 51457	all year
Ashe Memorial Hall, Denny St, **Tralee,** Co. Kerry	066 7121288	all year
Railway Square, **Tramore,** Co. Waterford	093 381572	June–Aug
The Mill Museum, **Tuam,** Co. Galway	093 24463	July–Aug
Williams St Shopping Centre, **Tullamore,** Co. Offaly	0506 52617	July–Aug
41 The Quay, **Waterford**	051 75788	all year
The Mall, **Westport,** Co. Mayo	098 25711	all year
Crescent Quay, **Wexford**	053 23111	all year
Rialto House, Fitzwilliam Square, **Wicklow**	0404 69117	all year
Market House, Market Square, **Youghal,** Co. Cork	024 92390	June–Sept

Northern Ireland

Corn Mill, **Annalong**, Co. Down	028 4376 8736	June–Aug
Pogue's Entry, Church Street, **Antrim**	028 9446 3113	all year
Old Bank Building, 40 English Street, **Armagh**	028 3752 1800	all year
Sheskburn House, 7 Mary Street, **Ballycastle**, Co. Antrim	028 2076 2024	all year
Council Offices, 80 Galgorm Rd, **Ballymena**, Co. Antrim	028 2565 3663	all year
Riada House,14 Charles Street, **Ballymoney**, Co. Antrim	028 2766 2280	all year
Gateway Centre, Newry Road, **Banbridge,** Co. Down	028 4062 3322	all year
Tower House, 34 Quay Street, **Bangor,** Co. Down	028 9127 0069	all year
St Anne's Court, 59 North Street, **Belfast,** Co. Antrim	028 9024 6609	all year
City Hall, Donegal Square, **Belfast**	028 9032 0202	all year
Belfast International Airport	028 9442 2888	all year
Belfast City Airport	028 9045 7745	all year
Post Office, 38 Harbour Road, **Carnlough**, Co. Antrim	028 2888 5210	all year
Antrim Street, **Carrickfergus,** Co. Antrim	028 9336 6455	all year
Swimming Pool, **Castlerock**, Co. Derry	028 7084 8258	July–Aug
Railway Road, **Coleraine**, Co. Derry	028 7034 4723	all year
Council Offices, 12 Burn Road, **Cookstown**, Co. Tyrone	028 8676 2205	all year
24b Mill Street, **Cushendall**, Co. Antrim	028 2177 1180	all year
8 Bishop Street, **Derry,** Co. Derry	028 7126 7284	all year
Town Hall, **Donaghadee,** Co. Down	028 9188 2087	all year
74 Market Street, **Downpatrick,** Co. Down	028 4461 2233	all year
Council Offices, Circular Road, **Dungannon,** Co. Tyrone	028 8772 5311	all year
Lakeland V.C., Wellington Rd, **Enniskillen,** Co. Fermanagh	028 6632 3110	all year
Library, Main Street, **Fivemiletown,** Co. Tyrone	028 8952 1409	all year
Visitor's Centre, **Giant's Causeway**, Co. Antrim	028 2073 1855	all year
Council Offices, The Square, **Hillsborough,** Co. Down	028 9268 2477	all year
Mourne Esplanade, **Kilkeel**, Co. Down	028 3076 4666	all year
Amenity Centre, Ballygawley Rd, **Killymaddy**, Co. Tyrone	028 8776 7259	all year
Narrow Gauge Road, **Larne,** Co. Antrim	028 2826 0088	all year
Council Offices, 7 Connell Street, **Limavady,** Co. Derry	028 7772 2226	all year
Town Hall, 6 Union Street, **Lurgan,** Co. Armagh	028 3832 3757	all year
Benone Tourist Complex, **Magillian**, Co. Derry	028 7775 0555	all year
Central Promenade, **Newcastle**, Co. Down	028 4372 2222	all year
Dublin–Newry Road, **Newry,** Co. Down	028 3026 8877	all year
Council Offices, 2 Church St, **Newtownards,** Co. Down	028 9181 2215	all year
Main Street, **Newtownstewart,** Co. Tyrone	028 8166 1560	June–Sept
1 Market Street, **Omagh,** Co. Tyrone	028 8224 7831	all year
Town Hall, Edward Street, **Portadown,** Co. Armagh	028 3835 3260	all year
Dunluce Centre, **Portrush,** Co. Antrim	028 7082 3333	April–Sept
Town Hall, The Crescent, **Portstewart,** Co. Derry	028 7053 2286	July–Aug
Abercorn Square, **Strabane,** Co. Tyrone	028 7188 3735	June–Sept
Carlingford Cruises, Marina, **Warrenpoint,** Co. Down	028 3077 2950	July–Aug

STORIES FOR JOURNEYS

County Wexford: you can visit a Holy Well at Carne that will cure toothache, or have a headache cured by lying in a stone sarcophagus in the old churchyard at Bannow.

Hook Peninsula, County Wexford: the famous phrase 'by Hook or by Crooke' originated here when Oliver Cromwell said he would take the city of Waterford by landing either on Hook Head or on the opposite side of the Suir Estuary at Crooke.

County Wexford: on the eastern coast of the peninsula is Tintern Abbey, the foundation of which can only be described as a maritime miracle. The Earl of Pembroke was crossing over to Wexford in the year 1200 when his ship was overwhelmed in a storm. Mastless, the stricken vessel was floundering in treacherous seas when the Earl, his wife and crew vowed that if they survived, they would found an abbey wherever they landed. The stricken vessel drifted into Bannow Bay and beached in the beautiful creek where the ruins of the majestic Cistercian abbey stand today. There are guided tours during June to September and the grounds are open throughout the year.

County Cork: in 1537 the village of Baltimore was sacked by the men of Waterford in revenge for the seizure of one of their ships. *The Sack of Baltimore* by Thomas David is a vivid poem describing a raid by Algerian pirates in 1631, when some of the villagers were slaughtered and others captured and taken as slaves to North Africa.

County Westmeath: There is a tragic legend associated with the Margy River. Queen Aoife is said to have pushed her four stepchildren into the water by the shore of Lough Derravaragh and turned them into swans. She decreed that they should remain so for the next 900 years. During the centuries of their enchantment, the children kept their human faculties and were endowed with the gift of song, singing so beautifully that all passers-by stopped to listen to them.

There are also fairies that live inside Tieveragh Hill, near Cushendall, reputed to be the capital of the fairies. And did you know about the mysterious vanishing lake at Loughareema? One day it can be full to overflowing, and the next completely empty, as though some mysterious monster with a great thirst has passed by in the night – or maybe someone simply pulled the plug out! Disappointingly, the real answer to the riddle of the changing water level is simply a geological one.

Every Westmeath lake has a myth or legend associated with it, guaranteed to capture children's imagination. The fairy queen Deirdre is said to have brought back Lough Owel as a present from King Dun of Connacht – she carried it in her white handkerchief over the mountains to the emerald hills of Westmeath.